Transforming Teaching with AI and Digital Tools:

Methods, Platforms, and Classroom Innovations

Antonio Cortijo Ocaña
University of California, Santa Barbara, USA

Javier Fernández-Molina
University of Alicante, Spain

IGI Global
Scientific Publishing
Publishing Tomorrow's Research Today

Vice President of Editorial Melissa Wagner
Director of Acquisitions Mikaela Felty
Director of Book Development Jocelynn Hessler
Production Manager Mike Brehm
Cover Design Jose Rosado

Published in the United States of America by
IGI Global Scientific Publishing
701 East Chocolate Avenue
Hershey, PA, 17033, USA
Tel: 717-533-8845 | Fax: 717-533-7115
Website: https://www.igi-global.com E-mail: cust@igi-global.com

Library of Congress Cataloging-in-Publication Data

(CIP Data Pending)
ISBN13: 979-8-2600-1568-1
Isbn13Softcover: 979-8-2600-1569-8
EISBN13: 979-8-2600-1570-4
British Cataloguing in Publication Data
A Cataloguing in Publication record for this book is available from the British Library.

Table of Contents

Preface xiii

Chapter 1
Digital Tools 1
Dini Febryana Sari, Universitas Esa Unggul, Indonesia
Binastya Anggara Sekti, Universitas Esa Unggul, Indonesia

Chapter 2
Minds and Machines: The Interdisciplinary Challenge of AI's Influence in Education 23
Pankaj Bhambri, Guru Nanak Dev Engineering College, Ludhiana, India

Chapter 3
Digital Tools and Computer Science for Transforming Modern Pedagogy: Bridging the Gap Between Innovation and Equity 39
Dini Febryana Sari, Universitas Esa Unggul, Indonesia
Binastya Anggara Sekti, Universitas Esa Unggul, Indonesia

Chapter 4
Ethical Perspectives of Teacher Trainees on the Use of Artificial Intelligence .. 63
María Soledad Villarrubia Zúñiga, University of Alicante, Spain

Chapter 5
Adaptive Learning System Implementation in LMS Platforms: Educator and Student Perceptions in a Scoping Review 83
Maximiliano Ernesto Merino Suárez, Universidad Santo Tomas, Chile
Jorge Fernández Herrero, University of Alicante, Spain

Chapter 6
Telegram as a Complementary Channel for Tutoring: Teaching Experience in Urbanism and Marketing 109
Francisco José Chamizo-Nieto, University of Seville, Spain
Claudia Prieto-Latorre, University of Malaga, Spain

Chapter 7
The Impact of Digital Tools on Students' Learning Experience: Teachers' Perceptions and Observations 127
Papagiannis Chrysovalantis, Independent Researcher, Greece

Chapter 8
E-Portfolio as an Alternative Method of Student Evaluation in Secondary Education in Greece 149
Maria Poulou, University of Alicante, Spain

Chapter 9
Innovative Educational Experiences: Exploring the Benefits of STEM Education 175
Stavroula Lada, University of Alicante, Spain

Chapter 10
Hybrid Pedagogies for STEAM Teacher Education: Integrating Games, Digital Tools, and Creative Practices in Portugal 205
Pedro Neves Rito, Polytechnic Institute of Viseu, Portugal

Chapter 11
From Analysis to Urban Project With an Eco-Social Approach: ECOLAB Reference Project Laboratory as a Teaching Methodology Applied to the Guadalmedina River 229
Rubén Mora-Esteban, Independent Researcher, Spain
Francisco Conejo Arrabal, Independent Researcher, Spain
Jorge Asencio-Juncal, Escuela Técnica Superior de Arquitectura, Universidad de Málaga, Spain
Nuria Nebot Gómez de Salazar, Independent Researcher, Spain

Chapter 12
Universal Design Learning Applied Through Gamification in Higher Education: An Experience From Two Gamification Innovations Implemented in the Course 'Sociology of Education' 251
Karla Berrens, CRIT Research Group, GIDASRES, CR Polis, University of Barcelona, Spain
Marina Elias, GIDASRES, CR Polis, University of Barcelona, Spain

Chapter 13
Gamification Learning for Urban Educational Challenges: A Mixed-Methods Quasi-Experimental Study in PGDM Programs 265
Senthil Kumar A. V., Nehru Institute of Information Technology and Management, India
Revati Ramrao Rautrao, Dr D.Y. Patil B-School, India
Sanjayan Thottapattunjalil Suseelan, GVM's Dr. Dada Vaidya College of Education, Ponda, India
Nagakishore Bhavanam S., Mangalayatan University, Jabalpur, India
Sambasiva Rao K. R. S., Dr. RVR NRI Institute of Technology (Deemed to be) University, India
Nasir Ahmad Ganaie, Department of Political Science, School of Social Sciences, University of Kashmir, Srinagar, India

Compilation of References 299

About the Contributors 339

Index 347

Detailed Table of Contents

Preface.. xiii

Chapter 1
Digital Tools 1
Dini Febryana Sari, Universitas Esa Unggul, Indonesia
Binastya Anggara Sekti, Universitas Esa Unggul, Indonesia

"Digital Tools" examines education's transformation by computer science, where technology is now fundamental. It maps the evolution from mainframes to AI, which drives active, personalized learning but also creates challenges like the digital divide, data privacy, and bias. Success requires interdisciplinary collaboration and critical digital literacy. International case studies illustrate diverse strategies. The future depends on balancing innovation (VR/AR) with ethical policies prioritizing equity and lifelong learning.

Chapter 2
Minds and Machines: The Interdisciplinary Challenge of AI's Influence in Education 23
Pankaj Bhambri, Guru Nanak Dev Engineering College, Ludhiana, India

Artificial Intelligence (AI) in education transcends its role as a mere tool, emerging as a formative force that shapes the very landscape of learning. This chapter argues that the most profound impacts of AI lie not in algorithmic efficiency, but in its capacity to reshape student cognition, attitudes, and pedagogical outcomes—a complex interplay demanding an interdisciplinary response. We move beyond technocentric views to explore how AI systems influence metacognitive skills and self-regulated learning (psychology), alter student-teacher dynamics and perpetuate biases (sociology), and demand new ethical frameworks and policy guidance (philosophy and law). The chapter concludes by proposing a collaborative framework for researchers, educators, and policymakers to harness AI's potential while safeguarding the human elements at the core of education.

Chapter 3
Digital Tools and Computer Science for Transforming Modern Pedagogy: Bridging the Gap Between Innovation and Equity 39
Dini Febryana Sari, Universitas Esa Unggul, Indonesia
Binastya Anggara Sekti, Universitas Esa Unggul, Indonesia

This chapter explores the impact of computer science and digital tools on modern pedagogy. The authors trace the evolution of educational technology, moving from legacy systems to artificial intelligence and adaptive learning. The text analyzes the integration of these tools into curricula, highlighting active learning and interdisciplinary collaboration. Additionally, the chapter addresses critical ethical challenges, including data security, algorithmic bias, and the digital divide. By examining global case studies from diverse nations, the authors illustrate how policy and infrastructure influence digital adoption. The work concludes by advocating for human-centric strategies that utilize technology to create inclusive, equitable, and efficient educational environments.

Chapter 4
Ethical Perspectives of Teacher Trainees on the Use of Artificial Intelligence .. 63
María Soledad Villarrubia Zúñiga, University of Alicante, Spain

The aim of this article is to present the perceptions of future teachers in the context of the Master's Degree in Educational Research at the University of Alicante on the ethical approaches to the implementation of AI in education. It demonstrates the necessity and relevance of integrating certain values, together with the teacher training indispensable for their application. The research was conducted using a qualitative-descriptive approach. The study took into account the work of a group of students with a solid academic background. The main objective is to recognise the ethical positioning regarding the use of artificial intelligence in the classroom. The results indicate a high degree of involvement and clear ideas on the subject. This study is not a survey but rather an argumentative analysis to evaluate the effectiveness and consistency of the ideas expressed in a class assignment to create a conceptual corpus to base future research.

Chapter 5
Adaptive Learning System Implementation in LMS Platforms: Educator and Student Perceptions in a Scoping Review 83
Maximiliano Ernesto Merino Suárez, Universidad Santo Tomas, Chile
Jorge Fernández Herrero, University of Alicante, Spain

The perceptions of university educators and students about the implementation of Adaptive Learning Systems (ALS) driven by artificial intelligence (AI) and integrated into Learning Management Systems (LMS) in higher education. The purpose of this chapter is to analyze empirical evidence published between 2020 and 2025 to identify key trends, facilitators, barriers, and perceived effects associated with the use of ALS in digital learning environments. The authors conducted a scoping review following the PRISMA-ScR framework, analyzing 12 studies selected from Web of Science, Scopus, and ProQuest. The findings reveal generally positive perceptions of ALS, particularly about learning personalization, automated feedback, and student engagement. However, significant challenges were also identified, including technical limitations, digital competency gaps, ethical concerns, and organizational resistance. This chapter highlights the significance of user perceptions in shaping the inclusive, sustainable, and pedagogically effective adoption of adaptive technologies.

Chapter 6
Telegram as a Complementary Channel for Tutoring: Teaching Experience in Urbanism and Marketing 109
Francisco José Chamizo-Nieto, University of Seville, Spain
Claudia Prieto-Latorre, University of Malaga, Spain

This research presents a pilot experience of using Telegram to facilitate communication between students and teachers as a complement to conventional tutoring. This messaging application took place during the 2021-2022 academic year in two subjects at the University of Malaga: Urbanism II and Statistics I. Both belong respectively to the Degree in Foundations of Architecture and the Degree in Marketing and Market Research. To evaluate the experience, a quantitative and qualitative methodology was used through the analysis of surveys and a critical reflection on the implementation. The results show a higher participation in Urbanism II (48%) compared to Statistics I (23%). However, in both cases, the attitude of the learners was passive, reading the publications, which were mostly text messages and images. Despite this, 71.4% of participants consider that its use has had a positive impact on their academic performance, so it shows support for tutoring in university teaching.

Chapter 7
The Impact of Digital Tools on Students' Learning Experience: Teachers' Perceptions and Observations 127
Papagiannis Chrysovalantis, Independent Researcher, Greece

The integration of digital tools in education has become increasingly vital, particularly in primary education, where innovative teaching approaches are crucial for fostering student engagement and deep learning. This study explores the impact of digital tools on students' learning experience, based on the perceptions and observations of 100 primary school teachers in Greece. The findings indicate that digital tools positively influence students' interest, participation, and understanding of content, while also supporting differentiated instruction and 21st-century skill development. However, concerns regarding access inequality and classroom management were also raised. The study concludes that while digital tools offer considerable pedagogical advantages, their effective integration requires ongoing teacher training, infrastructure support, and inclusive strategies to ensure equitable access for all learners. The research contributes to the broader discourse on technology-enhanced education and offers practical implications for policy and development in Greek education.

Chapter 8
E-Portfolio as an Alternative Method of Student Evaluation in Secondary Education in Greece 149
Maria Poulou, University of Alicante, Spain

This chapter refers to the views of secondary school teachers on alternative forms of students' assessment and specifically the e-portfolio. This study is a qualitative research that aims to gather the opinions of 14 teachers, through semi-structured interviews. It was observed that all teachers presented a positive attitude towards technology. Regarding the e-portfolio, teachers who had used it described it as very efficient, with obvious benefits. The majority of teachers who use it reported that they create it with the help of students alone, without collaborating with colleagues. Teachers who have not used this specific tool report that they either do not know about it or are not interested in investing more time in its design and preparation. It is concluded that there is a strong need to promote and use technological tools in education to improve the quality of the educational process and facilitate the work of teachers and students.

Chapter 9
Innovative Educational Experiences: Exploring the Benefits of STEM Education 175
Stavroula Lada, University of Alicante, Spain

STEM education, involving science, technology, engineering, and mathematics, is the pilar of modern educational initiatives. This chapter includes quantitative research related to the impact of STEM approach on students' performance, carried out among educators in Europe. The main research question is: How does STEM education shape students' achievements? Moreover, it measures educators' points of view of the challenges they meet while implementing STEM disciplines. According to the analysis of the data, the results of STEM implementation are not only academic. The researcher monitors educators' observations, and remarks on skills that are developed, which help students become problem-solvers, innovators, and pioneers who overcome the challenges of the contemporary world. The investigation is important for decision-making because it enables teachers, and education policymakers to form curriculums that meet the current requirements.

Chapter 10
Hybrid Pedagogies for STEAM Teacher Education: Integrating Games, Digital Tools, and Creative Practices in Portugal 205
Pedro Neves Rito, Polytechnic Institute of Viseu, Portugal

This chapter explores the integration of STEAM methodologies in Portuguese teacher training programs, emphasizing the pedagogical potential of hybrid approaches that combine digital and analog tools. Drawing on policy frameworks, it examines how accessible platforms such as Scratch, GeoGebra, and Arduino IDE, together with recyclable materials and educational board games, foster inclusive, creative, and practical learning experiences. Case studies from higher education institutions in Portugal demonstrate how structured training empowers educators with the confidence and skills necessary to implement interdisciplinary and student-centered learning. The chapter highlights the impact of these practices on teachers and students, noting increased engagement, collaboration, and equity in classrooms. It also addresses infrastructure, teacher preparation, and sustainability challenges, offering strategic recommendations for future training. This work contributes to the literature on equitable and effective STEAM education by implementing hybrid pedagogies.

Chapter 11
From Analysis to Urban Project With an Eco-Social Approach: ECOLAB Reference Project Laboratory as a Teaching Methodology Applied to the Guadalmedina River 229
Rubén Mora-Esteban, Independent Researcher, Spain
Francisco Conejo Arrabal, Independent Researcher, Spain
Jorge Asencio-Juncal, Escuela Técnica Superior de Arquitectura, Universidad de Málaga, Spain
Nuria Nebot Gómez de Salazar, Independent Researcher, Spain

This work presents an educational experience conducted within the context of the second-year Urban Planning 1 course at the School of Architecture in Málaga. Students are introduced to a public space project, for which they must consider ecological and social aspects. The difficulty the students encountered in transitioning from analysis and diagnosis to project implementation led the teachers to implement the ECOLAB Reference Project Laboratory teaching methodology, which provides resources and tools to facilitate critical and argumentative project implementation. The Guadalmedina river area becomes an open-air classroom where students can explore and learn about local issues and the consequences of meeting or not meeting ecological and social criteria for citizens and the environment.

Chapter 12
Universal Design Learning Applied Through Gamification in Higher Education: An Experience From Two Gamification Innovations Implemented in the Course 'Sociology of Education' 251
Karla Berrens, CRIT Research Group, GIDASRES, CR Polis, University of Barcelona, Spain
Marina Elias, GIDASRES, CR Polis, University of Barcelona, Spain

This article is based on two gamification innovations developed at the Faculty of Education of the University of Barcelona. They were implemented on the subject "Sociology of Education". During the 2023–2024 academic year, the project "Effects on Learning through Gamification as a Tool for Summative Assessment in the Sociology Course of the Primary Education Degree" invited students to use Wooclap for one of the course's summative assessments and to gamify the theoretical content. In the 2024–2025 academic year, the project "Fylki: strategic project, Education faculty" was implemented. It involved a board game designed to allow students to revisit key concepts addressed in the course through play, such as social structure, equality, justice, and equity. The objectives of the research projects were, through play, to generate an environment allowing students with diverse learning needs to engage with course content and take responsibility for their learning.

Chapter 13
Gamification Learning for Urban Educational Challenges: A Mixed-Methods Quasi-Experimental Study in PGDM Programs 265
Senthil Kumar A. V., Nehru Institute of Information Technology and Management, India
Revati Ramrao Rautrao, Dr D.Y. Patil B-School, India
Sanjayan Thottapattunjalil Suseelan, GVM's Dr. Dada Vaidya College of Education, Ponda, India
Nagakishore Bhavanam S., Mangalayatan University, Jabalpur, India
Sambasiva Rao K. R. S., Dr. RVR NRI Institute of Technology (Deemed to be) University, India
Nasir Ahmad Ganaie, Department of Political Science, School of Social Sciences, University of Kashmir, Srinagar, India

This study sees the new Gamification strategies used in the Post Graduate Diploma (PGDM) programs to solve urban educational challenges. The study uses a semi-professional approach with mixed methods to investigate how well the urban management improves the learning strategy for student engagement, knowledge retention, and skill development. According to its unique design, the research uses a mixture of quantitative and qualitative data collection methods such as study, performance reviews, focus groups and intensive interviews with coaches and students. According to the results, gamification improves the results of learning because it improves participants' motivation, accelerates their problems to solve problems, and helps them understand complex urban problems. The report's conclusions have ramifications for curriculum improvement, educational strategies, and the creation of customised gamification solutions for management packages with a city concentration.

Compilation of References 299

About the Contributors 339

Index 347

Preface

INTRODUCTION

As editors of *Transforming Teaching with AI and Digital Tools: Methods, Platforms, and Classroom Innovations*, we present this volume at a moment of profound change in education. The 21st century has ushered in a complex landscape shaped by rapid technological advancement, shifting societal expectations, and an urgent call for more inclusive and equitable learning environments. Among the many forces redefining education are the widespread integration of digital tools, the accelerating development of artificial intelligence, and the lasting impact of the COVID-19 pandemic on how teaching and learning are conceived and practiced worldwide.

This book emerges from the ICON-edu 2025 Conference, which brought together scholars, educators, and practitioners from diverse disciplines and cultural contexts. The contributions collected here reflect that diversity, offering a rich tapestry of perspectives grounded in both theory and practice. By bridging geographical, institutional, and disciplinary boundaries, this volume underscores the importance of collaboration in addressing the multifaceted challenges facing contemporary education.

The chapters included in this collection explore how emerging technologies and innovative pedagogies are reshaping educational experiences. They examine not only the opportunities afforded by digital transformation but also the responsibilities it entails—particularly in ensuring that no learner is left behind. Issues of accessibility, equity, and inclusion are central throughout the volume, with particular attention given to learners from marginalized communities and those with diverse educational needs.

In assembling this work, we sought to provide a comprehensive and interdisciplinary overview of current debates and practices. The contributions highlight empirical research, case studies, and conceptual frameworks that illuminate how educational innovation can be effectively implemented across varied contexts. Equally important, the volume fosters dialogue between disciplines, encouraging readers to consider how insights from different fields can inform more sustainable and adaptable educational practices.

This book is intended as a resource for a wide audience. Researchers and scholars will find valuable analyses and emerging lines of inquiry. Educators—both in schools and higher education—will encounter practical approaches and inspiring examples of innovation. Policymakers and administrators may draw on the insights presented here to inform decisions that promote inclusive and effective educational systems. Finally, graduate students and lifelong learning professionals will discover ideas and tools relevant to their ongoing work and development.

We hope this volume contributes meaningfully to the ongoing transformation of education and inspires continued exploration, collaboration, and innovation in teaching and learning.

ORGANIZATION OF THE BOOK

In this volume, each chapter contributes a distinct yet interconnected perspective on the evolving relationship between education, technology, and innovation. Together, they offer a layered understanding of how digital transformation is reshaping pedagogical theory and practice across contexts.

Chapter 1 introduces the foundational role of digital tools in contemporary education, tracing their evolution from early computational systems to advanced artificial intelligence. The chapter situates technology as both an enabler of personalized, active learning and a source of critical challenges, including issues of access, privacy, and bias. Through international case studies, it underscores the importance of interdisciplinary collaboration and ethical awareness, ultimately pointing toward a future that balances technological innovation with equity and lifelong learning.

Chapter 2 deepens this discussion by positioning artificial intelligence not merely as a tool, but as a transformative force that reshapes cognition, pedagogy, and educational relationships. Drawing on insights from psychology, sociology, philosophy, and law, the chapter examines how AI influences metacognitive development, student-teacher dynamics, and ethical considerations. It calls for a holistic, interdisciplinary framework that preserves the human dimensions of education while responsibly leveraging AI's capabilities.

Chapter 3 further explores the integration of digital tools and computer science into modern pedagogy, emphasizing the tension between innovation and equity. By examining global case studies, the chapter illustrates how policy, infrastructure, and institutional contexts shape technological adoption. It advocates for human-centered approaches that prioritize inclusivity and ethical responsibility while harnessing the benefits of adaptive and intelligent learning systems.

Chapter 4 shifts focus to the perspectives of future educators, offering a qualitative exploration of how teacher trainees conceptualize the ethical use of artificial intelligence in educational settings. The findings reveal a high level of critical engagement and awareness, highlighting the importance of embedding ethical reflection and value-based training within teacher education programs to ensure responsible implementation of emerging technologies.

Chapter 5 presents a comprehensive review of adaptive learning systems integrated into learning management platforms, synthesizing recent empirical research on educator and student perceptions. While the findings indicate strong support for personalization, engagement, and automated feedback, the chapter also identifies persistent barriers, including technical limitations, digital competency gaps, and ethical concerns. It emphasizes the central role of user experience in shaping sustainable and inclusive adoption.

Chapter 6 offers a practical case study on the use of a messaging platform as a complementary tutoring tool in higher education. The findings reveal increased participation and perceived academic benefits, despite largely passive engagement patterns. This chapter highlights the potential of informal digital communication channels to extend learning beyond traditional classroom boundaries while also raising questions about student interaction and engagement strategies.

Chapter 7 examines the impact of digital tools in primary education through the lens of teacher perceptions and observations. The study demonstrates clear benefits in student engagement, participation, and skill development, while also acknowledging challenges related to access and classroom management. The chapter underscores the need for ongoing professional development and infrastructure support to ensure equitable and effective implementation.

Chapter 8 explores the use of e-portfolios as an alternative assessment method in secondary education. Through qualitative insights from teachers, the chapter reveals both enthusiasm for the pedagogical benefits of e-portfolios and barriers related to awareness, time, and collaboration. It highlights the need for institutional support and professional development to promote broader adoption of innovative assessment practices.

Chapter 9 focuses on STEM education as a driver of innovation and skill development in contemporary learning environments. The findings extend beyond academic achievement, illustrating how STEM approaches foster critical thinking, problem-solving, and creativity. At the same time, the chapter acknowledges the challenges educators face in implementation, offering valuable insights for curriculum design and policy development.

Chapter 10 presents hybrid pedagogies within STEAM teacher education, demonstrating how the integration of digital tools, games, and creative practices can foster inclusive and engaging learning environments. Drawing on case studies from Portugal, the chapter highlights the importance of accessible technologies, interdisciplinary approaches, and teacher training in supporting sustainable and equitable educational innovation.

Chapter 11 provides an example of experiential and place-based learning through an eco-social urban planning project. By introducing the ECOLAB methodology, the chapter illustrates how students can bridge the gap between analysis and practical application. The use of real-world environments as learning spaces reinforces the importance of contextualized, socially and environmentally responsive education.

Chapter 12 examines the application of gamification within a framework of universal design for learning in higher education. Through two innovative projects, the chapter demonstrates how game-based approaches can support inclusive participation, engagement, and conceptual understanding. It highlights the potential of gamification to address diverse learning needs while fostering student autonomy and responsibility.

Finally, Chapter 13 explores the use of gamification strategies in postgraduate management education, particularly in addressing complex urban challenges. Using a mixed-methods approach, the chapter demonstrates how gamified learning enhances motivation, problem-solving, and knowledge retention. It concludes by emphasizing the potential of tailored gamification strategies to enrich curriculum design and respond to contemporary educational demands.

Taken together, these chapters reflect the breadth and depth of innovation currently shaping education. They collectively reinforce the importance of ethical awareness, inclusivity, and interdisciplinary collaboration in ensuring that technological advancements translate into meaningful and equitable learning experiences.

CONCLUSION

As this volume demonstrates, the transformation of education in the digital age is neither linear nor uniform; it is a dynamic and evolving process shaped by technological innovation, human values, and the diverse realities of educational contexts worldwide. The contributions gathered here collectively affirm that while digital tools and artificial intelligence offer unprecedented opportunities to enhance teaching and learning, their impact ultimately depends on how thoughtfully and ethically they are integrated into practice.

Across the chapters, a consistent theme emerges: innovation must be accompanied by critical reflection. The adoption of digital technologies is not simply a matter of access or implementation, but of purpose, design, and responsibility. Questions of equity, inclusion, data ethics, and pedagogical effectiveness are not peripheral concerns—they are central to ensuring that educational transformation benefits all learners. In this sense, the human dimension of education remains paramount, even as technological systems become more sophisticated and pervasive.

This volume also highlights the importance of interdisciplinary collaboration in addressing the complex challenges facing education today. Insights drawn from fields such as computer science, psychology, sociology, and the arts enrich our understanding of how learning occurs and how it can be supported in increasingly diverse and hybrid environments. The case studies and research presented here illustrate that meaningful innovation often arises at the intersections of disciplines, where new perspectives and practices can emerge.

Equally significant is the role of educators, whose adaptability, creativity, and critical engagement are essential to the success of any pedagogical innovation. Whether through the integration of adaptive learning systems, the use of gamification, or the application of hybrid and experiential methodologies, the chapters in this book underscore the need for ongoing professional development and institutional support. Empowering educators is, in many ways, the cornerstone of sustainable educational change.

Looking ahead, the future of education will require a careful balance between embracing technological possibilities and safeguarding the core values of teaching and learning. Lifelong learning, inclusivity, and global collaboration will continue to shape educational priorities, demanding flexible and resilient systems capable of responding to rapid change.

As editors, we hope this volume serves not only as a reference but also as an invitation—to question, to innovate, and to collaborate. The transformation of education is a shared endeavor, and it is through continued dialogue and critical inquiry that more equitable, inclusive, and meaningful learning environments can be realized.

Chapter 1
Digital Tools

Dini Febryana Sari
http://orcid.org/0009-0002-6540-3372
Universitas Esa Unggul, Indonesia

Binastya Anggara Sekti
http://orcid.org/0000-0001-5489-4888
Universitas Esa Unggul, Indonesia

ABSTRACT

"Digital Tools" examines education's transformation by computer science, where technology is now fundamental. It maps the evolution from mainframes to AI, which drives active, personalized learning but also creates challenges like the digital divide, data privacy, and bias. Success requires interdisciplinary collaboration and critical digital literacy. International case studies illustrate diverse strategies. The future depends on balancing innovation (VR/AR) with ethical policies prioritizing equity and lifelong learning.

1. INTRODUCTION

In the twenty-first century, computer science has emerged as a fundamental pillar underpinning almost every aspect of human endeavor, fundamentally reshaping the way individuals communicate, live their professional lives, and acquire knowledge. In the field of education, this transformation has proven to be very significant, as the application of various digital instruments that span the online learning ecosystem to systems supported by artificial intelligence has ushered in revolutionary changes in teaching methodologies. As noted by Sahayu et al. (2026) the framework linking pedagogy, science, and technology has birthed an entirely new paradigm wherein education is not simply transmitted through digital channels, but is systematically

DOI: 10.4018/979-8-2600-1568-1.ch001

analyzed and optimized through data-driven methodologies. This worldwide transition toward technology-enhanced education, accelerated dramatically by the global pandemic, has illuminated both the tremendous potential and considerable challenges inherent in depending upon digital environments for delivery. Contemporary scholars now recognize that comprehending the fundamental principles of computer science is indispensable not merely for creating innovative educational technologies, but equally for equipping learners to flourish in an increasingly interconnected global landscape by facilitating lifelong learning opportunities for all types of learners (Garzón et al., 2025). Consequently, algorithms and data architecture have transcended their traditional boundaries to become central elements in architecting adaptive learning ecosystems that generate personalized learning trajectories by tailoring learning activities to individual learners' prior knowledge (Fromm et al., 2025).

This integration of technology underscores the inherent interdisciplinary character of contemporary education, where computer science serves as a bridge that brings together traditionally different disciplines including psychology, linguistics, and mathematics. This evolution traces its roots back to the shift from mainframe computing to the democratization of personal computers in the 1980s. This historical transition represents a pivotal paradigm shift from teacher-centered instruction toward interactive, exploratory learning.

Figure 1. Evolution of digital tools in education

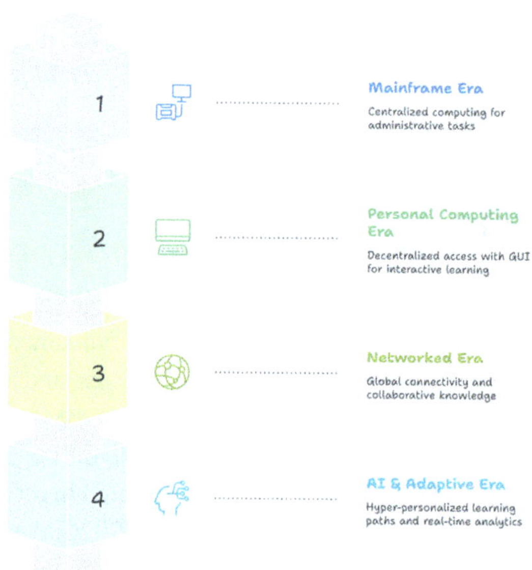

The development of digital educational tools has progressed through four distinct stages, as shown in Figure 1. It began with the Mainframe Era (1960s–1970s), which was characterized by centralized systems used mainly for research and administration. This gave way to the Personal Computing Era (1980s–1990s), which used interactive software and graphical user interfaces (GUI) to democratize technology. The next Networked Era (1990s–2010s) prioritized global connectivity and collaboration through the use of the internet and Learning Management Systems (LMS). The culmination of this journey is now the AI & Adaptive Era (2020s-Present), with active systems that dynamically customize the learning process. This development demonstrates a fundamental change from teacher-led, static technologies to adaptable, student-centered ecosystems.

Following the personal computing era, the advent of the internet and web-based learning management systems in the 1990s and 2000s fundamentally challenged traditional conceptions of the classroom by enabling unrestricted access to information and global connectivity. Moreover, the abundance of information available online necessitated new forms of digital literacy. Currently, the educational landscape is being reshaped by the most transformative force yet: Artificial Intelligence (AI) and adaptive learning systems. Rooted in machine learning and natural language processing, these systems analyze vast amounts of data to personalize learning experiences in real-time. Incorporating computer science into the education system will require a dedication to lifelong learning and innovation. Technology is no longer something to be considered an add-on rather, it has become an important part of the educational process, which must be governed by strong policies and moral principles.

2. THE EVOLUTION OF DIGITAL TOOLS IN EDUCATION

The historical traces of digital tools in education show the rapid advances in computer science and its great influence on the dissemination of knowledge. The use of technology began in the mid-20th century with the main computer, which was mainly used in academic institutions in the 60s for administrative tasks and complex data management. However, as these machines transform from tools that can only be used by researchers to widely usable platforms for teaching, there is a major shift that results in an interactive learning environment. This argument suggests that the early stages of computer thinking formed the foundation, moving from simply receiving data passively to encouraging active participation in logical structures, primarily through decomposition, pattern recognition, and abstraction capabilities (Fitrah et al., 2025). The initial focus was largely on computer-aided instruction (CAI), where linear algorithms guided students through drill-and-practice routines. This early system demonstrated the basic concept that learning materials could be converted into digital formats, stored, and accessed regularly, although their size is currently considered modest. The view of educational computing began to change with the advancement of technology. This was driven by far-ahead people who saw computers as not only a sophisticated computational tool but also as a "tool for thinking." Studies show that user perspectives and engagement in new technologies are essential.

This early system demonstrated the basic concept that learning materials could be converted into digital formats, stored, and accessed on a regular basis. While this looks simple by today's size, it's a first step. The view of educational computing began to change with the advancement of technology. This was driven by far-ahead people who saw computers as not only a sophisticated computational tool but also as a "tool for thinking." According to research, user perspectives and engagement in new technologies are essential. Levin et al. (2025) notes that this transition from centralized mainframe access to distributed personal computing represented a massive leap in how educational resources were recommended and utilized, marking the transformation of educational environments from hierarchical instructions to constructionist models, thus allowing for a foundational approach to personalized and democratized learning. The graphics-based user interface (GUI) developed today makes computers easier to understand, reducing technical issues that previously prevented ordinary people from using digital devices. This led to the school building different computer labs. In addition, educators are starting to look for ways to incorporate these new devices into their existing learning approaches.

With the advent of the internet in the 1990s and the advent of the World Wide Web, education shifted to the era of networking, removing physical limitations from traditional classrooms. The first web-based learning management systems (LMS), such as Blackboard and Moodle, emerged as a result of innovations in more advanced client-server architectures and standardized network protocols, which triggered this major change. In the 2000s and 2010s, the development of digital tools increased along with globalization and scale. This is characterized by the presence of Massive Open Online Courses (MOOCs) and cloud computing services. Platforms like Coursera and edX can serve millions of students simultaneously through distributed systems and advanced data analytics. Thus, the platform provides wider access to high-quality education from leading institutions. The researchers say that by using graph neural networks and advanced algorithms present in this platform, student performance analysis can be performed on an unprecedented scale. It also helps the system forecast results and optimize content delivery. Predictive capabilities are used to achieve this. Their findings suggest that the accessibility of digital devices, lack of infrastructure, and lack of digital literacy are major factors in higher education. The ability to access resources around the world is becoming a new indicator of privilege, suggesting that even as tools become more sophisticated, the digital divide continues to deepen existing educational inequalities.

Today, we are on the brink of an era of artificial intelligence and complex technologies, and the distinction between digital and physical learning is increasingly unclear. These developments have gone beyond simply connecting people with information Now concentrate on creating an intelligent and responsive environment that responds to students' emotional and cognitive states. They argue that this demonstrates transformative potential by creating adaptive, immersive, and inclusive learning environments, focusing on real-time adaptability to individual progress and addressing critical barriers such as static content and lack of inclusivity in existing systems. The current phase is defined by the integration of complex backend systems incorporating big data, machine learning, and IoT (Internet of Things) to create seamless educational ecosystems. However, this rapid technological progression requires a holistic approach to implementation. Tudor et al. (2025) suggest that just as in healthcare where tiered solutions are needed for equitable diagnosis, education systems must also develop multi-tiered digital strategies that account for varying levels of infrastructure readiness. They argue that structural changes in digital capacity and national readiness require policy change, which is critical to addressing structural inequalities in implementation. When we look at the shift from mainframes to AI-powered tutors, it's clear that the shift to digital tools isn't just about better hardware. It is also a constant story of how computer science is gradually opening up new opportunities for human potential, seeking to make learning more accessible, more personalized, and engaging for people around the world.

3. INTEGRATION OF TECHNOLOGY IN CURRICULUM AND ACTIVE LEARNING

Technology being incorporated into the curriculum is one of the most significant transformations in the way of thinking and practicing education today. It essentially shifts from a classical teaching model to a curriculum that encourages student engagement, cooperation, and participation. Instead of seeing technology as just an aid, the use of computer science in this educational design has resulted in an active, customizable, and data-driven learning environment. Xi et al. (2026) argue that stimulating innovative learning practices requires embedding technology at the core of instructional strategies, where artifacts and digital tools directly influence learners' actions and cognitive processes. The study shows how AI systems are able to encourage high-level thinking and assist in the design of human-AI collaborative learning systems. This integration allows teachers to transition from being sole information transmitters to facilitators of knowledge construction, empowering students to learn by exploring, analyzing, and creating through digital means. Figure 2 shows the recursive nature of the artificial intelligence-based adaptive learning cycle. The first step in the process is data input, which collects student interaction metrics such as assignment duration, assessment scores, and error frequency. Furthermore, the analysis engine uses machine learning algorithms to find knowledge gaps and learning preferences. This diagnosis informs the decision/intervention phase, in which the system dynamically changes the complexity of the content, suggests better exercises, or changes instructional modalities (e.g., switching from text to video). The resulting output results in a customized learning trajectory that re-enters the loop to ensure that learning continues to change as students grow. This closed-loop architecture allows for highly relevant, instant, and scalable interventions. For instance, Durango et al. (2025) explore how faculty experiences with integrating generative AI and other digital tools into second language curricula demonstrate that seamless technology use helps break down traditional disciplinary boundaries. The Creative Cross-Domain Synergy (CDCS) method they offer encourages creative collaboration involving various ways and fields that require interdisciplinary cooperation to optimize the potential of AI systems. This method encourages students to relate different areas of knowledge and use an integrated approach when they tackle complex problems. In addition, an iterative approach is required for strategic technology integration, which is in line with software development principles, such as prototyping, testing, and improvement.

After creating this structural integration, the pedagogical focus shifts to active learning, where digital devices help students engage in a way that focuses on themselves. Tools such as interactive whiteboards, gamified learning spaces, and cloud-based collaborative platforms encourage student participation by encouraging them to think and experience. Bottega et al. (2023) emphasize that these implicit game-based learning environments can make abstract concepts, such as historical consciousness, come alive by allowing students to experiment with strategies and experience consequences in safe virtual spaces, effectively bridging the gap between theoretical knowledge and practical application. They claim that the use of the Immersive Simulation Framework in cyberspace can significantly reduce the risk of testing in the real world, giving students the opportunity to improve their language skills in an active and interactive virtual environment.

However, the effective integration of technology into the curriculum is not without its hurdles, as it requires thoughtful planning, extensive teacher training, and continuous evaluation to overcome significant implementation challenges. Many educators face obstacles such as inadequate infrastructure, a lack of technical expertise, and limited time to redesign courses to accommodate new digital realities. Sidorkin (2025) highlights the necessity of high-level performance analysis, comparing AI capabilities with human expertise, to understand where technology can genuinely support instruction versus where it might fall short. This study shows that the development of proper cognitive models of AI's limitations and capabilities is needed. It's part of extended executive cognition, which is essential for strategically dividing cognitive attention, organizing tasks powered by AI, and handling problem-solving with hybrid intelligence. The problems associated with teacher preparation are urgent, and effective professional development requires more than basic technical training to help educators understand pedagogical application and increase their confidence in problem-solving. Technology can cause distractions and is not helpful if teachers feel uncomfortable using the tool. In addition, to ensure the sustainability of technology integration initiatives, institutions must commit beyond the initial implementation stage. To achieve long-term integration success, it is necessary to develop systems that support the technology innovation cycle and provide ongoing support. This is done to ensure that technological advances do not lead to burnout or disappointment when initial enthusiasm wanes and technical issues arise.

A critical dimension of these implementation challenges is the persistent issue of equity and the digital divide, which extends beyond simple access to hardware and connectivity to include disparities in the quality of technology experiences. Schools serving disadvantaged communities often struggle with outdated equipment and a lack of technical support staff, creating technology deserts where innovative practices are difficult to sustain. The research shows that structural limitations are major drivers of student attrition related to the digital divide, and dropout is not equally distributed but is shaped by socioeconomic and institutional factors. This inequity is not just about having a device it is about the structural disparities in readiness to adopt and utilize these tools effectively. Tudor et al. (2025) analyze national readiness for cloud adoption across the EU, revealing that structural disparities heavily influence how effectively digital ecosystems are established and maintained. They see that these differences in adoption indicate structural variations in digital capabilities Some countries face structural problems to achieve nation-level cloud readiness. Students who come from more affluent families typically have access to better home infrastructure and family support, while students from less affluent families are entirely dependent on limited school resources. Addressing these differences requires a comprehensive approach that takes into account regional and geographical differences.

Finally, the integration of technology plays a pivotal role in fostering global collaboration and digital citizenship, extending the learning community far beyond traditional institutional boundaries. Online communities and platforms allow students to work on real-world projects, share code, and receive peer feedback, illustrating how the principles of open-source computer science can enhance collaborative learning. Kong and Hu (2025) emphasize the importance of professional development in developing conceptual understanding of generative AI and digital tools among administrative staff and students alike, ensuring that the entire educational ecosystem is aligned in promoting responsible, collaborative, and innovative technology use. Based on a four-dimensional AI literacy framework, the study created a professional development program for administrative staff that demonstrated an improvement in participants' conceptual understanding of GenAI. The program aims to provide administrative staff with essential skills necessary for an AI work environment.

4. ARTIFICIAL INTELLIGENCE AND ADAPTIVE LEARNING

One of the most transformative technological forces in the world of education today is artificial intelligence (AI), which has significantly shifted learning towards a tailored and non-uniform approach. Artificial intelligence-powered systems can mimic aspects of human intelligence in education by leveraging more advanced areas of computer science such as machine learning, natural language processing, and neural networks. Alalawi et al. (2025), examining publication trends in this area, notes that the focus of research has shifted rapidly to systems that can precisely forecast student performance by analyzing large educational data. This change represents a significant paradigm shift. The conventional model of education, which treats students as a uniform group that receives the same instruction, is replaced by a more adaptive learning environment. Learning Analytics Intervention Studies (LAIs) emerged to address this issue by providing relevant information about issues such as customized lesson plans and students' lack of knowledge to help students implement interventions. These systems can identify and respond to profound differences in each student's learning style, prior knowledge, and cognitive abilities. Hakkal and Ait Lahcen (2025) demonstrate how leveraging technologies like graph neural networks allows for precise learner performance prediction, enabling interventions that were previously impossible at scale.

Figure 2. AI-driven adaptive learning loop

The recursive nature of the AI-driven adaptive learning cycle is illustrated graphically in Figure 2. Data input is the first step in the process, which gathers metrics from student interactions such as task duration, assessment scores, and error frequency. The Analysis Engine then uses machine learning algorithms to identify learning preferences and knowledge gaps. The Decision/Intervention phase, where the system dynamically modifies content complexity, recommends remedial exercises, or modifies instructional modalities (e.g., switching from text to video), is informed by this diagnosis. The resultant output creates a customized learning trajectory that re-enters the loop, ensuring that instruction keeps changing in tandem with the growth of the learner. Scalable, instantaneous, and highly relevant interventions are made possible by this closed-loop architecture.

As a result of this research, pictorial neural networks appear to be an effective tool for organizing complex relationships in educational data. Analysis of student interaction in the education system should be done to predict future success in predicting student performance. The ultimate goal is to build a scalable and generalized system to predict student performance. The merging of pedagogical theory with the power of computing in this new approach has opened up enormous opportunities to realize a long-desired vision of education: to bring students closer to where they are. AI can create dynamic and changing learning paths as student progress by analyzing millions of data in real-time. This ensures that the complexity of the material remains and is not lost or wasted, keeping students interested.

The mechanics of these adaptive learning systems represent one of the most practical and impactful applications of computer science in education today. By utilizing complex algorithms, these platforms assess a student's performance continuously, adjusting not just the pace of the lesson but also the mode of delivery. Feng et al.

(2025) describes how adaptive web-based frameworks integrating NLP enable students to interact with intelligent tutoring systems in a conversational manner, asking questions and receiving context-aware explanations as if they were speaking to a human tutor. An intelligent learning system based on a generative initial training model was used in this study to teach English. The system aims to help students learn through dialogue and provide relevant exercises, comparisons, and examples to improve their understanding of how to answer questions. In addition, the system also provides direct feedback, such as identifying errors and analyzing vocabulary, language coherence, and vocabulary selection. An interactive dialogue enhances cognitive participation and creates a mutually beneficial feedback cycle due to the shift from static information retrieval. Not only do students receive direction from these systems, but their interactions help the system understand their learning patterns.

Beyond the optimization of individual learning paths, the advent of Generative AI has introduced a new frontier of possibilities and challenges, expanding the scope of what adaptive systems can achieve. Large Language Models (LLMs), such as the GPT series, have demonstrated the ability to generate human-quality text, solve complex mathematical problems, and even engage in creative brainstorming, acting as on-demand collaborators for students. Souto et al. (2025) conduct a compelling analysis of this capability by comparing GPT-4o's performance against residency exams, illustrating that these tools can now function at a level of expertise comparable to advanced human learners in specific domains. The study found that GPT-4o has an accuracy of 85.88%, much higher compared to GPT-4, and shows that AI can be a useful tool in medical education, aid in residency exam preparation, and aid in understanding complex problems. However, the researchers also note that both models lose accuracy when faced with questions that require deep thought. Furthermore, the integration of Large Language Models introduces the critical need for 'prompt engineering' as a new literacy skill. Since these models generate outputs based on probabilistic patterns rather than sentient understanding, the quality of the educational output is directly dependent on the quality of the student's input. This interaction creates a unique cognitive loop: to effectively use an AI tutor, a student must first learn to articulate their problem clearly and logically. Therefore, the use of Generative AI paradoxically reinforces the need for strong communication and critical thinking skills, as students must constantly evaluate the AI's responses for 'hallucinations' or factual inaccuracies, turning every interaction into an exercise in verification and critical analysis.

With these capabilities, you can create unlimited and customizable practice materials, unique essay guides, coding problems, or historical scenarios tailored to the student's current interests and abilities. These forces require managers and educators to change the way they understand digital literacy. Kong and Hu (2025) emphasize that developing a conceptual understanding of generative AI among administrative staff and educators is crucial through professional development, as the indiscriminate use of these tools can lead to ethical pitfalls. Using a four-dimensional AI literacy framework, this study designed a professional development program for administrative staff. The program shows a significant improvement in participants' conceptual understanding of GenAI and aims to provide administrative staff with the essential skills needed in an AI-connected work environment, as well as to reduce AI literacy barriers in various industries. Therefore, the conversation has shifted from just "utilizing" technology to "cooperating" with it.

On an institutional level, the integration of AI extends to learning analytics and predictive modeling, which serve as the nervous system for modern educational administration. Universities and schools are increasingly relying on these data-driven insights to improve retention rates and optimize resource allocation. Their research develops a distributed collaborative learning framework that enables personalized learning among different clients. the findings indicate that the proposed framework reliably enables knowledge sharing in multimodal collaborative learning, while the privacy assessment demonstrates its robustness in safeguarding sensitive information. However, the rapid proliferation of AI in education is not without its profound ethical dilemmas and risks, particularly concerning the "black box" nature of many algorithms and the potential for bias. Because AI systems learn from historical data, they may inadvertently encode and perpetuate existing societal inequalities, leading to unfair assessment outcomes or discriminatory recommendations. Sidorkin (2025) argues that libraries and educational hubs must become centers for AI competency, fostering a culture where the limitations of AI are understood as clearly as its strengths. As a result of critical learning, the study introduced Extended Executive Cognition. The aim of this study is to create an accurate mental model of AI's limitations and capabilities for human-AI collaboration as well as metacognitive skills. The goal is to ensure that we retain empathy, creativity, and moral reasoning when utilizing algorithms.

5. INTERDISCIPLINARY COLLABORATION AND DIGITAL LITERACY

To achieve success in implementing digital transformation in education, there needs to be a strong premise that technological progress cannot be done independently, it is necessary to have very strong cooperation between disciplines such as computer science, education, psychology, sociology, and communication studies. This is important because educational technology carries values, assumptions, and priorities that need to be considered through a variety of lenses. The development of educational tools has gone from a purely technical engineering issue to a human-centered design process thanks to this collaborative ethic. This ensures that the technology created is not only useful but also pedagogically healthy and socially responsible. The redefinition of digital literacy is the goal of this interdisciplinary effort. Digital literacy has evolved from basic technical skills to complex competencies that include creative production, critical evaluation, and moral awareness. Digital literacy in the twenty-first century means more than just using software. It also means understanding the mechanisms behind the information ecosystem, such as how algorithms curate content, how data is harvested, and how bias is encoded in code.

The practical application of this interdisciplinary collaboration is most visible in the innovative design of learning experiences and the professional development of educators. When computer scientists and teachers collaborate, the result is often a transformation in instructional design where technology becomes an artifact that actively stimulates learning. However, educators need an interdisciplinary support structure for these innovations to take root. The main goal is to solve the problem of the "learning and use shift" that occurs during the training process and encourage teachers to acquire and apply their abilities to apply information technology. This supports the idea that cooperation should occur throughout the structure of the educational institution, not just between students.

Furthermore, interdisciplinary collaboration extends beyond the walls of the academy into the broader ecosystem of industry and community, fostering a culture of open innovation and lifelong learning. The rapid evolution of the digital economy means that the skills required in the workforce are constantly shifting, necessitating a tighter feedback loop between educational institutions and the industries they serve. This is seen in the increased use of digital badges and micro-credentials, which rely on secure data infrastructures to verify capabilities. This is possible because evidence allows for the integration of learning artifacts, such as writing samples or projects, into digital micro-credentials. It challenges traditional valuation and credentialing paradigms and allows for micro credentials. Educators can ensure that the "digital literacy" they teach is relevant and rigorous by working closely with industry partners, while computer scientists in industry can better understand the development needs of the future workforce and create effective cycles of improvement and adaptation.

Finally, the success of these collaborative efforts ultimately hinges on the ability to create engaging, immersive, and socially connected learning environments that resonate with the "digital native" generation. The integration of advanced technologies like virtual agents and alternate reality games into STEM education is a prime example of how computer science can serve pedagogical goals of engagement. Wang et al. (2025) present evidence that integrating Large Language Model-based virtual agents into alternate reality games significantly boosts student engagement, creating immersive narratives that compel students to solve problems. In their study mentioned below "Improving student engagement in STEM: Integrating virtual scaffolding based on large language models into alternate reality games," researchers found that LLM-ARG significantly improved students' learning outcomes and their metacognitive awareness. Additionally, LLM-driven scaffolding supports a variety of learning strategies and encourages flexible STEM learning. To create a learning experience that is greater than the sum of its parts, this approach blends art (game design), humanities (narrative structure), and artificial intelligence (AI). Nonetheless, such environmental design must be wary of "silosing" information.

6. ETHICAL AND DATA SECURITY CHALLENGES IN DIGITAL EDUCATION

The rapid digitization of the educational landscape has ushered in an era of unprecedented data accumulation, bringing with it a complex array of ethical dilemmas and security vulnerabilities that extend far beyond simple technical glitches. As learning management systems and educational applications collect vast troves of information ranging from academic grades and behavioral patterns to biometric data and social interactions the fundamental question of data ownership and privacy has become critical. Zichichi et al. (2022) argue that establishing and governing these data ecosystems requires a delicate balance between centralization for efficiency and decentralization for privacy, a tension that is palpable in how schools manage student records. They explain that the lack of transparency and centralization of data processing threatens the privacy of individuals. Having direct control over the flow of their personal data will help with privacy and "data altruism". Educational institutions are no longer just places where students learn now they are in charge of their own digital identity, which many people don't know. This has significant ethical consequences, especially considering the possibility that this data could be exploited or misused by third-party vendors. Barrera and Devechi (2024), in their analysis of the platformization of universities under surveillance capitalism, they criticize the broader capitalist structure of knowledge production and point out that the commercialization of educational data often prioritizes profit over student protection, treating student data as material to be extracted rather than a personal asset that must be protected. As a result, it is a moral obligation for organizations to implement a robust data governance system. The dangerous problem of algorithmic bias and injustice in the artificial intelligence (AI)-driven education system is closely related to data privacy issues. This is because schools are increasingly relying on algorithms to personalize learning, recommend courses, and even grade essays. There is a high probability that these systems will replicate and reinforce historical biases that exist in their education data. Roe et al. (2025), in their analysis of the algorithmic potential and its social consequences, examined the impact of

AI interventions in professional practice, noting that "black box" algorithms can obscure the decision-making process, making it difficult for stakeholders to understand why a student is given an opportunity or rejected. opportunity. In a high-risk educational environment, where decisions can change students' lives, these mistakes are untenable. If the algorithm is trained on specific demographic data, it may not be able to assess or support students from underrepresented groups. This would disguise discrimination as an unbiased science.

The adoption of digital tools is heavily influenced by national preparedness and structural deficiencies, especially in terms of resources, and points out that without ethical audits and inclusive design, AI in education may only become a tool of exclusion rather than empowerment. Th conventional "castle and moat" security model is no longer relevant as contemporary learning, in which students can access systems through personal devices on an unsecured home network, is on the rise. Securing this environment presents challenges in addition to technical issues. Therefore, cybersecurity must be treated as a pedagogical issue, not just an IT issue. The increasing use of proctoring technology, such as proctoring software that monitors students during exams to prevent academic dishonesty, raises many ethical and pressing issues. These tools are meant to be honest, but they often violate students' privacy and can cause psychological anxiety and mistrust. Students who are supervised by cameras that track eye movements or analyze background noise often report feeling criminalized, which can interfere with their academic performance and mental health. Vulnerable students are often disproportionately affected by this supervision, which brings socioeconomic bias into assessment as they may not have the personal and quiet space to take the exam.

Beyond the immediate stress of surveillance, there is a long-term concern regarding the creation of permanent 'data doubles' for students. Every click, pause, and interaction within a digital learning platform contributes to a behavioral profile that could theoretically follow a student throughout their academic and professional life. If this granular data originally intended for formative assessment is commodified or sold to third-party brokers, it risks pigeonholing students based on past performance, potentially limiting their future opportunities before they even enter the workforce. The "right to be forgotten", which ensures that a student's digital learning history does not become a permanent record that affects their classes in the future, is included in the ethical imperative. Ultimately, to address these ethical and data security issues, governance and institutional culture must be changed. Reactive compliance must be replaced by proactive ethical leadership. To build a transparent framework that puts human values above the benefits of technology, educators, students, policymakers, and technology must work together. This involves creating clear policies on data retention, consent, and algorithmic accountability. Ethics should be embedded in the design phase of every digital tool ("ethics-by-design"), ensuring that technology serves education, not the other way around.

7. CASE STUDIES OF DIGITAL TOOL IMPLEMENTATION ACROSS NATIONS

The global landscape of digital education reveals a striking diversity in how nations approach the integration of technology, a divergence shaped profoundly by differing cultural values, economic resources, and governance structures. While the aspiration to modernize education is universal, the pathways taken are distinct, offering a rich repository of case studies that highlight both successful strategies and cautionary tales. Aleca and Mihai (2025), in their analysis of cloud adoption and national readiness across the European Union, they emphasized that tailored strategies rather than a "one-size-fits-all" approach are needed to address disparities in digital infrastructure and workforce readiness. Finland is often cited as an example of educational excellence. Finnish strategies rely on teacher empowerment and pedagogical conviction. This sets it apart from other countries that prioritize mass deployment of hardware. The Finnish model concentrates on developing educators' digital competencies, ensuring that technology is a flexible tool for creativity rather than a rigid system for conveying information. Xie and Lu (2025) identifies cognitive gradients where different levels of digital literacy impact students' perception of information and innovation abilities, note that digital limitations are an important factor for student success. This is addressed in Finland by incorporating digital equality into its social welfare programs, ensuring that schools in remote areas receive the same services as those in Helsinki. The philosophy behind this success is that technology serves as a secondary component in human teaching. Using platforms like Opeka, teachers in Finland assess their own digital skills. It builds a culture of continuous and self-sustaining professional improvement that is in line with the principles of national autonomy and responsibility.

In sharp contrast to Finland's decentralized and teacher-centric model, Singapore offers a compelling example of a highly centralized, state-driven transformation under its "Smart Nation" initiative. Here, the integration of digital tools is systematic, uniform, and data-driven, reflecting a governance style that values efficiency and standardization. The curriculum is tightly integrated with advanced technologies, including AI-driven learning analytics that track student progress with granular precision Zhang (2025) provides an explanation of how dynamic learning path recommendation algorithms, driven by an analysis of user behavioural habits and learning preferences, are used to create personalised learning paths for students, which is characteristic of Singapore's approach to human resource development.

This top-down strategy ensures that all students, regardless of their background, have access to high-quality digital resources and instruction on cybersecurity. However, questions about the pressures students face and the room for unorganized creativity arise as a result of this data-centric approach. This approach shows the trade-offs of systems made for maximum efficiency.

Moving to the United States, the implementation of digital tools reflects the complexities of a highly decentralized and market-driven educational system. The landscape here is characterized by pockets of immense innovation coexisting with deep structural inequalities. Kistaubayev et al. (2025) addresses systems issues such as data centralization while emphasizing institutional governance and data sovereignty, studying the governance of data ecosystems amidst centralization and decentralization, a framework perfectly illustrates a situation in the United States where individual school districts, or even individual schools, make their own decisions about technology procurement. Rapid experimentation with cutting-edge tools such as Virtual Reality and adaptive learning platforms in wealthy districts is made possible by these autonomy. However, it also exacerbates the "digital divide", where urban and low-income rural districts face difficulties in getting basic connectivity. Countries. These diverse case studies converge on a singular lesson: the implementation of digital tools is less about the technology itself and more about the "human dynamics" and ecosystem design.

8. CONCLUSION: SOLUTIONS AND POLICY RECOMMENDATIONS FOR THE FUTURE OF DIGITAL EDUCATION

The future of education is marked by a radical departure from the "one size fits all" industrial model of the past, instead it can evolve into a dynamic blend of hyper-personalized learning and advanced computing intelligence. At a time when standing on the brink of transformation, traditional teaching models are changing very quickly to move towards an AI-based adaptive learning ecosystem that not only digitizes textbooks but also adapts materials, pace, and pedagogical strategies to specific student behaviors and needs. In a traditional classroom, a teacher must be able to cater to the needs of an average of thirty students, inevitably leaving some while holding others instead, an AI-based ecosystem uses predictive analytics and real-time data to create a unique profile for each learner. These changes show that education must be flexible, relevant, and highly aligned with human motivation, ensuring that learners remain the focal point of the technological revolution. As a result, educational institutions must be agile to support ever-evolving innovations, necessitating a shift in which teachers evolve from the sole distributor of knowledge to mentors and facilitators of curiosity that foster critical thinking and emotional intelligence while AI handles data processing and strengthening memorization skills.

The development of digital education is leading to immersive learning experiences through Virtual Reality (VR), Augmented Reality (AR), and space-based technologies, signaling a shift from the era of flat screens to the era of spatial computing. This environment it allows students to understand complex concepts through hands-on interaction that previously would not have been possible or too dangerous to replicate in class, such as medical students practicing surgery in hyper-realistic VR simulations or historians exploring ancient civilizations digitally reconstructed. The experience is supported by a Large Language Model (LLM)-based virtual agent that enhances students' understanding and achievement by acting as Socrates' tutor, asking questions, investigating and offering clues rather than simple answers. Above all, the design of future technologies should focus on the way humans process information, not on passive consumption. The architecture of these systems should be based on cognitive science to ensure that immersive graphics escalate the learning process rather than overwhelm learners, thereby maximizing knowledge retention and transfer rather than simply serving as entertainment.

This cognitive alignment is crucial for preparing the next generation for a workforce defined by 'Hybrid Intelligence' the collaborative relationship between human intuition and machine efficiency. As automation takes over routine cognitive tasks, the unique value of human workers will lie in their ability to empathize, interpret context, and make ethical judgments areas where AI currently lacks capacity. Therefore, digital education must not only teach technical skills but also nurture unique human traits that machines cannot replicate. The ability of these digital tools to enhance human intelligence without compromising fundamental cognitive and social skills is a key measure of their success. However, to drive digital transformation, public policies are needed that ensure digital equity, inclusive infrastructure, and strong data governance. This is because technology alone is not enough to cure the problem and we face the possibility that the digital divide will widen into an insurmountable economic canyon in the future. To prevent this from happening, governments must provide public digital infrastructure that includes high-speed internet and computing power, as well as electricity and clean water needs. In addition, policymakers ensure data privacy, algorithmic transparency, and interoperability so that technological advances can be balanced with student protection. Because AI systems process a lot of biometric and behavioral data, it's critical to ensure that this data is never used for business gain. We also have to understand why AI tutors recommend certain routes, so that our digital systems don't incorporate real-world biases. Without strategic efforts, immersive labs and personalized AI tutors will remain exclusive to the elite, leaving the less fortunate with outdated resources.

Ultimately, the success of digital education depends on the extent to which technology can empower people, foster trust, and create new value. It aims to build a better school system and make society ready for an uncertain future. The economy of the future will depend on continuous learning and new skills, not degrees accumulated over twenty years. We are heading towards a "digital proof of competency" system where blockchain-verified micro-credentials will replace or complement traditional diplomas. This will create an ecosystem where education is sustainable, accessible, and sustainable. We can build a future of education that is not only technologically advanced but also highly equitable, ensuring that innovation serves to enhance human potential in all demographics by aligning advanced computing intelligence with strong public policy and human-centered design.

REFERENCES

Alalawi, K., Athauda, R., & Chiong, R. (2025). An Extended Learning Analytics Framework Integrating Machine Learning and Pedagogical Approaches for Student Performance Prediction and Intervention. *International Journal of Artificial Intelligence in Education, 35*(3), 1239–1287. DOI: 10.1007/s40593-024-00429-7

Aleca, O. E., & Mihai, F. (2025). The Role of Digital Infrastructure and Skills in Enhancing Labor Productivity: Insights from Industry 4.0 in the European Union. *Systems, 13*(2), 113. Advance online publication. DOI: 10.3390/systems13020113

Barrera, D. F., & Devechi, C. P. V. (2024). Platformization of Brazilian Public Higher Education: Implications for the educational project. *Edutec, 87*, 101–114.

Bottega, J. A., Kich, V. A., de Jesus, J. C., Steinmetz, R., Kolling, A. H., Bedin Grando, R. B., da Silva Guerra, R. S., & Tello Gamarra, D. F. T. (2023). Jubileo: An Immersive Simulation Framework for Social Robot Design. *Journal of Intelligent & Robotic Systems, 109*(4), 91. Advance online publication. DOI: 10.1007/s10846-023-01991-3

Durango, I., Gallud, J. A., & Penichet, V. M. R. (2025). The data dance: Choreographing seamless partnerships between humans, data, and GenAI. *International Journal of Data Science and Analytics, 20*(4), 3613–3640. DOI: 10.1007/s41060-024-00684-w

Feng, W., Lai, X., Zhang, X., Fan, X., & Du, Y. (2025). Research on the construction and application of intelligent tutoring system for english teaching based on generative pre-training model. *Systems and Soft Computing, 7*, 200232. Advance online publication. DOI: 10.1016/j.sasc.2025.200232

Fitrah, M., Sofroniou, A., Setiawan, C., Widihastuti, W., Yarmanetti, N., Jaya, M. P. S., Panuntun, J. G., Arfaton, A., Beteno, S., & Susianti, I. (2025). The Impact of Integrated Project-Based Learning and Flipped Classroom on Students' Computational Thinking Skills: Embedded Mixed Methods. *Education Sciences, 15*(4), 448. Advance online publication. DOI: 10.3390/educsci15040448

Fromm, Y. M., Rasch, J., & Ifenthaler, D. (2025). Technology-enhanced personalized learning environments based on prior knowledge in continuing education: An experimental study. *Smart Learning Environments, 12*(1), 54. Advance online publication. DOI: 10.1186/s40561-025-00407-z

Garzón, J., Burgos, D., & Tlili, A. (2025). Advantages and challenges associated with mobile learning in education: A systematic literature review. *Journal of Computers in Education, 12*(4), 1173–1205. DOI: 10.1007/s40692-024-00342-x

Hakkal, S., & Ait Lahcen, A. A. (2025). Leveraging graph neural network for learner performance prediction. *Expert Systems with Applications, 293*, 128724. Advance online publication. DOI: 10.1016/j.eswa.2025.128724

Kistaubayev, Y., Liébana-Cabanillas, F., Shaikh, A. A., Mutanov, G., Ussatova, O., & Shinbayeva, A. (2025). Enhancing Transparency and Trust in Higher Education Institutions via Blockchain: A Conceptual Model Utilizing the Ethereum Consortium Approach. *Sustainability (Basel), 17*(20), 9350. Advance online publication. DOI: 10.3390/su17209350

Kong, S. C., & Hu, W. (2025). A study of developing administrative Staff's conceptual understanding of generative artificial intelligence through professional Development: Evaluation of a course using tests, surveys and thematic analysis of reflective writings. *Computers and Education: Artificial Intelligence, 9*, 100444. Advance online publication. DOI: 10.1016/j.caeai.2025.100444

Levin, I., Semenov, A. L., & Gorsky, M. (2025). Smart Learning in the 21st Century: Advancing Constructionism Across Three Digital Epochs. *Education Sciences, 15*(1), 45. Advance online publication. DOI: 10.3390/educsci15010045

Roe, J., Perkins, M., & Furze, L. (2025). Reflecting Reality, Amplifying Bias? Using Metaphors to Teach Critical AI Literacy. *Journal of Interactive Media in Education, 2025*(1). DOI: 10.5334/jime.961

Sahayu, W., Triyono, S., & Ungu, N. K. (2026). Digital Technology in Differentiated English Language Teaching: A Systematic Review with Bibliometric Insights. *Indonesian Journal of Science and Technology, 11*(1), 167–188. DOI: 10.17509/ijost.v11i2.89685

Sidorkin, A. M. (2025). Extended executive cognition, a learning outcome for the AI age. *Computers and Education Open, 9*, 100294. Advance online publication. DOI: 10.1016/j.caeo.2025.100294

Souto, M. E. V. C., Fernandes, A. C., Silva, A. B. S., de Freitas Ribeiro, L. H., & de Medeiros Fernandes, T. A. A. (2025). A multi-model longitudinal assessment of ChatGPT performance on medical residency examinations. *Frontiers in Artificial Intelligence, 8*, 1614874. Advance online publication. DOI: 10.3389/frai.2025.1614874 PMID: 40918587

Tudor, C., Florescu, M., Polychronidou, P., Stamatiou, P., Vlachos, V., & Kasabali, K. (2025). Cloud Adoption in the Digital Era: An Interpretable Machine Learning Analysis of National Readiness and Structural Disparities Across the EU. *Applied Sciences (Basel, Switzerland), 15*(14), 8019. Advance online publication. DOI: 10.3390/app15148019

Wang, M., Zhu, J., Hwang, G.-J., Chang, S.-C., Yang, Q.-F., & Zhang, D. (2025). Boosting Student Engagement in STEM: Integrating Large Language Model-Based Virtual Agents Into Alternate Reality Games. *Journal of Computer Assisted Learning*, *41*(6), e70139. Advance online publication. DOI: 10.1111/jcal.70139

Xi, L., Zhang, Y., & Wang, Q. (2026). Investigating the effects of an LLM-based Socratic conversational agent on students' academic performance and reflective thinking in higher education. *Computers & Education*, *241*, 105494. Advance online publication. DOI: 10.1016/j.compedu.2025.105494

Xie, X., & Lu, C. (2025). Bridging the Digital Gradient: How Digital Literacy and Information Perception Shape Innovation and Entrepreneurship Across Urban, County and Township Students. *Sustainability (Basel)*, *17*(22), 9942. Advance online publication. DOI: 10.3390/su17229942

Zhang, X. (2025). Research on the application of big data learning recommendation model driven by knowledge graph algorithm in educational information platform optimization. *Systems and Soft Computing*, *7*, 200298. Advance online publication. DOI: 10.1016/j.sasc.2025.200298

Zichichi, M., Ferretti, S., D'Angelo, G., & Rodríguez-Doncel, V. (2022). Data governance through a multi-DLT architecture in view of the GDPR. *Cluster Computing*, *25*(6), 4515–4542. DOI: 10.1007/s10586-022-03691-3

Chapter 2
Minds and Machines:
The Interdisciplinary Challenge of AI's Influence in Education

Pankaj Bhambri
http://orcid.org/0000-0003-4437-4103
Guru Nanak Dev Engineering College, Ludhiana, India

ABSTRACT

Artificial Intelligence (AI) in education transcends its role as a mere tool, emerging as a formative force that shapes the very landscape of learning. This chapter argues that the most profound impacts of AI lie not in algorithmic efficiency, but in its capacity to reshape student cognition, attitudes, and pedagogical outcomes—a complex interplay demanding an interdisciplinary response. We move beyond technocentric views to explore how AI systems influence metacognitive skills and self-regulated learning (psychology), alter student-teacher dynamics and perpetuate biases (sociology), and demand new ethical frameworks and policy guidance (philosophy and law). The chapter concludes by proposing a collaborative framework for researchers, educators, and policymakers to harness AI's potential while safeguarding the human elements at the core of education.

1 INTRODUCTION: THE UNSEEN CLASSROOM PARTNER

The integration of Artificial Intelligence (AI) into educational settings is often celebrated for its efficiency and personalization, promising a revolution in how we teach and learn. However, this narrative frequently overlooks a more profound and subtle transformation. Beyond the interactive tutors and automated grading systems, AI has become an "unseen classroom partner"—a pervasive force that actively, if imperceptibly, shapes the educational environment, influencing not just what students

DOI: 10.4018/979-8-2600-1568-1.ch002

learn, but how they think, feel, and perceive knowledge itself. This chapter moves beyond a technocentric view to investigate this multifaceted influence, arguing that to understand modern education, we must account for the silent, formative role of these intelligent systems. AI is not a neutral tool but an active participant in the educational dynamic (Lobanova et al., 2024). Its algorithms curate information, its feedback mechanisms guide behavior, and its very presence alters traditional classroom interactions and power structures. By framing AI in this way, we set the stage for a critical exploration of its cognitive, social, and ethical ramifications. The goal is to shift the conversation from what AI does for education to what AI is doing to education, prompting a necessary and interdisciplinary examination of our new learning reality.

1.1 From Tool to Agent: Redefining AI's Role

Traditionally, educational technology has been understood as a tool—an instrument wielded by human intention, like a calculator or a pencil. Its function was to augment human capability without independent influence. Contemporary AI, particularly with the advent of generative models and adaptive learning platforms, shatters this paradigm (Vatankhah et al., 2024). These systems are not passive instruments; they are active agents that make decisions, generate content, and provide personalized feedback based on complex, often opaque, internal logic. This shift from a static tool to a dynamic agent represents a fundamental change in the human-machine relationship within the learning process.

This redefinition is critical because an agent exerts a different kind of influence than a tool. An agent can initiate interaction, adapt strategies in real-time, and assert a form of "expertise." When a student interacts with an AI writing tutor that suggests structural changes to an essay, or an adaptive learning platform that alters the difficulty of problems based on performance, the AI is acting as a pedagogical agent (Yıldız, 2025). This agency directly impacts the learner's journey, delegating certain aspects of guidance and judgment to the machine. Consequently, we can no longer evaluate AI solely on its technical performance but must also assess its pedagogical actions and their consequences on student autonomy, trust, and intellectual development.

1.2 The Central Thesis: Why an Interdisciplinary Lens is Essential

The central thesis of this chapter is that the profound challenges and opportunities posed by AI in education are inherently interconnected and cannot be adequately understood or addressed through a single disciplinary silo (Creely &

Blannin, 2025). A computer scientist can optimize an algorithm for efficiency, but cannot alone grasp its potential to erode metacognitive skills. A psychologist might study learning outcomes, but may lack the framework to analyze how algorithmic bias perpetuates social inequities. Similarly, an ethicist can outline principles for fairness, but requires insights from sociology and education to implement them in practice. The complexity of AI's influence demands a synthesis of these perspectives. Therefore, an interdisciplinary lens is not merely beneficial but essential (Rani et al., 2024). It allows us to see the full picture: how a cognitive effect (e.g., algorithmic dependency) is linked to a technical design (e.g., high-powered recommendations), which in turn raises an ethical concern (e.g., diminished student agency) and a social consequence (e.g., changed classroom dynamics). This chapter argues that only by integrating insights from computer science, psychology, sociology, philosophy, and educational theory can we develop a holistic understanding of AI as an "unseen classroom partner" and craft effective, human-centric responses that harness its power while mitigating its risks.

1.3 Chapter Roadmap

This chapter is structured to systematically unpack the layered influence of AI, guiding the reader from the internal cognitive processes of the learner to the broader ethical and societal implications. We begin by exploring the Cognitive Layer, investigating how AI impacts thinking patterns, metacognition, and tangible learning outcomes. From there, we expand to the Affective and Social Layer, analyzing the formation of student attitudes, perceptions of AI reliability, and the reshaping of classroom relationships and social biases (Rana & Bhambri, 2024a). The third section delves into the Ethical and Philosophical Dimension, confronting the fundamental questions of autonomy, data privacy, and equity that AI introduces. The final section synthesizes these explorations to propose a way forward. In Toward an Interdisciplinary Response, we will integrate the threads from the preceding layers to construct a collaborative framework for researchers, designers, educators, and policymakers (Lamberti et al., 2025). This roadmap is designed to build a cumulative argument, demonstrating that each domain of influence is inextricably linked and that a siloed approach is insufficient for navigating the future of education in an age of intelligent machines. The conclusion will not merely summarize but will offer a forward-looking perspective on steering the symbiotic relationship between human minds and artificial agents.

2 THE COGNITIVE LAYER: AI'S IMPACT ON THINKING AND LEARNING OUTCOMES

2.1 Enhancing or Eroding Metacognition?

AI systems, particularly those offering real-time feedback and learning analytics, hold significant promise for enhancing metacognition—the awareness and understanding of one's own thought processes (Ng et al., 2024). By providing students with detailed dashboards on their performance, struggle points, and time management, these tools act as external mirrors, reflecting their learning journey back to them. This can help learners develop a more accurate sense of their knowledge gaps, strengthen their ability to self-assess, and make more informed decisions about what to study next, thereby fostering self-regulated learning (Parker et al., 2025). In this capacity, AI serves as a powerful scaffold, helping students "learn how to learn" by making the learning process visible and actionable.

Conversely, an over-reliance on AI-driven guidance risks eroding the very metacognitive skills it aims to build (Nishat, 2025). If an AI system consistently curates content, predicts difficulties before they are deeply felt, and provides immediate corrective feedback, the student may become a passive recipient of information rather than an active manager of their own cognition. The internal struggle to monitor one's comprehension and the crucial experience of working through confusion—key drivers of deep learning—can be short-circuited (Peters et al., 2024). The danger is that the AI becomes a cognitive crutch, leading to "metacognitive offloading," where students no longer develop the intrinsic ability to plan, monitor, and evaluate their learning independently, leaving them ill-equipped for complex tasks in non-scaffolded, real-world environments.

2.2 Personalized Learning Pathways and Knowledge Acquisition

The core promise of AI in education is the delivery of truly personalized learning pathways. By analyzing vast datasets of student interactions, AI can adapt the sequence, pace, and difficulty of content to match individual needs and aptitudes. This moves beyond the one-size-fits-all model, theoretically optimizing knowledge acquisition by ensuring students are consistently working within their "zone of proximal development." Such systems can identify and remediate specific misconceptions instantly, reinforce concepts as needed, and present information in modalities that align with a learner's preferences, potentially leading to more efficient and durable learning outcomes compared to traditional methods (Simões & Caldeira, 2024). However, this personalization raises critical questions about the nature of the knowledge being acquired. Highly algorithmically-curated pathways may lead to a fragmented or "siloed" understanding of a subject, where students miss the broader, interdisciplinary connections that a standardized curriculum often provides (Allison et al., 2025). Furthermore, the criteria for "optimal" pathways are defined by the algorithm's model of learning, which may prioritize measurable, short-term performance metrics (e.g., quiz scores) over deeper, more conceptual understanding or creative thinking. There is a risk of creating a generation of learners who are proficient in navigating narrow, pre-defined skill trees but lack the cohesive, integrated knowledge framework necessary for innovation and critical synthesis.

2.3 The Problem of "Algorithmic Dependency" and Critical Thinking

A primary cognitive risk associated with pervasive AI integration is the development of "algorithmic dependency"—a learned reliance on AI systems to the point where cognitive effort and intellectual autonomy diminish (Chen, 2025). When students habitually turn to an AI for answers, step-by-step solutions, or even ideation, they bypass the productive struggle that is essential for developing robust problem-solving skills and conceptual mastery. This dependency mirrors the "Google effect," where individuals forget information they believe can be easily retrieved, but extends it to the very process of thinking itself, potentially atrophying the cognitive muscles required for sustained intellectual effort.

This dependency poses a direct threat to critical thinking, the cornerstone of advanced learning. Critical thinking requires questioning assumptions, evaluating evidence, and constructing logical arguments—processes that are inherently internal and effortful (Khogali & Mekid, 2024). If an AI consistently provides pre-digested information, validated answers, and persuasive arguments, students may lose the motivation and capacity to engage in these foundational practices (Vatankhah et al., 2024). The challenge, therefore, is not just to prevent plagiarism, but to foster an environment where AI tools are used to stimulate and challenge thinking rather than replace it. Educators must design tasks that require students to critique, build upon, and apply AI-generated outputs, ensuring the technology serves as a catalyst for critical inquiry rather than a substitute for it (Kayyali, 2024).

3 THE AFFECTIVE AND SOCIAL LAYER: SHAPING ATTITUDES AND PERCEPTIONS

The chart of Figure 1 visualizes how an AI System directly influences three key affective and social domains (Trust & Relationships, Perception of Fairness & Bias, and Motivation & Engagement). These influences lead to specific alterations in classroom dynamics and student psychology, which collectively result in changed Student Attitudes and Learning Behaviours. Crucially, this outcome creates a feedback loop (indicated by the dotted line), as these new behaviours generate the data that is used to train and refine future AI systems, potentially creating a self-reinforcing cycle that can be either virtuous or vicious.

Figure 1. Cyclical relationship between AI systems and the affective/social dimensions of the learner

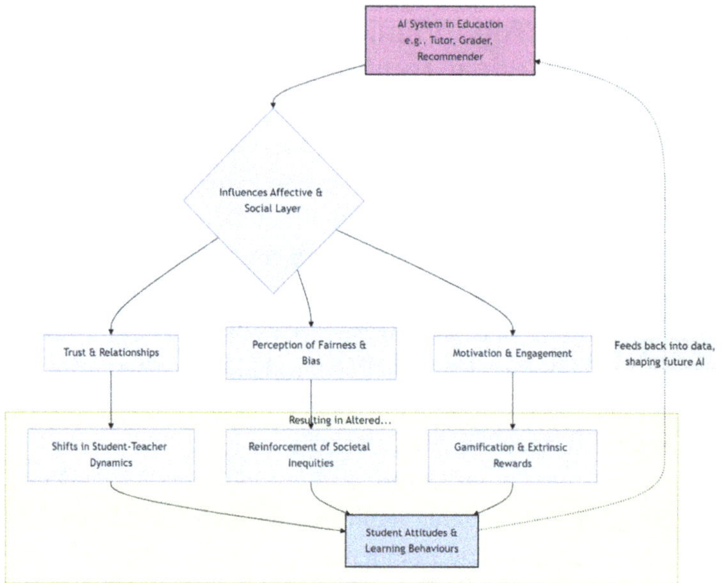

3.1 Trust, Reliability, and Student-Teacher Relationships

The integration of AI tutors and feedback systems fundamentally recalibrates the dynamics of trust in the classroom. Students may develop a transactional reliance on AI for immediate, unambiguous answers, which can erode their tolerance for the productive struggle essential for deep learning and diminish their perception of the teacher's role as the primary guide (Rong et al., 2024). Conversely, when AI systems provide erroneous or biased information, they can undermine student trust not only in the technology but also in the institution that deploys it. This shifting trust dynamic challenges educators to reassert their value as empathetic mentors and facilitators of critical thinking, moving beyond their traditional role as knowledge dispensaries to become interpreters and contextualizers of AI-generated information.

3.2 AI as a Mirror: Uncovering and Amplifying Societal Biases

AI systems in education do not operate in a vacuum; they are trained on data produced by a society laden with historical and social inequities. Consequently, these systems can act as a mirror, reflecting and often amplifying existing biases related to race, gender, socioeconomic status, and culture (Elamin, 2024). This can manifest in automated grading systems that penalize non-native language patterns, recommendation engines that steer students toward traditionally gendered career paths, or content that presents a predominantly Western canon. The peril lies in the perceived objectivity of the algorithm, which can cloak these biased outputs in a veil of neutrality, thereby legitimizing and institutionalizing discrimination under the guise of personalized, data-driven education.

3.3 Motivation, Engagement, and the Gamification of Learning

AI-driven platforms frequently employ gamification—using elements like points, badges, and leaderboards—to boost student motivation and engagement. While this can make learning more immediately appealing and increase time-on-task, it risks promoting extrinsic over intrinsic motivation, where students engage for the reward rather than a genuine love of learning. This can shallowify the educational experience, focusing on measurable metrics of completion rather than deep conceptual understanding (Bhambri & Kant, 2025a). The interdisciplinary challenge is to design AI systems that use these engaging mechanisms not as an end, but as a scaffold to foster a more profound, self-sustaining curiosity and a growth mindset, ensuring that the "game" of learning serves the deeper goal of mastery.

4 THE ETHICAL AND PHILOSOPHICAL DIMENSION: NAVIGATING THE NEW TERRAIN

4.1 Autonomy, Agency, and the Hidden Curriculum of AI

AI systems, through their recommendations and adaptive pathways, inherently shape student choice. While intended to personalize learning, this can inadvertently curtail intellectual autonomy by creating "filter bubbles" of knowledge and pre-empting the productive struggle essential for deep understanding (Stolpe & Hallström, 2024). The hidden curriculum here is one of deference to algorithmic authority;

students may learn to trust the machine's judgment over their own intellectual curiosity, potentially stifling the development of critical thinking and self-directed learning skills that are the hallmarks of genuine education (Huang & Qiao, 2024).

Furthermore, the very design of AI can compromise student agency. When a platform constantly dictates the "next best step," it reduces the learner's opportunity to make false starts, explore tangents, and exercise metacognitive control over their learning journey. Philosophically, this raises a critical question: are we educating students to be independent thinkers or efficient system-optimizers? Preserving human agency requires a deliberate design ethos that positions AI as a consultative tool that expands, rather than contracts, the space for authentic student choice and intellectual risk-taking (Bhambri & Rani, 2025).

4.2 Data Privacy, Surveillance, and the Digital Student

The data-driven nature of AI in education creates an unprecedented regime of surveillance, transforming the traditional classroom into a high-resolution panopticon. Every click, hesitation, and interaction can be captured, analyzed, and used to build a pervasive digital profile of the "digital student." This raises profound privacy concerns that extend beyond simple data security to the very right to learn in a space of intellectual safety, free from the constant pressure of performance monitoring and the potential for data to be repurposed in ways that harm a student's future opportunities (Storozhyk, 2024).

The ethical dilemma lies in the tension between personalized learning, which requires data, and the protection of a child's developmental right to anonymity and error. Constant monitoring can instill anxiety, discourage creative experimentation, and normalize a culture of surveillance that students may carry into adulthood. An interdisciplinary response must, therefore, integrate pedagogical goals with legal and ethical frameworks from data protection (e.g., GDPR, FERPA) to establish clear boundaries, ensure meaningful consent, and protect students from being reduced to their data points (Jain & Raghuram, 2024).

4.3 Defining Equity and Fairness in Algorithmic Systems

The promise of AI to democratize education is shadowed by the significant risk of exacerbating existing inequalities. Algorithmic systems are trained on historical data, which often contains societal and historical biases (Patel & Indurkhya, 2025). An AI trained on data from privileged school districts, for example, may develop a model of "success" that systematically disadvantages students from underrepresented or non-traditional backgrounds, mistaking correlation for causation and cementing inequity under a veneer of technological objectivity.

Achieving fairness, therefore, requires moving beyond a purely technical definition. It is not enough for an algorithm to be mathematically "blind"; it must be actively designed for equity and justice. This demands an interdisciplinary approach where computer scientists collaborate with sociologists, ethicists, and educators to critically audit datasets and models for bias (Bhambri & Kant, 2025b). The goal must be to create systems that are not only fair in procedure but also just in their outcomes, actively working to identify and remedy opportunity gaps rather than perpetuating the status quo.

5 TOWARD AN INTERDISCIPLINARY RESPONSE: A FRAMEWORK FOR INTEGRATION

The preceding analysis reveals that the challenges posed by AI in education are not siloed; they are woven from cognitive, social, and ethical threads (Tong, 2024). Addressing them requires moving beyond isolated solutions to an integrated, interdisciplinary framework (Chiu, 2024). This section proposes a structure for such collaboration, focusing on dialogue, design principles, and actionable recommendations that collectively steer AI's integration toward humane and effective ends.

5.1 Bridging the Silos: Dialogue Between Disciplines

To dismantle disciplinary silos, we must establish structured forums for sustained dialogue. This involves creating shared vocabulary and collaborative spaces where computer scientists, educators, psychologists, sociologists, ethicists, and policymakers can co-construct understanding. Practical mechanisms include interdisciplinary research consortia, "translator" roles for experts who can mediate between fields, and design charrettes that bring diverse stakeholders together at the inception of AIED projects, not merely as evaluators after the fact (Butson & Spronken-Smith, 2024).

The goal of this dialogue is to develop a holistic understanding of the "socio-technical-educational" system. For instance, a psychologist can illuminate how an AI's feedback mechanism impacts a student's self-efficacy (attitude), while a sociologist can examine how that same tool disproportionately affects students from different cultural backgrounds (perception). An ethicist can then frame these insights into guidelines for justice, and a computer scientist can implement technical safeguards (Allen & Kendeou, 2024). It is in this iterative exchange that truly robust and responsive educational AI can emerge.

5.2 Principles for Human-Centric AIED (AI in Education) Design

Moving from dialogue to design, we propose four core principles for Human-Centric AIED. First is Augmentation, Not Automation: AI systems should be designed to enhance and extend the capabilities of educators and learners, not replace them, preserving the irreplaceable human elements of mentorship, inspiration, and care (Nowrozy & Jam, 2024). Second is Equity and Justice by Design, requiring proactive auditing for bias, inclusive data practices, and designs that actively close—rather than widen—educational disparities, ensuring tools are accessible and fair for all learners.

The third principle is Transparency and Interpretability, mandating that AI systems provide intelligible explanations for their recommendations and outputs to both teachers and students, fostering trust and enabling informed oversight. Finally, Agency and Data Sovereignty must be central, ensuring that learners and educators retain control over their learning journey and personal data (Bhambri & Khang, 2024a). This means designing for meaningful consent, editable learner models, and options to opt-out of certain automated features, thereby reinforcing human autonomy within the technologically mediated environment (Hu, 2025).

5.3 Policy and Pedagogical Recommendations for the Future

Translating these principles into action requires concrete policy and pedagogical shifts. Policymakers must establish agile regulatory frameworks that set minimum standards for algorithmic fairness, data privacy, and accountability in educational tools, while also funding independent audits and long-term research on AI's societal impact. Simultaneously, institutions should develop "AI in Education" strategic plans that include infrastructure, professional development, and clear acceptable-use policies that align with their core educational mission (Kamali et al., 2024).

For educators, the recommendations focus on empowerment through continuous professional development. This includes training not just on how to use AI tools, but how to critically evaluate them, interpret their outputs, and integrate them pedagogically to support diverse learning objectives (Bhambri & Khang, 2024b). Furthermore, curriculum designers must embed digital and AI literacy for students, teaching them to be critical consumers of AI-generated content, to understand the ethical implications of these technologies, and to use them as powerful assistants in their own lifelong learning journeys, thus preparing them for a future of human-AI collaboration.

6 CONCLUSION: STEERING THE SYMBIOSIS

The integration of Artificial Intelligence into education is not a fleeting trend but a fundamental shift, demanding we move beyond viewing it as a simple tool. As this chapter has illustrated through interdisciplinary lenses, AI's most significant challenges and opportunities lie in its profound influence on the human dimensions of learning—how students think, what they believe, and how they relate to knowledge and each other. The cognitive, affective, and ethical layers of this integration are deeply intertwined; a change in one precipitates ripple effects across the others (Przegalinska & Triantoro, 2024). Therefore, the central challenge is no longer merely technical but socio-technical, requiring us to consciously steer the evolving relationship between human minds and machine intelligence toward a productive and ethical symbiosis, rather than allowing it to develop haphazardly.

To navigate this symbiosis, a proactive and collaborative framework is essential. This entails moving from isolated disciplinary actions to integrated responses where educators, technologists, psychologists, ethicists, and policymakers co-create the future of learning. Such a framework must be built on three pillars: first, Human-Centric Design, ensuring that AI tools are developed to augment, not replace, educator expertise and student agency. Second, Transparent Pedagogical Integration, where the use of AI is explicitly discussed in the classroom, its limitations are taught, and its outputs are critically evaluated as part of the curriculum (Bhambri & Khang, 2025). Third, Continuous Ethical Auditing, establishing ongoing processes to assess AI systems for bias, equity, and data privacy, with mechanisms for adaptation and accountability.

Ultimately, the goal is to forge a future where AI serves to amplify the best of human education: fostering creativity, critical thinking, and compassionate collaboration. By consciously steering this symbiosis, we can harness the power of AI to provide unparalleled personalization and support, freeing educators to focus on the deeply human acts of mentoring, inspiration, and care (Moemeke, 2024). The success of this endeavor will not be measured by the sophistication of the algorithms, but by our ability to cultivate wiser, more empathetic, and more empowered learners, prepared to thrive in a complex world alongside intelligent machines. The responsibility lies with us to ensure that in the classroom of the future, the mind remains firmly in the lead, with the machine as its most capable and carefully guided partner (Rana & Bhambri, 2024b).

REFERENCES

Allen, L. K., & Kendeou, P. (2024). ED-AI Lit: An interdisciplinary framework for AI literacy in education. *Policy Insights from the Behavioral and Brain Sciences*, *11*(1), 3–10. DOI: 10.1177/23727322231220339

Allison, J., Hwang, G. J., Mayer, R. E., Pellas, N., Karnalim, O., de Freitas, S., Ng, O.-L., Huang, Y.-M., Hooshyar, D., Seidman, R. H., Al-Emran, M., Mikropoulos, T. A., Schroeder, N. L., Roscoe, R. D., & Sanusi, I. (2025). From generative AI to extended reality: Multidisciplinary perspectives on the challenges, opportunities, and future of educational computing. *Journal of Educational Computing Research*, *63*(6), 1327–1363. DOI: 10.1177/07356331251359964

Bhambri, P., & Kant, S. (2025a, February 1-2). A taxonomy of bias in machine learning: Classification, sources, and implications for ethical AI [Paper presentation]. Lincoln-SPAST Global Sustainability Programme (SGS-24), 1st International Conference of L-GPR Program, Lincoln University College, Malaysia. SPAST Proceedings, 1(2). https://spast.org/techrep/article/view/5387/724

Bhambri, P., & Kant, S. (2025b, April 26-27). Ethical AI systems: A comprehensive framework for bias mitigation and fairness in machine learning [Paper presentation]. Lincoln-SPAST Global Sustainability Programme (SGS-24), 2nd International Conference of L-GPR Program, Lincoln University College, Malaysia. SPAST Proceedings, 1(2). https://spast.org/techrep/article/view/5385/698

Bhambri, P., & Khang, A. (2024a). The human-machine nexus with art-making generative AIs. In Hai-Jew, S. (Ed.), *Making art with generative AI tools* (pp. 73–85). IGI Global., DOI: 10.4018/979-8-3693-1950-5.ch004

Bhambri, P., & Khang, A. (2024b). Machine learning advancements in E-health: Transforming digital healthcare. In *Medical robotics and AI-assisted diagnostics for a high-tech healthcare industry* (pp. 174–194). IGI Global., DOI: 10.4018/979-8-3693-2105-8.ch012

Bhambri, P., & Khang, A. (2025). Edge computing for enhancing efficiency and sustainability in green transportation systems. In Khang, A. (Ed.), *Driving green transportation system through artificial intelligence and automation* (pp. 43–65). Springer., DOI: 10.1007/978-3-031-72617-0_3

Bhambri, P., & Rani, S. (2025). Advancements in educational technology: Navigating the landscape of user experience in Web 3.0. In Pelet, J.-É. (Ed.), *Architecting the digital future: Platforms, design, and application* (pp. 365–396). IGI Global., DOI: 10.4018/979-8-3693-2973-3.ch014

Butson, R., & Spronken-Smith, R. (2024). AI and its implications for research in higher education: A critical dialogue. *Higher Education Research & Development, 43*(3), 563–577. DOI: 10.1080/07294360.2023.2280200

Chen, J. J. (2025). From Turing's conception of machine intelligence to the evolution of AI in early childhood education: Conceptual, empirical, and practical insights. AI. *Brain and Child, 1*(1), 1. DOI: 10.1007/s44436-025-00002-6

Chiu, T. K. (2024). Future research recommendations for transforming higher education with generative AI. *Computers and Education: Artificial Intelligence, 6*, 100197. DOI: 10.1016/j.caeai.2023.100197

Creely, E., & Blannin, J. (2025). Creative partnerships with generative AI. Possibilities for education and beyond. *Thinking Skills and Creativity, 56*, 101727. DOI: 10.1016/j.tsc.2024.101727

Elamin, M. O. I. (2024). AI through the ages: Unlocking key opportunities and navigating challenges in the history and future of artificial intelligence. *International Journal of Religion, 5*(12), 1152–1166. DOI: 10.61707/tarzcj89

Hu, Y. (2025). Creating interactive AI learning environments: Integrating interdisciplinary approaches and Taoist art principles. *Interactive Learning Environments, 33*(6), 1–20. DOI: 10.1080/10494820.2025.2454442

Huang, X., & Qiao, C. (2024). Enhancing computational thinking skills through artificial intelligence education at a STEAM high school. *Science & Education, 33*(2), 383–403. DOI: 10.1007/s11191-022-00392-6

Jain, K., & Raghuram, J. N. V. (2024). Unlocking potential: The impact of AI on education technology. *Multidisciplinary Reviews, 7*(3), 2024049–2024049. DOI: 10.31893/multirev.2024049

Kamali, J., Alpat, M. F., & Bozkurt, A. (2024). AI ethics as a complex and multifaceted challenge: Decoding educators' AI ethics alignment through the lens of activity theory. *International Journal of Educational Technology in Higher Education, 21*(1), 62. DOI: 10.1186/s41239-024-00496-9

Kayyali, M. (2024). Future possibilities and challenges of AI in education. In *Transforming education with generative AI: Prompt engineering and synthetic content creation* (pp. 118–137). IGI Global Scientific Publishing. DOI: 10.4018/979-8-3693-1351-0.ch006

Khogali, H. O., & Mekid, S. (2024). Perception and Ethical Challenges for the Future of AI as Encountered by Surveyed New Engineers. *Societies (Basel, Switzerland), 14*(12), 271. DOI: 10.3390/soc14120271

Lamberti, P. M., Bombaerts, G., & IJsselsteijn, W. (2025). Mind the gap: Bridging the divide between computer scientists and ethicists in shaping moral machines. *Ethics and Information Technology*, *27*(1), 2. DOI: 10.1007/s10676-024-09806-1

Lobanova, A., Hrabovets, I., Prykhodko, O., Karytka, V., Kalashnikova, L., & Chernous, L. (2024). Artificial intelligence in teaching social disciplines: Opportunities and challenges of tools. *Educational Technology Quarterly*, *2024*(4), 360–377. DOI: 10.55056/etq.813

Moemeke, C. D. (2024). Artificial intelligence and machine learning in enhancing science learning experiences: Exploring possibilities and concerns. *NIU Journal of Educational Research*, *10*(2), 59–72.

Ng, D. T. K., Su, J., Leung, J. K. L., & Chu, S. K. W. (2024). Artificial intelligence (AI) literacy education in secondary schools: A review. *Interactive Learning Environments*, *32*(10), 6204–6224. DOI: 10.1080/10494820.2023.2255228

Nishat, A. (2025). Rethinking Intelligence: An Interdisciplinary Framework for AI Research. *Pioneer Research Journal of Computing Science*, *2*(2), 162–169.

Nowrozy, R., & Jam, D. (2024). Embracing the generative AI revolution: advancing tertiary education in cybersecurity with GPT. arXiv preprint arXiv:2403.11402.

Parker, J. L., Richard, V. M., Acabá, A., Escoffier, S., Flaherty, S., Jablonka, S., & Becker, K. P. (2025). Negotiating meaning with machines: AI's role in doctoral writing pedagogy. *International Journal of Artificial Intelligence in Education*, *35*(3), 1218–1238. DOI: 10.1007/s40593-024-00425-x

Patel, N. S., & Indurkhya, N. (Eds.). (2025). *The Rise of Intelligent Machines: A Multi-disciplinary Perspective from Industry and Impact on Higher Education*. CRC Press.

Peters, M. A., Jackson, L., Papastephanou, M., Jandrić, P., Lazaroiu, G., Evers, C. W., Cope, B., Kalantzis, M., Araya, D., Tesar, M., Mika, C., Chen, L., Wang, C., Sturm, S., Rider, S., & Fuller, S. (2024). AI and the future of humanity: ChatGPT-4, philosophy and education–Critical responses. *Educational Philosophy and Theory*, *56*(9), 828–862. DOI: 10.1080/00131857.2023.2213437

Przegalinska, A., & Triantoro, T. (2024). *Converging minds: The creative potential of collaborative AI*. CRC Press. DOI: 10.1201/9781032656618

Rana, R., & Bhambri, P. (2024a). Artificial Intelligence and Internet of Things (IoT) facilitated digital twin for Industry 4.0 application domains. In Rani, S., Bhambri, P., Kumar, S., Pareek, P. K., & Elngar, A. A. (Eds.), *AI-driven digital twin and Industry 4.0* (pp. 168–181). CRC Press., DOI: 10.1201/9781003395416-11

Rana, R., & Bhambri, P. (2024b). Generative AI in web application development: Enhancing user experience and performance. In Shah, I. A., & Jhanjhi, N. Z. (Eds.), *Generative AI for web engineering models* (pp. 471–486). IGI Global., DOI: 10.4018/979-8-3693-3703-5.ch021

Rani, S., Kataria, A., Bhambri, P., Pareek, P. K., & Puri, V. (2024). Artificial intelligence in personalized health services for better patient care. In Gupta, S. K., Karras, D. A., & Natarajan, R. (Eds.), *Revolutionizing healthcare: AI integration with IoT for enhanced patient outcomes* (pp. 89–108). Springer., DOI: 10.1007/978-3-031-65022-2_6

Rong, J., Terzidis, K., & Ding, J. (2024). Kids AI Design Thinking Education for Creativity Development. *Archives of Design Research, 37*(3), 119–133. DOI: 10.15187/adr.2024.07.37.3.119

Simões, J. M., & Caldeira, W. (2024). Ethics concerns in the use of computer-generated images for human communication. *Journal of Ethics in Higher Education*, (4), 169–192. DOI: 10.26034/fr.jehe.2024.5962

Stolpe, K., & Hallström, J. (2024). Artificial intelligence literacy for technology education. *Computers and Education Open, 6*, 100159. DOI: 10.1016/j.caeo.2024.100159

Storozhyk, M. (2024). Philosophy of future: Analytical overview of interaction between education, science, and artificial intelligence in the context of contemporary challenges. *Futurity Philosophy, 3*(1), 23–47.

Tong, Y. (2024). Integration of artificial intelligence into the general education curriculum: Importance, approaches, challenges, and a conceptual framework for liberal arts universities. In INTED2024 Proceedings (pp. 7582-7589). IATED.

Vatankhah, S., Bamshad, V., Arici, H. E., & Duan, Y. (2024). Ethical implementation of artificial intelligence in the service industries. *Service Industries Journal, 44*(9-10), 661–685. DOI: 10.1080/02642069.2024.2359077

Yıldız, T. (2025). The minds we make: A philosophical inquiry into theory of mind and artificial intelligence. *Integrative Psychological & Behavioral Science, 59*(1), 10. DOI: 10.1007/s12124-024-09876-2 PMID: 39743649

Zahra, S. T., Bibi, E., & Younus, Z. (2025). Artificial Intelligence (AI) and Human Mind: Struggles and Strengths in the Education Sector. In Artificial Intelligence and Human Agency in Education: Volume One: The Nexus Between AI and Human Agency in Educational Contexts (pp. 265-289). Springer Nature Singapore.

Chapter 3
Digital Tools and Computer Science for Transforming Modern Pedagogy:
Bridging the Gap Between Innovation and Equity

Dini Febryana Sari
http://orcid.org/0009-0002-6540-3372
Universitas Esa Unggul, Indonesia

Binastya Anggara Sekti
http://orcid.org/0000-0001-5489-4888
Universitas Esa Unggul, Indonesia

ABSTRACT

This chapter explores the impact of computer science and digital tools on modern pedagogy. The authors trace the evolution of educational technology, moving from legacy systems to artificial intelligence and adaptive learning. The text analyzes the integration of these tools into curricula, highlighting active learning and interdisciplinary collaboration. Additionally, the chapter addresses critical ethical challenges, including data security, algorithmic bias, and the digital divide. By examining global case studies from diverse nations, the authors illustrate how policy and infrastructure influence digital adoption. The work concludes by advocating for human-centric strategies that utilize technology to create inclusive, equitable, and efficient educational environments.

DOI: 10.4018/979-8-2600-1568-1.ch003

1. INTRODUCTION

In the twenty-first century, computer science has become a vital pillar that underpins almost every facet of human endeavor, radically altering how people communicate, carry out their professional lives, and gain knowledge. This change has been particularly noteworthy in the field of education, bringing about a radical transition from traditional, teacher-centered instruction to technology-enhanced ecosystems that give priority to each learner's distinct cognitive profile. The use of a variety of digital tools, from artificial intelligence-driven systems to online learning platforms, has highlighted both the enormous potential for individualized development and the significant difficulties associated with widespread digital delivery. Today's academics understand that understanding the foundational concepts of computer science is essential not only for developing new tools but also for preparing students to thrive in a world that is becoming more interconnected and technologically advanced. This change stems from the fact that in order to maximize learning in new, immersive environments like the Metaverse, digital educational technologies now take into consideration intricate neuropsychological maps and student psychotypes (Ldokova et al., 2025). Additionally, current publication trends in the field of Artificial Intelligence in Education (AIEd) show that research priorities have shifted from broad applications to more detailed, data-driven examinations of how technology permeates pedagogy itself (Zhu et al., 2025). An educator's technical literacy and willingness to accept immersive technologies, like augmented reality, as standard teaching tools rather than ancillary novelties frequently have an impact on this readiness to adopt such sophisticated tools (Sangodiah et al., 2023). Through interactive and gamified modalities, like digital escape rooms, which turn the static classroom into a dynamic laboratory for science, teamwork, and high-stakes problem-solving, the ultimate goal is to develop robust computational thinking (Tenorio-Sepúlveda et al., 2025).

The intrinsically multidisciplinary nature of modern education highlights the critical function of digital tools as a link between historically disparate fields, such as psychology, linguistics, and the creative arts. A fundamental reconceptualization of learning is made possible by computer science, where advanced tools like collaborative cloud platforms and simulation software enable students to explore abstract ideas through interactive modalities that were previously impossible to visualize. For example, it has been demonstrated that incorporating Large Language Model (LLM)-based virtual agents into alternate reality games greatly increases student interest in STEM subjects by offering a responsive, immersive narrative environment that changes based on the student's decisions (Wang et al., 2025). Similarly, faculty have been able to experiment with new instructional designs that offer instantaneous, context-aware feedback by strategically integrating generative AI tools into second language curricula. This has accelerated the learning curve for a variety of student populations and non-native speakers (Iqbal et al., 2025). Adaptive web-based educational search frameworks that use machine learning and natural language processing to provide individualized resources based on each learner's unique inquiry patterns further support these developments by guaranteeing that the information retrieved is highly relevant to the learner's current task (Li, 2025). In order to comprehend how human dynamics and geographic environments affect learning in the digital age, researchers are bridging the gap between space, mind, and computational urban science as education shifts toward a more computational and spatial model (Jiang et al., 2025). This convergence demonstrates that computer science is now a universal catalyst for interdisciplinary innovation across the whole educational spectrum rather than merely a technical subject for experts.

However, the quick spread of digital tools across educational systems has also brought about serious issues with security, ethics, and the ongoing digital divide that puts marginalized groups at risk of falling behind. Educators, technologists, and legislators must work together urgently to address critical issues like data privacy, algorithmic bias, and unequal access to high-speed resources. Since students without reliable connectivity or expensive devices are frequently routinely shut out of the advantages of contemporary innovation, the digital divide continues to be a key factor in explaining dropout rates in higher education (Barragán-Moreno & Guzmán-Rincón, 2025). Researchers are working hard to create privacy-preserving models to reduce these risks, especially in data-intensive industries like education or telecommunications, to make sure that performance tracking and predictive analytics don't jeopardize personal information or result in data misuse (Sana et al., 2025). Additionally, there are notable social, gender, and migration-related differences in the development of digital competencies during adolescence that call for focused, inclusive interventions to guarantee that digital literacy is a right rather than a privilege (Gnambs & Hawrot, 2025). The impact of AI interventions must be carefully examined through the lens of rural medical centers, even in the high-stakes fields of healthcare and medical education, to make sure that technological advancement does not unintentionally alienate providers or students in underserved geographic areas (Lintz, 2025). These difficulties highlight the necessity of maintaining the essential human component of teaching empathy, mentoring, and moral guidance while using technology as a sophisticated supplement rather than a complete replacement for human knowledge.

In summary, the incorporation of computer science into teaching practices represents a revolutionary period in which technology is an integral and fundamental component of education. Technology is now the technical foundation for contemporary knowledge transmission, and it is no longer appropriate to think of it as a simple accessory. We can create more reliable systems that forecast student outcomes while maintaining the complete integrity of student data by investigating the application of sophisticated concepts like federated learning and local-global collaboration (Ren et al., 2025). By ensuring that task relevance and "fit" drive engagement in video-based and lifelong learning contexts, the future vision entails developing holistic learning environments that serve all demographics, including older adults (Wang et al., 2025). To do this, a tiered, scalable solution that mimics the effective emerging models in digital medicine and healthcare diagnostics is needed. This solution must guarantee equitable diagnosis of knowledge gaps and access to high-quality resources across hierarchical systems (Zhu et al., 2025). Geographical analyses of regional differences will be essential in adjusting digital strategies to the unique sociocultural requirements of various countries as we look to the global development of smart cities and the further globalization of education (Tijjani et al., 2025). The ultimate goal of this academic work is to offer a nuanced understanding of how inclusive and prudent technology use can create learning ecosystems that are more productive, efficient, and compassionate. By means of interdisciplinary cooperation and forward-thinking legislation, we can equip the next generation with the skills necessary to successfully negotiate the intricacies of a technologically advanced world as critical thinkers, creative thinkers, and moral innovators who will mold the future of technology.

2. THE EVOLUTION OF DIGITAL TOOLS IN EDUCATION

From monolithic mainframe systems to the highly customized ecosystems of today, the evolution of digital instruments in educational settings can be traced back to the development of computer science in the middle of the 20th century. During the 1960s, computing was primarily used in large academic institutions as a centralized administrative function that was disconnected from the regular classroom pedagogical interactions. However, the advent of personal computers in the late 1970s and early 1980s brought computational power directly into the hands of individual students and teachers, causing a significant change. Students became active participants in their own cognitive development rather than passive recipients of processed data as a result of this democratization of technology, which went beyond simple hardware upgrades. Innovations such as the Logo programming language created the first frameworks for computational thinking by enabling students to learn technical skills through engaging, practical experimentation. This period demonstrated that, when incorporated into student-centered, exploratory learning environments rather than merely administrative databases, digital tools could function as potent cognitive tools. As contemporary research continues to investigate how digital escape rooms and interactive simulations can be used to foster the same computational thinking skills first envisioned during the personal computer revolution, the legacy of this era is still relevant today (Tenorio-Sepúlveda et al., 2025). Additionally, the success of technology integration has historically depended on educators' willingness to use such revolutionary tools this trend continues today as educators negotiate the challenges of augmented reality and other immersive teaching tools (Sangodiah et al., 2023). This early democratization of information processing is also the source of the shift toward collaborative knowledge creation, as demonstrated by modern models that make use of open platforms like Wikipedia (Evenstein Sigalov & Cohen, 2025). More advanced game-based learning environments that use implicit interaction and artificial intelligence to "come alive" abstract concepts were eventually made possible by this historical foundation (Madshaven et al., 2025).

With the introduction of the internet in the 1990s, education underwent a second significant change that ushered in a new era marked by interconnected networks and unrestricted access to global information. This internet revolution challenged the traditional location-bound nature of the classroom by radically changing how educational content was produced, disseminated, and consumed. Asynchronous communication and digital resource management were made possible by the emergence of web-based Learning Management Systems (LMS) like Blackboard and Moodle, which marked the first extensive use of networking protocols and database administration in educational institutions. This period gave rise to the idea of "e-learning," where multimedia experiences that included interactive exercises, animation, and video catered to a variety of learning styles that traditional textbooks were unable to accommodate. These systems' development necessitated a deep comprehension of client-server architectures and user interface design, bridging the gap between pedagogical theory and computer science. These early web-based foundations have developed into highly adaptive frameworks today, using machine learning and natural language processing to suggest particular resources based on a learner's individual profile (Li, 2025). As educational institutions strive to optimize how students navigate the vast amounts of information available on the web, research on the efficacy of these online resource recommendation methods has taken center stage. Furthermore, by offering structured process patterns and immediate feedback, the shift to gamified online environments has been demonstrated to enhance self-regulated learning and motivation, especially in specialized fields like second language acquisition (Maimaiti & Hew, 2025). A deeper comprehension of how "GeoAI" and computational science can bridge the gap between the physical mind and the digital space where learning now takes place is required as these digital networks grow and start to affect the very dynamics of human interaction (Jiang et al., 2025).

The emergence of Open Educational Resources (OER) and Massive Open Online Courses (MOOCs) propelled the globalization and democratization of digital education by the year 2000 and into the 2020s. Cloud computing and distributed system architectures were used by platforms like Coursera and edX to enable millions of people, regardless of location, to learn from top universities. The power of learning analytics was also introduced in this decade, enabling teachers to identify at-risk students through data-driven intervention and track student progress on a large scale. The current use of graph neural networks to predict learner performance with previously unheard-of accuracy is the best example of the shift toward these intelligent systems (Hakkal & Ait Lahcen, 2025). However, the ongoing "digital divide," in which students in underprivileged communities lack the resources or literacy skills required to fully engage in this new digital reality, has also been brought to light by this rapid globalization. According to research, this gap is still a major factor in higher education dropout rates, which calls for a more inclusive approach to technology policy (Barragán-Moreno & Guzmán-Rincón, 2025). In order to address these disparities, low-cost sensors and devices that can provide high-quality monitoring and digital access to schools in developing regions must be deployed along with affordable infrastructure solutions. The publication trends in the field of Artificial Intelligence in Education (AIEd) show a clear focus on improving these digital tools going forward to make sure they are not only technologically sophisticated but also morally sound and widely available (Zhu et al., 2025). The result of this evolution is a world in which education is a lifelong, digitally enhanced journey that adjusts to the changing social and economic demands of the global community rather than a static event.

3. INTEGRATION OF TECHNOLOGY IN CURRICULUM AND ACTIVE LEARNING

One of the biggest changes in educational philosophy and practice in the modern era is the incorporation of technology into the curriculum, which goes well beyond the conventional lecture-based model to create dynamic, adaptable, and data-driven environments. Modern educational institutions have started to incorporate computer science principles into their teaching strategies rather than viewing digital tools as merely supplemental tools. This has allowed teachers to develop from basic information transmitters into highly skilled facilitators of knowledge construction. This fundamental change effectively changes the role of the teacher from that of a lone authority to that of a guide who plans intricate discovery-based experiences, enabling students to learn through active exploration and the analysis of real-world data. This approach recognizes that in a time when information is widely available, the most beneficial results come from fostering critical thinking and innovative knowledge application. According to research on faculty experiences, a sophisticated grasp of both pedagogy and technology is necessary for the effective integration of generative artificial intelligence tools within particular curricula, such as second language acquisition (Iqbal et al., 2025). Additionally, utilizing collaborative knowledge platforms such as Wikipedia has been successful in improving student competencies and creating an atmosphere of open innovation in higher education (Evenstein Sigalov & Cohen, 2025). In addition to digitizing content, the strategic use of such technological artifacts actively promotes creative learning methods and affects students' direct actions (Velu et al., 2025). In the end, publication trends in the field of Artificial Intelligence in Education (AIEd) show that research on how these integrated systems can be optimized to satisfy various pedagogical needs is becoming more and more important (Zhu et al., 2025).

With the help of advanced digital engagement, active learning places a strong emphasis on student-centered methods where students develop their own understanding via a cycle of experience, introspection, and peer interaction. While teachers track students' progress using real-time analytics dashboards, technologies like immersive simulations, interactive whiteboards, and collaborative cloud-based platforms encourage students to contribute to collective knowledge. This data-driven approach guarantees that students gain the digital literacy and problem-solving abilities essential for the modern workforce by enabling prompt intervention and a deeper understanding of learning patterns. The rise of cutting-edge pedagogical models like blended learning and flipped classrooms further illustrates how technology can extend learning beyond conventional time and space constraints, enabling a customized pace and higher-order thinking during in-person sessions. According to studies, gamified self-regulated learning environments that offer structured process mining and immediate feedback can greatly increase reading comprehension and motivation (Maimaiti & Hew, 2025). Furthermore, abstract scientific or historical ideas can "come alive" through the use of artificial intelligence and game-based learning, encouraging a deeper level of conceptual engagement and historical consciousness (Madshaven et al., 2025). As researchers investigate the critical elements influencing a student's intention to use these interactive tools, the incorporation of mobile augmented reality (AR) applications also provides a potent modality for experiential learning (Cheng & Qian, 2025). In order to keep the curriculum interesting and adaptable to the needs of each individual student, educators use these technologies to strike a balance between autonomous digital exploration and social collaboration.

However, there are obstacles in the way of successfully integrating technology into the curriculum. To overcome ingrained implementation issues, careful planning, ongoing teacher preparation, and ongoing evaluation are necessary. Inadequate infrastructure, a lack of technical know-how, and a lack of time to update old courses to meet contemporary digital standards are three challenges that many educators must overcome. By creating user-friendly platforms and automated assessment tools that support instructional design without overburdening the practitioner, computer science plays a critical role in addressing these issues. Additionally, institutional commitment is required to guarantee that technology integration fosters inclusivity by offering supportive resources for students of all backgrounds and skill levels. The "digital divide" is still a serious issue since differences in access to technology can worsen already-existing educational disparities and serve as a major contributing factor to higher dropout rates in some student populations (Barragán-Moreno & Guzmán-Rincón, 2025). To maintain the accessibility and equity of digital resources, knowledge production and intellectual property management must be reevaluated within the larger framework of a capitalist educational system (Basilio, 2025). Machine learning analyses of cloud adoption across regions such as the EU reveal that structural disparities continue to impact how successfully schools can shift to digital-first models, and national readiness for these changes varies greatly (Tudor et al., 2025).The performance analysis of AI models against traditional residency exams challenges even the way we assess professional competency, necessitating a complete rethinking of how we measure human expertise in a world of capable machines (Shvartz et al., 2025).

In order to prepare students for the interconnected realities of the global workforce of the twenty-first century, technology integration also plays a crucial role in promoting global collaboration and digital citizenship. Students can work on practical projects, share code, and get peer feedback through online communities and open-source platforms, demonstrating how the concepts of collaborative computer science can improve group learning. These exchanges foster critical thinking and cross-cultural understanding, assisting students in navigating the challenges of remote work and distributed teams. Additionally, digital citizenship education which covers online safety, data privacy, and the ethical use of information has become a required part of the curriculum.

Institutions can create reliable predictive systems while upholding the strict data integrity requirements required for contemporary research by participating in federated learning and local-global collaboration (Ren et al., 2025). Additionally, academic libraries are becoming crucial centers for artificial intelligence proficiency, giving students the knowledge and resources they need to cultivate the moral consciousness required in a technologically advanced society (Sousa, 2025). Despite these developments, adolescents' digital competencies still differ significantly depending on their social, gender, and migration-related backgrounds, underscoring the need for focused educational policies (Gnambs & Hawrot, 2025). In the end, promoting open innovation in educational environments necessitates concentrating on organizational and strategic dynamics that can quickly adjust to technological change (Annamalah et al., 2025). Teachers enable students to become ethical innovators prepared to take the lead in a global society, rather than merely consumers of technology, by cultivating a responsible digital ecosystem.

4. ARTIFICIAL INTELLIGENCE AND ADAPTIVE LEARNING

One of the most revolutionary forces in contemporary education is artificial intelligence, which is radically changing how students learn, how teachers instruct, and how organizations function globally. AI, which has its roots in the fundamentals of computer science, includes a complex array of technologies, such as machine learning, natural language processing (NLP), and neural networks, all of which are intended to mimic and enhance aspects of human intelligence. AI-driven systems are able to analyze large, complex datasets in the current educational context in order to predict academic performance with previously unheard-of precision, identify latent knowledge gaps, and personalize learning experiences. Computer science is now the technical foundation of intelligent education systems, marking a fundamental evolution in pedagogy from one-size-fits-all instruction to adaptive, personalized learning environments. This change represents a significant paradigm shift in our understanding of the classroom, moving away from treating students as homogeneous groups and toward a model that acknowledges individual differences in motivational factors, learning styles, and prior knowledge. There has been a significant increase in research on these fine-grained pedagogical integrations, according to studies on publication patterns in Artificial Intelligence in Education (AIEd) (Zhu et al., 2025). Additionally, certain student psychotypes and neuropsychological maps can now be taken into account by contemporary AI systems, especially when digital technologies are used in the immersive Metaverse environments (Ldokova et al., 2025). Graph neural networks, which enable a more interconnected understanding of student data points, are helping to further improve the technical capacity to predict learner performance (Hakkal & Ait Lahcen, 2025). Adaptive web-based educational search frameworks that incorporate machine learning to provide learners with contextually relevant information in real-time support these developments (Li, 2025).

One of the most useful and significant uses of AI in the classroom is adaptive learning systems, which use algorithms to evaluate a student's performance in real time and modify the pace, content difficulty, and mode of delivery accordingly. By analyzing each student interaction to identify areas of strength and weakness, these platforms provide tailored feedback that guarantees students are continuously challenged at a suitable level. Because AI-powered chatbots and intelligent tutoring systems can now comprehend and react to human language, natural language processing has further transformed these interactions, making learning more conversational and approachable. With the ability to communicate with virtual assistants to summarize lectures or offer more examples, students can now transition from static information retrieval to dynamic, dialog-based learning. By offering responsive narrative environments, the incorporation of Large Language Model (LLM)-based virtual agents into alternate reality games has demonstrated a notable increase in student engagement for STEM subjects (Wang et al., 2025). Similarly, a greater level of instructional integration and instant feedback are made possible by the use of generative AI tools within curricula, such as second language learning (Iqbal et al., 2025). In addition to enhancing reading comprehension, these gamified self-regulated learning environments enable researchers to use process mining to identify patterns in student behavior (Maimaiti & Hew, 2025). Through implicit game-based learning and AI-enhanced simulations, educators can use these technologies to make abstract concepts "come alive," promoting a deeper historical and scientific consciousness (Madshaven et al., 2025).

Figure 1. AI-based adaptive learning cycle

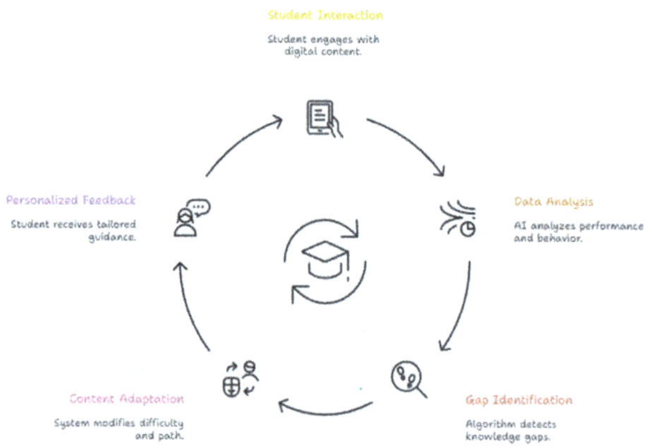

Beyond personalization, AI uses predictive modeling and institutional learning analytics to support more general educational decision-making. In order to identify at-risk students early, enhance curriculum design, and raise retention rates overall, universities and educational institutions can now examine trends in performance data. This proactive strategy shows how AI promotes institutional efficiency and equity by enabling administrative interventions prior to student failure. But integrating AI also poses difficult ethical issues, especially with regard to algorithmic bias, data privacy, and the "black box" nature of machine learning. AI systems may unintentionally perpetuate current disparities if they are not closely watched over by strict ethical frameworks because they learn from past data. Computer scientists and educators must work together to guarantee accountability and transparency in every algorithm in order to address these issues. To guarantee that predictive analytics do not jeopardize the identity of the students they are intended to assist, for example, privacy-preserving models must be developed (Sana et al., 2025). Additionally, policymakers must acknowledge that the "digital divide" is still a significant factor in explaining dropout rates, and the use of AI should not increase this disparity for students who do not have access to high-end technology (Barragán-Moreno & Guzmán-Rincón, 2025). It is crucial to foster trust and confidence in these digital spaces, particularly for vulnerable groups who might be inherently wary of automated surveillance (Durnell et al., 2025). To guarantee a balanced approach to technology adoption, practitioners must ultimately comprehend how these AI interventions affect their own professional practices (Lintz, 2025).

AI and adaptive learning have significant pedagogical ramifications because teachers can now create customized learning pathways that emphasize higher-order cognitive skills using AI-generated insights rather than being restricted to broad, group-based instruction. As a result, students have more freedom to learn at their own speed, acquire critical metacognitive abilities, and become more conscious of their own advantages and disadvantages. Intense discussions concerning the nature of learning and the abilities that are still exclusive to humans have been triggered by the development of generative AI, particularly Large Language Models like GPT-4o. Even though AI is capable of producing text and solving challenging mathematical puzzles, humans are still the only ones who can use ethical reasoning and apply real-world human experience to problem-solving. The need to reconsider assessment in order to prioritize critical thinking over rote memorization is highlighted by performance analyses of models such as GPT-4o against traditional residency exams (Shvartz et al., 2025). Professional development courses that assist teaching and administrative staff in comprehending the theoretical foundations of generative AI are therefore desperately needed (Kong & Hu, 2025). Additionally, academic libraries are changing their functions to become vital centers for AI competency where students can learn how to use these tools in an ethical and responsible manner (Sousa, 2025). Educational institutions can build a future where "hybrid intelligence" utilizes the best of both human and artificial capabilities by promoting open innovation through organizational and strategic dynamics (Annamalah et al., 2025). This guarantees that as technology develops, it stays rooted in human values, encouraging a more comprehensive and learner-centered approach to education for future generations.

5. INTERDISCIPLINARY COLLABORATION AND DIGITAL LITERACY

The ability of different disciplines to work well together across conventional boundaries is just as important to the success of digital transformation in education as technological innovation. Collaboration between computer science, education, psychology, sociology, and communication studies is necessary to make sure that digital tools support learning rather than impede it. A comprehensive framework that fosters social interaction, ethical awareness, and cognitive development is produced through interdisciplinary collaboration. No single discipline can handle the complexity of digital learning in today's educational environment instead, the convergence of several disciplines enable educators to create learning experiences that are socially conscious, pedagogically sound, and technologically sophisticated. This cooperative approach acknowledges that successful educational technology results from a thorough discussion between experts in human learning, technological system developers, and social dynamics and ethical implications. The development of contemporary educational technology reflects a sophisticated understanding that technology is never neutral rather, it embodies values, presumptions, and priorities that need to be analyzed from a variety of angles to guarantee that it benefits all students equally. For example, in the era of Geo AI, advancing translational human dynamics research necessitates using computational science to bridge space and mind (Jiang et al., 2025). Additionally, in order to preserve institutional integrity, creating and managing the data ecosystems that facilitate these partnerships necessitates negotiating the intersection of centralization and decentralization (Kernstock et al., 2025). In order to maintain the infrastructure's adaptability and responsiveness to change, driving this degree of open innovation requires an emphasis on both organizational and strategic dynamics (Annamalah et al., 2025). Lastly, the creation of hybrid adaptive models for complex monitoring guarantees that interdisciplinary feedback loops are used to continuously improve the technical apparatus of education (Liu et al., 2025).

One of the most important skills in the twenty-first century is digital literacy, which goes far beyond simple computer skills to include the capacity to critically assess, produce, and share information using advanced digital technologies. From an educational perspective, digital literacy entails developing the ability to learn on one's own and adjust to ongoing technological change, while from a computer science perspective, it entails comprehending how algorithms operate and identifying data biases. Through this synthesis, digital literacy is transformed from a purely technical ability into a lifelong ethical and cognitive practice that permeates every subject area. It equips students to deal with a world that is becoming more and more digital, where information is constantly flowing and technology is used to mediate almost every facet of both personal and professional life. However, the need for focused interdisciplinary interventions is highlighted by differences in teenage digital competencies, which are frequently connected to social, gender, and migration-related factors (Gnambs & Hawrot, 2025). In this field, academic libraries are becoming more and more important centers for ethical guidance and artificial intelligence competency (Sousa, 2025). In order to ensure that administrative staff members have a conceptual grasp of generative AI and its implications for the organization, professional development must be extended to them (Kong & Hu, 2025).

Furthermore, neuro-technological strategies that enhance privacy are necessary to foster confidence in these digital environments, especially for groups that might be distrustful of automated systems (Durnell et al., 2025). By incorporating these elements, teachers can assist students in acquiring the critical evaluation abilities required to evaluate the reliability of information and discern between trustworthy and dubious digital content.

Beyond the confines of formal education, interdisciplinary collaboration plays a crucial role in fostering a culture of adaptability and lifelong learning in communities, workplaces, and informal learning environments. By bridging the gap between academic theory and real-world application, industry partnerships with universities give students practical experience in fields like data science and software development. In addition to promoting innovation that benefits communities as a whole, this cross-sector collaboration guarantees that educational technologies continue to be relevant to societal needs. Collaborative knowledge creation can improve student competencies in higher education, as demonstrated by the use of platforms like Wikipedia for educational innovation (Evenstein Sigalov & Cohen, 2025). But in the capitalist system, knowledge production and intellectual property must be controlled from a viewpoint that guarantees scientific publications continue to be a public good rather than a restricted commodity (Basilio, 2025). In order to identify and address structural disparities across regions, the adoption of cloud technologies in the digital era must be analyzed using interpretable machine learning, as national readiness for these shifts varies (Tudor et al., 2025). In the end, integrating these digital tools with a thorough comprehension of student psychotypes is crucial for the future of education, especially when utilizing technologies in new environments like the Metaverse (Ldokova et al., 2025). Education becomes a place for empowerment rather than exclusion when human understanding and technological innovation are combined. With the help of interdisciplinary collaboration, digital literacy enables people to fully engage in the digital world, navigate complexity, and ethically contribute to technological advancement.

6. ETHICAL AND DATA SECURITY CHALLENGES IN DIGITAL EDUCATION

From highly effective administrative management systems to highly personalized learning experiences, the digital transformation of the global educational landscape has brought about an unmatched array of benefits. But these important developments also bring with them serious ethical issues and data security issues that need to be addressed immediately and methodically by all parties involved. The issue of how to handle, store, and safeguard the vast amounts of detailed data that digital tools gather about students, teachers, and institutional operations has emerged as a crucial component of maintaining educational integrity. A framework of fairness, transparency, and complete accountability must be used to assess the ethical ramifications of using sophisticated algorithms to track learning progress, forecast student success, and suggest particular academic paths. Opportunities for data collection at previously unthinkable scales have been made possible by the widespread use of educational technology, which raises important issues about who owns educational data and what rights students have over their digital identities. The inherent power dynamics between big institutions and individual students, as well as between third-party technology providers and users, make these issues especially complicated and raise a serious risk of sensitive information being exploited or misused. Researchers are concentrating more on creating privacy-preserving models in the context of predictive analytics to reduce these risks and make sure that student data does not jeopardize personal identity (Sana et al., 2025). Additionally, in order to preserve institutional values while permitting technical flexibility, the governance of these data ecosystems must be established at the intersection of centralization and decentralization (Kernstock et al., 2025). In order to stop student information from becoming a commodity, this also calls for a more comprehensive understanding of how knowledge production and intellectual property are handled within the current technological system (Basilio, 2025).

The widespread problem of bias and discrimination in AI-based educational systems, where algorithms intended to assess performance or customize content may unintentionally reflect the systemic biases found in their training data, presents another important ethical challenge. For example, rather than fostering the desired inclusivity, predictive systems may favor students from particular linguistic or cultural backgrounds, perpetuating current social inequalities. In order to create transparent and auditable AI systems, interdisciplinary teams comprising computer scientists, pedagogical specialists, and ethicists must actively participate in addressing this pernicious issue. It is notoriously difficult for families or educators to comprehend the rationale behind particular academic recommendations due to the "black box" nature of many machines learning algorithms, making the process of contesting unfair or incorrect decisions all but impossible. Research on how AI interventions affect professional practices shows how these automated systems can change the conventional dynamics of the provider-learner relationship, frequently necessitating a critical reevaluation of how technology is used (Lintz, 2025). In an effort to close the gap between technical proficiency and social responsibility, research on these particular ethical issues is becoming more prevalent, as evidenced by the current publication patterns in Artificial Intelligence in Education (AIEd) (Zhu et al., 2025). Furthermore, in order to avoid the automation of bias in high-stakes assessments, fairness and ethical auditing become even more crucial as AI models start to perform at levels comparable to human professional exams (Shvartz et al., 2025). To guarantee that digital environments, like the Metaverse, continue to be inclusive and equitable for all kinds of learners, educational systems must take into consideration a variety of neuropsychological maps and student psychotypes (Ldokova et al., 2025).

Figure 2. Digital education's ethical and security challenges

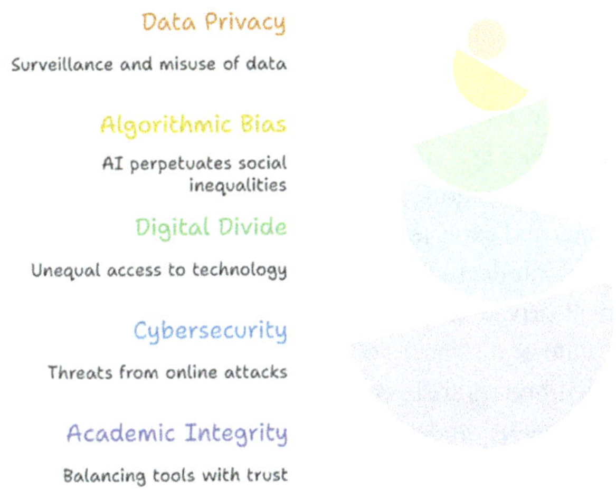

Since schools and universities depend more and more on cloud-based infrastructures and online platforms, which are naturally susceptible to malicious cyberattacks like ransomware, phishing, and unauthorized data breaches, cybersecurity is another essential component of the ethical conversation surrounding digital education. In addition to compromising data, these security incidents can seriously harm an institution's long-term integrity and interfere with the continuation of education. In order to lower the risks associated with human error, it is crucial to implement strong encryption protocols, frequent system updates, and multi-factor authentication. However, developing a deep culture of cybersecurity awareness among staff and students is frequently the most important defense. The abundance of personal data that educational institutions hold makes them appealing targets for cybercriminals, but they frequently lack the technical resources that the private sector has to fend off sophisticated threats. This problem is further complicated by disparities in digital competencies during adolescence, since different levels of technological literacy can result in different security practices among students (Gnambs & Hawrot, 2025). According to Barragán-Moreno and Guzmán-Rincón (2025), institutions that serve underprivileged communities may find it difficult to provide the high-end, secure infrastructure required to protect their users, which makes the digital divide a significant explanatory factor in these difficulties. To guarantee that all educational systems have the technological protections required for the digital age, national preparedness for cloud adoption must be examined through the prism of structural disparities (Tudor et al., 2025).

Lastly, a critical and ongoing analysis of the ethics of surveillance and its effects on academic freedom is necessary, especially as more educational institutions use digital monitoring tools to identify plagiarism or guarantee the integrity of remote exams. Although these tools are intended to support academic integrity, they may unintentionally violate the fundamental right to privacy and foster a culture of constant mistrust. The use of proctoring software, which records private home environments and tracks eye movements, has sparked serious worries about the psychological effects of ongoing surveillance on learning. Students often report feeling more anxious and experiencing "presumed guilt," which runs counter to the educational ideals of intellectual inquiry and trust. Digital environments must adopt neuro-technological privacy enhancements that respect user autonomy in order to transition from a state of distrust to one of confidence (Durnell et al., 2025). In this endeavor, academic libraries are becoming increasingly important hubs, acting as AI competency centers where students can learn to navigate these surveillance-heavy environments with a sense of ethical agency (Sousa, 2025). Additionally, in order to manage these tools with pedagogical sensitivity, administrative staff must receive specialized professional development to comprehend the conceptual foundations of generative AI (Kong & Hu, 2025). In the end, promoting open innovation in this field necessitates a deep comprehension of organizational and strategic dynamics that can strike a balance between the protection of human dignity and the requirement for security (Annamalah et al., 2025). The educational community can leverage technological innovation without sacrificing the fundamental principles of equality and trust by cultivating a responsible digital ecosystem based on ethics.

7. CASE STUDIES OF DIGITAL TOOL IMPLEMENTATION ACROSS NATIONS

There is a great deal of variation in the global landscape of digital education because national infrastructure, governmental policies, and unique cultural perspectives on innovation all play a fundamental role in how technological tools are implemented. Analyzing these various case studies provides important insights into the uneven effects of digital transformation, showing that social and political factors are just as important to success as technical ability. Finland is an example of a teacher-centered model where digital strategy puts professional trust and teacher agency ahead of top-down directives, enabling teachers to act as pedagogical experts and incorporate technology only when it helps achieve particular learning objectives. This contrasts sharply with Singapore's highly centralized and structured "Smart Nation" vision, which uses a technocratic approach to guarantee national digital literacy benchmarks, uniform standards, and fair resource distribution throughout its whole educational system. These variations demonstrate how different structural disparities and regional differences frequently lead to national preparedness for cloud technologies and digital adoption (Tudor et al., 2025). Additionally, how these national frameworks align with local cultural and tourist engagement strategies has a significant impact on the intention to use advanced tools, like mobile augmented reality (AR) educational applications (Cheng & Qian, 2025). The ability of these models to promote smart city environments and integrated geographical analyses that customize digital strategies to particular regional needs are frequently used to gauge their efficacy (Tijjani et al., 2025). The publication patterns of Artificial Intelligence in Education (AIEd), which increasingly concentrate on the nexus of national policy and pedagogical research focuses, ultimately reflect the shift toward these digital-first landscapes (Zhu et al., 2025).

The use of digital tools in the US is a reflection of a highly decentralized governance model in which state and local governments hold the majority of the power, creating an environment that is both highly innovative and markedly unequal. Localized initiatives like "Tech for All" are made possible by this decentralization, but it has also highlighted the severe "digital divide" that low-income and rural communities face due to poor internet access and a lack of digital literacy. These differences were brought to light by the COVID-19 pandemic, which showed that millions of students from underprivileged backgrounds were essentially shut out of the shift to remote learning. This gap has historically affected Black and Hispanic households at higher rates than white households, according to statistics from various educational reports. For instance, during the peak of the digital transition, approximately 13% of Black and 12% of Hispanic students lacked dependable access to devices or connectivity, compared to roughly 7% of their white counterparts. This highlights the fact that educational dropout rates are still primarily explained by the digital divide, which calls for systemic policy interventions rather than merely hardware distribution (Barragán-Moreno & Guzmán-Rincón, 2025). In order to ensure that even at-risk learners receive high-quality support, it is necessary to establish data ecosystems that can bridge the intersection of centralization and decentralization (Kernstock et al., 2025). Additionally, long-term research on teenage development demonstrates the persistence of social, gender, and migration-related differences in digital competencies, necessitating a sophisticated comprehension of how people from different backgrounds use technology (Gnambs & Hawrot, 2025). To guarantee that scientific and educational resources continue to be a public good rather than a tool for further marginalization, knowledge production must be strictly regulated within a capitalist system (Basilio, 2025).

Emerging models that combine national policy with grassroots, community-based innovation are increasingly driving the transformation of digital education in developing countries like Kenya and Indonesia. The adoption of local interactive platforms is encouraged by Indonesia's "Merdeka Belajar" (Freedom to Learn) initiative, but the country faces particular difficulties due to its extensive archipelagic geography, where thousands of islands need unique connectivity solutions. Similar to this, Kenya's Digital Literacy Programme has overcome systemic infrastructure barriers through context-specific innovation by utilizing public-private partnerships to supply solar-powered devices and tablets to elementary schools. These new models demonstrate that digital education can forge unique paths that capitalize on community strengths and strategic dynamics rather than adhering to the strict patterns of wealthy countries. A thorough understanding of organizational flexibility is necessary to drive this kind of open innovation, particularly in the context of SMEs and regional educational organizations (Annamalah et al., 2025). When technology combines implicit game-based learning and artificial intelligence (AI) to make difficult historical or scientific concepts understandable to students in settings with limited resources, the potential for technology to increase quality learning is further enhanced (Madshaven et al., 2025). Tiered AI solutions, like those used in digital healthcare, can be implemented to guarantee that high-quality diagnosis of learning gaps is available across all levels of the hierarchical system in order to achieve true equity at a national scale (Zhou et al., 2026). These countries are producing a more captivating and adaptable story for the upcoming generation of global learners as they continue to incorporate virtual agents and large language models into their STEM curricula (Wang et al., 2025).

8. CONCLUSION

The introduction of computer science into the classroom marks the beginning of a profound and long-lasting revolution in human learning and knowledge transfer. As this thorough analysis has shown, it is no longer sufficient or appropriate to think of technology as an add-on or accessory to conventional pedagogical approaches rather, it has developed into an essential and indispensable part of the educational process itself. The development of digital tools has been a constant path toward personal empowerment, from the early days of centralized mainframe systems to the democratization of computing through personal devices and the ensuing internet revolution. As a result of this journey, the learner's role has completely changed from that of a passive information consumer to that of an active participant and knowledge creator. Modern educational institutions have transcended the antiquated lecture-based model to create dynamic, data-driven, and highly interactive environments by integrating technology as a fundamental teaching strategy. Through simulation, international collaboration, and real-time experimentation, the curriculum is no longer a static collection of materials but rather a dynamic ecosystem that enables students to explore abstract ideas through previously unimaginable experiential modalities. With this integration, the classroom is fundamentally rethought, with the teacher serving as both a guide and an architect of learning experiences, assisted by a technological infrastructure that places an emphasis on exploration rather than memorization.

At the apex of this change is artificial intelligence, which provides the technical foundation for intelligent, adaptive educational systems that can analyze enormous amounts of data to customize instruction on a never-before-seen scale. AI-driven platforms can now detect latent knowledge gaps and predict academic performance with surgical precision by eschewing the constrictive "one-size-fits-all" approach. This allows them to provide customized trajectories that take into account individual differences in learning styles, prior knowledge, and cognitive abilities. This evolution aims to realize the long-held educational ideal of meeting every learner exactly where they are, rather than just attaining technical efficiency. Personalized feedback loops, conversational tutoring, and sophisticated problem-solving that adjusts to each student's individual pace are all made possible by the development of generative AI and large language models. As we embrace these amazing abilities, we must never lose sight of the fundamental human qualitie empathy, mentoring, and profound ethical reasoning that machines are unable to imitate. The idea of "hybrid intelligence," a cooperative partnership in which human educators concentrate on encouraging inspiration, character development, and the critical thinking abilities required for students to navigate an increasingly complex world, while automated systems handle the heavy lifting of data analysis and content delivery, holds the key to the future of education. This equilibrium guarantees that technology functions as an advanced supplement to the human element, augmenting rather than supplanting the crucial relational components of mentoring and instruction.

Our ability as a group to promote interdisciplinary cooperation and handle the major ethical and security issues that come with rapid innovation is also crucial to the success of this digital transformation. As we have shown, computer science alone cannot address the complexity of digital learning rather, a deep synthesis of knowledge from communication studies, psychology, sociology, and ethics is needed. The only practical approach to creating technologically sophisticated systems that are also inclusive, socially conscious, and culturally sensitive is through interdisciplinary cooperation. Algorithmic bias, data privacy violations, and the psychological effects of invasive surveillance on the student experience are just a few of the detrimental effects of digital proliferation that we must continue to watch out for. A sustainable digital future necessitates a cultural and institutional change in which ethical auditing, transparency, and privacy-preserving models become commonplace at every stage of technological advancement. Additionally, the ongoing digital divide continues to be a significant obstacle that poses a risk of using technological advancement as a means of social marginalization. The global lesson is the same whether we look at Finland's teacher-led innovation or Singapore's structured, technocratic approach: technology can only reach its transformative potential when it is paired with visionary policy, equitable infrastructure investment, and a resolute commitment to digital literacy for all members of society, regardless of their socioeconomic or geographic background.

Building a humane learning ecosystem that is essentially equitable, truly innovative, and accessible to everyone is the ultimate objective of incorporating digital tools into education. The role of education must grow into a lifetime endeavor supported by open educational resources, micro-credentials, and ongoing upskilling as we look to the creation of smart cities and the further globalization of knowledge. We are preparing the next generation to thrive in a world where they will not only utilize technology but also be the moral innovators and critical thinkers who mold its future. This calls for a curriculum that emphasizes digital responsibility, intercultural cooperation, and the capacity to discern between information and true wisdom. We can make sure that digital education becomes a potent force for global justice and empowerment by balancing technological innovation with human values. The way forward necessitates a prudent and inclusive strategy in which human dignity, equality, and trust are ingrained in every technological application. We can build a future where learning is a vibrant, diverse, and accessible gateway to human flourishing for all learners worldwide, equipping them to lead with confidence in a technologically advanced world, rather than being limited by physical boundaries or standardized limitations through interdisciplinary collaboration and thoughtful governance.

REFERENCES

Annamalah, S., Aravindan, K. L., & Ahmed, S. (2025). Driving open innovation in SMEs: The role of organizational and strategic dynamics. *Journal of Innovation and Entrepreneurship, 14*(1), 119. Advance online publication. DOI: 10.1186/s13731-025-00588-4

Barragán-Moreno, S. P., & Guzmán-Rincón, A. (2025). Digital divide as an explanatory variable for dropout in higher education. *International Journal of Educational Technology in Higher Education, 22*(1), 60. Advance online publication. DOI: 10.1186/s41239-025-00550-0

Basilio, S. G. (2025). Knowledge Production and Intellectual Property: A Perspective on Scientific Publications in the Capitalist System. *TripleC, 23*(1), 94–109. DOI: 10.31269/triplec.v23i1.1520

Cheng, J., & Qian, J. (2025). Exploring the key factors influencing tourists' intention to use mobile AR educational applications from the perspective of structural equation modeling. *NPJ Heritage Science, 13*(1), 119. Advance online publication. DOI: 10.1038/s40494-025-01575-4

Durnell, E., Howell, R. T., Okabe-Miyamoto, K., & Zizi, M. (2025). From mistrust to confidence: How NeuroTech improves privacy for mistrusted digital environments in a formerly incarcerated population. *Computers in Human Behavior, 173*, 108794. Advance online publication. DOI: 10.1016/j.chb.2025.108794

Evenstein Sigalov, S., & Cohen, A. (2025). Leveraging Wikipedia for educational innovation: A higher education course model for enhancing students' competencies and collaborative knowledge creation. *International Journal of Educational Technology in Higher Education, 22*(1), 27. Advance online publication. DOI: 10.1186/s41239-025-00518-0

Gnambs, T., & Hawrot, A. (2025). The development of social, gender, and migration-related disparities in digital competencies during adolescence. *Computers in Human Behavior, 173*, 108800. Advance online publication. DOI: 10.1016/j.chb.2025.108800

Hakkal, S., & Ait Lahcen, A. A. (2025). Leveraging graph neural network for learner performance prediction. *Expert Systems with Applications, 293*, 128724. Advance online publication. DOI: 10.1016/j.eswa.2025.128724

Iqbal, J., Asgarova, V., Hashmi, Z. F., Ngajie, B. N., Asghar, M. Z., & Järvenoja, H. (2025). Exploring faculty experiences with generative artificial intelligence tools integration in second language curricula in Chinese higher education. *Discover Computing, 28*(1), 128. Advance online publication. DOI: 10.1007/s10791-025-09655-6

Jiang, B., Cheng, T., Tsou, M.-H., Zhu, D., & Ye, X. (2025). Advancing translational human dynamics research: Bridging space, mind, and computational urban science in the era of GeoAI. *Computational Urban Science*, *5*(1), 12. Advance online publication. DOI: 10.1007/s43762-025-00171-3

Kernstock, P., Harms, C., Hein, A., & Krcmar, H. (2025). Establishing and governing data ecosystems at the crossroads of centralization and decentralization. *Electronic Markets*, *35*(1), 71. Advance online publication. DOI: 10.1007/s12525-025-00810-x

Kong, S. C., & Hu, W. (2025). A study of developing administrative Staff's conceptual understanding of generative artificial intelligence through professional Development: Evaluation of a course using tests, surveys and thematic analysis of reflective writings. *Computers and Education: Artificial Intelligence*, *9*, 100444. Advance online publication. DOI: 10.1016/j.caeai.2025.100444

Ldokova, G., Frumina, S., & Alwaely, S. A. (2025). Taking into account students' psychotypes and using their neuropsychological maps when implementing digital educational technologies within the Metaverse. *Smart Learning Environments*, *12*(1), 15. Advance online publication. DOI: 10.1186/s40561-024-00344-3

Li, J. (2025). Enhancing learning through an adaptive web-based educational search framework integrating natural language processing and machine learning techniques. *Discover Computing*, *28*(1), 213. Advance online publication. DOI: 10.1007/s10791-025-09732-w

Lintz, J. (2025). Exploring the impacts of artificial intelligence interventions on providers' practices: Perspectives from a rural medical center. *Journal of Medical Artificial Intelligence*, *8*, 39. Advance online publication. DOI: 10.21037/jmai-24-422

Liu, R., Wu, Y., Zhao, K., Zhou, Z., Gao, X., Lin, X., Zhang, X., Chen, X., & Lu, G. (2025). Online Resource Provisioning and Batch Scheduling for AIoT Inference Serving in an XPU Edge Cloud. *IEEE Transactions on Emerging Topics in Computing*, *13*(1), 234–249. DOI: 10.1109/TETC.2024.3403874

Madshaven, J. M., Omlin, C. W. P., & Spanos, A. (2025). Making Historical Consciousness Come Alive: Abstract Concepts, Artificial Intelligence, and Implicit Game-Based Learning. *Education Sciences*, *15*(9), 1128. Advance online publication. DOI: 10.3390/educsci15091128

Maimaiti, G., & Hew, K. F. (2025). Gamified self-regulated learning improves EFL Reading comprehension, motivation, self-regulation skills and process patterns: Quasi-experiment with process mining. *The Internet and Higher Education*, *67*, 101042. Advance online publication. DOI: 10.1016/j.iheduc.2025.101042

Ren, Y., Shang, J., Zhang, M., Xu, X., & Geng, Z. (2025). Federated learning with local–global collaboration for predicting acute coronary syndrome. *Chemometrics and Intelligent Laboratory Systems*, *267*, 105515. Advance online publication. DOI: 10.1016/j.chemolab.2025.105515

Sana, J. K., Rahman, M. S., & Rahman, M. S. (2025). Privacy-preserving customer churn prediction model in the context of telecommunication industry. *Engineering Applications of Artificial Intelligence*, *162*, 112514. Advance online publication. DOI: 10.1016/j.engappai.2025.112514

Sangodiah, A., Wei, W. C., Ayob, A. N. B., Jalil, N. B. A., Subramaniam, C. R. S. P. R., & Lirong, G. (2023). Machine Learning Clustering Analysis Towards Educator's Readiness to Adopt Augmented Reality as a Teaching Tool. *Mendel*, *29*(2), 147–154. DOI: 10.13164/mendel.2023.2.147

Shvartz, E., Zur, O., Attal, L., Nujeidat, Z., Plopsky, G., & Bahir, D. (2025). GPT-4o vs. residency exams in ophthalmology—A performance analysis. *Journal of Medical Artificial Intelligence*, *8*, 48. Advance online publication. DOI: 10.21037/jmai-24-269

Sousa, N. M. T. (2025). Academic libraries as hubs of artificial intelligence competency. *Discover Artificial Intelligence*, *5*(1), 221. Advance online publication. DOI: 10.1007/s44163-025-00490-8

Tenorio-Sepúlveda, G. C., Arguelles, A. J., Hernández-López, R., & Ramirez-Montoya, M. S. (2025). DIGITAL ESCAPE ROOMS TO DEVELOP COMPUTATIONAL THINKING: LEARNING ANALYTICS IN SCIENCE CLUB. *Journal of Information Technology Education*, *24*, 025. Advance online publication. DOI: 10.28945/5604

Tijjani, K. S., Levent, Y. S., & Levent, T. (2025). Smart Cities in the Global Context: Geographical Analyses of Regional Differentiations. *Systems*, *13*(4), 296. Advance online publication. DOI: 10.3390/systems13040296

Tudor, C., Florescu, M., Polychronidou, P., Stamatiou, P., Vlachos, V., & Kasabali, K. (2025). Cloud Adoption in the Digital Era: An Interpretable Machine Learning Analysis of National Readiness and Structural Disparities Across the EU. *Applied Sciences (Basel, Switzerland)*, *15*(14), 8019. Advance online publication. DOI: 10.3390/app15148019

Wang, M., Zhu, J., Hwang, G.-J., Chang, S.-C., Yang, Q.-F., & Zhang, D. (2025). Boosting Student Engagement in STEM: Integrating Large Language Model-Based Virtual Agents Into Alternate Reality Games. *Journal of Computer Assisted Learning*, *41*(6), e70139. Advance online publication. DOI: 10.1111/jcal.70139

Zhou, T., Liu, K., Li, X., Jiang, N., & Chunguo, C. (2026). Joint Data Compression, Secure Multi-Part Collaborative Task Offloading and Resource Assignment in Ultra-Dense Networks. *IEEE Transactions on Network Science and Engineering*, *13*, 278–295. DOI: 10.1109/TNSE.2025.3582977

Zhu, W., Wei, L., & Qin, Y. (2025). Artificial Intelligence in Education (AIEd): Publication Patterns, Keywords, and Research Focuses. *Information (Basel)*, *16*(9), 725. Advance online publication. DOI: 10.3390/info16090725

Chapter 4
Ethical Perspectives of Teacher Trainees on the Use of Artificial Intelligence

María Soledad Villarrubia Zúñiga
http://orcid.org/0000-0003-4955-7849
University of Alicante, Spain

ABSTRACT

The aim of this article is to present the perceptions of future teachers in the context of the Master's Degree in Educational Research at the University of Alicante on the ethical approaches to the implementation of AI in education. It demonstrates the necessity and relevance of integrating certain values, together with the teacher training indispensable for their application. The research was conducted using a qualitative-descriptive approach. The study took into account the work of a group of students with a solid academic background. The main objective is to recognise the ethical positioning regarding the use of artificial intelligence in the classroom. The results indicate a high degree of involvement and clear ideas on the subject. This study is not a survey but rather an argumentative analysis to evaluate the effectiveness and consistency of the ideas expressed in a class assignment to create a conceptual corpus to base future research.

INTRODUCTION

In the 21st century, most educational institutions and their teachers are committed, in different areas, to incorporating educational technology to improve our students'

DOI: 10.4018/979-8-2600-1568-1.ch004

academic results. To achieve this goal, it is necessary to analyse the technological and teaching skills of teachers from early childhood education to university. However, appropriate use of technology requires more than basic continuous training in these tools. It is equally important to recognise that this context entails the acquisition of various competencies, notably ethical values. This study will focus specifically on ethical values in the application of artificial intelligence within education.

In 2008, UNESCO highlighted the need to learn and teach technological tools to solve everyday problems. It outlined three approaches concerning the digital skills and competencias that teachers should have to implement in their pedagogical practice with students: 1) Basic notions of technology; 2) Deepening this knowledge; and finally, 3) Generating technological knowledge. However, the emergence of computational intelligence in 2021 forced the organisation to focus on promoting the use of ethical, inclusive and human rights-centred artificial intelligence. Thus, in November 2021, it approved the Recommendation on the Ethics of Artificial Intelligence, supported by 193 member states, becoming the first global regulatory instrument in this field. It is interesting to learn about some basic principles related to this intelligence: first, the transparency of AI systems; non-discrimination and fairness to avoid so-called "algorithmic biases"; the protection of personal data and user privacy; responsibility and accountability for the design and use of AI; and finally, the promotion of sustainable development and digital inclusion. Also, UNESCO undertakes other tasks, such as organising global forums to promote dialogue between countries and public and private institutions on responsibility for academic and societal issues relating to AI.

There is currently an academic debate on how to address the challenge posed by artificial intelligence (AI) to ensure that its use is consistent with the principles of technological innovation, ethics, inclusion, and sustainability. This can be considered a highly relevant and priority issue due to the malpractices that are being detected. In this context, this article is based on the perceptions of the ethical use of AI as a teaching tool among a group of students in a postgraduate training course. The ideas and concepts expressed are essential for designing future studies with a broader scope and strategies that allow for the proper inclusion of AI in the classroom in accordance with UNESCO guidelines. It is clear that in the field of education today, there is an urgent need to establish specific standards and programmes for the ethical use of AI. The aims and efforts of institutions should focus on promoting pedagogical integration that, on the one hand, strengthens teaching and supports students and, on the other, serves as a normative guide that directs both towards critical, responsible and sustainable educational practice. It is not a question of prohibiting the use of AI in classrooms, but rather of regulating it.

BACKGROUND

Ethical Codes

In recent years, education reflections on AI and ethics have generated extensive and multidisciplinary academic research. Numerous studies have examined this relationship from philosophical, pedagogical, social, educational and technological perspectives, thereby revealing the inherent complexity of AI's use and developmente across different contexts. The following recent contributions serve to corroborate this perspective.

Bicharra García (2020) analyses the use of AI and the social prejudices it generates. The cases analysed reveal how AI techniques intensifies distortions, but also perpetuates racial or gender biases and related inequalities. Data is not neutral, it reflects human choices. According to Marín García (2019), the relationship between AI and ethics presents two fundamental challenges: first, to define exactly what AI is and how it manifests itself; and second, to understand the process from design of algorithms to their autonomous decisions, a crucial aspect in the designation of ethical responsibilities.

Recent studies explore these ethical issues from different perspectives. Dávila Morán and Agüero Corzo (2023) focus on the social and economic implications of AI's ethical challenges. Maldonado (2024a, 2024b) examine AI ethic through complexity sciences, with particular focus to Educational pedagogy. Some studies (Stark and Crawford, 2019; Amanbay, 2023) highlight ethical dilemmas related to AI-generated artistic production and its impact on artists. AI is a valuable resource, but at the same time it posses risk to human art and creativity.

Nevertheless, this topic is not new. Previous studies have already explored the philosophical foundations of ethics information and considered AI as a crucial domain for the future of humanity (Bostrom, 2014).

The study by Silvera and Reyes Alvarado (2023) is particularly relevant, as they conducted a descriptive, retrospective, and documentary analysis using a cross-sectional, non-experimental design on codes of ethics in higher education institutions. The authors aimed to examine the codes of ethics of universities in Panama. First determining which universities have a code of ethics published on their websites, and then identifying the ethical foundations embedded in these codes and reflect within the Panamanian educational context. The results showed the existence of 20 ethical principles, and indicated that private universities have more comprehensive codes than public universities. The study also revealed the widespread presence of ethical gaps resulting from the omission of principles included in the code of ethics for public institutions. As we can see, the research on AI is large. This can be seen in studies on the state of the art by Espinoza Freire and Calva Nagua (2020) or González

Fernández et al. (2025), which present a documentary study to investigate the regulatory and ethical frameworks for the use of AI in higher education institutions.

Teachers and Technology in the Classroom

Another factor that support this study relates to teachers' trust about the use of technology in the classroom. These beliefs are fundamental to this study. Some of them have a tendency to implement AI as tools (Núñez et al., 2015). Others explore the benefits, drawbacks, and challenges for teachers in integrating educational technology (Camacho Marín & Semanate Zapata, 2023) or demonstrate its impact in the attitudes in training with less resources (Gómez-Marí et al., 2023). There are even studies (Arancibia et al., 2020) that identify teaching profiles (constructivist or behaviourist) base on the use of platforms (Moodle).

While these references outline the state of the art and highlight concerns about the impact of technology in the classroom, the main focus should be on how teachers perceive the use of these technologies and their impact on learning and inclusion–integration (Núñez et al., 2015; Saladino et al., 2020). The primary concern has shifted to how teachers' can help and provide the integration of ICT in education environment, or not (Ertmer, 2005; Tirado-Morueta and Aguaded-Gómez, 2014).

The articles since the early 2000s are extensive and cover a wide range of perspectives that demonstrate the important role of teachers as facilitators. However, it is important to observe the study attending to the purpose and guiding thread.

However, in the case of our study, we find Cabero's work (Cabero, 2016) as relevant, as it sets out certain guidelines for research in accordance with this article: 1) The expansion of the subjects surveyed or informants for the reconstruction and contextualisation of the knowledge acquired; 2) The inclusion in studies of a greater number of teachers' perceptions on the subject; 3) The analysis of specific results taking into account different dimensions (communicative, affective, social, cognitive, ethical-moral components, etc.). Therefore, the main focus of the research is on teachers and their ideas and opinions, as they are responsible for using technological tools in the classroom with students. The teacher profile and their education and training demonstrate the teaching skills required to implement technologies and, in the specific case at hand, AI (Dorfsman, 2012; Tello and Cascales, 2015).

Teacher's Perceptions

To conclude this overview of values, it is necessary to review the concept of 'perception', since the analysis carried out is focused on this concept.

Neisser (1981) specifies that 'perception' is an active-constructive process in which the perceiver, before processing new information and with the data in their consciousness, develops an anticipatory information schema. This schema considers a mental image that is constructed through experience and needs. Guardiola Jiménez (2014) said that perception derives from a process of selection, analysis and rectification of each individual's own sensations.

For Neisser (1981), it is essential to consider two elements linked to perception: sensations and internal inputs, the latter consisting of three factors: need, motivation and experience, without which the perception process would be incomplete. Each of these factors contributes to perceptions being personal and subjective in nature and, therefore, varying from one subject to another. The author therefore asserts that subjects actively construct their perceptions of the context through anticipatory schemas, which implies constant interaction between sensory information and memory in specific frameworks.

Ghitis and Alba (2019), following the idea about teaching materials established by Guardiola Jiménez (2014), suggest a perceptual process that interprets stimuli according to each subject's understanding in three phases: 'selection', 'organisation' and 'interpretation'. In the first phase, according to the authors, the individual selectively perceives one stimulus among several presented to them, depending on their interests and needs. In the organisation phase, the stimulus is classified, and the characteristics that are relevant to the person are highlighted. Finally, the interpretation phase is based directly on the individual's previous experience (motivations, personal interests, and their interaction with other people).

Many of the studies reviewed focus on teachers' perceptions as the basis for their research, while others focus specifically on teachers' perceptions of technology in relation to ethics. For example, we found the article by Ghitis and Alba (2019). It bases its study on teachers' perceptions of the use of technology focusing on early childhood education and whose work presents relevant information on ethics and perceptions. Terán Torres' research (2023) is a study on ethics in the use of ChatGPT through motivation as a form of perception. It is a kind of combination of cognitive processes through sensory codes or inferences that stem from our knowledge of the world (Vergara León, 2012, p. 15).

However, Briceño Caballero's study (2024) is a fundamental reference for the work developed in this article. The author presents research on perceptions of integrity in university teaching. This practice involves values and ethical principles that guide interactions and the exchange of ideas within an educational community, which takes on special relevance in the university context. In this study, the role of the teacher in the training of professionals is central, and a lack of academic integrity can significantly undermine the quality of education. The bibliography on professional teaching ethics is extensive.

The research by Morán-Ortega et al. (2024) also raises the barriers of AI in higher education students from the teachers' perspective. The opinions on the potential benefits and associated ethical challenges are conveyed. In their conclusion, the responses highlight the urgent need to address the risks associated with the misuse of AI in an ethical and legal manner, especially in the field of academic research.

In conclusion, the previous experience of trainee teachers in the use of any technological tool, including AI, influences their perception, as explained by Vergara León (2012). These perceptions involve subjective interpretation, although rather than a strictly sensory phenomenon, the perceptions of future teachers in training must be understood, according to Vergara, as complex psychological behaviour linked to a specific set of references and preferences, created from their own personal, social and academic experience.

METHODOLOGY

The research was conducted using a qualitative-descriptive approach with a cross-sectional design that includes quantitative data to demonstrate the results. The group from which the data was collected consisted of 30 students, but only 23 completed activity. The subject in which the activity is framed is Research in Teaching: *Development of Reading, Writing and Oral Communication Skills, from the Master's Degree in Educational Research* at the University of Alicante for the 2025 academic year.

It is assumed that a low sampling rate for a qualitative study may not meet the standards of assurance, rigour and reliability. However, its use is justified because it is considered a preliminary study to determine a conceptual corpus on which to base future research related to ethics in the use of intelligent computer technologies at different educational levels.

The selection criteria for the group were not random. Instead, a Master's degree programme focused on educational research was chosen, whose participants are future teachers who, in some cases, have already studied educational artificial intelligence at the postgraduate level, have enrolled in the doctoral programme, and some will write a thesis on this topic. Therefore, the first indicator for beginning this study was to choose a profile that responded to a subject related to education, with knowledge of computational intelligence and an interest in research, to see their reflections, which we intuitively believe will be solid and serious. The aims was to obtain opinions based on a critical and argumentative attitude that was effective for the purpose. Students are aware that the purpose of the activity is twofold: 1) to serve as a part of assessment for the course; and 2) to generate materials for future work. It is explained that this work is not an opinion poll and that the identities of the group members will never be disclosed.

The classroom activity is built around three main items. These will serve to categorise the study on the ethical use of AIEd at any educational stage (from early childhood education to university), with appropriate variables based on the student's profile: benefits, limitations of use, and ethical use per se (Table 1).

Table 1. Categories and descriptors

Items	Categories	Descriptors
1	Improvement.	Educational Artificial Intelligence (AIEd) as a tool for teacher-researchers and students (teaching-learning).
2	Limitation.	Advantages and disadvantages of using AI in different educational settings.
3	Ethical use.	Impact and ethical considerations of using AI.

Note. Own elaboration for the study.

This Table 1 is used as a basis for developing the class activity based on three questions to be answered openly in a maximum of 150 words (Table 2). It is a reflective classroom task collected through *Google Form* so that it can be shared and reviewed by everyone. This format is easily accessible to students and allows information to be dumped for analysis. Data is obtained to assess the maturity of the students' reflection, but at the same time, the text produced allows items related to the use of IAE in educational contexts to be obtained as a conceptual corpus. The activity is anonymous and remains open and available for educational and research purposes. The task is considered an "initial and facilitating task" that allows for a final task consisting of a reflective debate based on a critical, non-directed attitude towards the information obtained.

The dynamic proposed in the Master's course, in the subject *Research in didactics: developing reading, writing, and oral communication skills*, opens up the possibility of future lines of research into how students construct their critical thinking in the face of artificial intelligence and how these reflections can be integrated into school curricula. In this way, the proposed task serves an immediate formative function but also becomes a valuable tool for analysing trends, perceptions, and attitudes towards the ethical use of AI in education, providing evidence that can inform educational policies and teaching innovation strategies. This type of dynamic moves beyond traditional perception surveys that only capture item selection, fostering instead a deeper and more detailed analysis of student responses and reflections.

The evaluation grade obtained was 'pass' or 'fail'. This kind of grading system emphasises participation and reflective engagement rather than the accuracy of answers. It aims to focus away from achieving higher or lower scores. The procedure encourages students to express their ideas freely without the pressure of traditional grades. The focus and assessment are on the quality of critical thinking and the ability to articulate perspectives on the ethical use of AI in education. When students develop a deeper and more thoughtful learning process, we need an open and formative, less traditional, approach for the evaluation.

Table 2 presents the categories and descriptors used as a reference for the reflective classroom activity. This table organises the contest but also serves as a conceptual framework for guiding the critical opinion. Each item highlights a different dimension of the use of AI (improvement, limitation, and ethical consideration), providing students with a structured process through which to analyse their own experiences and perspectives. This structure ensures that the responses are focused on the engagement with the topic.

The following table (Table 2) are activities based on three questions to be answered openly in a maximum words. It is a reflective classroom task collected through Google Form so that it can be shared and reviewed by everyone. This format is easily accessible to students and allows information to be dumped for analysis. Data is obtained to assess the maturity of the students' reflection, but at the same time, the text produced allows items related to the use of IAE in educational contexts to be obtained as a conceptual corpus. The activity is anonymous and remains open and available for educational and research purposes. The task is considered an "initial and facilitating task" that allows for a final task consisting of a reflective debate based on a critical, non-directed attitude towards the information obtained. The grade obtained is pass or fail:

Table 2. Categories and descriptors for the activities (Activities question header)

Items	Categories	Activities
1	Improvement.	Reflect on the importance of Educational Artificial Intelligence (EAI) for the teacher-researcher (Maximum 150 words).
2	Limitation.	You must create a list of the advantages and disadvantages of the IAE (10 respond for the list. Maximum 150 words).
3	Ethical use.	Answer the following question (maximum 100 words): What should be the ethical framework for the use of AI in education by teachers and students?

Note: Personal study schedule table.

Table 2 represents a highly significant exercise because it does not use closed-ended questions but invites students to reflect critically and openly on three key dimensions of the use of Educational Artificial Intelligence (EAI): improvement, limitations, and ethical use. By asking them to write brief, structured texts, synthesis skills and critical thinking are fostered. Superficial answers are avoided, and deeper, more critical analysis is encouraged. Furthermore, the anonymous and accessible nature of the activity, along with a subsequent discussion, provides a space for sharing through group dialogue. Here, students can identify perspectives and build a shared conceptual corpus on the integration of AI in education. In this sense, the table serves as a bridge between individual reflection and the construction of collective knowledge, laying the groundwork for a broader ethical and academic discusión.

Only 23 out of the 30 students completed the class assignment. The results were excellent, and therefore all students successfully met the objectives. Beyond the course assignment, this article presents a qualitative-descriptive analysis of the data collected through this formative activity. This methodology is proposed as a strategy for observing, recording, and analysing a phenomenon—in this case, an educational one—as it occurs in the classroom setting, without intervening or modifying students' responses. Its main objective has been to describe in detail the responses, ideas, and concepts based on professional and academic experiences with the IAE.

The metodologhy has steps were taken to ensure the success of the process:

Table 3. Description of the stages of the process

	Categories	Process descriptors
1	Contextualisation of the topic.	Problem delimitation to defines what you want to study and why (AIEd + ethics).
2	Tecnics/procedure.	Choos and Development Activities (Table 2).
3	Information gathering.	Choose the plataform (*Google Form*).
4	Organising data.	Table 1 and choose the programme (*Taguette*).
5	Interpretation.	Interpretation based on AI and ethics in Education (bibliography).
6	Discussion.	Students' final assignment and debate.
7	Results.	Final analysis.

Note: Personal study schedule table.

The Table 3 provides an ordered description of the stages of the work process. This is offering a clear, sequential overview of how the reflective activity on Educational Artificial Intelligence (EAI) and ethics is structured. Each category serves a specific function: first, the problem is defined, and then the topic is contextualised. This ensures a precise approach. Next, the techniques and procedures are selected (in relation to Table 2), and the information collection platform (*Google Form*) is defined. The aim is to ensure the accessibility and systematic nature of the process.

As we have seen, the Taguette program was used to organise and evaluate the data (Rampin & Rampin, 2021). This qualitative analysis tool is very useful for generating histograms and descriptors. It provides the frequency of occurrence of themes. The codes are generated after coding the text that appears in the responses. This is a visual complement to the research. Also, this tool (Taguette) facilitates the systematisation of information for qualitative studies and allows the results to be interpreted and compared more clearly within the framework of this education research.

RESULTS

The process of analysing and cataloguing the items found in the activities yielded a result of 38 elements in activities related to the ethical use of IAE in the classroom through Taguette tool. This finding of recurring concepts is an excellent starting point for structuring future work on the subject (guides, pedagogical proposals, studies of frequency of use, quantitative and qualitative studies, the impact of AI on educational institutions' regulations, etc.).

The organisation of the conceptual corpus with the results obtained allows for the creation of eight tables based on a common factor found in the different responses. The information was organised in a table to identify the result more easily.

To describe the results obtained, we have used three different generative artificial intelligence tools: *Microsoft Copilot*, *Gemini* (Flash 2.5), and ChatGPT (based on OpenAI's GPT-5.1model). Each of these platforms has enabled us to compare the information obtained in the classroom exercise with quality, accuracy, and coherence, facilitating a more reliable comparative analysis. The combination of these tools provided a more accurate view of students' responses by interpreting and synthesising the information in the tables below.

The first table brings together elements within the term and meaning of 'equity'. This term is taken as a category that not only seeks to give each subject their fair share but also to create environments where all people, regardless of their social or economic differences, feel valued and can develop fully. This involves recognising the barriers faced by certain groups and actively working to remove them:

Table 4. Concepts related to equity

	Categories	Descriptors	Frequency
1	Inequalities.	Described Corrects structural imbalances.	1
2	Discrimination.	Promote social justice.	1
3	Inclusion.	Ensures everyone's participation.	4
4	Respect.	Promote equitable and dignified relationships.	2
4	Fair education.	Right to fair and equal treatment.	1
5	Equity.	Equanimity.	6
Total			15

Note: Personal study schedule table.

The results of Table 4 show how students understand equity in education, highlighting six categories that total 15 mentions: equity appears as the most frequent concept (6); followed by inclusion (4); underscoring the importance of ensuring everyone's participation; d) respect (2) reinforces the need for dignified and fair relationships, while inequalities, discrimination, and fair education (1 each) complement the view by linking equity to social justice and the correction of structural imbalances. Taken together, the results reflect that equity is not limited to equal treatment but involves creating inclusive, respectful, and fair educational environments where existing barriers are recognised and actively addressed.

Another group of items is categorised under the concept 'digital training and competence'. It is key to ensuring the ethical and effective use of Educational Artificial Intelligence (EAI) in classrooms. If you have already identified a group of items under this category, we could use them to build a solid structure that promotes professional development for teachers and meaningful learning for students.

Table 5. Digital training and competence

	Categories	Descriptors	Frequency
1	Knowledgeable about usage.	Skills to use technologies.	1
2	Knowledgeable about plagiarism.	Identification of dishonest practices.	6
3	Knowledge of copyright law.	Laws and regulations that protect creations.	3
4	Previous training.	Knowledge and skills.	4
5	Support tool.	AI as supplementary resources.	10
6	Adapted Education.	Personalised strategies and resources.	1
7	Verify data.	Capacity to compare the information obtained.	1
Total			26

Note: Personal study schedule table.

The results of Table 5 highlight the main areas students associate with digital training and competence. The most frequently mentioned category is 'AI as a support tool' (10 mentions), which suggests that learners view artificial intelligence primarily as a supplementary resource to enhance their educational experience. Another concept, 'knowledgeable about plagiarism' (6) and 'previous training' (4), reflects a strong concern with academic integrity and the importance of prior preparation in developing digital skills. 'Knowledge of copyright law' (3) indicates awareness of the legal framework protecting intellectual creations, while categories such as 'Knowledge about usage', 'Adapted education', and 'Verify data' have 1 mention each. It shows less emphasis but still points to relevant aspects of digital competence, including basic technological skills, personalisation of learning, and critical evaluation of information. Overall, the 26 elements reveal that students perceive digital competence not only as technical proficiency but also as ethical responsibility, legal awareness, and the effective integration of AI into educational contexts.

On the other hand, a broad respond is observed that is ultimately classified under the concept "Responsible use of artificial intelligence". It is suggests that this theme acts as an umbrella—encompassing ethical, pedagogical, and technical dimensions of AI integration in education.

Table 6. Responsible use of artificial intelligence

	Categories	Descriptors	Frequency
1	Ethical promote.	Promote ethical with the educational technology	1
2	Misuse.	Pursuing the use of AI for dishonest or inappropriate purposes (copying, impersonating, manipulating)	1
3	Use and critical attitude.	Using AI reflectively, questioning results, comparing sources, and making informed decisions.	7
4	Supervise and control.	Establish AI control mechanisms.	1
5	Algorithm control.	Ensure that AI systems are understandable, so that users understand how and why an algorithm acts.	1
6	Bias control.	Identify and reduce prejudices and inequalities.	6
7	Don't be alarmed about AI.	AI is not a cause for concern.	1
8	Clear rules. Responsible protocol.	Establish explicit rules on how AI should be used and define procedures in case of misuse or conflict.	2
9	AI doesn't replace.	Recognise that, although AI can be a valuable resource, the human role of the teacher is irreplaceable.	7
Total			27

Note: Personal study schedule table

Table 6 shows students' perspectives on the responsible use of artificial intelligence in education. It has a total of 27 references distributed across nine categories. The most frequently mentioned aspects are the need for a critical attitude towards the use of AI (7) and the recognition that AI cannot replace the teacher's role (7). Both responses emphasise both a reflective engagement with technology and the value of human guidance in learning. Bias control (6) is close at hand. This reveals a strong concern for fairness and the reduction of inequalities in AI systems. Other categories, such as establishing clear rules and responsible protocols (2) and ensuring ethical promotion, oversight, algorithm control, and the prevention of misuse (each has one entry). This response reflects an awareness of the importance of transparency and control. Overall, the results suggest that students view the responsible use of AI as a balance between leveraging its benefits and maintaining an ethical stance. This, therefore, confirms the importance of human educators in the teaching process.

Table 7 compiles the items related to "Ethical and Social Values" in relations with AIEd. A table focused on this topic in relation to Artificial Intelligence in Education (AIEd) can serve as a foundation for both policy development and classroom practice.

Table 7. Ethical and social values

	Categories	Descriptors	Frequency
1	Honesty.	Work with transparency and truthfulness.	1
2	Humanity.	Recognise and value the dignity and emotions of others.	1
3	Responsibility.	Take responsibility for decisions, actions, and their consequences.	14
4	Principles and ethical compliance.	Act with universal values (justice, equality, truth) that guide right action.	2
5	Moral principles.	Internal norms that guide behaviour according to what an individual or society considers.	1
6	Legal principles.	Rules established by laws that guarantee the rights and duties of everyone.	1
7	Respect.	Recognise and value the diversity, opinions, spaces, and rights of others.	2
Total			22

Note: Personal study schedule table.

The results of the Table 7 reveals that students place great importance on responsibility (14 mentions), making it the most prominent ethical and social value. This highlights their awareness of the importance of being responsible for decisions, actions, and their consequences when interacting with educational technologies such as AI. Other values, although less frequent, still contribute to a broader ethical framework: respect (2) and ethical principles and compliance (2) underscore the need for justice, equality, and recognition of diversity, while categories such as honesty, humanity, moral principles, and legal principles (each with one mention) show that transparency, dignity, and adherence to the law are also considered relevant. Overall, the 22 references suggest that students view ethical and social values as essential for guiding responsible behaviour, highlighting responsibility as the cornerstone for ensuring integrity and equity in educational contexts.

In the next table, number 8, we offfer the list the items that students considered important in the AI and ethics relationship on topics such as empowerment and autonomy; data protection and privacy; and transparency. That's a rich and meaningful dataset. The fact that students themselves identified key items under empowerment and autonomy, data protection and privacy, and transparency shows a growing awareness of the ethical dimensions of AI in education. These insights can be used to shape more inclusive and student-centered policies and practices.

Table 8. Empowerment and autonomy

	Categories	Descriptors	Frequency
1	Autonomy.	Ability to act and make decisions independently.	1
2	Empowerment.	Acquiring or possessing confidence, resources and skills.	1
3	Awareness.	Reflective recognition of oneself or others.	1
4	Creativity.	Ability to generate new and useful ideas.	2
5	Critical thinking.	Ability to analyse, evaluate and question information or ideas.	6
Total			11

Note: Personal study schedule table.

Table 8 highlights the students' perspectives on empowerment and autonomy, with a total of 11 references distributed across five categories. The most prominent aspect is 'critical thinking' (6 mentions), which underscores the importance of analysing, evaluating, and questioning information as a key skill for independent learning and responsible use of AI in education. The concept to 'Creativity' (2 mentions) also emerges as a valued competence, pointing to the ability to generate innovative and useful ideas. Meanwhile, 'autonomy', 'empowerment', and 'avareness' (with one mention each) reflect recognition of the need for self-confidence, independent decision-making, and reflective self-awareness, even if they appear less frequently. Overall, the data suggest that students view empowerment and autonomy primarily through the lens of critical thinking, complemented by creativity and personal growth, which together form the foundation for active, responsible, and self-directed participation in educational contexts.

In Table 9, 'Privacy and data protection,' we present two fundamental categories in the debate on the ethical use of artificial intelligence and digital technologies in education: 1) privacy and data protection; 2) transparency. Both concepts are directly linked to individuals' rights and the need to ensure a safe and trustworthy environment for handling personal information.

Table 9. Privacy and data protection

	Categories	Descriptors	Frequency
1	Privacy, data protection and processing.	Right to confidentiality and privacy. Every person's right to control their personal information.	10
2	Transparency.	Practice of sharing information in a clear, accessible and honest manner.	6
Total			16

Note: Personal study schedule table.

The results show that the category most frequently mentioned by participants is 'privacy and data protection' (10 references), followed by 'transparency' (6 references). In total, 16 mentions were recorded, reflecting the importance that future teachers place on these aspects in the educational context.

The last table, number 10, includes a total of five references distributed across three categories that reflect essential values for the educational use of artificial intelligence: humanised information, human interaction, and sustainability. Although the frequency is low, the results are significant because they show that students not only perceive AI as a technical tool, but also recognise the need for data to be presented in a comprehensible and empathetic manner, for interpersonal relationships to be maintained through dialogue and collaboration, and for responsible, lasting habits to be fostered. In this regard, the table demonstrates a concern for integrating technology into education without losing sight of human and social values, underscoring that innovation must be accompanied by sustainable practices and a people-centered approach. This invites reflection on the importance of balancing technological advancement with the preservation of the ethical and human dimension in educational processes.

Table 10. Human and social dimension

	Categories	Descriptors	Frequency
1	Humanised information.	Present data or content in a relatable, understandable, and empathetic way.	1
2	Human interaction.	Interpersonal relationships based on dialogue, listening, empathy, and collaboration.	2
3	Sustainability.	Encourage responsible and lasting habits.	2
Total			5

Note: Personal study schedule table.

From the compilation of these 10 tables on ethics in the use of AI, valuable conclusions can be drawn that reflect both the level of ethical awareness among students and the educational opportunities that arise from the use of artificial intelligence in the classroom.

Although the corpus is small, the reflections gathered demonstrate a critical awareness of the risks and opportunities posed by AI, and highlight the need for clear frameworks to guide its integration into the classroom. Taken together, the tables not only reveal students' level of ethical awareness but also provide an empirical basis for designing educational policies, curricular proposals, and teaching practices that promote the responsible, sustainable, and inclusive use of technology.

FUTURE RESEARCH DIRECTIONS

The tables analysed reveal a growing ethical awareness among students in training, future teachers, regarding the use of artificial intelligence in education. These elements reflect a conceptual value and legitimate concerns about privacy and control of information and text production, but also a desire to understand and actively participate in the technological processes that affect teaching and learning, which are already closely related to AI. Adding both together, we have a result of the necessity to incorporate ethics in digital technology as an integral part of the school curriculum.

The ideas presented are aimed at encouraging critical thinking about AI to promote spaces for dialogue where students and teachers can participate in digital development in an informed and responsible manner. Much work remains to be done, such as the development of regulations and guidelines, but a study such as this demonstrates that banning AI in the classroom is not an acceptable solution. The objective should be focused on integration, taking into account certain factors that may pose a personal, but also an academic, risk. The presence of artificial intelligence in the educational field must be approached from a critical, reflective, and regulated integration perspective. The focus should be on how to respond to academic challenges through consistent and responsible use. The arguments developed in the article can serve as a basis for further study to shed more light on this topic.

Based on the findings presented, it is essential to direct future research towards the development of pedagogical frameworks and curricula that integrate digital ethics into teacher training, and to explore the use of methodologies that allow for the systematic evaluation of artificial intelligence's impact on teaching and learning processes. It is essential to delve deeper into the institutions that have already activated a protocol for the ethical use of AI. Furthermore, it will be essential to conduct comparative studies across diverse educational contexts to analyse how regulations within and outside countries can be adapted to educational settings. We will need to examine students' and teachers' perceptions of the automation of academic tasks through AI. It will be no less important to investigate critical digital literacy strategies that strengthen the ability to detect algorithmic biases and the use of data for unethical purposes. These lines of work will help consolidate a comprehensive vision that not only addresses the risks but also leverages the opportunities of AI as a transformative educational tool. In conclusion, it is important to note that studies should not only focus on highlighting the dangers of AGI in academia; they must also propose ways to gradually implement usage guidelines and evaluation criteria for integrating activities based directly or indirectly on AGI into course curricula.

CONCLUSION

We have seen the study presented here is based on a classroom task carried out in a master's degree in educational research. The aims of this study was not to be an opinion poll, it is rather a reflective exercise based on the excellent abilities and preparation of a group of students. The students were informed of the purpose all time. The work was anonymised to be used and shared by all the participans.

As noted, the homeworks presented form a very small corpus; however, the information provided in the three activities has allowed us to create tables that show the position and concerns of trainee teachers on the ethics of AI use. It is clear that this data could be a reference for organising and developing future works. The research in this area is important because it highlights the real concerns of trainee teachers regarding the ethical challenges posed by artificial intelligence in educational contexts. In addition, they contribute to building an empirical basis from reflective practice, which can guide future research, curriculum proposals, and institutional policies.

Integrating the voice of students into the analysis strengthens the participatory approach and promotes a critical and responsible culture around the use of emerging technologies in teaching. Currently, many schools are considering banning or limiting the use of technology in the classroom. This is partly due to a lack of planning and clear guidelines to guide teachers and students.

These rules for ethical use already exist in many institutions. Instead of restricting access, it is essential to commit to the conscious and educational integration of technologies, especially artificial intelligence, that takes into account ethical, pedagogical, and inclusion criteria. The key is to provide teachers with clear tools and frameworks that enable them to guide the responsible use of technology and to train students to actively participate in their own digital development, with critical thinking, responsibility and autonomy.

This study demostrates the necessity of dialogue between researchers, teachers, and educational policymakers to guarantee that the integration of artificial intelligence in education is not only viable but also socially and ethically sustainable. We can advance towards an educational model where technology serves as a tool to enhance teaching methods and strengthen students' use of AI by encouraging cooperation and introspection. However, it is necessary to promote the ethical use of computational intelligence to guarantee data privacy, prevent bias and discrimination, strengthen democratic education through transparent information, and ensure responsible academic production in order to safeguard intellectual and creative work. In a certain sense, it is about promoting a form of sustainability based on responsible innovation that benefits the entire community without jeopardizing the fundamental pillars of society.

REFERENCES

Amanbay, M. (2023, April 4). *The ethics of AI-generated art. SSRN*. https://ssrn.com/abstract=4551467

Arancibia, M. L., Cabero, J., & Marín, V. (2020). Creencias sobre la enseñanza y uso de las tecnologías de la información y la comunicación (TIC) en docentes de educación superior. *Formación Universitaria, 13*(3), 89–100. Advance online publication. DOI: 10.4067/S0718-50062020000300089

Bicharra García, A. C. (2020). Ética e Inteligência Artificial. *Computação Brasil*, (43), 14–22. DOI: 10.5753/compbr.2020.43.1791

Bostrom, N. (2014). *Superintelligence: Paths, Dangers, Strategies*. Oxford University Press.

Briceño Caballero, M. M. (2024). Percepciones de la integridad en la docencia universitaria: Perspectiva del alumnado. *Praxis Educativa (Santa Rosa), 19*, 1–20. Advance online publication. DOI: 10.5212/PraxEduc.v.19.22859.004

Cabero, J. (2016). ¿Qué debemos aprender de las pasadas investigaciones en Tecnología Educativa? *Revista Interuniversitaria de Investigación en Tecnología Educativa, 0*, 23–33. DOI: 10.6018/riite/2016/256741

Camacho Marín, R. J., & Semanate Zapata, R. D. (2023). Percepciones de los docentes sobre la implementación de tecnología en el aula. *Revista Ciencia y Descubrimiento, 1*(3). Advance online publication. DOI: 10.70577/c0gcrz88RCD

Dávila Morán, R. C., & Agüero Corzo, E. C. (2023). Desafíos éticos de la inteligencia artificial: Implicaciones para la sociedad y la economía. *Revista Conrado, 19*(94), 137–144. DOI: 10.52575/rc.v19i94.3326

Dorfsman, M. I. (2012). La profesión docente en contextos de cambio: el docente global en la sociedad de la información. *Revista de Educación a Distancia - Docencia Universitaria en la Sociedad del Conocimiento*, 6, 1-23. https://www.um.es/ead/reddusc/6/marcelo_dusc6.pdf

Ertmer, P. A. (2005). Teacher pedagogical beliefs: The final frontier in our quest for technology integration? *Educational Technology Research and Development, 53*(4), 25–39. DOI: 10.1007/BF02504683

Freire, E., Enrique, E., Nagua, C., & Xavier, D. (2020). La ética en las investigaciones educativas. *Revista Universidad y Sociedad, 12*(4), 333-340. Epub 02 de agosto de 2020. Retrieved from 21th October 2025. http://scielo.sld.cu/scielo.php?script=sci_arttext&pid=S2218-36202020000400333&lng=es&tlng=es

Ghitis, T., & Alba, A. (2019). Percepciones de futuros docentes sobre el uso de tecnología en educación inicial. *Revista Electrónica de Investigación Educativa, 21*(e23), 1–12. DOI: 10.24320/redie.2019.21.e23.2034

Gómez-Marí, I., Lacruz-Pérez, I., & Sanz-Cervera, P. (2023). Percepciones y actitudes del profesorado hacia el uso de la tecnología como herramienta inclusiva. *REIDOCREA, 12*(8), 86–97. DOI: 10.30827/Digibug.81000

González Fernández, M. O., Romero-López, M. A., Sgreccia, N. F., & Latorre Medina, M. J. (2025). Marcos normativos para una IA ética y confiable en la educación superior: Estado de la cuestión. *RIED-Revista Iberoamericana de Educación a Distancia, 28*(2). Advance online publication. DOI: 10.5944/ried.28.2.43511

Guardiola Jiménez, P. F. (2014). *Mis publicaciones de sociología.* https://www.um.es/docencia/pguardio/

Maldonado, C. E. (2024a). El problema de la ética: El convivio. Ética e Inteligencia Artificial. *Revista Iberoamericana de Complejidad y Ciencias Económicas, 2*(2), 31–48. DOI: 10.48168/ricce.v2n2p31

Maldonado, C. E. (2024b). *Inteligencia artificial y ética.* Ediciones desde abajo.

Marín García, S. (2019). *Ética e inteligencia artificial.* Cuadernos de la Cátedra CaixaBank de Responsabilidad Social Corporativa, No. 42. IESE Business School. https://dx.doi.org/DOI: 10.15581/018.ST-522

Morán-Ortega, S.-A., Ruiz-Tirado, S.-G., Simental-López, L.-M., & Tirado-López, A.-B. (2024). Barreras de la Inteligencia Artificial generativa en estudiantes de educación superior. Percepción docente. *Revista De Investigación En Tecnologías De La Información, 12*(25), 26–37. DOI: 10.36825/RITI.12.25.003

Neisser, U. (1981). *Cognición y realidad: principios e implicaciones de la psicología cognitiva.* Marova.

Núñez, L., Conde, S., Ávila, J., & Mirabent, M. (2015). Implicaciones, uso y resultados de las TIC en educación primaria. Estudio cualitativo de un caso. *Edutec. Revista Electrónica de Tecnología Educativa,* 53, 1-17. https://dx.doi.DOI: 10.21556/edutec.2015.53.581

Rampin, R., & Rampin, V. (2021). Taguette: Open-source qualitative data analysis. *Journal of Open Source Software*, *6*(68), 3522. DOI: 10.21105/joss.03522

Saladino, M., Marín Suelves, D., & San Martín Alonso, Á. (2020). Percepción docente del aprendizaje mediado tecnológicamente en aulas italianas. *Revista Interuniversitaria de Formación del Profesorado, 34*(3), 175–194. DOI: 10.47553/rifop.v34i3.80593

Silvera, L., & Reyes Alvarado, S. (2023). Análisis de los Códigos de Ética de las Universidades en Panamá. *Sapientia*, *14*(3), 26–39. DOI: 10.54138/27107566.465

Stark, L., & Crawford, K. (2019). The work of art in the age of artificial intelligence: What artists can teach us about the ethics of data practice. *Surveillance & Society, 17*(3/4), 442-455. https://dx.doi.DOI: 10.24908/ss.v17i3/4.10821

Tello, I., & Cascales, A. (2015). Las TIC y las necesidades específicas de apoyo educativo: Análisis de las competencias TIC en los docentes. *Revista Iberoamericana de Educación a Distancia*, *18*(2), 355–383. DOI: 10.5944/ried.18.2.13536

Terán Torres, H. (2023). *La implementación de la Inteligencia Artificial en la enseñanza de la programación: Un estudio sobre el uso ético de ChatGPT en el aula. Encuentro Internacional de Educación en Ingeniería.* EIEI ACOFI., DOI: 10.26507/paper.2768

Tirado-Morueta, R. J., & Aguaded-Gómez, J. I. (2014). Influencias de las creencias del profesorado sobre el uso de la tecnología en el aula. *Review of Education*, (363), 230–255. DOI: 10.4438/1988-592X-RE-2012-363-179

UNESCO. (2008). Estándares de competencias en TIC para docentes. Retrieved from www.oei.es/historico/tic/UNESCOEstandaresDocentes.pdf

UNESCO. (2021). *Recomendación sobre la ética de la inteligencia artificial*. Organización de las Naciones Unidas para la Educación, la Ciencia y la Cultura. Retrieved from https://www.unesco.org/es/artificial-intelligence/recommendation-ethics

Vergara León, M. J. (2012). *Percepción de docentes y estudiantes sobre el currículo de estudios de una universidad privada de Lima* [Tesis de maestría, Universidad San Ignacio de Loyola]. Repositorio USIL. https://repositorio.usil.edu.pe/handle/20.500.14005/1348

Chapter 5
Adaptive Learning System Implementation in LMS Platforms:
Educator and Student Perceptions in a Scoping Review

Maximiliano Ernesto Merino Suárez
http://orcid.org/0009-0004-8799-3371
Universidad Santo Tomas, Chile

Jorge Fernández Herrero
http://orcid.org/0000-0003-1545-8906
University of Alicante, Spain

ABSTRACT

The perceptions of university educators and students about the implementation of Adaptive Learning Systems (ALS) driven by artificial intelligence (AI) and integrated into Learning Management Systems (LMS) in higher education. The purpose of this chapter is to analyze empirical evidence published between 2020 and 2025 to identify key trends, facilitators, barriers, and perceived effects associated with the use of ALS in digital learning environments. The authors conducted a scoping review following the PRISMA-ScR framework, analyzing 12 studies selected from Web of Science, Scopus, and ProQuest. The findings reveal generally positive perceptions of ALS, particularly about learning personalization, automated feedback, and student engagement. However, significant challenges were also identified, including technical limitations, digital competency gaps, ethical concerns, and organizational resistance. This chapter highlights the significance of user perceptions in shaping the inclusive, sustainable, and pedagogically effective adoption of adaptive technologies.

DOI: 10.4018/979-8-2600-1568-1.ch005

INTRODUCTION

LMSs have emerged as pivotal tools in the ongoing digital transformation of higher education. These platforms have enabled the systematic organization and delivery of teaching and learning processes in virtual environments. In parallel, the advent of ALS, driven by AI technologies, has marked a significant advancement in the personalization of education by allowing instructional pathways to be tailored to the specific characteristics of individual learners (Andhika et al., 2024).

The relatively new novelty of these technologies in the market makes academic literature scarce and speculative concerning ALS. However, there is evidence that these systems do improve student engagement and achievement in comparison to conventional LMS. Benefits include decreased optimum idle time in virtual classrooms, enhanced engagement with content, and a lower abandonment rate. Nevertheless, although there is access and training on these technologies, learners and teachers have not fully incorporated them into their regular teaching and learning activities (Mukhamadiyeva & Hernández-Torrano, 2024).

Therefore, the perception of the major stakeholders must be investigated thoroughly. It is important to understand the views, experiences, and problems of teachers and students when considering the use of ALS within LMS, since this will allow for the identification of the barriers to adoption as well as strategies that can facilitate successful deployment. Moreover, such understanding may contribute to uncovering institutional or pedagogical environments that can directly impact how technological tools can or cannot be effectively used (Harati et al., 2021).

A deeper understanding of these perceptions serves to provide insight into the phenomenon and to offer input for the development of pedagogical interventions, faculty development initiatives, and strategic institutional policies. For example, an exploration of students' perception of adaptive pathways as a motivational tool or instructors' experience of the system's feedback mechanisms may provide a critical distinction between the success and misalignment of implementation (Koh et al., 2022; Lindholst et al., 2024).

So, this chapter aims to synthesize empirical evidence on the perceptions and experiences of faculty and students regarding AI-based adaptive learning systems integrated into LMS platforms.

From this objective, the following research questions have been formulated to guide the analytical process:

1. What are the most common perceptions and evaluations of university students regarding their learning experiences in LMS environments that integrate adaptive learning systems, and how do these influence their motivation and academic engagement?

2. What opinions and experiences do university instructors express concerning the use of adaptive learning systems (ALS) within LMS platforms, particularly in terms of pedagogical utility, ease of implementation, and institutional support?
3. What barriers and facilitators are identified by students and faculty for the effective adoption of adaptive learning systems in higher education settings?
4. How are the perceptions of faculty and students related to perceived outcomes in terms of academic performance, feedback received, and personalization of the learning process?

Research into these perceptions is essential to ensure the effective and sustainable implementation of adaptive learning systems in the future.

BACKGROUND

The integration of digital technologies into higher education has radically restructured how teaching and learning processes are conceived and delivered. At the core of this transformation is LMS, which is a digital platform designed to structure, administer, and monitor educational experiences in online or hybrid environments (Mukerji & Tripathi, 2014). LMSs have become essential for enabling access to content, facilitating communication, and managing assessments, particularly in response to the increasing demand for flexibility and scalability in academic institutions.

Matching the rise of LMS, ALS has gained prominence as tools that leverage AI to personalize learning experiences. ALS can monitor learner behaviors and performance in real time, using this data to adjust the sequence, pace, and difficulty of instructional content. The adaptive approach represents a significant evolution in educational technology, shifting from static content delivery to dynamic, individualized pathways (Andhika et al., 2024). The promise of ALS lies in its potential to enhance learner engagement, motivation, and performance by accommodating individual needs and learning styles.

Despite these capabilities, the current body of literature reveals that the implementation and sustained use of ALS in higher education remains limited and uneven. Preliminary studies have shown that these systems can reduce cognitive overload, increase time-on-task, and decrease dropout rates compared to conventional LMS environments (Mukhamadiyeva & Hernández-Torrano, 2024). However, as Harati et al. (2021) emphasize, the success of ALS is contingent not solely upon their technical design, but upon their contextual integration into educational settings.

Crucially, user perceptions—specifically those of educators and students—have emerged as decisive factors in determining the effectiveness of ALS. Recognizing how these stakeholders experience, interpret, and interact with adaptive technologies is essential to guiding both their development and institutional deployment. As noted by Lindholst et al. (2024), users' daily experiences, motivations, and levels of resistance significantly influence the acceptance and pedagogical value of these tools (Gârdan et al., 2025). In this context, perceptions are not passive responses but strategic inputs that can inform critical areas such as system design, faculty training, and alignment between technological features and authentic teaching practices.

Also, viewing ALS through the lens of user experience provides actionable insights to enhance their adoption. Understanding whether students find adaptive feedback meaningful or whether faculty consider system suggestions pedagogically sound can make the difference between a successful integration and a misalignment that erodes trust and usability (Koh et al., 2022). This perspective positions user perception not as an outcome but as a driver of educational innovation.

ALS, when meaningfully implemented, offers a pathway toward more personalized, inclusive, and effective higher education. Yet their impact is not guaranteed by their algorithms alone. Their success depends on meaningful integration that honors the voices of those who use them. So, a comprehensive examination of empirical studies focused on these perceptions is needed to map current evidence, identify barriers and facilitators, and generate practical guidance for future deployment.

METHODOLOGY

The methodology employed in this chapter adheres to the PRISMA-ScR guidelines, which provide a structured framework for conducting scoping reviews of the literature. This approach was selected to map the existing body of research on the implementation of artificial intelligence (AI)-driven adaptive learning systems in the context of higher education, specifically in the training of future professionals.

Eligibility Criteria

To ensure the rigor and relevance of this scoping review, specific inclusion and exclusion criteria were established to select only studies that demonstrated academic quality and direct relevance to the research questions. These criteria helped delimit the scope and ensured that the analysis was grounded in credible and meaningful empirical evidence.

Table 1. Inclusion and exclusion measure

Measure	Inclusion	Exclusion
Publication Period	Articles published between 2020 and 2024.	Articles published before 2020.
Language	Publications written in English or Spanish.	Publications in other languages without a reliable or accessible translation.
Target Population	Studies involving higher education faculty and/or students as primary participants.	Studies focused exclusively on primary or secondary education, or other non-tertiary educational contexts.
Intervention or Phenomenon of Interest	Research analyzing the implementation, perception, experience, or acceptance of Adaptive Learning Systems (ALS) within Learning Management Systems (LMS) such as Moodle, Blackboard, Canvas, etc.	Research addressing general educational technologies or traditional LMS without adaptive components; studies solely focused on academic performance without explicit reference to faculty or student perceptions or experiences.
Type of Study	Empirical studies employing qualitative, quantitative, or mixed methods.	Opinion pieces, essays, editorials, or technical reports lacking empirical methodology or a structured systematic review approach.

Literature Search Strategy

To ascertain pertinent studies, a sophisticated search methodology was executed across three prominent databases: Web of Science (WOS), ProQuest Central, and Scopus. Boolean operators were employed to amalgamate principal terms pertinent to the deployment of adaptive learning systems within Learning Management Systems (LMS), in conjunction with terminology related to faculty and student perceptions. This search methodology was formulated to guarantee an exhaustive and focused exploration of the extant literature within the discipline.

The search methodology was organized around six conceptual categories that corresponded with the research inquiries. Boolean operators (OR, AND) were utilized to link synonymous terms within each category and to integrate disparate categories. The ensuing table encapsulates the principal variables and their associated search terminologies:

Table 2. Search terms by conceptual category

Variable	Search Terms
Adaptive Learning System	*"Adaptive learning system" OR "intelligent tutoring system" OR "Recommender system"*
Learning Management Platforms	*"Learning management system" OR LMS OR Moodle OR Blackboard OR Canvas OR "e-learning"*
Perception / Experience	*perception* OR attitude* OR experience* OR acceptance OR usability OR "user satisfaction" OR engagement
Population – Students	*student* OR undergraduate* OR "graduate student"*
Population – Faculty	*faculty OR teacher* OR professor* OR lecturer*
Educational Context	*"Higher education" OR university OR college OR "tertiary education"*

Study Selection Process

The study selection process was carried out in multiple phases following the PRISMA-ScR guidelines. Initially, a systematic search was conducted across three databases: Web of Science (WOS), Scopus, and ProQuest Central, resulting in the identification of 94 records. After an initial screening for duplicates, 8 entries were removed, yielding 86 unique studies for the initial screening phase.

Two independent reviewers then evaluated the titles and abstracts of the retrieved studies, applying the previously defined inclusion and exclusion criteria. Discrepancies between reviewers were resolved by consensus. During this stage, 36 studies were excluded for not meeting the eligibility criteria, and 50 full-text articles were selected for in-depth review. The next step was excluded.

Zotero software was used to manage references and facilitate the screening process, while a validated data extraction template was employed for organizing and coding the selected studies. No automation tools were used at any stage of the review.

During the full-text review phase, the same two reviewers independently assessed the remaining articles. Ultimately, 12 studies were included in the final synthesis, having fully met the eligibility criteria and provided relevant evidence concerning the perceptions and experiences of faculty and students with adaptive learning systems (ALS) integrated into LMS platforms in higher education settings.

The complete selection process is illustrated in a PRISMA 2020 flow diagram, which transparently outlines the phases of identification, screening, eligibility, and final inclusion.

Figure 1. PRISMA ScR model

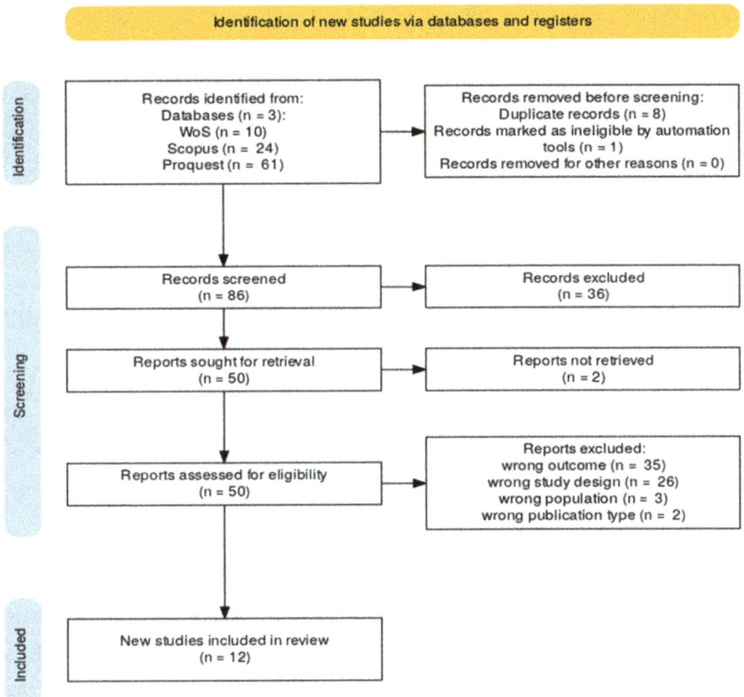

Risk of Bias and Data Integration Approach

Given that this scoping review focused on the qualitative analysis of perceptions, attitudes, and subjective experiences reported in empirical studies, no standardized formal tool for assessing risk of bias was applied. However, methodological quality was considered during the selection process, prioritizing studies with clearly defined research designs, appropriate sampling strategies, and transparent data collection procedures.

Studies lacking structured empirical methodology were excluded, which contributed to mitigating the risk of bias in interpreting the findings. For future systematic reviews, it is recommended to employ critical appraisal tools such as the MMAT or CASP to evaluate the quality of included studies.

Also, the nature of this scoping review did not involve conducting a meta-analysis or calculating quantitative effect measures (such as risk ratios or mean differences). However, some of the included studies reported relative frequencies or percentages regarding faculty and student perceptions. These data were used contextually to illustrate patterns or trends in the findings and were integrated as complementary qualitative evidence, without engaging in comparative statistical analysis.

The review identified and categorized key variables of interest based on the guiding research questions to map the perceptions of faculty and students regarding the implementation of ALS within LMS environments.

RESULTS

The results of this scoping review were organized into four thematic dimensions that informed both the coding and the analysis of the included studies:

1. Student Perceptions and Evaluations
2. Faculty Perceptions and Experiences
3. Organizational and Managerial Challenges

All results compatible with these categories were considered, regardless of measurement type, level of analysis, or timeframe, provided that the information was directly derived from the reported perceptions, experiences, or attitudes of the participants. This inclusive approach ensured that both qualitative and descriptive data could be integrated to reflect the lived experiences of users interacting with ALS within LMS environments.

A summary table is presented below to visualize the set of studies selected for full-text analysis and inclusion in this review, along with the thematic dimension(s) each study contributed to.

Table 3. Thematic dimensions by study

APA Reference	1. Student Perceptions and Evaluations	2. Faculty Perceptions and Experiences	3. Ethical Challenges	4. Organizational and Managerial Challenges
Al-Shaikhli, 2023	Yes	No	No	Yes
Al-Shanfari et al., 2023	No	Yes	No	Yes
Baba et al., 2024	Yes	Yes	Yes	Yes
Contrino et al., 2024	Yes	No	No	Yes
Lim et al., 2022	Yes	No	No	Yes
Majjate et al., 2025	Yes	No	Yes	Yes

continued on following page

Table 3. Continued

APA Reference	1. Student Perceptions and Evaluations	2. Faculty Perceptions and Experiences	3. Ethical Challenges	4. Organizational and Managerial Challenges
Moradi et al., 2023	Yes	No	No	Yes
Kovan Mzwri & Turcsányi-Szabo, 2025	Yes	No	Yes	Yes
Panjaburee et al., 2022a	Yes	No	No	Yes
Plaza et al., 2023	No	Yes	No	Yes
Rodríguez et al., 2021	Yes	No	Yes	Yes
Troussas Christos et al., 2021	Yes	Yes	No	No

To accurately elucidate the intricate study selection methodology employed in this scoping review, a PRISMA-SCR flow chart has been painstakingly constructed. This graphical representation encapsulates each phase of the systematic search process, encompassing the removal of duplicates, the assessment of eligibility criteria, and the conclusive selection of articles for subsequent analysis.

In alignment with the overarching objective and the formulated research inquiries, the following dimensions pertinent to the analysis of the literature search outcomes were delineated. The dimensions cover students' insights on ALS usage, educators' or scholars' views on ALS deployment within LMS, the challenges linked to ALS integration in LMS, and the aspects that enable ALS within LMS. The findings are subsequently articulated following the dimensions.

1. Student Perceptions and Assessments

The findings derived facilitate the discernment of a predominantly affirmative evaluation by higher education students concerning the implementation of ALS within the LMS frameworks. Nevertheless, concomitant with these advantageous evaluations, critical perspectives also arise that elucidate technical, pedagogical, and emotional obstacles that directly influence the educational experience, as well as the levels of motivation and academic engagement.

a. Positive Assessments

One of the elements most prominently acknowledged by the participants was the efficacy of these systems in enhancing educational outcomes. A substantial proportion of students indicated that ALS contributes to a deeper comprehension of the material and an enhancement in academic performance. In essence, it emerged that 84% (Baba et al., 2024) of individuals surveyed considered a platform powered by AI as either "moderately effective" or "highly effective" for enhancing their learning, and 88% believed their experience was "slightly better" or "much better" than that of conventional educational approaches (Baba et al., 2024).

The customization of the educational process was another salient characteristic. The students appreciated the system's capacity to accommodate their learning styles, particular needs, and individual paces, underscoring hybrid models that integrate sensory and cognitive preferences as especially effective (Troussas Christos et al., 2021). This adaptability was perceived as a potent strategy to facilitate access to and mastery of content (Al-Shanfari et al., 2023).

The usability of the platforms was also favorably evaluated. Most of the participants regarded the systems as "very user-friendly" or "somewhat user-friendly" (Kovan Mzwri & Turcsányi-Szabo, 2025), directly linking this perception to the educational utility of the virtual environment. This correlation between user-friendliness and perceived utility is crucial for the acceptance of innovative educational technologies (Lim et al., 2022).

Concerning feedback mechanisms, there was a high appraisal of automated systems that provide immediate, detailed, and pertinent comments. Forty-four percent of the students indicated that this feedback enabled them to distinctly recognize their strengths and weaknesses, while 35% reported receiving partial yet significant assistance (Kovan Mzwri & Turcsányi-Szabo, 2025; Majjate et al., 2025).

Finally, a positive perception was noted regarding the security and reliability of online assessments, particularly when the platforms incorporated authentication mechanisms. This sense of transparency and ethical oversight fostered trust among students, thereby enhancing their concentration and alleviating anxiety during evaluations.

b. Perceived Challenges and Negative Evaluations

Although numerous students recognized the prospective advantages of ALS, a considerable corpus of scholarly literature delineates a spectrum of challenges and negative assessments that adversely influenced their comprehensive learning experience. One of the most frequently articulated concerns pertained to the opacity surrounding the mechanisms by which ALS customized content, resulting in confusion and a perceived erosion of autonomy over the educational process. Students articulated ambiguity regarding the rationale underlying system-generated recommendations, adjustments in pacing, or the sequencing of content, which ultimately undermined their confidence in the platform.

Technical complications and platform instability further intensified these apprehensions. In environments characterized by inadequate digital infrastructure or prohibitively expensive internet access, students reported ongoing difficulties, including connectivity disruptions, protracted loading times, and system failures. These issues were consistently correlated with feelings of frustration, anxiety, and detachment from the educational milieu (Moradi et al., 2023). Usability constraints, including non-intuitive interfaces, ambiguous AI-generated feedback, and a deficiency of interactive components, were similarly identified as detrimental to the educational experience (Mirata et al., 2020).

A disjunction between adaptive logic and individual learning preferences constitutes another prevalent challenge. Certain students perceived themselves as constrained by the algorithmic determinations of the system, particularly when it inadequately acknowledged their prior knowledge or provided limited flexibility. This misalignment was frequently associated with a decline in motivation, particularly when students regarded the learning trajectory as excessively rigid or incongruent with their academic objectives.

Additionally, students expressed concerns about the reduced interpersonal engagement common in ALS environments. While the advantages of automation and personalization were widely recognized, the lack of significant instructor involvement, collaborative peer interaction, and dialogic educational opportunities was viewed as a major limitation. For students in more complex or theoretical fields, this lack of interaction hindered deep learning and the development of higher-order cognitive skills, such as critical analysis and problem-solving (Moradi et al., 2023).

Other challenges were related to digital preparedness and equity issues. Learners with limited prior experience in online education, especially those in the social sciences, reported facing greater difficulties adapting to Learning Management System (LMS) interfaces compared to their peers in technology-focused fields. This disparity underscored the need for customized onboarding methods and inclusive design principles.

Also, concerns were raised about assessment methods, particularly the emphasis on rote memorization rather than analytical reasoning in online adaptive evaluations, as well as the constraints placed on creativity and decision-making skills (Moradi et al., 2023). Additionally, students criticized content design for its lack of interactivity, variety in activities, and clear pedagogical feedback.

Ultimately, numerous studies highlighted ethical considerations, including risks related to data privacy and a perceived "excessive transparency" within the system

(Majjate et al., 2025). In some cases, this resulted in a sense of information overload and discomfort. Furthermore, elements of social visibility, such as comparisons of progress among peers, were viewed unfavorably, as they negatively affected self-esteem and detracted from the individual learning experience.

To conclude, these perceived limitations emphasize the critical importance of developing adaptive learning systems that are rooted in pedagogical principles, contextually aware, and responsive to the diverse needs, expectations, and experiences of the student population.

c. Influence on Motivation and Academic Commitment

The observation that ALS is efficacious and tailored to individual needs exerted a favorable influence on students' scholarly motivation (Baba et al., 2024). Those individuals who perceived themselves as comprehended by the system and discerned enhancements in their academic performance conveyed elevated levels of dedication and contentment. Indeed, 80% of participants reported a heightened dedication to their academic pursuits following the utilization of platforms integrated with artificial intelligence (Troussas Christos et al., 2021).

Immediate feedback, a feeling of assurance in evaluations, and the opportunity to monitor the collective activity of the group without engendering individual comparisons were also factors that bolstered self-regulation, self-efficacy, and the intention to persist in utilizing the system.

On the contrary, technical impediments, an absence of significant interaction, inadequacies in system architecture, and apprehensions regarding privacy led to a diminishment in motivation and commitment, thereby negatively impacting the continuity of the learning trajectory and overall satisfaction with the educational experience (Al-Shaikhli, 2023).

2. Perceptions and Encounters of Tertiary Education Instructors Concerning the Utilization of ALS in LMS

The incorporation of AI-driven ALS methodologies into LMS has elicited varied perspectives among academic faculty (Guerra et al., 2024). The academic discourse underscores both its transformative potential and the myriad challenges that its implementation entails.

a. Opportunities and Positive Perception of Postsecondary Education Instructors

Educators markedly acknowledge the efficacy of ITS in pedagogy (Al-Shanfari et al., 2023). They assert that these instruments contribute to enhanced comprehension and performance by learners, particularly in intricate disciplines such as programming.

They also underscore that ITS enables the extension of learning durations and facilitates individualized instruction, which is particularly advantageous in courses characterized by elevated attrition rates. In particular circumstances, such as what has been demonstrated in Oman, where educators articulate that their readiness to embrace these frameworks is contingent upon the presence of training institutions and sufficient technical assistance (Al-Shanfari et al., 2023; Guerra et al., 2024; Ortiz et al., 2025).

In general terms, educational professionals appreciate the potential of artificial intelligence to customize instruction and optimize pedagogical methodologies. They posit that its judicious application can augment the effectiveness of learning, streamline feedback mechanisms, and diminish administrative encumbrances, thereby enabling a more pronounced focus on strategic planning within the educational framework (Kovan Mzwri & Turcsányi-Szabo, 2025).

Also, instruments such as recommendation systems and chatbots facilitate the modification of content to the distinct requirements of students, fostering more inclusive learning experiences. Activities formulated in LMS environments that integrate adaptive learning systems are perceived as more appealing than conventional methods, permitting students to progress at their own pace (Guerra et al., 2024; Mirata et al., 2020).

Those educators who have employed adaptive functionalities on platforms such as Moodle concur that adaptive learning paradigms enhance the caliber of academic instruction and promote its practical execution within the classroom. In this regard, the integration of artificial intelligence within LMS is regarded as a pivotal resource for bolstering student engagement, personalizing educational trajectories, and improving overall academic achievement.

b. Educators' Challenges and Concerns

Notwithstanding the perceived advantages, instructors also caution against considerable impediments to the implementation of ALS in LMS.

i. Technical and Infrastructure Constraints

One of the principal apprehensions resides in the deficiency of trained personnel and specialized technical assistance for the development, application, and maintenance of these technologies. The intricacy of integration with extant platforms constitutes a significant hindrance, compounded by the limitations of connectivity and access to devices in underprivileged contexts, which exacerbate digital divides and undermine educational equity (Al-Shanfari et al., 2023; Mirata et al., 2020).

ii. Data Prerequisites and Usability

Adaptive systems necessitate substantial volumes of annotated content and high-caliber data, which entails a considerable investment in their development and upkeep. Furthermore, challenges related to the usability of interfaces and the imperative for ongoing evaluative processes are acknowledged (Panjaburee et al., 2022)

iii. Complex Content and Pedagogical Limitations

Administering intricate resources, such as diagrams or mathematical equations, can prove challenging on certain platforms. Ultimately, deficiencies are discerned in the oversight of the emotional dimension of learning, an element regarded as essential to a comprehensive educational experience (Baba et al., 2024; Moradi et al., 2023).

3. Organizational and Management Obstacles

At the organizational level, the findings demonstrated that successful execution of AI-based technologies also encounters impediments at the organizational level (Mirata et al., 2020). This process necessitates a considerable allocation of time, financial resources, and skilled personnel, which is not universally accessible across all institutions (Al-Shanfari et al., 2023; Mirata et al., 2020).

The participants additionally recognized a prevalent obstacle as the lack of a definitive institutional strategy that associates the adoption of these technologies with the university's educational and innovative objectives. In the absence of a collective vision and explicit institutional commitment, endeavors tend to become disjointed. Also, governance challenges are identified, such as inadequate project planning, vague delineation of roles and responsibilities, and difficulties in managing resistance to transformation among certain segments of the teaching staff (Lim et al., 2022; Sajja et al., 2024).

Ultimately, perceptions and levels of adoption of ALS fluctuate depending on the institutional context. Factors such as the socioeconomic status, the type of university (public or private), and the phase of technological implementation influence the disposition of the involved actors. For instance, research conducted in Oman indicates that educators in private institutions exhibited a greater receptiveness to the adoption of intelligent tutoring systems in comparison to their counterparts in public universities, emphasizing the impact of the institutional environment on the readiness for change.

In tandem with pedagogical considerations, significant ethical challenges arise. A significant concern pertains to the protection of the privacy and security of the personal data that these platforms consistently gather and process. The potential for the emergence of algorithmic biases also constitutes a risk, as it could precipitate automated decisions that perpetuate inequalities or discriminatory tendencies, particularly in contexts characterized by substantial social vulnerability (Baba et al., 2024; Guerra et al., 2024).

These elements underscore the pressing necessity to establish robust institutional ethical frameworks that direct the responsible utilization of artificial intelligence. Such frameworks should safeguard the rights of students and educators, guarantee system transparency, and foster the formulation of explicit policies regarding the utilization of these tools within educational settings. Moreover, the discourse continues regarding the authorship and originality of the academic work produced with the assistance of AI, which raises concerns about academic integrity and the equitable assessment of student performance(Guerra et al., 2024; Majjate et al., 2025; Mukhamadiyeva & Hernández-Torrano, 2024).

DISCUSSION

The examined literature illustrates that university scholars predominantly articulate favorable perceptions regarding ALS and ITS integrated within LMS platforms. These perceptions are mediated by variables that exert a direct influence on their motivation, dedication, and readiness to utilize these technologies to facilitate self-regulated and significant learning.

In this section, we shall provide a comprehensive account of the formulated research inquiries, thus initiating the discourse concerning what constitutes the most prevalent perceptions and evaluations of university scholars regarding the educational experience in LMS environments that incorporate adaptive learning systems, and how these perceptions impact their motivation and academic dedication. Also, we shall address the inquiry: How are the perceptions of educators and students interconnected with perceived outcomes in terms of academic performance, feedback received, and customization of learning? These inquiries will be our primary focus initially.

Among the most esteemed elements are the customization of content by individual requirements, immediate and tailored feedback, enhancement of academic performance, and the usability of the systems (Al-Shanfari et al., 2023; Baba et al.,

2024; Troussas Christos et al., 2021), which is corroborated (Andhika et al., 2024; Koh et al., 2022) through the individualization of the content's structure, aligned with the student's learning profile, which is pertinent to the students enabling them to progress at their tempo, plan and monitor their advancement, and engage in more flexible, interactive, and accessible learning, particularly in mobile formats. Additionally, the perception of trust and transparency in the platforms fortifies their inclination to actively engage in educational processes (Al-Shanfari et al., 2023).

Nevertheless, considerable apprehensions also surface that constrain their experience. These encompass technical and infrastructural challenges, deficiencies in digital competencies, subpar quality or pedagogical relevance of the content, absence of meaningful human interaction, and ethical dilemmas associated with data privacy, algorithmic biases, and digital equity (Kovan Mzwri & Turcsányi-Szabo, 2025). Such factors can engender anxiety, distrust, demotivation, and a sense of isolation that diminishes sustained commitment to the platform (Panjaburee et al., 2022).

To contextualize these disparities, Table 4 encapsulates the primary contrasting attributes between traditional LMS and adaptive LMS, as substantiated by the reviewed literature.

Table 4. Traditional LMS v/s adaptive LMS

Feature	Traditional LMS	Adaptive LMS
Content Delivery	One-size-fits-all approach	Personalized based on learning styles and preferences (Arsovic & Stefanovic, 2020; El-Sabagh, 2021; Sayed et al., 2023).
Feedback	Limited, often delayed	Immediate and tailored to individual learner needs (Papamitsiou et al., 2020; Sayed et al., 2023)
Engagement Strategies	Lacks interactive elements	Incorporates adaptive and gamified components (Hellín et al., 2023; Zourmpakis et al., 2023).
Learning Analytics	Basic progress tracking	Advanced analytics using multimodal data (Essa et al., 2023; Papamitsiou et al., 2020).
Motivation	Relies on intrinsic motivation	Enhances motivation through personalized and engaging experiences (Apoki et al., 2022; Zourmpakis et al., 2023)

The role of adaptive learning platforms influencing student motivation is intricate. While customization, prompt feedback, and autonomy enhance engagement (du Plooy et al., 2024; Ling & Chiang, 2022), technical, ethical, and pedagogical obstacles also arise that adversely impact the experience. Deficiencies in digital competencies, inadequate human interaction, and apprehensions regarding privacy can diminish motivation and sustained utilization (Al-Shaikhli, 2023). Consequently, its efficacy is contingent upon the institutional capability to furnish meaningful experiences, uphold the ethics surrounding the utilization of AI, and mitigate existing digital disparities (Panjaburee et al., 2022).

Conversely, the gathered evidence suggests that university educators regard ALS and Intelligent Tutoring Systems as instruments with substantial pedagogical potential, particularly due to their capacity to tailor instruction, automate responsibilities, and facilitate self-regulated learning. The article by Aroca (2024) highlights that over 10% improvement was observed in advancing students to higher grades, a finding corroborated by the research conducted by Sari et al. (2024), which indicates that the mean score before the assessment was 68.4, whereas the mean score post-evaluation rose to 82.7. Additional literature also substantiates the claims, which were previously presented in the results section. However, this affirmative appraisal coexists with considerable technical, pedagogical, and ethical issues, alongside an explicit demand for structured institutional support to facilitate its effective and continuous adoption.

In summary, it is articulated that ALS has indeed been esteemed by both educators and learners. Educators indicate that the customization of learning is valued, emphasizing that the personalization of instruction allows for the acquisition of individualized feedback and the provision of autonomous learning opportunities (Katonane Gyonyoru & Katona, 2024; Mukhamadiyeva & Hernández-Torrano, 2024). Also, based on the review conducted, it can be asserted that the educators utilizing ALS benefit from the ability to concentrate on the instructional process of learning, thereby alleviating academic burdens.

Based on the inquiry presented regarding the pertinent question, what specific barriers and facilitators can be identified that influence both students and teachers about the effective adoption of adaptive learning systems within the contexts of higher education environments? It is worth noting that when it comes to the multifaceted challenges associated with the implementation of such adaptive learning systems, particularly the ALS, educators encounter a plethora of significant obstacles. In the realm of challenges, a multitude of technical and infrastructural obstacles surface, encompassing yet not restricted to, the deficiencies in smooth incorporation with existing LMS, the constraints presented by usability considerations, the economic factors associated with the execution phase, and the lack of adequate technical strength that can be noted in specific educational environments.

From a pedagogical standpoint, there exists a palpable concern regarding the potential for these adaptive learning systems to inadvertently foster a form of superficial learning, which could severely constrain the cultivation of critical thinking skills and prove to be ill-suited for addressing intricate content or specific disciplinary contexts that require a nuanced approach. Also, the necessity to undertake a comprehensive redesign of educational materials and curricular frameworks to align with the principles of adaptive logic introduces an additional layer of workload that is not always adequately managed or supported by educational institutions (Baba et al., 2024; Panjaburee et al., 2022).

A particularly salient barrier that has been identified within this discourse is the pronounced lack of digital competencies and specialized training among educators, which consequently engenders feelings of insecurity, an inherent resistance to change, and an apprehension regarding a perceived loss of control over the training processes that they are responsible for facilitating (Al-Shanfari et al., 2023; Mirata et al., 2020). Furthermore, there are substantial concerns articulated about the potential diminishment of the teaching role itself and the concomitant reduction in meaningful human interaction, which could ultimately serve to impoverish the essential pedagogical connection that is vital for effective teaching and learning (Panjaburee et al., 2022).

Finally, how are the conceptualizations of educators and learners associated with perceived outcomes in terms of scholarly performance, feedback received, and customization of learning? With regard to affirmative evaluations and pedagogical efficacy, educators predominantly appreciate the customization of learning, indicating that ALS/ITS facilitate the modification of instructional content and paces to the individual attributes of each learner, fostering autonomous advancement and profound comprehension. They also acknowledge significant enhancements in learner scholarly performance, reporting superior knowledge retention and elevated levels of achievement in comparison to traditional methodologies (González et al., 2022; Panjaburee et al., 2022).

Another pivotal aspect is automated feedback, which is regarded as timely, precise, and beneficial for bolstering learner self-efficacy. At the operational stage, ALS is perceived as a remedy that can optimize educator administration, automating fundamental assessments, diminishing repetitive inquiries, and permitting improved management of extensive cohorts (Waldeck, 2007). Also, educators recognize the merit of these systems to encourage self-regulated learning and to furnish multimodal and interactive resources that enrich the educational experience (Cianciolo & Regehr, 2023).

Ethical apprehensions are recurrent: they underscore the anxiety of infringing upon the confidentiality of learner data, the potential algorithmic partiality in personalization and evaluation, and the misuse of AI by learners, such as plagiarism or delegation of responsibilities. Confidence in the outcomes produced by AI is not absolute, particularly when scrutinizing the precision and validity of its automated pedagogical choices.

Regarding perceptions nearby institutional endorsement, it is noted that the conditions which educators deem essential for a successful integration of ALS/ITS include active institutional engagement. The necessity for affirmative leadership, technical and financial resources, and continuous technical-pedagogical support is accentuated. It also underscores the urgency of formulating clear policies and ethical guidelines that govern the responsible utilization of AI in educational contexts.

FUTURE RESEARCH DIRECTIONS

Future inquiries should prioritize the advancement and assessment of equitable adaptive learning systems that explicitly confront digital disparity. An adequate and equitable technological infrastructure is imperative to guarantee that all learners, irrespective of socioeconomic status, can wholly engage in adaptive learning environments. The deficiency of digital equity constitutes a substantial threat, potentially intensifying existing educational inequities and undermining the inclusive potential of adaptive learning technologies.

Also, subsequent investigations should endeavor to expand the linguistic and cultural breadth of the current evidence corpus. This review was constrained to studies published in English and Spanish, which may have omitted valuable insights from regions where other languages are predominant. Broadening the spectrum of languages and cultural contexts examined would augment the global applicability of findings and facilitate more context-sensitive implementations.

Another pivotal domain for future inquiry is the methodological standardization of research concerning adaptive learning systems. The existing corpus of literature exhibits considerable heterogeneity in study designs, ranging from qualitative case analyses to extensive quantitative surveys, rendering it challenging to undertake meta-analytic syntheses. Future studies could contribute by employing comparable instruments, longitudinal frameworks, and robust evaluative structures to enable cross-study comparisons and enhance generalizability.

Finally, approaching research should investigate triangulated data sources that extend beyond self-reported perceptions. While comprehending user experiences remains crucial, amalgamating subjective feedback with behavioral data, system logs, learning analytics, and performance outcomes can provide a more holistic perspective on how adaptive learning systems influence learning. This would assist in alleviating biases related to self-disclosure, social desirability, or institutional expectations, and fortify the evidence base for pedagogical decision-making.

CONCLUSION

University educators acknowledge the potential of ALS and ITS as formidable pedagogical instruments, with the capacity to significantly enhance teaching methodologies, tailor educational experiences, and facilitate improved learning outcomes.

However, the deployment of these technologies encounters considerable impediments related to infrastructural capabilities, pedagogical efficacy, educator training, interpersonal engagement, and the ethical quandaries inherent in the application of artificial intelligence. The acceptance, efficacy, and sustainability of these technological advancements are substantially contingent upon robust institutional backing, ongoing professional development for educators, and the formulation of ethical, transparent, and actionable policies that ensure equitable, pertinent, and humane educational applications.

However, these positive evaluations coexist with considerable challenges that hinder their effective integration. These challenges encompass technical difficulties concerning digital infrastructure and system usability; pedagogical issues such as inadequate meaningful human interaction or superficial development of critical analytical skills; and ethical apprehensions regarding data privacy, algorithmic biases, and digital equity.

The outcomes of this review align with the findings presented by du Plooy et al. (2024), who assert that 59% of the analyzed studies indicate enhancements in academic performance through Peer-Assisted Learning (PAL), while 36% report an increase in student engagement. However, they also caution that 41% of studies reveal no measurable impact on performance, and 64% fail to document improvements in engagement, thereby underscoring the necessity to regard motivation and institutional support as critical determinants that influence the effectiveness of these systems, as elucidated in our review.

In the context of educators, the propensity to employ ALS is influenced by institutional variables, including the availability of technical and pedagogical support, institutional leadership, and the presence of clear policies governing the responsible utilization of artificial intelligence. The results imply that technological acceptance is influenced by more than just system functionalities; it is also molded by the organizational environment and the educational practices in place where they are used.

Also, student perspectives indicate that while ALS possesses the potential to enhance motivation and self-regulation, its efficacy is considerably compromised when issues such as digital divides, foundational technological competencies, and the emotional and cognitive requirements of users remain unaddressed.

Consequently, the meaningful incorporation of ALS within higher education necessitates not only the establishment of technological infrastructure but also a comprehensive transformation of institutional frameworks, curricula, and training paradigms. The effectiveness of these systems is predicated upon their capacity to be humanized, contextualized, and aligned with the educational objectives of institutions, transcending the mere implementation of adaptive algorithms.

As a result, it is concluded that adaptive learning systems present substantial opportunities to advance towards a more personalized, equitable, and effective educational paradigm, provided their implementation is accompanied by initiatives aimed at teacher training, institutional fortification, ethical governance, and collaborative development with users. This review thus furnishes an empirical foundation for informing policies, practices, and future inquiries that advocate for a transformative and critical engagement with artificial intelligence in university learning environments.

ACKNOWLEDGMENT

This research received no specific grant from any funding agency in the public, commercial, or not-for-profit sectors. However, the authors acknowledge the institutional support provided by the University of Alicante, which granted access to its academic databases through its library system, and by the Universidad Santo Tomás, which supported the development of this study by facilitating bibliographic and research resources.

REFERENCES

Al-Shaikhli, D. (2023). The effect of the tracking technology on students' perceptions of their continuing intention to use a learning management system. *Education and Information Technologies, 28*(1), 343–371. ProQuest Central; Social Science Premium Collection. DOI: 10.1007/s10639-022-11156-8

Al-Shanfari, L., Abdullah, S., Fstnassi, T., & Al-Kharusi, S. (2023). Instructors' Perceptions of Intelligent Tutoring Systems and Their Implications for Studying Computer Programming in Omani Higher Education Institutions. *International Journal of Membrane Science and Technology, 10*(2), 947–967. *Scopus*. Advance online publication. DOI: 10.15379/ijmst.v10i2.1395

Andhika, A., Aldila, A. S., Supriyono, L. A., Previana, C. N., & Habibie, D. R. (2024). The Effectiveness of Adaptive Learning Systems Integrated with LMS in Higher Education. *Jurnal KomtekInfo*, 49–56. DOI: 10.35134/komtekinfo.v11i2.505

Apoki, U. C., Ali Hussein, A. M., Humam K Majeed Al-Chalabi, Costin Badica, & Mocanu, M. L. (2022). The Role of Pedagogical Agents in Personalised Adaptive Learning: A Review. *Sustainability, 14*(11), 6442. ProQuest Central. DOI: 10.3390/su14116442

Arsovic, B., & Stefanovic, N. (2020). E-learning based on the adaptive learning model: Case study in Serbia. *Sadhana, 45*(1), 266. DOI: 10.1007/s12046-020-01499-8

Baba, K., El Faddouli, N.-E., & Cheimanoff, N. (2024). Mobile-Optimized AI-Driven Personalized Learning: A Case Study at Mohammed VI Polytechnic University. *International Journal of Interactive Mobile Technologies, 18*(4), 81–96. *Scopus*. Advance online publication. DOI: 10.3991/ijim.v18i04.46547

Cianciolo, A. T., & Regehr, G. (2023). The Case for Feedback-in-Practice as a Topic of Educational Scholarship. *Academic Medicine : Journal of the Association of American Medical Colleges, 98*(3), 317–321. DOI: 10.1097/ACM.0000000000005013 PMID: 36222528

Du Plooy, E., Casteleijn, D., & Franzsen, D. (2024). Personalized adaptive learning in higher education: A scoping review of key characteristics and impact on academic performance and engagement. *Heliyon, 10*(21), e39630. DOI: 10.1016/j.heliyon.2024.e39630 PMID: 39524879

El-Sabagh, H. A. (2021). Adaptive e-learning environment based on learning styles and its impact on the development of students' engagement: Revista de Universidad y Sociedad del Conocimiento. *International Journal of Educational Technology in Higher Education, 18*(1). ProQuest Central; Social Science Premium Collection. DOI: 10.1186/s41239-021-00289-4

Essa, S. G., Celik, T., & Human-Hendricks, N. E. (2023). Personalized Adaptive Learning Technologies Based on Machine Learning Techniques to Identify Learning Styles: A Systematic Literature Review. *IEEE Access : Practical Innovations, Open Solutions, 11*, 48392–48409. DOI: 10.1109/ACCESS.2023.3276439

Gârdan, I. P., Manu, M. B., Gârdan, D. A., Negoi ă, L. D. L., Pa tiu, C. A., Ghi ă, E., & Zaharia, A. (2025). Adopting AI in education: Optimizing human resource management considering teacher perceptions. *Frontiers in Education, 10*, 1488147. DOI: 10.3389/feduc.2025.1488147

González, L. A., Neyem, A., Contreras-McKay, I., & Molina, D. (2022). Improving learning experiences in software engineering capstone courses using artificial intelligence virtual assistants. *Computer Applications in Engineering Education, 30*(5), 1370–1389. *Scopus.* Advance online publication. DOI: 10.1002/cae.22526

Guerra, V. E. B., O'Brien, M. I. Z., Bajaña, V. P. M., Villacrés, E. B. R., Pacheco, M. de J. N., Rodríguez, N. E. C., & Zúñiga, W. W. B. (2024). Percepciones y experiencias de docentes universitarios sobre la inteligencia artificial: Transformación, ética y desafíos en el uso académico por estudiantes. *LATAM Revista Latinoamericana de Ciencias Sociales y Humanidades, 5*(6), Article 6. DOI: 10.56712/latam.v5i6.3204

Harati, S., Perez, L., Molowny-Horas, R., & Pontius, R. G.Jr. (2021). Validating models of one-way land change: An example case of forest insect disturbance. *Landscape Ecology, 36*(10), 2919–2935. DOI: 10.1007/s10980-021-01272-0

Hellín, C. J., Calles-Esteban, F., Valledor, A., Gómez, J., Otón-Tortosa, S., & Tayebi, A. (2023). Enhancing Student Motivation and Engagement through a Gamified Learning Environment. *Sustainability (Basel), 15*(19), 19. Advance online publication. DOI: 10.3390/su151914119

Katonane Gyonyoru, K. I., & Katona, J. (2024). Student Perceptions of AI-Enhanced Adaptive Learning Systems: A Pilot Survey. *2024 IEEE 7th International Conference and Workshop Óbuda on Electrical and Power Engineering (CANDO-EPE)*, 93–98. DOI: 10.1109/CANDO-EPE65072.2024.10772884

Koh, J., Cowling, M., Jha, M., & Sim, K. N. (2022). Collaborating with AI for better student-teacher reconnection. *ASCILITE Publications*, e22126–e22126. DOI: 10.14742/apubs.2022.126

Kovan Mzwri, & Turcsányi-Szabo, M. (2025). The Impact of Prompt Engineering and a Generative AI-Driven Tool on Autonomous Learning: A Case Study. *Education Sciences, 15*(2), 199. ProQuest Central; Social Science Premium Collection. DOI: 10.3390/educsci15020199

Lim, L., Lim, S. H., & Lim, R. W. Y. (2022). Measuring Learner Satisfaction of an Adaptive Learning System. *Behavioral Sciences (Basel, Switzerland), 12*(8), 264. Advance online publication. DOI: 10.3390/bs12080264 PMID: 36004835

Lindholst, A. C., Eriksen, T. B., & Knudsen, S. V. (2024). Danish school pupils' perception of their learning outcomes from participating in computer-based adaptive tests: A pressure for just clicking something? *Scandinavian Journal of Educational Research, 68*(6), 1186–1202. DOI: 10.1080/00313831.2023.2228823

Ling, H.-C., & Chiang, H.-S. (2022). Learning Performance in Adaptive Learning Systems: A Case Study of Web Programming Learning Recommendations. *Frontiers in Psychology, 13*, 770637. Advance online publication. DOI: 10.3389/fpsyg.2022.770637 PMID: 35153951

Majjate, H., Bellarhmouch, Y., Jeghal, A., Yahyaouy, A., Tairi, H., & Zidani, K. A. (2025). Assessing the impact of ethical aspects of recommendation systems on student trust and engagement in E-learning platforms: A multifaceted investigation. *Education and Information Technologies, 30*(3), 3953–3977. DOI: 10.1007/s10639-024-12979-3

Mirata, V., Hirt, F., Bergamin, P., & Van Der Westhuizen, C. (2020). Challenges and contexts in establishing adaptive learning in higher education: Findings from a Delphi study. *International Journal of Educational Technology in Higher Education, 17*(1), 32. DOI: 10.1186/s41239-020-00209-y

Mukhamadiyeva, S., & Hernández-Torrano, D. (2024). Adaptive Learning to Maximize Gifted Education: Teacher Perceptions, Practices, and Experiences. *Journal of Advanced Academics*, *35*(4), 652–670. DOI: 10.1177/1932202X241253166

Ortiz, É. R. C., & Cruz, D. del P. P., Ortiz, D. M. C., Sánchez, M. F. P., & Sánchez, L. F. C. (2025). Integración de la Inteligencia Artificial en la Educación: Desafíos y Oportunidades para el Aprendizaje Personalizado. *Polo del Conocimiento*, *10*(2), 2. Advance online publication. DOI: 10.23857/pc.v10i2.8879

Panjaburee, P., Komalawardhana, N., & Ingkavara, T. (2022). Acceptance of personalized e-learning systems: A case study of concept-effect relationship approach on science, technology, and mathematics courses. *Journal of Computers in Education, 9*(4), 681–705. ProQuest Central; Social Science Premium Collection. DOI: 10.1007/s40692-021-00216-6

Papamitsiou, Z., Pappas, I. O., Sharma, K., & Giannakos, M. N. (2020). Utilizing Multimodal Data Through fsQCA to Explain Engagement in Adaptive Learning. *IEEE Transactions on Learning Technologies*, *13*(4), 689–703. DOI: 10.1109/TLT.2020.3020499

Sajja, R., Sermet, Y., Cikmaz, M., Cwiertny, D., & Demir, I. (2024). Artificial Intelligence-Enabled Intelligent Assistant for Personalized and Adaptive Learning in Higher Education. *Information (Basel)*, *15*(10), 596. DOI: 10.3390/info15100596

Sayed, W. S., Noeman, A. M., Abdellatif, A., Abdelrazek, M., Badawy, M. G., Hamed, A., & El-Tantawy, S. (2023). AI-based adaptive personalized content presentation and exercises navigation for an effective and engaging E-learning platform. *Multimedia Tools and Applications, 82*(3), 3303–3333. ProQuest Central. DOI: 10.1007/s11042-022-13076-8

Troussas Christos, Chrysafiadi Konstantina, & Virvou, M. (2021). Personalized tutoring through a stereotype student model incorporating a hybrid learning style instrument. *Education and Information Technologies, 26*(2), 2295–2307. ProQuest Central; Social Science Premium Collection. DOI: 10.1007/s10639-020-10366-2

Waldeck, J. H. (2007). Answering the Question: Student Perceptions of Personalized Education and the Construct's Relationship to Learning Outcomes. *Communication Education*, *56*(4), 409–432. DOI: 10.1080/03634520701400090

Zourmpakis, A.-I., Kalogiannakis, M., & Papadakis, S. (2023). Adaptive Gamification in Science Education: An Analysis of the Impact of Implementation and Adapted Game Elements on Students' Motivation. *Computers*, *12*(7), 7. Advance online publication. DOI: 10.3390/computers12070143

Chapter 6
Telegram as a Complementary Channel for Tutoring:
Teaching Experience in Urbanism and Marketing

Francisco José Chamizo-Nieto
http://orcid.org/0000-0002-7752-1248
University of Seville, Spain

Claudia Prieto-Latorre
http://orcid.org/0000-0002-6510-3057
University of Malaga, Spain

ABSTRACT

This research presents a pilot experience of using Telegram to facilitate communication between students and teachers as a complement to conventional tutoring. This messaging application took place during the 2021-2022 academic year in two subjects at the University of Malaga: Urbanism II and Statistics I. Both belong respectively to the Degree in Foundations of Architecture and the Degree in Marketing and Market Research. To evaluate the experience, a quantitative and qualitative methodology was used through the analysis of surveys and a critical reflection on the implementation. The results show a higher participation in Urbanism II (48%) compared to Statistics I (23%). However, in both cases, the attitude of the learners was passive, reading the publications, which were mostly text messages and images. Despite this, 71.4% of participants consider that its use has had a positive impact on their academic performance, so it shows support for tutoring in university teaching.

DOI: 10.4018/979-8-2600-1568-1.ch006

INTRODUCTION

Using a mobile phone is a daily habit within the digitalized context in which Generation Z—known as Gen Z—has grown up. The use of social network applications has allowed them to access content in real time. This fact makes them especially appreciate the immediacy in how they interact with each other and relate to the whole world. The use of social media within the university education system is now widely accepted despite initial resistance with the emergence of smartphones in the early 2010s (e.g., Barrot, 2021). Therefore, the implementation of social media applications in class has facilitated student-teacher communication (e.g., Matos Lopes, 2017). One of the benefits of messaging applications is the promotion of tutoring as a complement to traditional communication channels, such as email and virtual learning platform forums (i.e., e-learning). Both are characterized as being less fluid and in a very formal language that does not invite intervention by the students, so that multimedia content applications become a more supportive way of tutoring by sharing text messages, images, and links to current news or even videos.

This research studies the implementation of the Telegram channel to support tutoring within the university context. To this end, a pilot performance was conducted in the subjects Urbanism II and Statistics I at the University of Malaga during the 2021-2022 academic year. Both subjects are integrated into the Degrees of Foundation of Architecture and Marketing and Market Research, respectively. The Telegram messaging application was chosen over others based on an analysis of its design, functionalities, and associated tasks. Compared to other applications, such as WhatsApp or Line, Telegram has the following advantages. First, it facilitates the creation of private channels, where users can only become members of the group with an invitation link or scanning a QR code facilitated by the teachers involved. Second, in terms of privacy and security, Telegram has end-to-end encryption of messages, leaving no trace on the servers. It also allows a thorough and very specific privacy adjustment of members' information with their own contacts and users without information. Third, it has high accessibility, since it can be installed on various operating systems, and it is compatible with any device with an internet connection via Telegram Web. Fourth, a capacity of up to 200,000 contacts can be accommodated within the same channel, which is another advantage it possesses.

Considering the digital competences of Gen Z, the use of Telegram for tutoring channels allows collaborative and peer-learning. In both subjects in which the program was implemented, the teachers involved created a Telegram channel with the aim of raising questions and sharing content related to the subject, such as articles, blog posts, or current news. The students who subscribed to the Telegram channel of each subject assumed the role of administrator, which only enabled students to publish messages. Once a member of the channel, the first post published by the teacher shows not only welcoming and description but also presents the rules of use: appropriate use of language, not publishing off-topic content, online schedule for the teaching team to publish content related to the subject, answer messages, and encourage students to participate, among others.

From the methodological point of view, a quantitative and qualitative method is used to evaluate the experience of the Telegram channel used by students. To do so, the same survey was conducted among members of each channel created for the two subjects concerned. The survey mainly includes questions with a single answer option, but it is also allowed to answer some items in an open way to justify the chosen answer option. This last qualitative answer deepens the user's experience in a more personal way. Thus, this survey allows the collection of information, which is qualitative and quantitative, and different statistical analyses were conducted. Moreover, the teaching team also conducted an evaluation of the pilot experiences to identify the modifications and improvements to be considered for future implementations of the intervention program. This method was carried out to verify if the implementation of a Telegram channel to support tutoring at the university positively contributes to the process of knowledge and has a beneficial effect on the academic success of the students involved. Thus, the overall objective of this research is to analyze whether the Telegram application facilitates student-teacher communication to support tutoring in the university context. This research contributes to the literature on Telegram use in higher education by creating a communication channel, as an alternative to traditional tutoring, implemented in subjects of different disciplines. It also evaluates student perception after the implementation of the program to identify aspects that need improvement in future interventions.

BACKGROUND

The Mobile Learning Ecosystem

The integration of mobile phones into formal education is based on the use of mobile data services, such as Wi-Fi networks, messaging, or GPS location data, mobile tools embedded into the device—known as hardware (e.g., camera)—, and applications downloaded from the Internet (e.g., games, books, or social media applications) (Grant, 2019). Mobile phones mediate the interaction between the learning community, creating a dynamic and interconnected system. Ng et al. (2010) stated that mobile learning is not limited by space or time, while Vavoula and Sharples

(2002) explained that thanks to this tool, learning can take place anywhere, at any time, and in different areas of life.

The Framework for the Rational Analysis of Mobile Education (FRAME) model developed by Koole (2009) is one of the first comprehensive models to analyze mobile learning. According to this conceptual model, mobile learning is the result of the intersection of three elements: the mobile device, the learner, and social interaction. Regarding the mobile device, the characteristics of the device, such as its physical characteristics (e.g., size and weight), input capabilities, and processor speed, can affect the user experience. In relation to the learner, aspects that significantly affect the structure, retention, and exchange of information are cognitive skills, memory, previous knowledge, emotions, and motivations. Lastly, the social aspect considers the process of social interaction and cooperation, highlighting that following rules and paying attention to each other during conversations are key aspects for communicating. The convergence of all three leads to mobile education.

The systematic review by Kyslova et al. (2025) examines the evolution of mobile learning from 2014 to 2023. This meta-analysis of 97 articles shows a significant positive effect of mobile learning on student outcomes at different educational levels and subject areas. Specifically, it has more effect in languages and biology, while a moderate effect is found in mathematics, physics, and chemistry. In addition, the pedagogical approach conditions the effectiveness of mobile learning. According to the results, the most effective method is project-based learning, followed by collaborative learning. The review also emphasizes that despite increased use of mobile learning, barriers remain, including technological challenges, pedagogical hurdles, and accessibility issues, as well as institutional and policy-related obstacles.

The Use of Social Media in Higher Education

The use of social media in education has become relatively common (Barrot, 2021). Such tools are used to support a blended learning methodology, and according to their utility, they have different applications in the teaching-learning process. According to Manca (2020), students mostly use Instagram, Pinterest, Snapchat, and WhatsApp for development and conversations concerning peer learning and assessment. In particular, the use of WhatsApp for learning—formally or informally—comes from the creation of groups, which may include or not the teacher (Jordan, 2023). Regarding Instagram, the project of Hernández-Falagán (2020) used it as a visual repository of ideas. Regarding Facebook, Matos Lopes (2017) highlight the versatility of this application, which is used by teachers and students for sharing synchronous and asynchronous information and discussing course content across different disciplines. In the field of architecture, Nicolau-Corbacho et al. (2019)

emphasize the significance of Facebook as a mentoring tool that supports students throughout their creative process.

The related literature has shown that such platforms could form an effective tool to support learning and exhibit some benefits compared to traditional communication channels used in education. For instance, Lee (2020) found that students are significantly more likely to read information and material posted on Facebook than on official university campus platforms. She also found that students with lower physical participation in classes are characterized by higher participation in online discussions, which ultimately has a positive effect on their academic performance. Besides this, social media have a positive impact on students' satisfaction in higher education (Rahman et al., 2020). This effect is mediated by the perceived utility of social media in the learning process.

Al-Bahrani et al. (2015) found that platforms such as Twitter, Instagram, YouTube, and Facebook increase communication between students by allowing a more spontaneous connection, compared to traditional email. Specifically, Kassens (2014) highlights the development of transversal skills such as writing and reflection using Twitter, given that the briefness required by tweeting forces students to express their thoughts concisely, which enhances their reflection and writing skills. The use of Twitter in teaching also exhibits the development of critical thinking and creativity (Nogués-Pedregal & Carmona-Zubiri, 2024).

Judging from the above, online social media applications appear to facilitate sharing knowledge with peers and are characterized by greater participation and engagement, as well as developing a more active role in the teaching process. It has also been documented as having a positive effect on grades and students' satisfaction.

The Case of Telegram

Regarding the use of Telegram in education, there is a scarce number of studies that explore its application. Of note is the research by Iqbal et al. (2020), in which Telegram was used during the SARS-CoV-2 pandemic (COVID-19) as a complementary online tool in the educational process of medical students. Most of the students who participated in this study stated that this application had multiple utilities: easy access to educational resources and the ability to add unlimited members, as well as exchanging and accessing files in all formats and sizes. In addition, the application helped students engage in collaborative learning, maintain their well-being, and ensure their safety. However, they also stated that it had some drawbacks, such as its complex interface, which at times led to information overload and a tendency to distract.

Yinka and Queendarline (2018) investigated students' usage of Telegram and their perception in the Faculty of Education at the University of Port Harcourt (Rivers

State, Nigeria). Their results show that Telegram can provide desirable aspects as a platform for learning through functions such as group chat, options for sharing files in different formats (i.e., messages, images, videos, and documents), and, at the time, elevated privacy. Students also value that they can log on to multiple devices at the same time. In general, students were satisfied with the use of this tool in university courses. Nevertheless, there is no significant relationship between the usage level of Telegram and students' perception.

The study by Md Yusof and Abdullah (2025) shows evidence of the effectiveness of Telegram in enhancing argumentative writing skills among distance learning students in Malaysian higher education. They employ a quasi-experimental design comprising a treatment group—consisting of students using Telegram—and a control group—the complement—, also assessing the characteristics of both groups in terms of academic performance before and after the application of the program. Their results show that students using Telegram are characterized by significantly improved academic performance, and their writing process was more engaging and interactive.

Conde et al. (2021) analyzed the use of WhatsApp and Telegram by Computer Engineering students when engaging in group work. They revealed that the most interactive groups used WhatsApp and Telegram to a greater extent, whereas groups with a lower level of interaction used Skype, Facebook, and Discord. The overall tendency as they show is a noticeable increase in communication between students via WhatsApp and Telegram regardless of the level of interaction.

Lastly, the experience of post-graduate students with the use of Telegram was also perceived as positive (Iksan & Saufian, 2017). Students highlighted that the multimedia and visual content of the lecturer's interventions enriches the learning process. They also emphasized that unlike in face-to-face classes, they felt freer to express their ideas and experienced less pressure because of the relaxed, flexible, and accessible environment, which they could access from anywhere. They also found it easy to catch up by reviewing previous conversations. Overall, Telegram encouraged active student participation, creativity, and engagement. According to the previous research mentioned above, it shows how Telegram has potential as an educational tool. These teaching experiences are the basis for the present study, with the aim of supporting virtual tutoring, which is more popular for Gen Z than email or forum.

METHODOLOGY

The Case of Telegram in Urbanism and Market Research

The program was implemented during the second term of the 2021-2022 academic year in the subjects Urbanism II and Statistics I, corresponding to the second and first year of studies, respectively. These subjects belong, respectively, to the Degrees in Fundamentals of Architecture and the Degree in Marketing and Market Research, both at the University of Malaga.

During the class sessions, the teachers created a Telegram channel for students who voluntarily subscribed via a QR code or invitation link. The Telegram channel was presented as an additional means of communication for students to use alongside tutorials, email, and the Virtual Campus platform. Students could use it to ask and resolve any questions that arise during the course, as well as share content related to the subject (i.e., research articles, blog posts, or current news). By using the Telegram channel, students engage actively in the construction of their knowledge through collaborative learning and mutual support. Once the students had subscribed, a welcome message and channel description were posted first. A set of rules regulates aspects such as appropriate language use, the type of content to be posted on the channel, useful timetables, and the role of the teaching team. Students who subscribe to the channel assume the role of administrator and have the option to post messages. Regarding this aspect, the teachers' role was to moderate the channel, encouraging participation, reminding users of the rules if necessary, and answering questions that have not been resolved.

A Telegram channel was implemented in the following subjects separately: Urbanism II and Statistics I. Both subjects are theoretical and practical in nature. Notably, a total of 25 students were enrolled in Urbanism II and 85 in Statistics I, but only 48% and 22.4% of the students subscribed to the Telegram channel in each subject, respectively.

Evaluation of the Program Implementation

A survey was conducted to assess the implementation of the Telegram application. Survey data were collected at the end of the course (June 2022). Students completed the questionnaire anonymously in a physical format during class. Through this survey, we gathered information on how the platform is used, how often it is used, and how long it is used. To analyze the impact on communication, we assessed the perceived fluency of teacher-student communication and the perceived benefit of channel support measured in terms of students' satisfaction and the expected effect on grades. It was also considered cases in which, for various reasons, students had not used the tool. To determine the reasons for a passive role, the survey is composed of closed and open questions, where students had the opportunity to express their thoughts and opinions about the experience of using Telegram.

The data collected were analyzed from a quantitative and qualitative perspective. Likewise, the teaching team also conducted a critical reflection for the evaluation of the results of the pilot experience to identify the strengths, weaknesses, and improvements in future program interventions. Regarding the quantitative analysis, descriptive statistics for the recruited sample are provided. This research also focused on assessing whether students' perceptions differed according to the degree they were studying. To this end, it was tested whether the variables were equally distributed between the two independent samples, that of Architecture and Marketing students. For those qualitative ordinal variables measured using a Likert scale ranging from 1 to 5 (1 means "Strongly disagree" and 5 means "Strongly agree"), it was performed a Mann-Whitney U test or Wilcoxon rank-sum test, a non-parametric test. The null hypothesis is that the distribution of the variable X is the same for the two independent samples:

$$H_0{:}X_{architecture} \sim X_{marketing}$$

For the remaining variables—binary or nominal—the Fisher exact test was used. If the null hypothesis cannot be rejected, it would be concluded that there is no association between the variable under analysis and the two subsamples. For each variable X, the hypothesis to be tested is:

$$H_0{:}p_{i,\,architecture} = p_{i,\,marketing} = p_{i.}\ \forall i = 1,2,\ldots r$$

Where i=1,2,…,r is the number of categories of the variable X. $p_{i,\,architecture}$/ $p_{i,\,markeitng}$ is the join probability of a student to belong to the category i in architecture or marketing, respectively. p_i is the distribution of the variable in the full sample.

RESULTS

Table 1 shows the descriptive statistics—mean and standard deviation—of the variables collected in the survey and the descriptive analysis by field of knowledge. The last column provides the p-values of the hypothesis tests that examine the equality of distribution of each variable over the two groups (subsamples of Architecture and Marketing students). This allows us to compare whether the observed differences are statistically significant—when the p-value is less than or equal to the significance level (α= 1%, 5%, and 10%) the null hypothesis is rejected.

Table 1. Descriptive statistics of the survey by field of knowledge and test of difference between subsamples

		Full sample		Subsample of Architecture – Urbanism II		Subsample of Marketing – Statistics I		Test of difference between subsamples
		Mean	**SD**	**Mean**	**SD**	**Mean**	**SD**	*p*-value
Degree	Architecture	0.550	0.504					
	Marketing	0.450	0.504					
Sex	Male	0.400	0.496	0.500	0.512	0.278	0.461	0.203
	Female	0.600	0.496	0.500	0.512	0.722	0.461	
Are you subscribed to the Telegram channel?	Yes, and I have shared content	0.050	0.221	0.045	0.213	0.056	0.236	0.333
	Yes, but I have not shared content	0.600	0.496	0.500	0.512	0.722	0.461	
	No, I have not	0.350	0.483	0.455	0.510	0.222	0.428	
If you are a subscriber, have you read your colleagues' messages?	Yes	0.618	0.493	0.421	0.507	0.867	0.352	0.013
	No	0.382	0.493	0.579	0.507	0.133	0.352	
If you have read the messages, have you responded to any of them to help your colleagues?	Yes	0.576	0.502	1.000	0.000	0.067	0.258	0.000
	No	0.424	0.502	0.000	0.000	0.933	0.258	
For what reason have you not used the platform? Note: You can select more than one option.	I was not interested	0.081	0.277	0.048	0.218	0.125	0.342	0.568
	I was not motivated enough	0.108	0.315	0.095	0.301	0.125	0.342	1.000
	I didn't have time	0.459	0.505	0.333	0.483	0.625	0.500	0.104
	I had no doubts	0.250	0.439	0.286	0.463	0.200	0.414	0.705

continued on following page

Table 1. Continued

		Full sample		Subsample of Architecture – Urbanism II		Subsample of Marketing – Statistics I		Test of difference between subsamples
		Mean	SD	Mean	SD	Mean	SD	*p*-value
I feel that I can make appropriate and effective use of the Telegram platform to raise questions or doubts (*)	Strongly disagree	0.083	0.280	0.050	0.224	0.125	0.342	0.121
	Somewhat disagree	0.000	0.000	0.000	0.000	0.000	0.000	
	Neither disagree nor agree	0.139	0.351	0.150	0.366	0.125	0.342	
	Somewhat agree	0.167	0.378	0.050	0.224	0.313	0.479	
	Strongly agree	0.611	0.494	0.750	0.444	0.438	0.512	
Do you think that your academic performance may have been affected by not participating in the Telegram channel?	Yes	0.714	0.458	0.950	0.224	0.400	0.507	0.001
	No	0.286	0.458	0.050	0.224	0.600	0.507	
I consider that the relationship with the teacher has influenced my use of Telegram (*)	Strongly disagree	0.167	0.378	0.190	0.402	0.133	0.352	0.337
	Somewhat disagree	0.111	0.319	0.048	0.218	0.200	0.414	
	Neither disagree nor agree	0.472	0.506	0.429	0.507	0.533	0.516	
	Somewhat agree	0.139	0.351	0.190	0.402	0.067	0.258	
	Strongly agree	0.111	0.319	0.143	0.359	0.067	0.258	
I consider that the involvement of the teacher has been adequate (taking into account the availability contemplated in the decalogue and the help provided through the channel) (*)	Strongly disagree	0.056	0.232	0.048	0.218	0.067	0.258	0.292
	Somewhat disagree	0.000	0.000	0.000	0.000	0.000	0.000	
	Neither disagree nor agree	0.083	0.280	0.095	0.301	0.067	0.258	
	Somewhat agree	0.139	0.351	0.048	0.218	0.267	0.458	
	Strongly agree	0.722	0.454	0.810	0.402	0.600	0.507	

continued on following page

Table 1. Continued

		Full sample		Subsample of Architecture – Urbanism II		Subsample of Marketing – Statistics I		Test of difference between subsamples
		Mean	SD	Mean	SD	Mean	SD	*p*-value
If you had the opportunity to use the tool in another subject, would you consider using it?	Yes	0.474	0.506	0.190	0.402	0.824	0.393	0.000
	No	0.526	0.506	0.810	0.402	0.176	0.393	
Do you think it can be applied to other subjects?	No, I do not think it is useful for other subjects.	0.263	0.446	0.381	0.498	0.118	0.332	0.000
	Yes, in more practical subjects	0.211	0.413	0.048	0.218	0.412	0.507	
	Yes, in subjects of a more theoretical nature	0.342	0.481	0.524	0.512	0.118	0.332	
	Yes, in both practical and theoretical subjects	0.184	0.393	0.048	0.218	0.353	0.493	
In your opinion, which channel do you think would be more suitable than Telegram? Note: You can select more than one option.	Face-to-face tutorials	0.684	0.471	0.714	0.463	0.647	0.493	0.734
	Virtual tutorials	0.342	0.481	0.333	0.483	0.353	0.493	1.000
	Emails	0.184	0.393	0.095	0.301	0.294	0.470	0.207
	Virtual Campus Forums	0.054	0.229	0.048	0.218	0.063	0.250	1.000

continued on following page

Table 1. Continued

		Full sample		Subsample of Architecture – Urbanism II		Subsample of Marketing – Statistics I		Test of difference between subsamples
		Mean	SD	Mean	SD	Mean	SD	*p*-value
I would recommend the use of Telegram to colleagues who will take the subject in the future (*)	Strongly disagree	0.083	0.280	0.050	0.224	0.125	0.342	0.041
	Somewhat disagree	0.000	0.000	0.000	0.000	0.000	0.000	
	Neither disagree nor agree	0.194	0.401	0.150	0.366	0.250	0.447	
	Somewhat agree	0.250	0.439	0.150	0.366	0.375	0.500	
	Strongly agree	0.472	0.506	0.650	0.489	0.250	0.447	
Number of observations		40		22		18		

Source: Authors' own elaboration based on the survey conducted. Note: "SD" stands for standard deviation. For those variables marked with (*), the p-value provided comes from the Mann-Whitney U test or Wilcoxon rank-sum test. In the rest of the variables, the test of difference between subsamples applied is the Fisher exact test.

DISCUSSION

In Table 1, the results show similarities and differences between the implementation of the Telegram channel in Urbanism II and Statistics I. The proportion of participants from both degrees is nearly equal, with 55% in Urbanism II and 45% in Statistics. It is also highlighted that the female and male representation is equal in the case of Urbanism II but differs in the case of Statistics I with 28% and 72%, respectively. This is explained in the case of Statistics I for several reasons: (1) male students were less involved and engaged in the subject, (2) male students used to miss class while female students attended regularly, so the invitation to the Telegram channel through scanning a QR code facilitated in class also explains why the representation of male students is lower. However, this difference is not statistically significant (p-value = 0.203).

Most students who completed the survey subscribed to the channel. In particular, 65% of students subscribed to the channel, sharing or not sharing content with other channel users. However, students who subscribed to the Telegram channel took a passive role in both subjects, focusing mainly on reading the content published by other channel members. Students' participation is the same in Architecture and Marketing, given the p-value of the test of differences between subsamples (0.333).

In addition, it is also pointed out that there are students subscribed to the Telegram channel who did not read the posted content, with 57.9% in Urbanism II and 13.3% in Statistics I. This difference is statistically significant (p-value = 0.013). Despite participation in the two Telegram channels mainly through posting text messages and images, about 5% of students involved not only read the published content but also shared content. This could be explained by the fact that both Telegram channels were implemented almost halfway through the semester, so that students did not integrate the application from the beginning.

It is also noted that all the respondents in Urbanism II declared having replied at least once to give support to other colleges, but over 7% did the same in Statistics I—a significant difference at the 1% confidence level. This could be explained by the fact that the assessment process differs among the subjects tested. On the one hand, Urbanism students are continuously assessed through urban design projects. Therefore, students' interaction with the teacher during the course is very relevant. On the other hand, in Statistics, although students have to complete tasks, the main assessment method is a final exam. For those students who did not use the Telegram channel in both subjects, the main reason they declared was for not having time, with 33.3% in Urbanism I and 62.5% in Statistics I—the p-value of the test of difference between subsamples is 0.104. It might also be explained by the fact that they became familiar with Telegram nearly at the end of the semester when they had to meet several deadlines for different subjects. The survey also asked whether students felt that they could make appropriate and effective use of the platform—not significant differences between subsamples (p-value = 0.121). Most of the students strongly agreed (61.1%), while 8.3% strongly disagreed. Considering the full sample, the participants connected their active role with academic success. This is observed clearly in the case of Urbanism II, but 60% in Statistics I believe there is no relation. This difference between subjects is statistically significant (p = 0.001), so it could be explained by the differences in the methodological approaches previously argued above.

This lack of active role of subscribed students contrasts with the fact that they positively consider the role of the teachers taking part in the channel. In both subjects, students were satisfied with teachers' communication and their involvement in the platform—p-values of difference between subsamples of 0.337 and 0.292 for each question, respectively. For instance, 81% and 60% of students in Architecture and Marketing strongly agree that the involvement of the teacher has been adequate. Moreover, 80% of students in Urbanism II considered using this application in other subjects. This percentage has decreased to less than 20% for Statistics I. Notably, there is a statistical difference (p-value = 0.000). According to the application of Telegram in other subjects, 52.4% of students surveyed in Urbanism II believe that it could be applied in theoretical subjects, whereas 41.2% of students in Statistics believe that the use of Telegram could be positive in practical subjects. This could be explained by the application of the channel that differs in both subjects statistically (p-value = 0.000). On the one hand, urban design students might think that a message application in practical lessons is not appropriate since the creative project in urban and building design requires an in-person tutorial. On the other hand, in Statistics I, the main use given to the channel was to discuss exercises.

Regarding the suitability of other applications compared to Telegram, students of both grades agreed (p-values > 0.2). Despite the potential of a virtual channel for tutoring, the students in both subjects chose as an alternative to Telegram the face-to-face tutorials (68.4%), followed by other ways of virtual tutoring (34.2%). It is also pointed out that students involved are interested in using this application in these subjects in the future. However, there are differences between subjects (p-value = 0.041). While most students in Urbanism strongly recommended using this application in the future (65%), the majority agreed in Statistics (37.5%).

The implementation of the Telegram tutoring channel in two subjects served as a pilot study for its subsequent replication in university education after incorporating any improvements. To do this, it is necessary to identify any limitations observed in this first test. They can be summarized in the following two aspects: (1) the Telegram channel was presented and implemented halfway during the semester, which added to the lack of knowledge of the Telegram application by some students as it was first introduced in the academic context; (2) student perception was only evaluated through a survey, but it does not include measures of usability or academic achievement.

Firstly, because of its introduction during the semester, many students became familiar with the messaging application weeks later near the end of the semester. As a result, the use of the application was not exploited until the end of the course. To solve this issue in future experiences, it could be useful for students to take part in an introductory course on the use of Telegram to familiarize themselves with this application at the beginning of the subject. It could promote participation by exploring all the tutoring possibilities beyond sending texts. Secondly, the program was evaluated only according to the student's perception at the end of the subject. However, the evaluation of the usability of the tutoring channel during the semester was not available. To address Telegram usage issues, it might be useful to discuss how the tutoring channel works in class to identify and resolve problems promptly. These review sessions on the use of Telegram throughout the semester could also reflect on how students feel about the tutoring channel contributing to their academic performance. Moreover, it could be beneficial to transfer some of the questions resolved in the chat during class time to highlight the possibilities and effectiveness of Telegram for tutoring. This could promote engagement beyond just reading posted messages and encourage students to share content to address doubts and questions raised on Telegram.

CONCLUSION

This pilot experience shows that the overall perception of students on the use of a Telegram channel for tutoring was positive. The student-teacher communication improved and served as a complement to face-to-face tutorials, but it did not replace it. However, traditional channels such as email or virtual forums are on the way out according to the perception of the student involved once they have used Telegram for tutoring. Despite the positive implications of the Telegram channel for tutoring, the pilot experience presented was not exempt from limitations that could be addressed in future implementations considering the following improvements: (1) the Telegram channel for tutoring has to be presented at the beginning of the subject, considering an introductory course on the use of Telegram as a way to promote participation; (2) to assess the impact of the program on academic performance, usability, and students' perception, a control group has to be defined.

Artificial intelligence poses a threat to the entire education system and could replace tutoring tasks. However, a recent report by the Organization for Economic Co-operation and Development (OECD, 2026) warns of the negative effects of using artificial intelligence to answer students' questions and perform tutoring tasks, particularly the reduction in active student participation, improving task performance without the corresponding learning benefits. This highlights the value of promoting the use of Telegram in the teaching-learning process, avoiding the use of artificial intelligence, and encouraging interaction between students and teachers. This teaching experience can serve as a basis for the implementation of new channels closer to Generation Z that facilitate tutorial action in the university context. These new applications, such as Telegram, could also be supported by universities through their integration into their official virtual learning platforms, along with tutorials and guides on usage and good practice by university publishers in institutional repositories.

ACKNOWLEDGMENT

This research was supported by the University of Malaga - *Plan de Formación del Personal Docente e Investigador 2022* [course number D048.22 – *Iniciación a la innovación educativa del profesorado Universitario (3.ª fase)*].

REFERENCES

Al-Bahrani, A., Patel, D., & Sheridan, B. (2015). Engaging students using social media: The students' perspective. *International Review of Economics Education, 19*, 36–50. DOI: 10.1016/j.iree.2015.06.001

Barrot, J. S. (2021). Scientific Mapping of Social Media in Education: A Decade of Exponential Growth. *Journal of Educational Computing Research, 59*(4), 645–668. DOI: 10.1177/0735633120972010

Conde, M. Á., Rodríguez-Sedano, F. J., Rodríguez Lera, F. J., Gutiérrez-Fernández, A., & Guerrero-Higueras, Á. M. (2021). WhatsApp or Telegram. Which is the Best Instant Messaging Tool for the Interaction in Teamwork? In Zaphiris, P., & Ioannou, A. (Eds.), *Learning and Collaboration Technologies: New Challenges and Learning Experiences* (pp. 239–249). Springer., DOI: 10.1007/978-3-030-77889-7_16

Grant, M. M. (2019). Difficulties in defining mobile learning: Analysis, design characteristics, and implications. *Educational Technology Research and Development, 67*(2), 361–388. DOI: 10.1007/s11423-018-09641-4

Hernández-Falagán, D. (2020). Pedagogía colaborativa y redes sociales. Diseñar en cuarentena. In Bardí i Milà, B., & García-Escudero, D. (Eds.), *VIII Jornadas sobre Innovación Docente en Arquitectura (JIDA'20)* (pp. 186–197). Iniciativa Digital Politècnica Oficina de Publicacions Acadèmiques Digitals de la UPC, Publicaciones y Divulgación Científica de la Universidad de Málaga., DOI: 10.5821/jida.2020.9336

Iksan, Z. H., & Saufian, S. M. (2017). Mobile Learning: Innovation in Teaching and Learning Using Telegram. *International Journal of Pedagogy and Teacher Education, 1*(1), 19–26. DOI: 10.20961/ijpte.v1i1.5120

Iqbal, M. Z., Alradhi, H. I., Alhumaidi, A. A., Alshaikh, K. H., AlObaid, A. M., Alhashim, M. T., & AlSheikh, M. H. (2020). Telegram as a Tool to Supplement Online Medical Education During COVID-19 Crisis. *Acta Informatica Medica, 28*(2), 94–97. DOI: 10.5455/aim.2020.28.94-97 PMID: 32742059

Jordan, K. (2023). How can messaging apps, WhatsApp and SMS be used to support learning? A scoping review. *Technology, Pedagogy and Education*, *32*(3), 275–288. DOI: 10.1080/1475939X.2023.2201590

Kassens, A. L. (2014). Tweeting Your Way to Improved #Writing, #Reflection, and #Community. *The Journal of Economic Education*, *45*(2), 101–109. DOI: 10.1080/00220485.2014.889937

Koole, M. L. (2009). A Model for Framing Mobile Learning. In Ally, M. (Ed.), *Mobile Learning: Transforming the Delivery of Education and Training* (pp. 25–47). AU Press., DOI: 10.15215/aupress/9781897425435.01

Kyslova, M. A., Semerikov, S. O., & Slovak, K. I. (2025). Mobile learning evolution: A decade of developments (2014-2023). *Educational Technology Quarterly*, *2025*(2), 186–208. DOI: 10.55056/etq.25

Lee, C. E. (2020). Facebook Use in Malaysian Higher Education Classroom. In Tatnall, A. (Ed.), *Encyclopedia of Education and Information Technologies* (pp. 751–758). Springer., DOI: 10.1007/978-3-030-10576-1_141

Manca, S. (2020). Snapping, pinning, liking or texting: Investigating social media in higher education beyond Facebook. *The Internet and Higher Education*, *44*, 100707. DOI: 10.1016/j.iheduc.2019.100707

Matos Lopes, R. (2017). Facebook in educational research: A bibliometric analysis. *Scientometrics*, *111*(3), 1591–1621. DOI: 10.1007/s11192-017-2294-1

Md Yusof, N., & Abdullah, A. (2025). The efficacy of Telegram Messenger as a tool for enhancing argumentative writing among students in open and distance learning. *Asian Association of Open Universities Journal*, *20*(1), 4–16. DOI: 10.1108/AAOUJ-07-2022-0091

Ng, W., Nicholas, H., Loke, S., & Torabi, T. (2010). Designing Effective Pedagogical Systems for Teaching and Learning with Mobile and Ubiquitous Devices. In Gogh, T. T. (Ed.), *Multiplatform E-Learning Systems and Technologies: Mobile Devices for Ubiquitous ICT-Based Education* (pp. 42–56). IGI Global., DOI: 10.4018/978-1-60566-703-4.ch003

Nicolau-Corbacho, A., Verdú-Vázquez, A., & Gil-López, T. (2019). Incorporación del *blended learning* al taller de proyectos arquitectónicos. In García-Escudero, D., & Bardí i Milà, B. (Eds.), *VII Jornadas sobre Innovación Docente en Arquitectura (JIDA'19)* (pp. 648–662). Iniciativa Digital Politècnica Oficina de Publicacions Acadèmiques Digitals de la UPC., DOI: 10.5821/jida.2019.8391

Nogués-Pedregal, A. M., & Carmona-Zubiri, D. (2024). Twitter as an instructional tool for critical thinking and creativity in Higher Education. In *10th International Conference on Higher Education Advances (HEAd'24)* (pp. 186–193). Universitat Politecnica de València. https://doi.org/DOI: 10.4995/HEAd24.2024.17272

Organization for Economic Co-operation and Development [OECD] (2026). *OECD Digital Education Outlook 2026: Exploring Effective Uses of Generative AI in Education.* OECD Publishing. https://doi.org/DOI: 10.1787/062a7394-en

Rahman, S., Ramakrishnan, T., & Ngamassi, L. (2020). Impact of social media use on student satisfaction in Higher Education. *Higher Education Quarterly*, *74*(3), 304–319. DOI: 10.1111/hequ.12228

Vavoula, G., & Sharples, M. (2002). KLeOS: A Personal, Mobile, Knowledge and Learning Organisation System. In M. Milrad, U. Hoppe, & Kinshuk (Eds.), *Proceedings of the IEEE International Workshop on Wireless and Mobile Technologies in Education (WMTE 2002)* (pp. 152–156). IEEE. https://doi.org/DOI: 10.1109/WMTE.2002.1039239

Yinka, A. R., & Queendarline, N. N. (2018). Telegram as a social media tool for teaching and learning in tertiary institutions. *International Journal of Multidisciplinary Research and Development*, *5*(7), 95–98.

Chapter 7
The Impact of Digital Tools on Students' Learning Experience:
Teachers' Perceptions and Observations

Papagiannis Chrysovalantis
Independent Researcher, Greece

ABSTRACT

The integration of digital tools in education has become increasingly vital, particularly in primary education, where innovative teaching approaches are crucial for fostering student engagement and deep learning. This study explores the impact of digital tools on students' learning experience, based on the perceptions and observations of 100 primary school teachers in Greece. The findings indicate that digital tools positively influence students' interest, participation, and understanding of content, while also supporting differentiated instruction and 21st-century skill development. However, concerns regarding access inequality and classroom management were also raised. The study concludes that while digital tools offer considerable pedagogical advantages, their effective integration requires ongoing teacher training, infrastructure support, and inclusive strategies to ensure equitable access for all learners. The research contributes to the broader discourse on technology-enhanced education and offers practical implications for policy and development in Greek education.

DOI: 10.4018/979-8-2600-1568-1.ch007

INTRODUCTION

In the modern era of the digital revolution, technology has permeated every aspect of human activity, including education. The use of digital tools in the classroom has transformed the way teachers teach and students learn. From interactive whiteboards and learning software to mobile devices and virtual learning environments, digital tools have added new dimensions to the teaching and learning experience.

As technology evolves at a rapid pace, it is imperative to explore its impact on the learning process. Although many studies have been conducted on the pedagogical benefits of technology, it remains necessary to understand the views and observations of teachers themselves, who are the main implementers of digital innovations in the classroom. Teachers' perceptions, attitudes and experiences can significantly determine the effectiveness of digital tools in enhancing learning.

This research paper aims to explore the impact of digital tools on students' learning experiences, through the perceptions and observations of primary and secondary school teachers. Focusing on teachers' perspectives, it attempts to capture the benefits, limitations and challenges that accompany the integration of technology into school practice.

BACKGROUND

Definition and Categories of Digital Tools

The concept of digital tools in the educational process has evolved significantly in recent years, reflecting technological progress and the need to modernize teaching. Digital tools are considered to be all those technological means and platforms that are used to support learning, facilitate communication and improve the educational experience. These tools cover a wide range, from simple presentation applications to complex virtual reality environments.

According to Heafner and Fitchett (2015), digital tools can be defined as technological solutions used in educational environments to support and/or enhance teaching and learning. Such tools can be software, electronic platforms, digital devices, online applications and other forms of technology used by teachers and students.

The categorization of digital tools can be based on their function, purpose, and use. The main categories include:

1. Learning Management Systems (LMS)

Platforms such as Moodle, Google Classroom, and Edmodo allow the creation of virtual classrooms, posting educational materials, assigning assignments, and providing feedback to students (Almusharraf & Khahro, 2020). These tools make it possible to continue the educational process even in remote conditions.

2. Interactive Learning Tools

Applications such as Kahoot!, Quizlet, and Mentimeter offer the ability to create knowledge games, quizzes, and interactive activities that increase student participation and interest. Such tools often incorporate mechanisms for immediate feedback and reinforcement of knowledge.

3. Multimedia and Presentation Tools

PowerPoint, Prezi and other software allow for the visualization of information, facilitating the understanding of difficult concepts. The use of videos, images and diagrams enhances multimodal learning (Mayer, 2009).

4. Collaboration and Communication Tools

Platforms such as Google Docs, Padlet and Microsoft Teams facilitate teamwork and the exchange of ideas, while cultivating students' digital and interpersonal skills (Cohen et al., 2017).

5. Augmented and virtual reality (AR/VR) tools

The use of augmented and virtual reality introduces students to highly interactive environments, offering experiential learning in areas such as history, geography and natural sciences (Radianti et al., 2020).

6. Adaptive Learning Tools

Applications such as Smart Sparrow and DreamBox Learning use performance data to adapt teaching to the needs of each student, promoting differentiated teaching.

The use of these tools in the educational process is not uniform, as it depends on factors such as the subject area, the level of students, the digital competence of teachers and the school infrastructure.

The Role of Digital Tools in Improving Learning

The use of digital tools in the educational process has brought about significant changes in the way students interact with knowledge, classmates and teachers. Digital media are no longer just auxiliary tools, but critical components of a modern, dynamic and personalized learning experience. Their role is not limited to transmitting information, but extends to enhancing student engagement, supporting differentiated teaching and developing 21st century skills.

One of the main ways in which digital tools improve learning is by enhancing active participation and motivation of students. Through interactive applications, videos, games and quizzes, students acquire an active role in the learning process. Tools such as Kahoot!, Nearpod and Socrative, through the use of gamification elements, enhance competitiveness and collaboration, creating an attractive learning environment. Students often perceive the use of digital tools as a more "natural" and familiar experience, since they are already familiar with the use of technology in their daily lives (Prensky, 2001).

Technology provides opportunities to adapt teaching to the individual needs and pace of students. Adaptive learning applications analyze student performance in real time and adjust learning content accordingly. A typical example is DreamBox Learning, which adapts mathematical exercises according to the user's performance.

The integration of technology is not limited only to the acquisition of knowledge but is directly linked to the development of key skills required in the modern world: digital literacy, problem solving, collaboration, creativity and critical thinking (Voogt et al., 2015).

For example, when students use tools such as Google Docs for group writing or Padlet for collective brainstorming, they learn to collaborate in real time, communicate effectively, and organize their thinking. At the same time, exposure to digital media helps them develop research, evaluation, and information management skills that are essential for their participation in the digital society.

Digital tools offer opportunities to include and support students with special educational needs. Applications with audio narration, text-to-speech conversion, video captions, and interactive learning games can be used as tools to enhance the participation of these students (Al-Azawei et al., 2016).

Digital tools contribute to the systematic and immediate provision of feedback, which is crucial for students' educational progress. Through quizzes, tests and interactive activities, students are immediately informed about their performance, recognizing their mistakes and identifying areas that need reinforcement (Hattie, 2012).

Furthermore, these tools allow students to monitor their own progress (self-monitoring), cultivating autonomy and a sense of responsibility for their learning.

Thus, metacognitive ability, i.e. the conscious understanding of the learning process, is promoted.

This sub-chapter shows how digital tools are not just means of supporting traditional teaching, but can redefine learning, making it more participatory, personalized and inclusive.

Teachers' Perceptions of Technology in Education

The successful integration of digital tools into teaching depends largely on teachers' perceptions and attitudes towards technology. Teachers act as mediators between technology and students; therefore, their views play a crucial role in the acceptance, adoption and pedagogical use of digital tools in the classroom.

Many teachers recognize the advantages of digital tools, both at the learning and teaching levels. According to research by Ertmer and Ottenbreit-Leftwich (2010), teachers who believe in the pedagogical value of technology tend to integrate it more systematically and creatively into their daily practice.

Research at the European level shows that over 70% of teachers believe that digital tools can significantly improve the quality of teaching. Furthermore, in a study by Tondeur et al. (2017), it was found that teachers with positive attitudes towards technology show higher levels of creative and student-centered use of digital tools.

Despite positive expectations, many teachers express reservations or experience difficulties when integrating digital media into teaching. These difficulties are not only related to technical knowledge but also to deeper pedagogical and institutional challenges.

According to Inan and Lowther (2010), barriers to technology integration fall into two main categories: external barriers (e.g. lack of logistical infrastructure, limited time, insufficient technical support) and internal barriers (e.g. attitudes, beliefs, lack of self-confidence) (Koehler & Mishra, 2009).

Finally, the teacher's pedagogical philosophy plays an important role. Teachers who adopt a learner-centered approach are more likely to creatively integrate digital tools, seeing them as means of empowering students rather than simply as technical solutions. In contrast, those who follow a traditional, teacher-centered approach may use them primarily for reproducible, passive forms of learning.

MAIN FOCUS OF THE CHAPTER

1. To explore teachers' perceptions of the use of digital tools in the educational process.

2. To identify the observed effects of digital tools on student learning engagement and performance.
3. To document the challenges teachers face when integrating digital media into the lesson.

Research Questions

1. What are teachers' perceptions of the effectiveness of digital tools in improving the learning process?
2. How do teachers observe that students are affected in terms of their participation and academic progress?
3. What are the main difficulties teachers face in utilizing digital tools?

METHODOLOGY

This research follows the quantitative methodological approach, aiming to collect and analyze structured data that capture teachers' opinions and experiences regarding the use of digital tools in the learning process. The quantitative design was chosen as it offers the possibility of generalizing the results to a wider population and enhances the objectivity and reliability of the study (Creswell & Poth, 2018).

Specifically, the structured questionnaire method was used, which was distributed to a sample of 100 primary education teachers in primary schools in Greece. The choice of this specific method is based on its ability to provide clear, comparable and statistically processable information, facilitating the analysis of trends, attitudes and correlations between variables (Cohen et al., 2017).

The research design is non-experimental and descriptive, as it aims to record the views of teachers and not to investigate causal relationships. In addition, it is a cross-sectional study, since the data were collected at a single point in time, which makes it suitable for studying current perceptions and attitudes.

This particular approach is considered appropriate in the context of educational research, as it focuses on real classroom conditions, giving a voice to education professionals. At the same time, the use of quantitative methods is aligned with modern research practices that utilize technology in educational imaging.

Sample and Population

The population of this study consists of primary school teachers working in primary schools in Greece. This population was selected as primary school teachers play a crucial role in introducing and utilizing digital tools from a very early stage in students' learning process, directly influencing children's attitudes and relationships with technology (Tondeur et al., 2017).

The sample included male and female teachers, with varying years of service (from newly appointed to teachers with many years of experience) and different levels of training in the use of digital technologies. This diversity ensured the diversity of opinions and strengthened the validity of the results in terms of the representativeness of the range of experiences in the educational field (Cohen et al., 2017).

The selection of 100 participants was deemed sufficient for statistical analysis, in accordance with the rules of quantitative research, where a sample of more than 30 people is considered acceptable for simple descriptive statistics. Also, the sample size allows for the extraction of general trends and the extraction of comparisons between subgroups, such as in relation to age, years of service or training.

Participation in the research was voluntary and anonymous, and teachers' consent was ensured in accordance with the principles of ethics in educational research (BERA, 2018).

Research Tool

A structured questionnaire was used to collect research data, which was created specifically for the purposes of this study. The questionnaire was designed to explore teachers' opinions, experiences and observations regarding the use of digital tools in teaching and the learning process.

The structure of the questionnaire was based on previous relevant research (e.g. Tondeur et al., 2017) and was adapted to the Greek educational context, taking into account the specificities of primary education. The tool was designed to be clear, short and easy to complete, without requiring special technical knowledge.

The questionnaire includes a total of 4 sections:

1. Demographic characteristics (5 questions)
2. Frequency and type of use of digital tools (6 questions)
3. Perceptions of the effectiveness of digital tools (5 questions)
4. Observations on the impact on the students' learning experience (5 questions)

Most questions are closed-ended and use a four- or five-point Likert scale (e.g. from "Not at all" to "Very much" or from "Strongly disagree" to "Strongly agree"), allowing statistical processing of the responses.

There were also 1-2 open-ended questions, to give participants the opportunity to express personal opinions or comments.

The questionnaire was piloted with 10 teachers before the main distribution, in order to check the clarity, content validity and understanding of the questions

(Creswell & Poth, 2018). After the test, minor corrections were made to the wording of some questions.

Data Collection Process

The data collection process took place during the period March – April 2025. The questionnaire was distributed electronically via Google Forms, in order to facilitate the participation of teachers from various geographical areas of Greece, both urban and rural. The choice of electronic distribution was deemed necessary and functional, as it allows for the rapid dissemination of the tool and the collection of data with security and accuracy.

Teachers were identified and invited to participate through:

- Educational groups on social media (Facebook, Viber).
- Teachers' associations that had previous collaboration with the researcher.
- Sending emails to school units.

At the beginning of the questionnaire there was an introductory note, which stated the objectives of the research, the voluntary nature of participation, as well as the assurance of confidentiality and anonymity. In addition, participants were asked to declare that they freely consented and that they could withdraw at any time without any consequences.

Participation in the research was voluntary and no personal information (name, school, region) was requested or recorded, respecting the principles of ethical conduct in educational research, in accordance with the guidelines of the British Educational Research Association and the National Committee on Bioethics and Technoethics.

During data collection:

- There was a reminder to participants one week after the initial mailing.
- An active access link to the questionnaire was maintained for a total of three weeks.
- Regular checks were made for the number and completeness of responses to ensure the adequacy and validity of the sample.

In total, 110 teachers responded, of which 100 questionnaires were deemed complete and suitable for analysis. The remaining 10 questionnaires were excluded either due to incomplete responses or due to violation of the basic participation criteria (e.g. non-teachers or irrelevant level of education).

The choice of the electronic form in combination with clear instructions and user-friendly design contributed to the efficiency and validity of the data collection process (Creswell & Poth, 2018).

Data Analysis Methods

The data analysis of this quantitative research was carried out using Microsoft Excel and IBM SPSS Statistics (version 26) software. The selection of these tools was based on their reliability and their ability to support statistical processing appropriate for questionnaire data.

The analysis included descriptive statistics as well as comparative analysis, depending on the type of variables and the objectives of the research. Specifically:

Descriptive Statistics

The first phase of the analysis included the calculation of frequencies, percentages, means (Mean) and standard deviations (Standard Deviation). Through these indicators, the basic characteristics of the sample and the general trends in the teachers' responses were captured, such as:

- The percentage of use of digital tools.
- The opinions on the effectiveness of ICT in teaching.
- The observed effects on the students' learning experience.

The closed questions of the Likert scale were analyzed as ordered quantitative variables. Means were used to express the general attitude of teachers in each thematic unit (e.g. positivity towards the use of ICT).

Data Visualization

Bar charts and tables were used to support the interpretation of the results. The visual representation of the data enhanced the understanding of the findings and made their presentation more readable to the reader (Creswell & Poth, 2018).

RESULTS

Frequency of Digital Tool Usage in the Classroom

Question 1: How often do you use digital tools (e.g., interactive whiteboards, educational software, tablets) in your teaching?

Figure 1. Frequency of use of digital tools in teaching

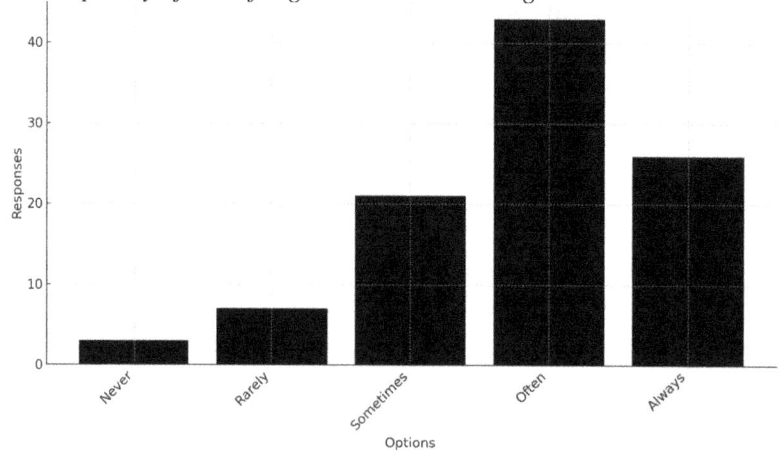

Analysis

The results show that a significant majority of teachers (43%) report using digital tools **often**, while an additional 26% use them **always**. Combined, nearly **70%** of the sample integrates technology into their daily or frequent teaching practices. Only 10% report using them **rarely** or **never**, indicating that the digital integration in primary classrooms is now widespread.

This aligns with findings from relevant literature emphasizing the growing prevalence of digital tools in teaching across European educational systems. It also reflects the increased accessibility of ICT infrastructure in schools and the broader pedagogical shift towards digital literacy (Selwyn, 2012; Voogt et al., 2015).

Such frequent use suggests not only a familiarity with digital environments but also a recognition of their **added value** in enhancing classroom engagement and learning outcomes, as supported by Ertmer and Ottenbreit-Leftwich (2010).

Teachers' Perceptions of the Impact of Digital Tools on Student Engagement

Question 2: To what extent do you agree with the statement: "Digital tools enhance student engagement during lessons"?

Figure 2. Teachers' perceptions of student engagement through digital tools

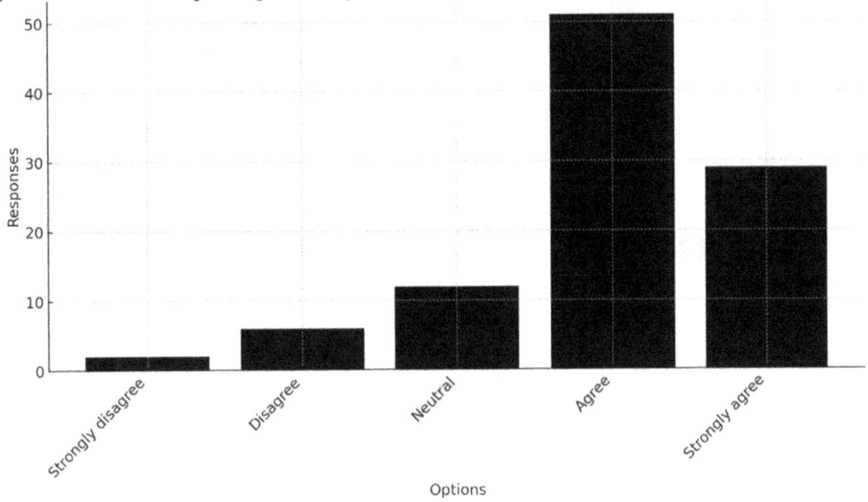

Analysis

According to the data, **80%** of respondents either **agree** or **strongly agree** that digital tools enhance student engagement, which underscores a generally positive perception among educators. Only **8%** express disagreement, while **12%** remain neutral.

This high level of agreement highlights that digital tools are not only present in classrooms but are also **valued for their pedagogical impact**, particularly in increasing student attention, motivation, and participation. As Kozma (2003) and Passey (2019) suggest, when integrated effectively, digital technologies can transform passive learners into active participants by fostering **interactivity** and **multimodal engagement**.

Furthermore, these results support earlier findings by Tondeur et al. (2017), which indicated that teachers who perceive a positive impact on engagement are more likely to continue adopting and experimenting with technology-based strategies.

Perceived Improvement in Students' Learning Outcomes Due to Digital Tools

Figure 3. Perceived improvement in student learning outcomes

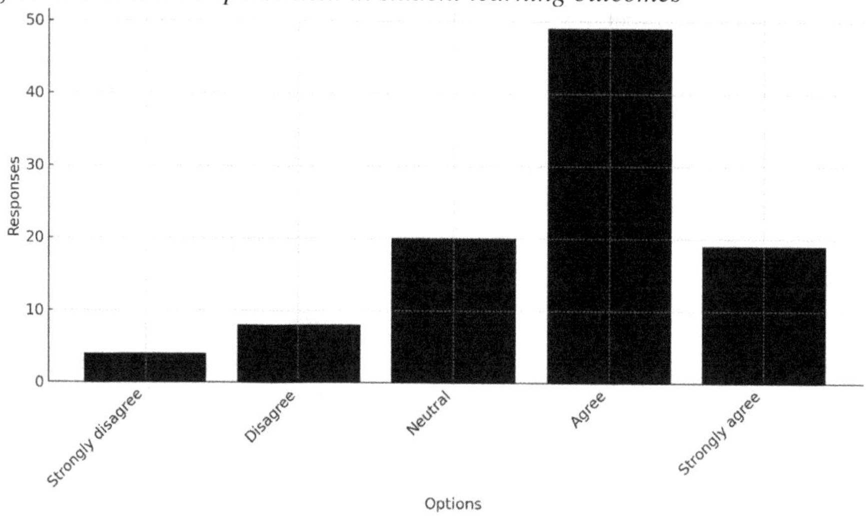

Analysis

Nearly **70%** of participants (Agree + Strongly agree) believe that digital tools contribute positively to students' learning outcomes. This suggests a prevalent belief among educators that technology use is not merely engaging, but also **pedagogically effective**.

The **20% neutral** response rate may indicate either uncertainty regarding measurable learning benefits or variability based on context (e.g., subject, student level, type of digital tool). Meanwhile, only **12%** express outright disagreement.

These findings are in line with studies emphasizing the **constructivist affordances** of digital tools, which enable student-centered learning, formative assessment, and differentiated instruction (Mishra & Koehler, 2006). Teachers' positive perceptions also reflect experiences where technology is used to support **critical thinking, creativity, and deeper understanding** (Fullan & Langworthy, 2014).

However, the fact that not all teachers strongly agree suggests a need for **targeted training** and **evidence-based practice** to ensure that technology is applied in ways that clearly support learning.

Teachers' Confidence in Using Digital Tools

Question 4: How confident do you feel in using digital tools for teaching purposes?

Figure 4. Teachers' confidence in using digital tools

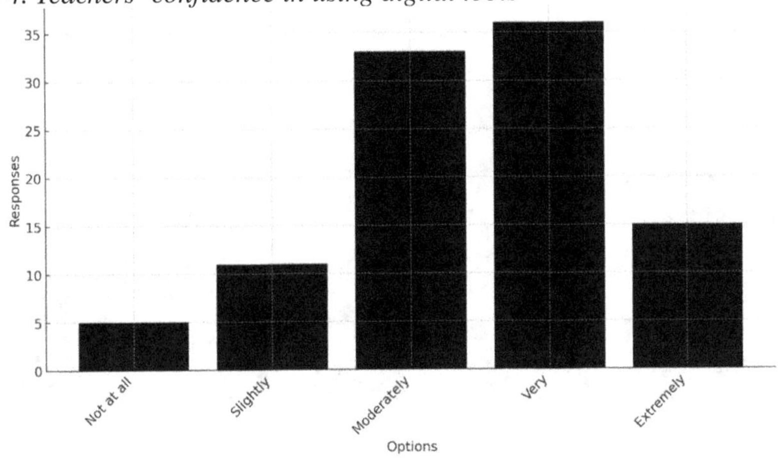

Analysis

According to the results, the majority of respondents feel confident using digital tools: 51% report being either very or extremely confident, while an additional 33% describe themselves as moderately confident. Only 16% fall on the lower end of the scale.

These findings suggest that a substantial number of teachers possess a positive self-efficacy regarding digital technology use—an essential factor for successful integration in the classroom (Bandura, 1997; Tschannen-Moran & Hoy, 2001). Teachers' confidence is often linked with both frequency of use and innovative practices, as noted by Ertmer and Ottenbreit-Leftwich (2010).

However, the presence of a small but noteworthy group (16%) with low confidence signals a need for ongoing professional development, especially for those who may lack previous training or experience.

Providing structured support can increase confidence and competence, thereby enabling teachers to leverage digital tools more effectively for pedagogical purposes.

Barriers to the Effective Use of Digital Tools

Question 5: What is the main barrier you face when trying to integrate digital tools into your teaching?

Figure 5. Barriers to the effective use of digital tools

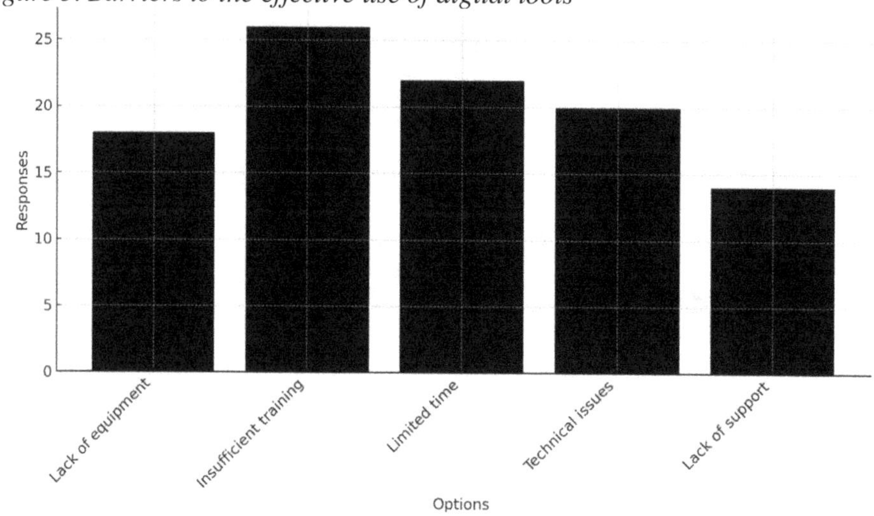

Analysis

The most frequently cited barrier is insufficient training (26%), followed by limited time during lessons (22%) and technical issues (20%). Lack of equipment also presents a significant obstacle (18%), while lack of administrative support was selected by 14% of respondents.

These results highlight both technical and systemic challenges in digital integration. The prominence of training-related concerns suggests that even when infrastructure exists, the professional capacity of educators to use it meaningfully may be lacking (Tondeur et al., 2017).

Similarly, limited instructional time reflects constraints within the current curriculum and classroom structure that prevent teachers from experimenting with or fully utilizing digital tools. Technical problems, still cited by 1 in 5 teachers, further reinforce the importance of reliable infrastructure and ongoing IT support in schools.

Addressing these barriers through policy reforms, professional development, and institutional support can significantly improve the educational value derived from digital technologies (Voogt et al., 2015).

Teachers' Interest in Further Training on Digital Tools

Question 6: Would you be interested in attending further training or professional development seminars related to the use of digital tools in teaching?

Figure 6. Interest in further training related to digital tools

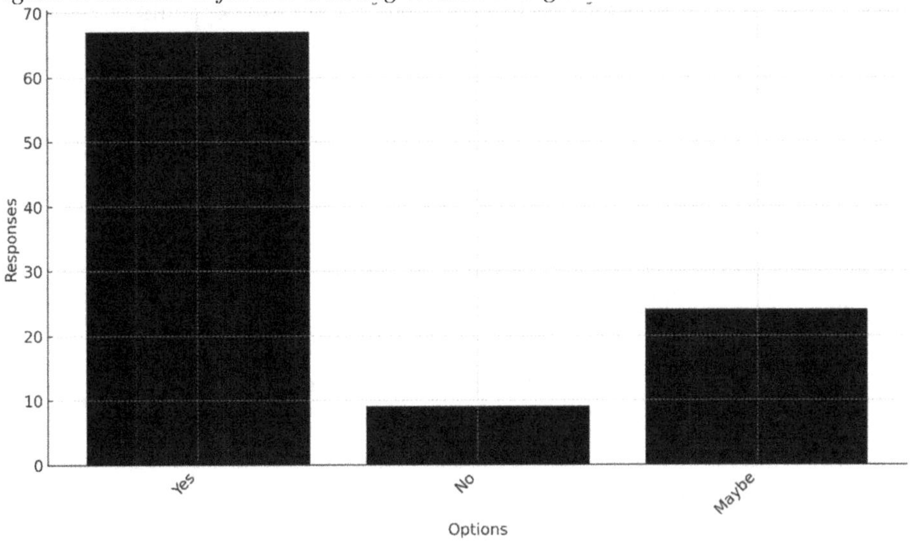

Analysis

The majority of respondents (67%) expressed a clear interest in participating in further training on digital tools, while 24% answered maybe, and only a small minority (9%) indicated no interest.

This strong interest in continuous professional development reflects a proactive attitude among teachers toward improving their digital competencies. It aligns with recent educational research that highlights how ongoing, targeted training is essential for the effective pedagogical use of ICT (Koehler & Mishra, 2009; OECD, 2021).

The high percentage of "maybe" responses also suggests that, for many teachers, training content, timing, and accessibility may influence their decision. These findings emphasize the need for flexible, context-relevant, and well-supported training programs that are tailored to the specific needs of teachers in primary education.

Such programs could focus not only on technical skills but also on didactic strategies, assessment integration, and student-centered digital teaching approaches.

SOLUTIONS AND RECOMMENDATIONS

This chapter presented the quantitative data collected from 100 primary school teachers in Greece regarding their perceptions and experiences with digital tools in the classroom. The findings reveal several key insights:

Frequency of Use: The majority of teachers (75%) use digital tools regularly (daily or weekly), indicating a high level of integration of technology into their teaching practices.

Perceived Impact on Engagement: A substantial 80% of respondents agreed or strongly agreed that digital tools enhance student engagement. This supports the notion that digital technologies can motivate learners and foster more interactive learning environments.

Perceived Impact on Learning Outcomes: While slightly more moderate, 68% of teachers agreed or strongly agreed that digital tools improve learning outcomes. This suggests a general belief in the educational value of technology, though some teachers remained neutral or unconvinced.

Confidence in Use: More than half of the respondents (51%) reported high levels of confidence in using digital tools, while 33% felt moderately confident. This reflects the growing digital competence among educators, although a small percentage (16%) still feel underprepared.

Barriers to Integration: The most commonly reported barriers were insufficient training (26%), limited instructional time (22%), and technical issues (20%). These findings underline the importance of both infrastructure and support systems in ensuring the effective use of technology.

Willingness to Pursue Further Training: A significant 67% of participants expressed interest in further training, showing a clear desire for professional growth in digital pedagogy. An additional 24% responded "maybe," suggesting that with the right opportunities and conditions, even more teachers could engage in professional development.

FUTURE RESEARCH DIRECTIONS

- Expand the sample to include teachers from different levels and regions of Greece.
- Combine quantitative and qualitative methods to more fully understand teachers' attitudes and experiences.
- Focus on specific categories of digital tools (e.g. STEM tools, gamification applications, virtual and augmented reality).

- Investigate the impact of digital technology on students' academic performance and psychosocial development, with measurable data.

CONCLUSION

This research has highlighted essential aspects of the impact of digital tools on students' learning experience, as perceived by primary education teachers in Greece. Through the quantitative analysis of data collected from 100 teachers, the following key findings were recorded. The frequency of use of digital tools in daily teaching is relatively high, with a significant percentage of teachers stating that they use them on a regular basis. Most teachers consider that digital tools contribute positively to students' learning, enhancing engagement, understanding and willingness to participate.

Teachers' self-confidence in using technologies is directly related to how often they use them, which underlines the importance of professional empowerment (Ertmer & Ottenbreit-Leftwich, 2010). Teachers with lower self-confidence are those who show greater willingness to participate in training, confirming the literature-based need for differentiated training programs (Desimone, 2009).

These findings confirm previous research that argues that the successful integration of technology into teaching depends not only on the logistical infrastructure, but mainly on human factors such as teachers' attitudes, beliefs and digital skills (Tondeur et al., 2017; Voogt et al., 2015).

Research Limitations

Despite the important findings, this study faced certain limitations:

- The sample is limited to 100 primary school teachers and cannot be considered fully representative.
- The quantitative approach, although analytical, did not record in depth the personal experiences and concerns of the participants.
- The self-referential nature of the responses may involve subjectivity or socially desirable responses.

REFERENCES

Al-Azawei, A., Serenelli, F., & Lundqvist, K. (2016). Universal Design for Learning (UDL): A content analysis of peer reviewed journals from 2012 to 2015. *The Journal of Scholarship of Teaching and Learning, 16*(3), 39–56. DOI: 10.14434/josotl.v16i3.19295

Bandura, A. (1997). Self-efficacy: The exercise of control. *The Freeman.*

Cohen, L., Manion, L., & Morrison, K. (2017). *Research Methods in Education* (8th ed.). Routledge., DOI: 10.4324/9781315456539

Creswell, J. W., & Poth, C. N. (2018). *Qualitative inquiry and research design: Choosing among five approaches* (4th ed.). Sage Publications.

Desimone, L. M. (2009). Improving impact studies of teachers' professional development: Toward better conceptualizations and measures. *Educational Researcher, 38*(3), 181–199. DOI: 10.3102/0013189X08331140

Ertmer, P. A., & Ottenbreit-Leftwich, A. T. (2010). Teacher technology change: How knowledge, confidence, beliefs, and culture intersect. *Journal of Research on Technology in Education, 42*(3), 255–284. DOI: 10.1080/15391523.2010.10782551

Fullan, M., & Langworthy, M. (2014). *A rich seam: How new pedagogies find deep learning*. Pearson.

Hattie, J. (2012). *Visible learning for teachers: Maximizing impact on learning*. Routledge. DOI: 10.4324/9780203181522

Heafner, T. L., & Fitchett, P. G. (2015). Principals' and teachers' reports of instructional time allocations in third grade abstract. *Journal of International Social Studies, 5*(1), 81–100.

Inan, F. A., & Lowther, D. L. (2010). Factors affecting technology integration in K-12 classrooms: A path model. *Educational Technology Research and Development, 58*(2), 137–154. DOI: 10.1007/s11423-009-9132-y

Koehler, M. J., & Mishra, P. (2009). What is technological pedagogical content knowledge (TPACK)? *Contemporary Issues in Technology & Teacher Education, 9*(1), 60–70.

Kozma, R. B. (2003). Technology and classroom practices: An international study. *Journal of Research on Technology in Education, 36*(1), 1–14. DOI: 10.1080/15391523.2003.10782399

Mishra, P., & Koehler, M. J. (2006). Technological pedagogical content knowledge: A framework for teacher knowledge. *Teachers College Record, 108*(6), 1017–1054. DOI: 10.1111/j.1467-9620.2006.00684.x

Passey, D. (2019). Technology-enhanced learning: Rethinking the term, the concept and its theoretical background. *British Journal of Educational Technology, 50*(3), 972–986. DOI: 10.1111/bjet.12783

Prensky, M. (2001). Digital natives, digital immigrants part 2: Do they really think differently? *On the Horizon, 9*(6), 1–6. DOI: 10.1108/10748120110424843

Radianti, J., Majchrzak, T. A., Fromm, J., & Wohlgenannt, I. (2020). A systematic review of immersive virtual reality applications for higher education: Design elements, lessons learned, and research agenda. *Computers & Education, 147*, 103778. DOI: 10.1016/j.compedu.2019.103778

Selwyn, N. (2012). *Education and technology: Key issues and debates*. Bloomsbury Academic.

Tondeur, J., van Braak, J., Ertmer, P. A., & Ottenbreit-Leftwich, A. (2017). Understanding the relationship between teachers' pedagogical beliefs and technology use in education: A systematic review of qualitative evidence. *Educational Technology Research and Development, 65*(3), 555–575. DOI: 10.1007/s11423-016-9481-2

Tschannen-Moran, M., & Hoy, A. W. (2001). Teacher efficacy: Capturing an elusive construct. *Teaching and Teacher Education, 17*(7), 783–805. DOI: 10.1016/S0742-051X(01)00036-1

ADDITIONAL READING

Almusharraf, N., & Khahro, S. (2020). Students satisfaction with online learning experiences during the COVID-19 pandemic. [iJET]. *International Journal of Emerging Technologies in Learning, 15*(21), 246–267. DOI: 10.3991/ijet.v15i21.15647

Blikstad-Balas, M., & Klette, K. (2020). Still a long way to go: Narrow and transmissive use of technology in the classroom. *Nordic Journal of Digital Literacy, 15*(2), 55–68. DOI: 10.18261/issn.1891-943x-2020-01-05

Darling-Hammond, L., Hyler, M. E., & Gardner, M. (2017). *Effective teacher professional development*. Learning Policy Institute. https://learningpolicyinstitute.org/product/effective-teacher-professional-development-report

Ertmer, P. A., & Ottenbreit-Leftwich, A. T. (2010). Teacher technology change: How knowledge, confidence, beliefs, and culture intersect. *Journal of Research on Technology in Education*, *42*(3), 255–284. DOI: 10.1080/15391523.2010.10782551

Hammond, M., & Reynolds, L. (2021). Understanding teachers' digital competence: A review of the literature. *Technology, Pedagogy and Education*, *30*(1), 109–127. DOI: 10.1080/1475939X.2020.1865096

Mayer, R. E. (2009). Constructivism as a theory of learning versus constructivism as a prescription for instruction. In *Constructivist instruction* (pp. 196–212). Routledge.

OECD. (2021). *21st-century readers: Developing literacy skills in a digital world.* OECD Publishing., DOI: 10.1787/a83d84cb-

Selwyn, N. (2016). *Education and technology: Key issues and debates* (2nd ed.). Bloomsbury Academic.

Voogt, J., Erstad, O., Dede, C., & Mishra, P. (2015). Challenges to learning and schooling in the digital networked world. *Journal of Computer Assisted Learning*, *31*(5), 473–481. DOI: 10.1111/jcal.12107

KEY TERMS AND DEFINITIONS

Blended Learning: A teaching model that combines traditional face-to-face instruction with online learning activities, providing flexibility and personalization for students.

Digital Competence: The ability to use digital technologies effectively, critically, and responsibly in a variety of contexts, including teaching and learning environments.

Digital Divide: The gap between individuals or communities who have access to digital tools and internet connectivity and those who do not, often influenced by socioeconomic or geographic factors.

Differentiated Instruction: An educational approach in which teachers adapt content, process, and assessment methods to meet diverse student needs and learning preferences.

Educational Technology: Tools and processes that integrate digital technologies into teaching and learning to enhance educational outcomes and support pedagogy.

Gamification: The use of game design elements in non-game contexts such as classrooms to increase student motivation, engagement, and participation.

ICT (Information and Communication Technologies): A broad term referring to all technologies used to handle telecommunications, broadcast media, intelligent building management systems, audiovisual processing and transmission systems, and network-based control and monitoring functions.

Student Engagement: The level of interest, motivation, and active involvement that a student exhibits in the learning process, which is often linked to academic success.

TPACK (Technological Pedagogical Content Knowledge): A framework that identifies the types of knowledge educators need to effectively integrate technology into their teaching, balancing technology, pedagogy, and subject content.

Virtual Learning Environment (VLE): An online platform or software that facilitates digital interaction between teachers and students, offering tools for content delivery, communication, and assessment.

Chapter 8
E-Portfolio as an Alternative Method of Student Evaluation in Secondary Education in Greece

Maria Poulou
http://orcid.org/0009-0005-2372-4970
University of Alicante, Spain

ABSTRACT

This chapter refers to the views of secondary school teachers on alternative forms of students' assessment and specifically the e-portfolio. This study is a qualitative research that aims to gather the opinions of 14 teachers, through semi-structured interviews. It was observed that all teachers presented a positive attitude towards technology. Regarding the e-portfolio, teachers who had used it described it as very efficient, with obvious benefits. The majority of teachers who use it reported that they create it with the help of students alone, without collaborating with colleagues. Teachers who have not used this specific tool report that they either do not know about it or are not interested in investing more time in its design and preparation. It is concluded that there is a strong need to promote and use technological tools in education to improve the quality of the educational process and facilitate the work of teachers and students.

DOI: 10.4018/979-8-2600-1568-1.ch008

INTRODUCTION

In contemporary societies characterized by rapid technological, economic, and socio-cultural change, the acquisition of new skills throughout one's lifetime has become essential for personal development and professional success. Education systems are therefore expected to cultivate not only disciplinary knowledge but also transversal competencies such as autonomy, collaboration, creativity, and digital literacy. Within this context, student assessment constitutes a central mechanism for monitoring learning, providing feedback, fostering self-regulation, and informing educational decision-making at individual and institutional levels.

Traditional forms of assessment—mainly examinations, tests, and grading—have been increasingly criticized for promoting anxiety, competition, and score-seeking behaviors, often at the expense of deeper learning, reflection, and inclusive participation. Internationally, this critique has reinforced interest in alternative assessment methods that are formative, qualitative, process-oriented, and student-centered. Among these, the electronic portfolio (e-portfolio) has attracted considerable attention because it enables the collection, organization, and presentation of students' work over time, while integrating multiple media formats and opportunities for self-evaluation and feedback.

In Greece, the integration of digital tools in education has progressed unevenly due to infrastructural constraints, limited training opportunities for teachers, and the heavy reliance on summative assessments embedded in the national examination system. Nonetheless, the digital transformation of education—accelerated by global technological developments and recent shifts to online and blended learning environments—has renewed academic and policy interest in tools that can support more holistic and authentic forms of assessment.

This chapter investigates the perceptions of secondary school teachers regarding the use of e-portfolios as an alternative method of student evaluation in Greece. Through qualitative semi-structured interviews with fourteen teachers from diverse professional backgrounds, the chapter explores perceived benefits, challenges, and implementation conditions, and discusses the extent to which e-portfolios can complement traditional assessment practices. The chapter argues that e-portfolios may contribute to a more inclusive, reflective, and competence-based culture of assessment, provided that adequate institutional, technical, and pedagogical support is offered.

BACKGROUND

Assessment constitutes a core component of the educational process, allowing teachers to form judgments about students' learning, identify strengths and weaknesses, and determine the effectiveness of instruction. Conceptually, assessment encompasses evaluation, measurement, and grading, and is grounded in criteria of validity, reliability, and objectivity (Polyzos, 2007). While traditional assessment practices primarily emphasize summative judgments through examinations, alternative assessment approaches seek to document learning as a dynamic and reflective process. Such approaches align with broader shifts towards competence-based education and lifelong learning.

E-portfolios have been defined as digital collections of artefacts—such as texts, images, audio, videos, or presentations—that document learning outcomes, achievements, reflections, and professional development over time (Barrett, 2007; Lorenzo & Ittelson, 2005). E-portfolios differ from traditional portfolios in their enhanced multimodality, accessibility, interoperability, and potential for feedback and communication. Research also highlights their role in fostering self-regulated learning, metacognitive reflection, and autonomy (Andrade & Valtcheva, 2009; Berrill & Addison, 2010).

Internationally, e-portfolios have been adopted across different levels of education and for diverse purposes, including assessment, accreditation, student progression, faculty development, and continuing professional learning (Gibson & Barrett, 2003; Hallam & Creagh, 2010). Although terminology varies, the literature generally distinguishes between assessment portfolios, presentation portfolios, and development portfolios (Davis & Ponnamperuma, 2005; Buzzetto, 2010). Empirical studies report positive attitudes among students and teachers, increased engagement, evidence-based evaluation, and improved communication between stakeholders; however, concerns remain regarding workload, technical support, data security, and institutional readiness (Deneen & Shroff, 2014; Bryant & Chittum, 2013).

Recent studies emphasize the importance of ethical, legal, and social considerations in digital assessment, particularly regarding privacy, data ownership, and compliance with data protection frameworks such as the General Data Protection Regulation (GDPR) in Europe (Lam, 2023). Issues of digital equity, access, and inclusion are also recognized as critical determinants of successful implementation, especially for learners with unequal technological resources or special educational needs. In this regard, e-portfolios may contribute to greater inclusivity insofar as they allow students to demonstrate learning through diverse modalities; yet digital divides may simultaneously reinforce inequalities if institutional support is inadequate.

In Greece, research on e-portfolios is limited and largely focused on primary education or specific subject areas such as foreign languages and computer science. The adoption of digital tools in secondary education remains fragmented, constrained by infrastructural limitations, limited teacher training, and the predominance of high-stakes summative assessment at national level. Nevertheless, educational policies highlight the need to modernize evaluation processes and promote the integration of Information and Communication Technologies (ICT) to support holistic learning and assessment.

Against this backdrop, this chapter contributes to the literature by examining teachers' perceptions of e-portfolios in secondary education in Greece and exploring their potential as a complementary assessment tool.

Assessment has long been characterized as a process of collecting, interpreting, and utilizing evidence of student learning for decision-making at multiple levels: classroom instruction, student progression, feedback, and system accountability. In contemporary scholarship, distinctions are commonly made between measurement, evaluation, and assessment, with each term reflecting different epistemological assumptions about learning, performance, and knowledge representation. Traditional assessment, dominated by tests and examinations, prioritizes standardization, reliability, and comparability across students. While such practices provide structure and serve certification purposes, they have been criticized for promoting score competition and anxiety, rather than fostering deep learning, critical thinking, and self-regulation.

Alternative forms of assessment emerged as part of broader curricular reforms and progressive pedagogical movements emphasizing student agency, competence-based learning, and formative feedback. Within this paradigm, learning is conceptualized not as the acquisition of static knowledge but as a dynamic and iterative process shaped by reflection, feedback, collaboration, and contextual application. Portfolios, and subsequently electronic portfolios (e-portfolios), gained traction as tools capable of capturing learning processes and trajectories over time, aligning with constructivist and socio-cultural theories of learning.

From a theoretical standpoint, the shift towards formative and authentic assessment is supported by scholarship highlighting the importance of metacognition, self-regulation, and reflective practice. Zimmerman's (2002) models of self-regulated learning emphasize goal setting, self-monitoring, and reflection, while Andrade and Valtcheva (2009) argue that self-assessment contributes to higher performance outcomes by engaging students cognitively and affectively in the evaluation of their work. E-portfolios align with these frameworks by providing environments where students can curate artifacts, articulate learning goals, reflect on progress, and identify areas for improvement. Such processes are fundamental to competence-based education, which aims to equip learners with transversal skills applicable across academic and professional contexts.

Internationally, the adoption of e-portfolios varies significantly across educational levels and systems. In some higher education institutions, e-portfolios serve accreditation and certification purposes, enabling students to document professional competencies and achievements. In K–12 contexts, e-portfolios are used to showcase learning products, foster parent-teacher communication, and support formative and summative assessment. Countries such as the United States, Australia, and Singapore have experimented with digital portfolio initiatives in secondary education, integrating them into broader digital transformation agendas. Research in these contexts highlights gains in motivation, engagement, and reflective learning, yet also acknowledges challenges related to teacher workload, platform usability, and curricular alignment.

The European context presents a unique set of considerations, particularly due to regulatory frameworks concerning data protection and digital rights. The implementation of the General Data Protection Regulation (GDPR) has influenced how educational institutions manage, store, and safeguard student data, requiring explicit consent, transparency, and security measures. Scholars such as Lam (2023) argue that e-portfolios intersect with ethical and legal concerns in ways that demand interdisciplinary approaches, combining pedagogy, technology, and policy. Issues of privacy, ownership, and data portability become particularly salient in the design and institutional adoption of e-portfolio systems.

Digital inclusion constitutes another dimension of international discourse on digital assessment. UNESCO and OECD reports emphasize that digital transformation in education must address inequalities related to access, infrastructure, and digital literacy. The COVID-19 pandemic magnified these disparities by shifting learning online and exposing gaps in connectivity, device ownership, and teacher readiness. In this context, e-portfolios can serve as inclusive tools that enable multimodal expression and differentiated performance; however, they can also exacerbate inequities if technological access is uneven. Empirical research indicates that disadvantaged students may face disproportionate barriers in adopting digital assessment tools, raising critical questions about equity, justice, and educational opportunity.

The concept of digital competence has been formalized in European policy frameworks such as the Digital Education Action Plan (2021–2027), which underscores the importance of equipping students and teachers with the skills required for effective participation in digital societies. E-portfolios can contribute to the development of digital competence by requiring learners to curate, organize, communicate, and reflect upon digital artifacts. Moreover, competence-based learning frameworks emphasize transversal skills—critical thinking, creativity, collaboration—linked to workforce readiness and lifelong learning, aligning with the pedagogical affordances of e-portfolios.

Research also distinguishes between different types of portfolios, including learning portfolios, assessment portfolios, and showcase portfolios, each serving distinct purposes. Learning portfolios emphasize reflection and growth, assessment portfolios are designed for evaluation, and showcase portfolios highlight achievements. E-portfolios retain these distinctions but expand the multimodal possibilities of artifact creation and display. Digital platforms enable the integration of videos, images, hyperlinks, and text, facilitating richer and more authentic representations of learning.

Despite these advantages, teachers and scholars note that e-portfolio adoption requires substantial institutional support. Without adequate infrastructure, training, and curricular integration, e-portfolios risk remaining peripheral tools used irregularly or experimentally. Studies in Spain, Portugal, and Finland demonstrate that teacher attitudes and confidence significantly influence adoption rates, while systemic support and policy alignment play decisive roles in sustainability. In some cases, national digital strategies or innovation programs have facilitated wider adoption of digital assessment tools; however, such initiatives are uneven across Europe and globally, reflecting broader disparities in digital transformation.

The pedagogical rationale for e-portfolios is also grounded in socio-cultural models of learning which emphasize interaction, mediation, and the situated nature of knowledge. Vygotskian perspectives on learning highlight the role of tools and artifacts in cognitive development, suggesting that learning occurs through the active construction of meaning within social contexts. From this standpoint, e-portfolios may be interpreted not merely as repositories of student work but as mediating artifacts that facilitate communication, reflection, and co-construction of learning between students and teachers. This theoretical lens further aligns e-portfolios with collaborative learning models in which feedback and peer interaction play central roles.

From a psychological perspective, e-portfolios engage affective dimensions of learning by providing students with greater ownership of their learning processes. When students can select, curate, and justify artifacts for assessment, they are more likely to experience autonomy, competence, and relatedness—constructs associated with intrinsic motivation according to Self-Determination Theory. Empirical studies indicate that students who participate in portfolio assessment demonstrate increased motivation, deeper reflection, and a greater sense of identity as learners. These findings suggest that e-portfolios may support both cognitive and socio-emotional growth, which are increasingly recognized as integral to holistic education.

A growing body of literature also examines the role of reflection in e-portfolio implementation. Reflection is commonly conceptualized as an iterative cognitive process through which learners make sense of their experiences, evaluate their progress, and identify strategies for improvement. Within portfolio assessment, reflection is operationalized through journal entries, commentary on artifacts, or structured prompts guiding learners to articulate learning goals and evaluate their attainment. Scholars in the field argue that reflection is essential for transforming portfolios from collections of products into tools of metacognitive development. Barrett (2007) and subsequent researchers have emphasized that the pedagogical value of e-portfolios lies not in the artifacts themselves but in the reflective processes that accompany their selection and interpretation.

In addition to pedagogical perspectives, research from the fields of innovation adoption and educational change provides insights into the systemic factors that shape e-portfolio implementation. The diffusion of innovation theory suggests that new technologies are adopted when they align with users' needs, values, and expectations, and when they offer clear advantages relative to existing practices. In the case of e-portfolios, teachers' perceptions of relative advantage, compatibility with pedagogical goals, and complexity influence adoption decisions. Moreover, institutional support structures—such as leadership vision, professional development, and resource allocation—play decisive roles in sustaining innovation beyond initial pilot projects.

Comparative studies indicate that national policy frameworks and cultural norms influence how e-portfolios are conceptualized and operationalized. In some contexts, e-portfolios are primarily used for high-stakes assessment and certification, whereas in others they function as formative tools for reflection and self-regulation. The choice of approach often reflects broader educational philosophies and priorities concerning accountability, autonomy, and competence development. For example, countries with strong competence-based curricula may be more inclined to integrate e-portfolios as authentic assessment instruments, while countries with centralized examination systems may encounter greater resistance due to entrenched summative practices.

The European Union has articulated strategic priorities related to digital education through initiatives such as the Digital Education Action Plan (2021–2027), which emphasizes digital competence, innovation, and inclusion. These policy frameworks encourage member states to integrate digital tools into teaching, learning, and assessment and to support teachers in acquiring relevant competencies. E-portfolios can be situated within this policy landscape as instruments that promote learner autonomy, digital literacy, and competence-based evaluation, aligning with European agendas on lifelong learning and workforce readiness. However, the realization of these policy ambitions varies significantly across member states, reflecting disparities in funding, infrastructure, and institutional capacity.

Inclusion and equity constitute critical dimensions of digital assessment discourse. The Universal Design for Learning (UDL) framework, developed by the Center for Applied Special Technology (CAST), provides a conceptual foundation for designing inclusive learning environments that accommodate diverse learner needs (CAST, 2018). UDL principles advocate multiple means of representation, expression, and engagement, which resonate strongly with the multimodal affordances of e-portfolios. By enabling students to demonstrate knowledge and competencies through varied formats—textual, visual, oral, or multimedia—e-portfolios can support differentiated assessment practices. This alignment positions e-portfolios as potentially powerful tools for inclusive education, particularly for students with diverse learning profiles or linguistic backgrounds.

However, inclusion must be understood holistically, taking into consideration access, support, and policy frameworks. Digital divides represent a persistent obstacle to equitable participation in digital assessment activities. Students with limited access to devices, internet connectivity, or supportive learning environments may be disadvantaged in e-portfolio implementation. UNESCO reports underscore the importance of systemic interventions to address infrastructure gaps, provide assistive technologies, and ensure that digital transformation does not exacerbate existing inequalities. In this context, e-portfolios can contribute to inclusion only if equity considerations are embedded into implementation strategies.

Ethical considerations extend beyond inclusion to encompass data protection, privacy, and ownership. The GDPR establishes strict requirements regarding the collection, processing, and storage of personal data, including student artifacts in digital learning environments. Educational institutions must ensure that e-portfolio platforms adhere to privacy-by-design principles, offer transparency regarding data use, and secure informed consent from students and parents. Questions of data ownership and portability also arise, particularly in contexts where e-portfolios serve as long-term records of learning that students may wish to retain beyond their schooling years. These issues highlight the need for collaboration among educators, policymakers, and technology providers to establish ethical and sustainable digital assessment ecosystems.

Within the Greek context, digital transformation in education has been influenced by policy initiatives, national examinations, and socio-economic factors. While digital tools have been integrated into certain aspects of schooling, assessment practices remain predominantly summative and oriented towards certification. These conditions shape teachers' perceptions of e-portfolios, as they navigate tensions between innovative assessment approaches and traditional institutional demands. The limited institutional recognition of alternative assessment tools further constrains experimentation, despite teachers' positive attitudes toward digital learning technologies. This interplay of policy, culture, and infrastructure underscores the complexity of implementing e-portfolios at scale.

Taken together, the literature suggests that e-portfolios occupy an intersectional space between pedagogy, technology, policy, and inclusion. Their affordances cannot be reduced to technical features alone; instead, their educational value emerges from the pedagogical principles and institutional conditions that shape their use. This implies that successful implementation requires not only digital infrastructure and software but also pedagogical alignment, curricular coherence, teacher readiness, ethical governance, and policy support.

Teacher attitudes emerge as a critical factor in determining adoption and sustainability. Studies in European secondary education contexts indicate that teachers who possess strong digital literacy and positive beliefs about technology's pedagogical value are more likely to experiment with e-portfolios and integrate them into classroom practice. Conversely, teachers who perceive digital tools as burdensome, complex, or insufficiently supported by their institutions tend to avoid innovative assessment practices. Teacher beliefs thus operate as a mediating variable between technological affordances and pedagogical enactment.

Institutional culture and assessment regimes also influence adoption patterns. In systems characterized by high-stakes examinations and centralized curriculum control, innovation in assessment tends to be limited. Greece represents such a context, where national examinations exert strong influence over teaching and evaluation, shaping classroom practices towards summative assessment and content coverage. Under these conditions, alternative tools such as e-portfolios may be viewed as supplementary rather than integral components of learning and evaluation, even if teachers recognize their pedagogical value.

The literature also emphasizes the role of technological platforms and interoperability in shaping e-portfolio practices. Commercial and open-source e-portfolio platforms differ in their usability, privacy settings, integration with learning management systems, and archiving capabilities. Usability studies highlight that user-friendly interfaces, customizable templates, and efficient feedback mechanisms enhance student and teacher engagement. In contrast, platforms that impose rigid structures or require extensive technical knowledge may discourage adoption. Cross-platform integration is particularly relevant in secondary education, where teachers often use multiple tools for instruction, communication, and assessment.

Recent developments in artificial intelligence and learning analytics are generating new discourse around digital assessment and e-portfolios. Learning analytics can provide students and teachers with visualizations of progress, patterns of engagement, and performance metrics, potentially enhancing reflection and feedback. However, these technologies introduce additional ethical considerations concerning data privacy, algorithmic transparency, and consent. Scholars warn against reductive datafication of learning and emphasize the need for critical frameworks to evaluate the epistemic assumptions underlying digital analytics. Although AI-enabled e-portfolios remain emergent in K–12 education, their potential raises important questions for future research and policy.

Finally, e-portfolios must be situated within broader conversations about the purpose of assessment in schooling. Contemporary debates increasingly challenge the notion that assessment should merely certify learning outcomes. Instead, assessment is framed as an integral element of learning, emphasizing process, reflection, and self-regulation. E-portfolios align with this reconceptualization by enabling students to document and narrate learning trajectories over time. Such practices foster metacognitive awareness, which is fundamental to lifelong learning. They also encourage constructive dialogue between teachers and learners, positioning assessment as a collaborative practice rather than a unidirectional judgment.

MAIN FOCUS OF THE CHAPTER

Issues, Controversies, Problems

Assessment practices in secondary education must address the diversity of students' cultural, linguistic, socio-economic, and developmental characteristics. A central controversy concerns whether assessment should primarily serve selection and certification purposes or whether it should support learning, inclusion, and personal development. Traditional practices in Greece and internationally continue to emphasize standardized examinations that prioritize summative judgments over formative feedback, thereby generating competition, anxiety, and score-oriented behaviors rather than reflection, collaboration, or lifelong learning dispositions.

The integration of digital tools into school assessment processes introduces both opportunities and challenges. On one hand, e-portfolios can support more authentic and process-oriented evaluation, enabling students to document learning trajectories, demonstrate competencies through multimodal artefacts, and engage in self-evaluation. On the other hand, the implementation of e-portfolios raises concerns regarding workload, digital infrastructures, teacher training, curriculum alignment, and institutional recognition of alternative assessment modes.

In the Greek context, teachers reported that digital tools are increasingly present in classroom environments; however, their pedagogical use remains uneven due to infrastructural deficiencies, insufficient support for ICT integration, and the absence of systematic digital assessment policies. High-stakes examinations at the national level further constrain innovation in school assessment, reinforcing summative traditions and limiting the uptake of formative alternatives such as e-portfolios.

Teachers' perceptions thus illuminate a tension between educational aspirations for more inclusive, personalized, and competence-based assessment and the structural constraints of the existing system. This tension constitutes the central focus of the present chapter.

Uses of E-Portfolios

Previous studies classify e-portfolios into different functional categories, including assessment, presentation, and development portfolios (Buzzetto, 2010). In practice, e-portfolios may be used:

- by students to demonstrate knowledge, skills, and behaviours for academic or professional purposes;
- by teachers as tools for formative and summative assessment;
- by educational institutions to support accreditation processes and quality assurance;
- for self-evaluation, reflection, documentation, and instructional feedback; and
- in distance learning environments to organize content and support asynchronous communication.

Such versatility distinguishes e-portfolios from traditional assessment tools, enabling educators to capture not only learning outcomes but also learning processes and metacognitive growth over time.

Challenges and Barriers

Despite reported advantages, teachers identified several limitations associated with e-portfolio implementation:

- digital competence gaps among teachers and students;
- limited infrastructure (hardware, connectivity, software);
- time constraints for design, feedback, and maintenance;
- insufficient institutional support;
- lack of curricular integration; and
- uncertainty concerning assessment criteria and validation procedures.

From a broader digital ethics perspective, issues of privacy, data ownership, consent, and GDPR compliance were also highlighted as essential considerations in European educational settings. Furthermore, teachers noted concerns about student equity and digital divides, stressing that technological resources and support are not uniformly distributed across learners.

METHODOLOGY

Research Design

A qualitative research design was adopted to investigate teachers' perceptions of e-portfolios as an alternative assessment tool in secondary education. Qualitative approaches enable researchers to explore participants' experiences, beliefs, and interpretations in depth, while preserving the contextual complexity surrounding educational practices (Fossey et al., 2002; Pathak et al., 2013). Semi-structured interviews were selected as the primary method of data collection, as they provide an optimal balance between comparability across participants and flexibility to explore emerging themes.

Participants

The study involved fourteen (n=14) secondary school teachers, selected based on their familiarity with educational technologies and their willingness to participate. Participants differed in age, teaching experience, employment status, qualifications, and prior exposure to ICT. Ten participants were women (71%) and four were men (29%). Three age groups were represented: 20–29 years (21%), 30–39 years (50%), and 40–49 years (29%). Six participants (43%) held postgraduate degrees in fields such as information systems, special education, and teaching, whereas nine (64%) reported previous training related to educational technologies. This diversity was considered a strength, as it enriched the variability of perspectives captured in the study.

Data Collection

Semi-structured interviews were conducted through online platforms (Google Meet and Skype), facilitating participation and ensuring data continuity during remote communication. A pilot interview was conducted to refine the protocol and verify the clarity and flow of the questions. Participants received information regarding the purpose, procedures, and ethical considerations of the study, including anonymity and confidentiality. Informed consent was obtained prior to participation. Interview duration ranged from 15 to 25 minutes, depending on the participant's familiarity with the topic and willingness to elaborate.

Ethical Considerations

The research adhered to standard ethical guidelines for qualitative research. Participants provided informed consent and were assured that no identifying information would be disclosed. In line with European data protection principles, care was taken to anonymize responses during transcription and analysis. Issues related to privacy, data storage, and GDPR compliance were addressed, reflecting broader ethical and legal concerns in digital assessment environments.

Data Analysis

Interviews were video recorded, transcribed verbatim, and analyzed using thematic content analysis. Transcripts were read multiple times to identify recurring patterns and thematic categories. Responses were organized around thematic axes corresponding to the research questions and conceptual framework. Preliminary codes were grouped into broader themes, for example: (a) perceptions of technology and digital learning tools; (b) perceptions of current assessment practices; (c) advantages and disadvantages of e-portfolios; (d) institutional and infrastructural constraints; and (e) future intentions and recommendations. For visualization purposes, descriptive categorizations and simple frequency counts were supported using spreadsheet software.

Validity, Credibility, and Reflexivity

To enhance credibility, the research incorporated the following validation strategies:

- Pilot testing of interview protocol;
- Triangulation of sources via participant diversity;
- Peer debriefing during instrument design;
- Systematic thematic analysis; and
- Reflexive review to minimize researcher bias.

Acknowledging the interpretive nature of qualitative inquiry, reflexivity was maintained throughout the process. The researcher recognized potential biases related to personal assumptions, experience with technology, and expectations about educational innovation. Such transparency strengthens the methodological rigor and interpretive trustworthiness of the findings.

RESULTS AND FINDINGS

Findings from the semi-structured interviews were organized into three main thematic categories: (1) teachers' perceptions of educational technology, (2) views on existing assessment practices and alternative methods, and (3) e-portfolios as a tool for student evaluation. Within each theme, sub-categories emerged relating to perceived benefits, challenges, institutional conditions, and future intentions.

Perceptions of Educational Technology

All participants reported regular engagement with digital tools in their professional or personal lives, albeit at varying levels of frequency and competence. Teachers highlighted the pedagogical value of technology in enhancing visualization, promoting interaction, and facilitating communication. Reported advantages included improved lesson preparation, better organization of instructional materials, and increased student participation.

However, teachers also noted systemic challenges, primarily related to infrastructural deficiencies in Greek schools. These included outdated equipment, limited internet connectivity, insufficient laboratory spaces for science subjects, and the financial burden associated with software and technological upgrades. A minority of teachers expressed concerns regarding their own digital competence, although younger participants reported fewer difficulties, suggesting an age-related gradient in confidence and familiarity with ICT.

Perceptions of Current Assessment Practices

When reflecting on existing assessment methods, teachers described the current system as predominantly summative, emphasizing grades, examinations, and performance-based comparisons. The majority of participants considered this approach stressful for students and insufficiently aligned with contemporary learning objectives. Challenges included limited time for individualized feedback, disparities in students' levels of prior knowledge, and the large number of students per classroom, which constrained opportunities for continuous evaluation.

Despite these limitations, teachers acknowledged that traditional assessment provides standardized, certifiable outcomes that remain institutionally recognized. As such, participants framed alternative assessment as complementary rather than substitutive. Tools such as descriptive evaluation, projects, experiments, and digital platforms (e.g., e-me, e-class) were mentioned as viable supplements to traditional tests, especially for formative purposes.

Advantages of Using E-Portfolios

Teachers familiar with e-portfolios identified multiple pedagogical and affective benefits. These included reduced student anxiety, enhanced collaboration, improved self-evaluation, long-term documentation of learning, and opportunities for personalized feedback. E-portfolios were perceived as promoting a more holistic understanding of students' competencies beyond test scores, aligning with student-centered pedagogies and competence-based curricula.

Participants also emphasized the value of e-portfolios for communication with parents and teachers, who can monitor progress and view students' artefacts over time. Several teachers highlighted the potential role of e-portfolios in facilitating smoother transitions between educational stages, given their archival and reflective functions.

Barriers to Implementation

Despite the reported benefits, significant barriers emerged. Time constraints were identified as the most pressing challenge, as designing, maintaining, and evaluating e-portfolios requires sustained effort. Institutional support was considered insufficient, with limited training opportunities and minimal curricular integration. Participants also referred to digital equity issues, noting that not all students possess adequate devices or stable internet access, potentially reinforcing existing inequalities.

In addition, teachers expressed concerns regarding data security, privacy, and compliance with GDPR. These considerations were particularly salient in the Greek context due to the lack of standardized digital infrastructures at the school level and the absence of explicit national policies governing digital assessment tools.

Use vs. Non-Use Patterns

A clear distinction emerged between teachers who had prior experience with e-portfolios and those who had not. Experienced users framed e-portfolios as pedagogically meaningful and expressed willingness to continue using them in the future. By contrast, non-users cited lack of familiarity, perceived complexity, and insufficient institutional incentives as deterrents. Notably, non-users did not dismiss the pedagogical value of e-portfolios; rather, they highlighted structural obstacles and the need for professional development.

Influence of Demographic Factors

Demographic variables interacted with teachers' perceptions in nuanced ways. Younger teachers and those with postgraduate qualifications in areas related to ICT or education expressed higher levels of confidence and stronger advocacy for digital assessment tools. Conversely, older teachers and those without technological training tended to report greater uncertainty, despite acknowledging potential benefits. Employment status did not appear to significantly influence perceptions, although part-time or substitute teachers reported fewer opportunities for experimentation due to workload and classroom continuity constraints.

Future Intentions

Most participants expressed openness to integrating e-portfolios in the future, provided that adequate training, time, and technical support are offered. Teachers emphasized that innovation in assessment requires systemic rather than individual efforts and should be accompanied by curricular reform, infrastructural investment, and explicit institutional recognition of alternative evaluation methods.

DISCUSSION AND IMPLICATIONS

The findings of this study suggest that teachers perceive e-portfolios as a pedagogically meaningful and potentially transformative alternative to traditional assessment practices. In line with international literature (Andrade & Valtcheva, 2009; Barrett, 2007), the results highlight e-portfolios' capacity to foster reflective learning, provide authentic evidence of student competencies, and support formative feedback processes. Participants viewed e-portfolios not merely as artifacts for documenting achievement but as tools capable of promoting autonomy, collaboration, and self-evaluation—competencies endorsed by contemporary educational frameworks and EU policy agendas related to lifelong learning and digital competence.

The reported benefits also resonate with broader critiques of summative evaluation in secondary education. Traditional grading practices, while institutionally entrenched and socially legitimized, were perceived as insufficiently sensitive to individual learning trajectories and as contributors to student anxiety and competition. E-portfolios, by contrast, were associated with reduced performance stress and enhanced learner engagement. Such perceptions are consistent with scholarship emphasizing the motivational advantages of formative and process-oriented assessment, particularly in relation to student agency and metacognition (Bryant & Chittum, 2013).

However, the findings also underscore significant structural and systemic barriers that constrain the integration of e-portfolios in Greek secondary education. These include limitations in digital infrastructure, insufficient professional development opportunities for teachers, and ambiguous curricular expectations regarding alternative assessment tools. These barriers mirror international concerns that successful implementation of digital assessment tools requires alignment across pedagogical, organizational, and policy levels (Deneen & Shroff, 2014; Lam, 2023). In this study, teachers consistently emphasized that innovation in assessment cannot be sustained through individual initiatives alone but must be embedded within broader institutional frameworks.

Issues of digital equity, privacy, and GDPR compliance emerged as particularly salient in European educational contexts. Teachers' concerns regarding data security, ownership, and consent reflect ethical debates surrounding digital assessment and highlight the need for clear governance mechanisms. Moreover, access disparities among students raise important considerations for inclusion. While e-portfolios can democratize assessment by enabling multimodal expression and differentiated performance, they may simultaneously exacerbate inequalities if technological resources and support are unevenly distributed. These findings point to the necessity of policy interventions to ensure equitable implementation.

Implications for practice include the need to reconceptualize teacher professional development as a collaborative and reflexive process that encourages experimentation with digital assessment tools. Participants articulated a desire for more structured training in both the technical and pedagogical dimensions of e-portfolio use. At the curricular level, assessment policies should provide clearer guidance on how e-portfolios can complement summative evaluation, while institutions should establish infrastructures and recognition mechanisms that legitimize alternative assessment methods.

Finally, the study contributes to ongoing academic debates regarding the future of assessment in secondary education. It positions e-portfolios not merely as technological artifacts but as instruments capable of supporting broader shifts towards competence-based, inclusive, and student-centered learning. The implications are therefore multi-level, extending across classrooms, schools, and policy systems.

The findings indicate strong alignment with literature emphasizing the formative and reflective functions of e-portfolios. Teachers in this study consistently highlighted reduced anxiety, increased engagement, and enhanced self-evaluation as benefits for students. These perceptions resonate with scholarship arguing that e-portfolios promote autonomy, metacognition, and self-regulation, which are central to constructivist theories of learning. Andrade and Valtcheva (2009) demonstrate that self-assessment facilitates cognitive engagement and performance improvement, while Bryant and Chittum (2013) synthesize evidence supporting e-portfolios' motivational and reflective value.

The present study also corroborates findings from international research showing that e-portfolios foster communication among teachers, students, and parents. Participants noted that portfolio artifacts allow parents to monitor learning outcomes and observe progress over time, facilitating more informed dialogue about student learning. Gibson and Barrett (2003) similarly identify communication and documentation as core affordances of e-portfolios. This communicative function aligns with broader shifts toward learner-centered pedagogies and transparency in assessment.

Despite these advantages, teachers emphasized systemic barriers that constrain adoption. These barriers—insufficient training, limited infrastructure, and the dominance of summative practices—mirror challenges identified in other European contexts. Deneen and Shroff (2014) argue that institutional conditions and teacher beliefs jointly shape innovation sustainability in digital assessment. The present findings suggest that without coherent institutional frameworks, e-portfolios risk becoming optional add-ons rather than embedded assessment practices. Teachers expressed willingness to adopt e-portfolios but stressed that innovation requires support beyond individual initiative.

A key contribution of this study lies in highlighting the tension between formative and summative assessment cultures in secondary education. Participants characterized summative assessments as unavoidable due to national examination systems that determine academic progression and university admission. This tension is not unique to Greece; comparative research in countries with centralized examinations reveals similar constraints on assessment innovation. Nonetheless, the teachers' expressed desire for more holistic evaluation aligns with international calls to integrate formative assessment into secondary education. E-portfolios could represent a bridge between these paradigms by complementing summative measures with qualitative evidence of learning.

Moreover, teachers recognized that e-portfolios could contribute to the development of digital competence, a priority articulated in European policy frameworks. The ability to curate, reflect upon, and present digital artifacts represents a transversal skill with relevance beyond schooling. The study findings thus support policy arguments linking assessment reform to digital transformation and competence-based education. However, these potential contributions remain unrealized without systemic commitment and curricular alignment.

The study also reveals nuanced differentiation in perceptions across demographic variables. Younger teachers and those with postgraduate training in ICT or education exhibited stronger advocacy for e-portfolios. This suggests that digital competence and pedagogical confidence influence perceived feasibility and value. Such patterns are consistent with research identifying teacher digital literacy as a predictor of digital innovation adoption. Conversely, older teachers reported uncertainty, although they did not dismiss the pedagogical benefits of e-portfolios. This finding supports targeted professional development strategies that address heterogeneous competence profiles within teaching staff.

Finally, inclusion and equity emerged as cross-cutting themes. Teachers acknowledged that students possess uneven access to devices, connectivity, and supportive learning environments. These disparities raise ethical concerns about fairness in digital assessment. While e-portfolios can support inclusive practices through multimodal assessment, they may also exacerbate inequities if material and infrastructural barriers remain unaddressed. This dual potential reflects broader debates about digital transformation in education and underscores the importance of policy interventions that mitigate digital divides.

The findings of this study also contribute to theoretical debates surrounding the epistemic functions of reflection in assessment. Reflection has been theorized as a transformative process that enables learners to externalize knowledge, negotiate meaning, and articulate their evolving understanding of concepts. Within e-portfolio environments, reflection operationalizes metacognition through written commentary, artifact selection, and narrative justification. Such reflective processes support the internalization of learning goals and performance criteria, aligning with competence-based models of assessment in which the demonstration of understanding is prioritized over the reproduction of content.

Moreover, e-portfolios allow for pluralistic representations of learning, challenging the assumption that academic achievement must be reduced to numerical scores or standardized outputs. By integrating multimodal artifacts—textual, visual, audio, and multimedia—e-portfolios expand the semiotic resources available to students and enable differentiated pathways for demonstrating knowledge. This resonates with UDL principles, which emphasize the importance of multiple means of representation and expression. Through this lens, e-portfolios not only assess learning but also democratize visibility in the classroom, allowing students with diverse profiles to showcase strengths that may remain invisible in traditional examinations.

The study's findings also invite consideration of the cultural dimensions of assessment. In educational systems where examinations are deeply embedded in societal expectations and institutional routines, reform in assessment practices encounters cultural resistance. The reluctance to depart from established norms may be rooted not in pedagogical disagreement but in broader socio-political concerns regarding accountability, meritocracy, and selection. In the Greek context, high-stakes examinations serve multiple purposes—certification, ranking, and access to higher education—thereby consolidating their legitimacy. Teachers' hesitations to adopt alternative assessment tools can therefore be interpreted as expressions of systemic alignment rather than pedagogical conservatism.

Comparative analyses highlight that countries with decentralized curricula and school-level autonomy exhibit greater flexibility in assessment innovation. In such contexts, portfolios and e-portfolios have been adopted as mechanisms for documenting competence and supporting personalized learning trajectories. By contrast, countries with centralized examinations face structural obstacles that limit experimentation. These comparative observations underscore the need to situate e-portfolio adoption within broader governance and policy structures rather than reducing it to teacher choice or technological capability.

In addition, the findings reveal important policy implications concerning digital transformation agendas in education. The European Union and international organizations such as UNESCO and OECD have called for assessment systems that reflect the complexity of learning in contemporary societies and that prepare students for a dynamic labor market. Competencies such as collaboration, creativity, communication, and digital literacy are difficult to capture through traditional examinations. E-portfolios offer means to document these transversal competencies through authentic tasks and real-world artifacts. This alignment between e-portfolios and policy objectives strengthens the argument for their integration into secondary education.

However, policy aspirations alone are insufficient to generate change. Without operational frameworks for implementation—curricular guidelines, institutional support, teacher training, and infrastructure—the adoption of e-portfolios remains aspirational. The findings from this study suggest that teachers recognize the alignment between e-portfolios and educational goals but require systemic support to enact innovation. This indicates that assessment reform must be understood as a multi-level process involving classrooms, schools, ministries, and international actors. Such multi-level complexity is typical of digital transformation in education, which intersects with technological capacity, pedagogical knowledge, and governance systems.

Finally, the study contributes to methodological discussions about how qualitative research can illuminate the subtle dynamics influencing assessment innovation. Teacher perceptions offer insight into both the affordances and constraints of digital assessment tools. Qualitative methodologies are particularly well-suited for examining the subjective, interpretive, and socio-cultural dimensions of educational change. By capturing teachers' experiences and reflections, qualitative research can inform policy and practice in ways that quantitative analyses may overlook. This underscores the importance of mixed-methods approaches in future research, which could triangulate teacher perceptions with student perspectives, policy documents, and learning outcomes.

When interpreted through a policy lens, the findings point toward the need for coordinated efforts to modernize assessment in secondary education. Digital transformation strategies must integrate assessment reform, recognizing that tools such as e-portfolios can serve as levers for broader pedagogical change. The alignment between e-portfolios and competence-based education suggests that ministries and educational authorities should provide clearer curricular and assessment frameworks that legitimize alternative evaluation methods. Similarly, investments in digital infrastructure and teacher training are essential for ensuring that implementation does not exacerbate inequalities or generate new forms of exclusion.

International frameworks such as the European Commission's Digital Education Action Plan and UNESCO's guidelines on inclusive digital learning emphasize the importance of equitable access, ethical governance, and digital competence. The study's findings support these priorities and suggest that e-portfolio adoption could contribute to the attainment of these goals if embedded within comprehensive implementation strategies. However, the barriers identified by teachers indicate that current conditions are insufficient to sustain innovation. Policy interventions must therefore address both material and cultural dimensions of assessment reform, supporting teachers as agents of change and ensuring that institutional environments facilitate rather than impede pedagogical experimentation.

This chapter contributes to ongoing academic debates on assessment innovation by illustrating how e-portfolios can serve as formative and reflective tools within secondary education. At a theoretical level, the chapter advances the understanding of how digital portfolio practices align with constructivist and competence-based learning frameworks, emphasizing the role of reflection, self-regulation, and multimodal knowledge representation. At a pedagogical level, the findings highlight teachers' perceptions of the practical benefits and barriers of e-portfolios, offering insights into how classroom practices can evolve toward more student-centered and inclusive assessment approaches. At a policy and system level, the chapter underscores the importance of aligning assessment reform with digital transformation agendas, infrastructure development, and professional development frameworks. Together, these contributions support the argument that e-portfolios can complement traditional assessment and foster more holistic, equitable, and future-oriented evaluation practices.

SOLUTIONS AND RECOMMENDATIONS

Based on the findings and supporting literature, several recommendations can be formulated to enhance the integration of e-portfolios in secondary education:

Pedagogical Integration and Curriculum Alignment. The effective use of e-portfolios requires explicit curricular embedding. Clear guidelines regarding assessment criteria, learning objectives, and expected artefact types should be provided to ensure coherence and consistency across subjects and grade levels. Curricular alignment would also facilitate institutional recognition of e-portfolios as legitimate assessment instruments rather than supplementary activities.

Teacher Training and Professional Development. Professional development initiatives should address both technical skills and pedagogical approaches related to digital and alternative assessment. Training should emphasize student-centered learning, formative assessment, feedback strategies, and reflective practices. Collaborative learning communities can support sustained knowledge exchange among teachers.

Institutional Support and Infrastructure. Adequate infrastructure—hardware, connectivity, software platforms, and technical support—is essential for widespread adoption. Schools require stable digital environments that respect privacy, data protection, and interoperability standards. Without such conditions, e-portfolios remain dependent on individual teachers' voluntary efforts.

Student Empowerment and Digital Competence. Students should be introduced to e-portfolios as tools for reflection, self-regulation, and documentation of learning trajectories. Instructional scaffolding should support the development of digital literacy, organizational strategies, and metacognitive skills, enabling students to assume ownership of their learning artifacts.

Equity and Inclusion Considerations. Policies must address digital divides that disproportionately affect learners with fewer resources, special educational needs, or limited access to technological devices. Inclusive implementation strategies may include device provision, accessible platform design, and differentiated support mechanisms.

Data Security, Privacy, and GDPR Compliance. Schools and educational authorities should develop explicit guidelines for managing digital assessment data. Compliance with GDPR, data encryption, parental consent, and ownership of artifacts must be clarified to build trust among stakeholders and safeguard sensitive information.

Communication and Stakeholder Engagement. Transparent communication among students, teachers, parents, and administrators can strengthen shared understanding of e-portfolios' role, benefits, and evaluation processes. Engagement enhances acceptance and contributes to sustainable implementation.

FUTURE RESEARCH DIRECTIONS

Future research could explore several areas identified in this study:

- **Longitudinal studies** examining how e-portfolios shape student learning, self-regulation, and motivation over extended periods.
- **Comparative analyses** between schools or educational systems with different infrastructural and policy contexts.
- **Experimental or quasi-experimental designs** investigating the impact of e-portfolios on academic performance relative to traditional assessment methods.
- **Equity-focused research** on access barriers for students with limited technological resources or special educational needs.

- **Policy-oriented studies** assessing how national frameworks and digital transformation agendas influence adoption and sustainability.
- **Design-based research** testing platform usability, interoperability, and features supporting multimodal reflection and feedback.

These directions highlight the need for multi-level, interdisciplinary approaches that bridge pedagogy, technology, and policy.

CONCLUSION

The chapter examined secondary school teachers' perceptions of e-portfolios as an alternative method of assessment in Greece. The findings reveal a predominantly positive stance towards digital assessment tools and highlight e-portfolios' potential to reduce student anxiety, promote collaboration, support self-evaluation, and enable holistic documentation of learning. Nevertheless, systemic barriers—particularly infrastructural limitations, insufficient training, and the dominance of summative assessment cultures—pose challenges for widespread implementation.

The study contributes to international debates on assessment innovation by illustrating the conditions under which e-portfolios could complement traditional practices in secondary education. It argues that policy reform, institutional support, and professional development are necessary to align assessment with contemporary educational goals, especially in relation to digital competence, inclusion, and learner-centered pedagogies. With appropriate support, e-portfolios may serve as catalysts for transforming assessment cultures towards greater transparency, reflection, and equity.

REFERENCES

Andrade, H. L., & Valtcheva, A. (2009). Promoting learning and achievement through self-assessment. *Theory into Practice*, *48*(1), 12–19. DOI: 10.1080/00405840802577544

Barrett, H. (2007). Researching electronic portfolios and learner engagement: The REFLECT Initiative. *Journal of Adolescent & Adult Literacy*, *50*(6), 436–449. DOI: 10.1598/JAAL.50.6.2

Berrill, D., & Addison, E. (2010). 'Professional learning portfolios' for teachers: A site for understanding, improving practice and leadership. *Professional Development in Education*, *36*(4), 639–665.

Bryant, L. H., & Chittum, J. R. (2013). E-portfolio effectiveness: A broad synthesis of research findings. *International Journal of E-Portfolio*, *3*(2), 111–131.

Buzzetto, M. (2010). Assessing the efficacy and effectiveness of an e-portfolio used for summative assessment. *Interdisciplinary Journal of E-Learning and Learning Objects*, *6*, 61–85.

CAST. (2018). *Universal Design for Learning guidelines version 2.2*. CAST.

Davis, M. H., & Ponnamperuma, G. G. (2005). Portfolio assessment. *Journal of Veterinary Medical Education*, *32*(3), 279–284. DOI: 10.3138/jvme.32.3.279 PMID: 16261482

Deneen, C., & Shroff, R. H. (2014). Empowering students through e-portfolio assessment: Interrelationships among feedback, self-regulated learning and e-portfolio use. *Assessment & Evaluation in Higher Education*, *39*(7), 1–17.

Fossey, E., Harvey, C., McDermott, F., & Davidson, L. (2002). Understanding and evaluating qualitative research. *The Australian and New Zealand Journal of Psychiatry*, *36*(6), 717–732. DOI: 10.1046/j.1440-1614.2002.01100.x PMID: 12406114

Gibson, D., & Barrett, H. (2003). Directions in electronic portfolio development. *Canadian Journal of Learning and Technology*, *31*(3), 1–15.

Hallam, G., & Creagh, T. (2010). E-portfolios for the trades: Can they work? *Education + Training*, *52*(6/7), 500–513.

Lam, B. H. (2023). E-portfolios, assessment and data ethics in higher education. *Assessment & Evaluation in Higher Education*, *48*(3), 1–16.

Lorenzo, G., & Ittelson, J. (2005). *An overview of e-portfolios*. Educause Learning Initiative.

OECD. (2020). *Digital education outlook 2020: Delivering digital skills*. OECD Publishing.

Pathak, V., Jena, B., & Kalra, S. (2013). Qualitative research. *Perspectives in Clinical Research*, *4*(3), 192–197. DOI: 10.4103/2229-3485.115389 PMID: 24010063

Polyzos, N. (2007). *Assessment in contemporary school settings*. Grigoris Publications. [In Greek]

UNESCO. (2022). *Reimagining our futures together: A new social contract for education*. UNESCO Publishing.

Zimmerman, B. J. (2002). Becoming a self-regulated learner: An overview. *Theory into Practice*, *41*(2), 64–70. DOI: 10.1207/s15430421tip4102_2

KEY TERMS AND DEFINITIONS

Alternative Assessment: Evaluation practices emphasizing qualitative, formative, and process-oriented approaches rather than summative grading.

Assessment: A process of collecting and interpreting evidence of learning for decision-making regarding student performance.

Digital Literacy: Competencies enabling effective and responsible use of digital tools for communication, learning, and problem-solving.

E-Portfolio: A digital collection of artifacts documenting learning, skills, reflection, and achievement over time.

Formative Assessment: Assessment designed to support learning through feedback, revision, and ongoing improvement.

GDPR Compliance: Adherence to European regulatory requirements related to privacy, data ownership, and personal data protection.

Reflection: A metacognitive process through which learners evaluate their experiences and performance to guide improvement.

Self-Evaluation: Learners' ability to assess their own progress, strengths, and weaknesses based on specified criteria.

Summative Assessment: Evaluation conducted at the end of a learning period to certify performance, typically associated with grading or certification.

Chapter 9
Innovative Educational Experiences:
Exploring the Benefits of STEM Education

Stavroula Lada
http://orcid.org/0000-0002-6666-8711
University of Alicante, Spain

ABSTRACT

STEM education, involving science, technology, engineering, and mathematics, is the pilar of modern educational initiatives. This chapter includes quantitative research related to the impact of STEM approach on students' performance, carried out among educators in Europe. The main research question is: How does STEM education shape students' achievements? Moreover, it measures educators' points of view of the challenges they meet while implementing STEM disciplines. According to the analysis of the data, the results of STEM implementation are not only academic. The researcher monitors educators' observations, and remarks on skills that are developed, which help students become problem-solvers, innovators, and pioneers who overcome the challenges of the contemporary world. The investigation is important for decision-making because it enables teachers, and education policymakers to form curriculums that meet the current requirements.

INTRODUCTION

STEM education (Science, Technology, Engineering, and Mathematics) education is indicated as a pillar of current curricula, showing the progressing demands of a rapid-changing world. As industries progressively add greater value on tech-

DOI: 10.4018/979-8-2600-1568-1.ch009

nological creativity, and cross-disciplinary problem-solving skills, schools, and educators are assigned to equip learners to succeed in STEM fields. The increasing universal attention on STEM education is not simply due to academic tendencies but an important action to address workforce shortage in STEM field professions, world-wide challenges, and the needs of a progressively interconnected society (Molina-Ascanio et al., 2023). According to the National Science Foundation (2024), in the near future millions of positions may likely be unclaimed because of deficiency of qualified professionals. This implies the urgency of preparing, and equipping future generations with relevant competences, and knowledge which are acquired in STEM areas of study.

However, in STEM education special challenges in implementation broadly feature, especially from the viewpoint of educators. As agents of instruction, they contribute critically in forming the effectiveness of STEM curricula. Educators' opinion holds a pivotal role in students' engagement, their academic success, and their focus on future STEM domains. Nonetheless, educators often face challenges like shortage of supplies, lack of time due to outdated curricula, and professional development opportunities deficiency.

The focus of this research is to concentrate on educators' perspectives, beliefs, and experiences on STEM approach. By investigating their attitudes, this study points at clarifying the practical challenges they face, and the techniques they utilize to overcome them. In addition, this research aims to determine ways to aid educators in their initiatives to enhance STEM teaching, whether through professional development activities, allocation of assets, or curriculum restructure.

The outcomes of this research offer the possibility to communicate policy decisions and educational approaches which encourage efficient STEM education. Through hearing the voices of teachers, this research encourages a greater understanding of how to enhance STEM education and implement it to benefit learners, teachers, and society as a whole. Since the need for STEM knowledge does not abate, constructing teachers to provide quality STEM education will be essential to resolving workforce requirements, and driving innovation.

BACKGROUND

Educators' view-points and attitudes of STEM instruction impact on academic performance are investigated in previous studies. Still, the findings vary in relation to national curricula, educational levels (primary or secondary), and research methods. Margot and Kettler (2019) found that educators refer to the multiple benefits of STEM education, but encounter considerable challenges, including teaching-related obstacles, systemic setbacks, and shortage of assistance. Tunc &

Bagceci in their research in 2021 mention that the collaboration between educators, effective professional development, and updated curricula are pillars for enhancing the implementation of STEM education. Moreover, according to the outcomes of the same analysis, educators underlined the substantial effect of STEM activities on students, particularly in developing 21st-century skills, like the 4 c's (collaboration, creativity, communication, and critical thinking). However, educators encountered setbacks in implementing STEM approach, including limited means, insufficient infrastructure, and lack of management assistance. Despite these barriers, teachers acknowledged STEM education's capability to improve student skills, knowledge, and overall learning experiences. Another research (Bal & Bedir, 2021) aimed to interpret the perspectives of four educators who are trained and use STEM disciplines in science and math lessons. The research was based in semi-structured interviews. The findings outlined the enhancement in skills in science, math, engineering, and technology. They stated that there was positive academic performance, the students' self-esteem was elevated, and the lesson was mentioned as more pleasant and engaging. Moreover, according to the data, hands-on activities improved students' knowledge and skills. However, the educators faced setbacks, like classrooms with shortage of supplies and lack of institutional support.

For Papagiannopoulou and Vaiopoulou (2024), in their research about teachers' attitudes towards STEM education, they explored the role of their readiness. According to the outcomes, educators who in general have a positive attitude towards teaching, have also a positive opinion on STEM instruction. Their beliefs are mostly affected by their knowledge and skills, that means, by their cognitive readiness, as well as by their emotions and feelings (emotional readiness). Another element that effects their beliefs is the teachers' devotion on STEM and their self-image and self-effectiveness. Moreover, in case educators are in state of being well aware of what STEM is and how they can teach based on this philosophy, their attitude becomes more favorable than the one of those who do not understand the foundation of STEM principles. In other words, self-efficacy and self-confidence play a crucial role on the ways of adopting STEM approach in educators' teaching.

In another research, STEM curricula affected in a positive way academic achievements, in comparison to conventional teaching. According to this meta-analysis, learners excelled, mainly due to the combination of STEM approach and inquiry-based learning. These findings offer useful recommendations for enhancing STEM educational disciplines and boosting student performance.

Drawing from the literature review, the opinions of educators related to how STEM instruction can be effectively implemented at school converge on a variety of factors. Continuous professional development, on-going training sessions seminars and instructional improvement initiatives are key factors for enforcing educators' ability to enhance STEM strategies' integration (Papagiannopoulou & Vaiopoulou,

2024; Margot & Kettler, 2019; Shahali & Halim, 2024; Nadelson & Seifert, 2017; El-Deghaidy, Mansour, Alzaghal & Alhammad, 2021). Another factor that influences educators' views is support, resources, instructional materials, educational assets and guidance (Kelley & Knowles, 2016; Honey et al., 2014; English, 2016; Becker & Park, 2011; Wang, Moore, Roehrig & Park, 2011; Park, Byun & Sim, 2020). Some researchers propose the reduction of non-instructional duties to allow time for STEM lesson planning, minimize educators' extracurricular responsibilities and alleviate teachers' administrative and non-teaching tasks to support effective STEM curriculum development (Papagiannopoulou & Vaiopoulou, 2024; Dare, Ellis & Roehrig, 2018; Thibaut, Ceuppens, De Loof et al., 2018; Vaiopoulou, Papagiannopoulou & Stamovlasis, 2023).

The current research monitors viewpoints of European educators regarding STEM's role in academic success and in improvement of 21st century skills. The study focuses in a holistic perspective of the ways STEM education influences both short-term learning outcomes and future accomplishments. It also takes into account the attitudes of educators who implement STEM practices as experts, since the majority of the participants are members of Scientix community.

METHODOLOGY OF THE RESEARCH

This research utilizes a quantitative survey study approach to investigate educators' views on STEM education, its influence on learners, and the barriers encountered in implementing STEM-related activities. 144 educators took part in the survey, by diverse countries. Almost half of the sample consisted of Scientix ambassadors—participants of the European STEM education network—whose competence added valuable insight to the results.

Quantitative research is widely implemented in educational science. It helps researchers to investigate and study phenomena and measure elements in an objective way (Ary, Jacobs, Irvine & Walker, 2018; Cohen, Manion & Morrison, 2018; Johnson & Christensen, 2017; Lodico, Spaulding & Voegtle, 2019). Quantitative research collects numeric data which are analyzed statistically. A common tool of collecting data is the questionnaire (Holmes et al., 2022; Bartram, 2019; Bihu, 2020). In this kind of research, investigators measure opinions, attitudes and behaviors of participants. An example can be the study of the ways educators use collaborative methods in the classroom, and its effectiveness in learning outcomes. The quantitative approach deals with topics like how often a set of conditions happens or what is the relation between two or more variables. It examines the factors that play a role in an attitude or behavior. The questionnaire actually serves as a tool (Cohen, Manion & Morrison, 2018; Ary, Jacobs, Irvine & Walker, 2018). It is structured and has closed-ended questions. It may be in multiple-choice mode or Likert scales. Sometimes open-ended questions are included.

The questions have to be clear, specific, well-defined, and understandable to the participants. They must be relevant to the research, without bias or guidance. It helps to measure the intensity of an opinion or attitude (Taylor et al., 2025; Bartram, 2019; Bihu, 2020; Kafyulilo & Fisser, 2015). Concerning the success of the research, it depends on the quality of the design. The researcher defines the research question (what exactly they want to know and measure), and the variables (which are the factors to be studied - for example, attitudes towards STEM education, self-confidence, experience). Moreover, the researcher investigates the sample, that means, who are participating, the proper number of people taking part in order for the outcomes of the research to be reliable, and the method of data collection. Questions like how the questionnaire will be distributed or how much time is needed are essential for the procedure of the research. The sample must be representative in order for the results to be generalized. For instance, if the research is targeted to educators of primary education, the sample has to include people from different geographical areas, ages, and experience levels.

The next step of the research is data analysis. After collecting the responses, statistical tools are used. For analysis, descriptive statistics are common. Means, percentages, standard deviations are used in statistic methods. Concerning correlations, the researcher studies how two variables are related, for instance, what is the relation between self-confidence and attitude towards STEM practice. Group comparisons take place as well. For example, if younger teachers differ from experienced ones. There are also structural models that measure the relationships of many variables together. The analysis of data is objective when it is based on specific criteria. Results are presented clearly, with a set of figures that make the findings visually clearer and more obvious (Gall, Gall & Borg, 2015; Muijs, 2021; Fraenkel, Wallen & Hyun, 2019; Johnson & Christensen, 2017; Lodico, Spaulding & Voegtle, 2019).

The advantages of quantitative research are various. It offers clear and measurable results. It allows generalization in large populations and it helps in educational policy decisions (Taylor et al., 2025). Quantitative research may be combined with qualitative research in order to gain a complete picture of the studied phenomena (Creswell, 2015). However, challenges and limitations exist in this kind of research. Numbers do not always show the reason why behind a case, behind attitudes or behaviors (Rauteda, 2025). The quality of the questionnaire plays a key role in reliability. Participants may not answer honestly. This is the reason why statistics require attention and specialization by the researcher, well-designed research, with statistically weighted questionnaires and well interpreted results. In conclusion, quantitative research with a questionnaire is a powerful tool for educational research.

It reveals trends, relationships, factors that influence teaching and learning. However, it requires a properly designed planning and correct interpretation of the results.

In the present study, the researcher used the quantitative method and chose participants who are extensively experienced with STEM learning. Scientix ambassadors' viewpoints are critical for this analysis. They are connected with the European STEM community, and implement STEM disciplines, guaranteeing reliable finding on the field. This selection corresponds to outcomes that emphasize the significance of examining biases in research and exploring more focused, tailored groups to reveal detailed barriers and opportunities (Winkler & Wofford, 2024). The study's approach also recognizes the importance of picking participants who provide wide-ranging yet experienced perspectives to encourage meaningful outcomes. By focusing on these participants, the researcher confronts structural deficiencies and supports that the information gathered advances to a more equitable, more inclusive perspective of STEM education's effects on academic development and career readiness.

Quantitative data analysis comprised explanatory metrics (e.g., frequencies, ratios) and inferential approaches, such as Pearson correlation evaluations, to investigate connections between factors, such as learners' involvement during STEM lessons and its impact on future scholarly and career decisions. Results were methodically grouped to emphasize patterns across answers and provide practical insights.

In line with Rauteda (2025), traditionally, quantitative research is connected with physical sciences, conducted for testing theories and hypotheses by conducting experiments. Nevertheless, it is applied in social sciences and education to a greater extent, and it is very effective in measuring the success of educational approaches. Nevertheless, in quantitative studies there is always the risk to ignore issues, such as bias, privacy and generalizability. This is the reason why the author of this study has taken into account experience-based, and varied perspectives of educators, eventually encouraging a more thorough comprehension of educational trends in STEM system.

Ethical standards were rigorously followed, with notified consent acquired from participants and anonymity assured. The incorporation of unequal sampling sizes, as well as with the focused expertise of Scientix ambassadors, guarantees that the research showcases a thorough and detailed perception of educators' opinions, enhancing the discussion on STEM education.

DATA OF THE RESEARCH

Demographic Characteristics

First of all, the identity of the survey participant is essential. The questionnaire was shared among the educators in the platform of Scientix ambassadors, as well as in the European School Education Platform, and more concisely, as a post in eTwinning community forum. Figure 1 shows the country of each participant. 144 educators of multiple countries corresponded, with Greece having the highest participation at 29.9%, followed by Turkey (15.3%), and Romania (9.7%). Other countries, like France, Estonia, Lithuania, and others, provided around 1% to the sample. This leads to unequal sample proportions among groups, a frequent phenomenon in research due to functional limitations including participant availability and operational issues.

Figure 1. Which country are you in?

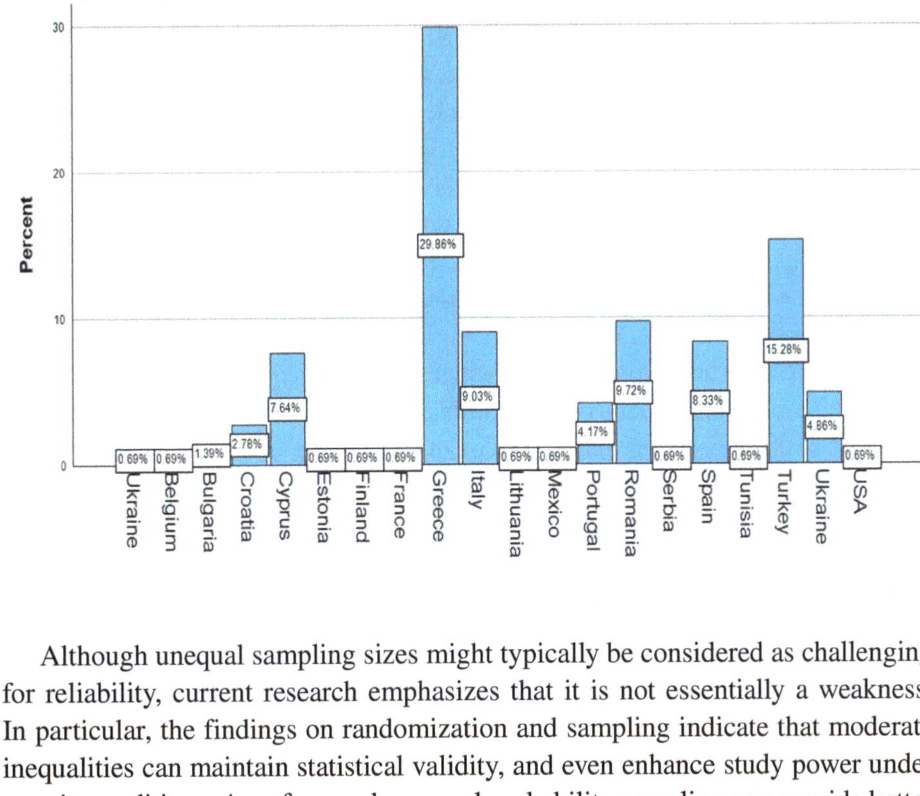

Although unequal sampling sizes might typically be considered as challenging for reliability, current research emphasizes that it is not essentially a weakness. In particular, the findings on randomization and sampling indicate that moderate inequalities can maintain statistical validity, and even enhance study power under certain conditions. As referenced, unequal probability sampling can provide better population estimates than equal sampling, especially when auxiliary variables like geographic diversity are involved. As a consequence, the participation of Greek educators offers important insights into regional patters, but this does not exclude other nationalities to provide valuable data in the comparative analysis, as mentioned in several studies concerning unequal sampling (Oldfield, 2016; Schulz & Grimes, 2002; Grafström, 2010; Elliott & Valliant, 2017). Besides that, by forcing equal group sizes in sampling may result in bias, and harm unpredictability in the research. For Aires (2000), when the researcher allows natural discrepancies, there is an alignment with scientifically valid randomization methods which relates to real-world diversity.

During the last years, the diversity of the sample that proves to be unequal plays a key role for capturing varied perspectives on STEM education (Elliott & Valliant, 2017). As a consequence, the data represent the spectrum of contexts, and provide insights about the dominant trends, like the impact of STEM education in Greece. As a conclusion around the unequal sampling in quantitative research, based on the previous studies, demonstrate the importance of handling both larger and smaller group contributions to draw meaningful conclusions.

As far as the relation of educators with STEM is concerned, more than 60% of the them are Scientix ambassadors, where Scientix is the European community of STEM education that means, they advocate who are members of the international network committed to STEM education. Scientix acts as a significant platform for exchanging resources, expertise, and effective strategies among teachers globally, promoting innovation and teamwork in STEM teaching (www.scientix.eu/). The participation of Scientix ambassadors adds significant value to the research, as these participants bring informed perspectives and expertise shaped by their active engagement with STEM initiatives. The researcher is also a Scientix ambassador. The inclusion of STEM related teachers in the study guarantees that the data collected are credible and grounded in practical experience. As a consequence, this representative sample underscores the strength and the reliability of the findings, providing a robust basis for the advancement in STEM educational strategies.

Figure 2 shows the identity of the highest academic background of the participants in the survey. The predominant group possess superior degrees. 62.5% of educators hold a Master's degree, 23.6% hold a Bachelor's degree, and 13.2% of them hold a PhD, indicating a considerable representation of expert-level educators.

Figure 2. What is your highest level of education?

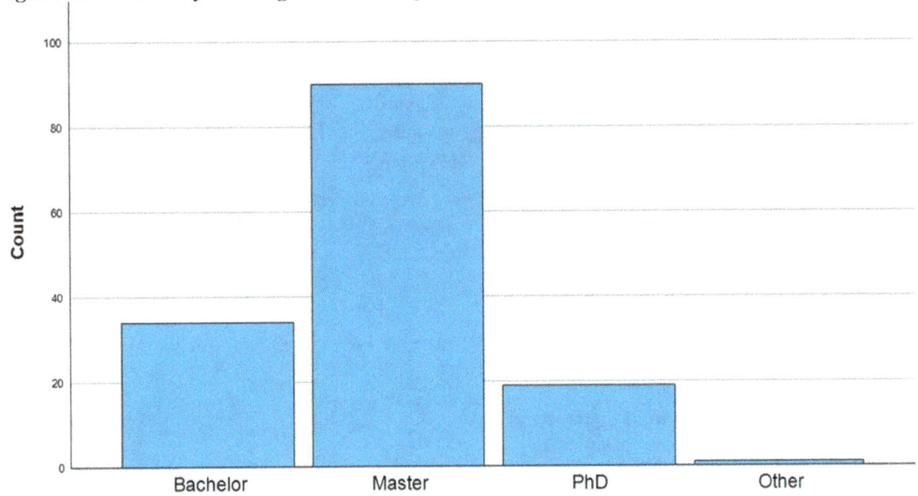

As shown in Figure 3, the majority of educators (66.7%) belong to primary school education, while a smaller group (22.2%) refers to secondary education. 9.0% of the participants are kindergarten educators and 1.4% represent special education teachers.

Figure 3. What grade level do you teach?

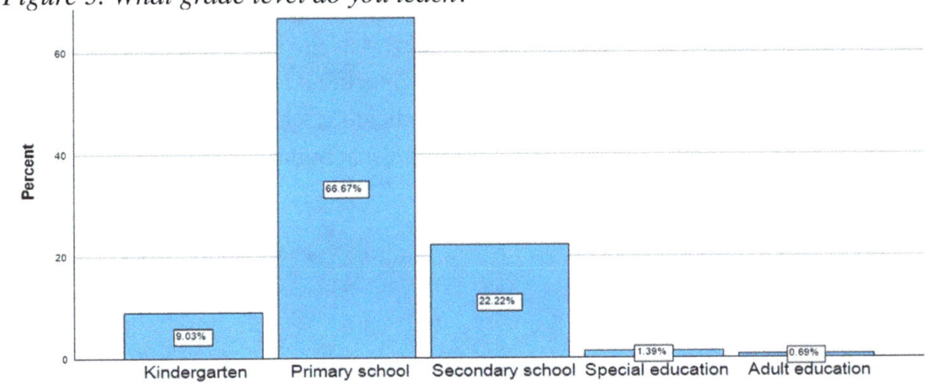

Table 1 shows that there exists a weak yet statistically significant positive correlation ($r = 0.234$, $p = 0.002$) between the number of years of teaching experience and familiarity with STEM standards. That is, the more experienced teachers are more familiar with STEM subjects. A sample of 144 responses guarantees consistency and accuracy, and provides evidence that teaching experience affects familiarity with STEM education comparatively.

Table 1. Teaching experience and STEM familiarity

Correlations[b]

		How many years of teaching experience do you have?	How familiar are you with the principles of STEM education?
How many years of teaching experience do you have?	Pearson Correlation	1	.234**
	Sig. (1-tailed)		.002
	Sum of Squares and Cross-products	90.639	23.972
	Covariance	.634	.168
How familiar are you with the principles of STEM education?	Pearson Correlation	.234**	1
	Sig. (1-tailed)	.002	
	Sum of Squares and Cross-products	23.972	115.306
	Covariance	.168	.806

**. Correlation is significant at the 0.01 level (1-tailed).
b. Listwise N=144

STEM Implementation Practices

The statistics indicate that the highest proportion of respondents use STEM activities in their schools on a regular basis, with 43.1% using them weekly, and 20.1% using them every day. As Figure 4 shows, a quarter of the respondents (25.0%) use STEM activities every month, with a lower proportion, 11.8% collectively, using them sometimes or never. What these results indicate is a high rate of use of STEM education by respondents, with potential for further enactment among incidental users.

Figure 4. Frequency of STEM activities incorporation

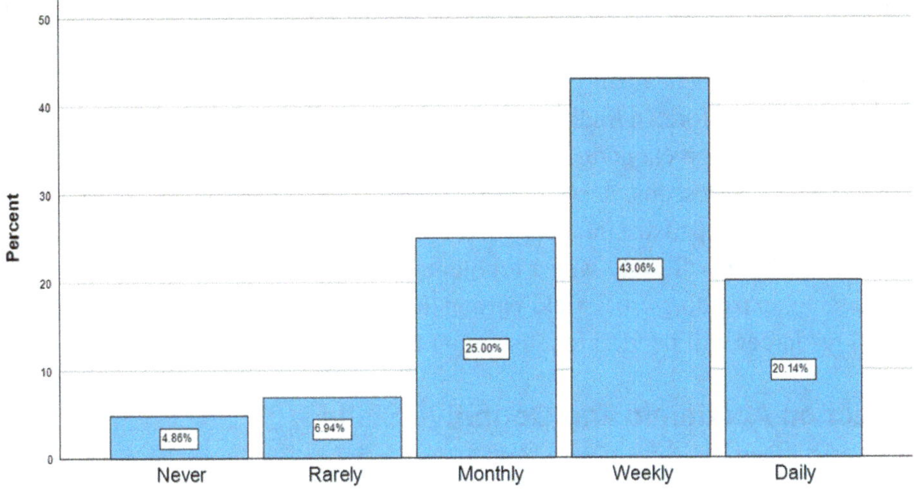

Ways of Implementing STEM Education Into Teaching Practices

According to the results, project-based learning is the most favored practice, referenced in 42 answers (29.2%), reflecting its common preference among instructors. Experimentation through hands-on activities comes next with 39 answers (27.1%), indicating a strong preference for participatory and experiential education. Technology deployment, such as programming software and virtual experiments, features in 37 answers (25.7%), reflecting its extensive incorporation into pedagogical practices. Cross-subject lessons, as stated in 35 responses (24.3%), also mirror how teachers value bringing STEM concepts across subjects together.

These findings indicate a balanced application of various STEM strategies, where project-based and experiential learning are greatly valued. The continued blending of technology, inter-disciplinary studies, and hands-on approaches indicates a leaning towards blended teaching strategies, where teachers use various tools to enhance student participation. This blending supports the notion that effective STEM instruction involves a blended and interactive approach, as opposed to a focus on a single method. Further examination might explore to what degree educators who adopt various strategies exhibit higher levels of student engagement and learning outcomes.

Notable Outcomes From Implementing STEM Disciplines

Participants state that incorporating STEM approach in diverse educational settings has shown notable beneficial outcomes on student involvement, creativity, and educational achievements. Through initiatives like Erasmus and eTwinning projects, learners collaborate on international platforms, share knowledge, and acquire skills in coding, robotics, and scientific inquiry. In addition, STEM activities advance self-esteem and engagement, mainly in Science and Mathematics, mainly in students who weren't engaged before, in traditional learning environments. Students with special needs who often face challenges in learning also benefit from hands-on activities and STEM-based lessons, according to educators. The experiences presented in various projects emphasize the importance of STEM in shaping equipped scholars, skilled in tackling with real-world problems through forward-thinking strategies. Progressing, expanding cross-field partnerships and delivering balanced access to STEM resources will be vital for sustaining these beneficial results.

Impact on Academic and Cognitive Skills

The correlation between STEM effectiveness in learning and in skills improvement, as shown in Table 2, is examined in a crosstabulation analysis.

Table 2. Impact of STEM programs in improving educational progress and their effect on problem-solving

			How does STEM education influence students' problem-solving and critical thinking skills? Significantly improves skills	Total
How effective do you find these programs in enhancing student learning?	Not effective	Count	0	1
		% within How effective do you find these programs in enhancing student learning?	0.0%	100.0%
		% of Total	0.0%	0.7%
	Somewhat effective	Count	9	34
		% within How effective do you find these programs in enhancing student learning?	26.5%	100.0%
		% of Total	6.3%	23.6%
	Very effective	Count	82	109
		% within How effective do you find these programs in enhancing student learning?	75.2%	100.0%
		% of Total	56.9%	75.7%
Total		Count	91	144
		% within How effective do you find these programs in enhancing student learning?	63.2%	100.0%
		% of Total	63.2%	100.0%

Chi-Square Tests

	Value	df	Asymptotic Significance (2-sided)
Pearson Chi-Square	64.405[a]	4	<.001
Likelihood Ratio	38.159	4	<.001
Linear-by-Linear Association	36.609	1	<.001
N of Valid Cases	144		

According to the cross-analysis results, there is a significant relationship between the impact of STEM education in educational progress and the improvement in problem-solving and critical thinking skills. The majority of educators identified STEM lessons as "very effective" and 75.2% of them replied that problem-solving and critical thinking competences were improved. Relatively, participants who deemed STEM approach as "ineffective" or "somewhat effective" stressed low levels of competence improvement. The Chi-Square tests advocate this relationship (<,001). This results in a strong statistical connection between the effectiveness of STEM curricula and the improvement of skills. This indicates that cognitive competences may be improved by thoughtfully designed STEM curricula.

How STEM Education Impact Students' Academic Performance in Subjects Like Science and Mathematics

The outcomes present that STEM education is effective in scholarly success in the courses of science and mathematics, as shown in Figure 5. More than half of the respondents, that is, 56.3%, believe that it "significantly improves performance," and another 42.4% believe that it "improves performance." Collectively, these results indicate that nearly all the survey respondents (98.7%) recognize improvement in students' learning outcomes through STEM education.

Figure 5. Impact of STEM programs in academic performance

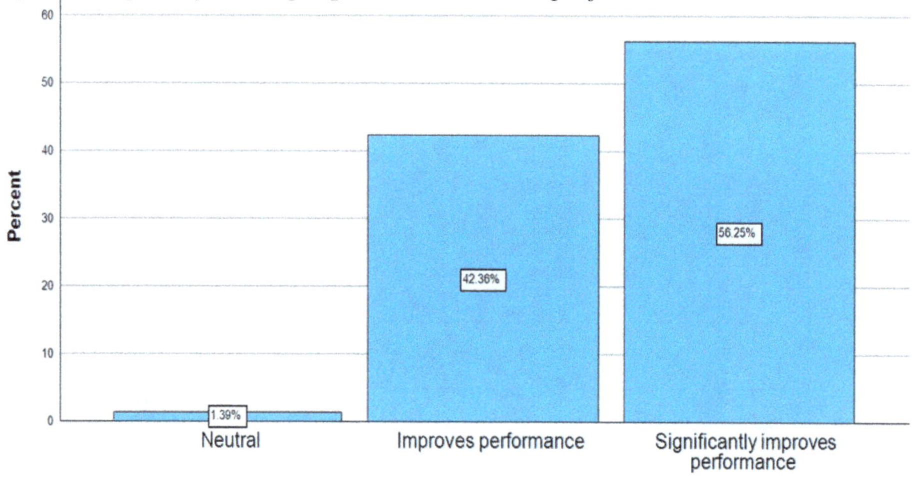

Student Collaboration and Teamwork Competences

Figure 6 presents that STEM education effects pupils' collaboration and teamwork skills. 52.1% mentioned a major improvement, and a 41.7% of educators noted progress. This results in a considerable 93.8% of statements that acknowledge STEM's impact in promoting teamwork. A small percentage (5.6%) recorded minor adjustments.

Figure 6. Impact of STEM programs in collaboration skills

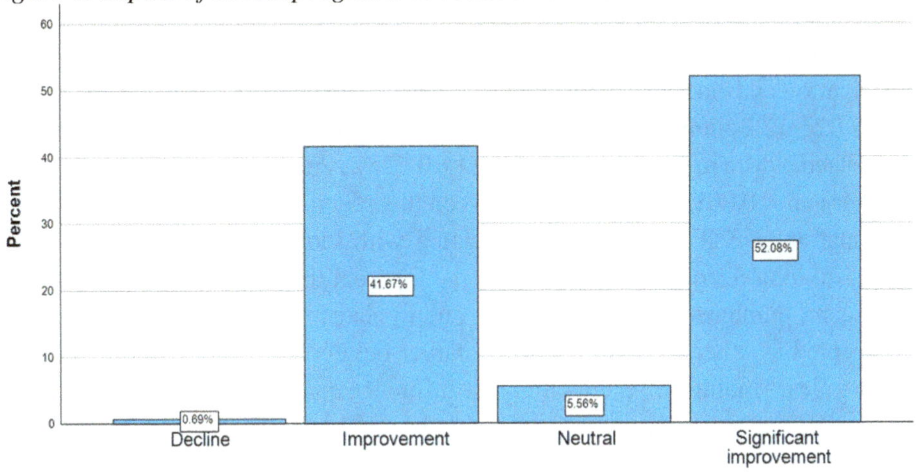

How STEM Education Affects Students' Creativity and Innovation

According to the findings in Figure 7, STEM education supports student creativity and innovation. 57.6% of participants note that STEM education "significantly enhances" creativity and innovation, while 38.2% state that it "enhances" these capabilities. As a whole, these categories represent 95.8% of the answers. These results support STEM curricula as a factor of advancement of these skills in students' future success.

Figure 7. Impact of STEM programs in creativity and innovation skills

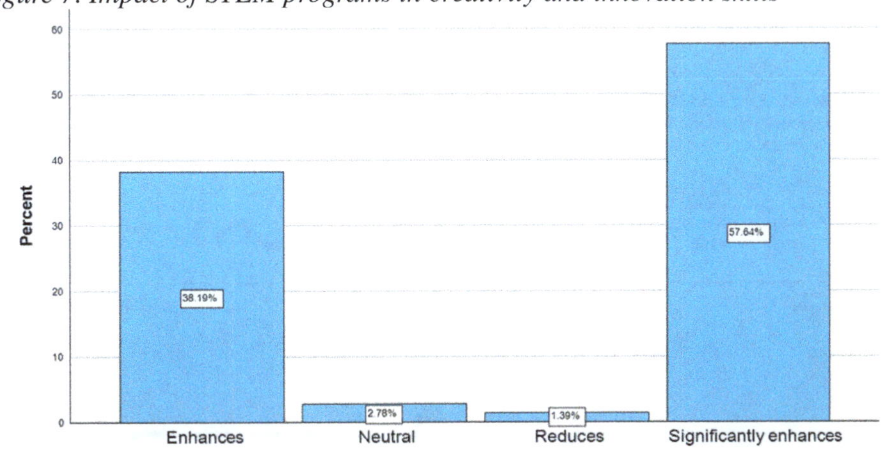

Engagement and Future Careers

As shown in Table 3, the results of the survey reveal an average level of learners' participation and enthusiasm throughout STEM courses, with a mean score of 2.56 (SD = 0.589). Beliefs of STEM's impact on academic and professional paths are diminished, with a mean score of 1.53 (SD = 0.528). A moderate positive correlation ($r = 0.418$, $p < 0.001$) was recorded between these factors, indicating that increased participation in STEM lessons is associated with more robust convictions in its impact on long-term decisions. Despite the fact that the correlation is statistically significant, demonstrating it is unlikely due to chance, direct effect is not able to be accepted as other factors may affect career beliefs. Future research could lead in more clear findings on the factors that influence career paths, since the relation between STEM programs participation and professions' choices.

Table 3. Correlation between engagement and future career choices

Descriptive Statistics

	Mean	Std. Deviation	N
How engaged and motivated are students during STEM lessons compared to traditional lessons?	2.56	.589	143
How do you think STEM education influences students' future academic and career choices?	1.53	.528	143

Correlations[b]

		How engaged and motivated are students during STEM lessons compared to traditional lessons?	How do you think STEM education influences students' future academic and career choices?
How engaged and motivated are students during STEM lessons compared to traditional lessons?	Pearson Correlation	1	.418**
	Sig. (2-tailed)		<.001
	Sum of Squares and Cross-products	49.245	18.483
	Covariance	.347	.130
How do you think STEM education influences students' future academic and career choices?	Pearson Correlation	.418**	1
	Sig. (2-tailed)	<.001	
	Sum of Squares and Cross-products	18.483	39.608
	Covariance	.130	.279

**. Correlation is significant at the 0.01 level (2-tailed).
b. Listwise N=143

CHALLENGES AND STRATEGIES

Frequency Analysis of the Challenges Faced by Educators

According to the survey, lack of time and limited educational materials are the two main barriers in STEM incorporation. The necessity for professional training arises as a key component, with educators supporting organized development initiatives to strengthen their skills in STEM instruction. Moreover, learner hesitation, though less frequently mentioned, propose that interactive techniques require improvement to cultivate passion for STEM disciplines. Challenges such as the above can be confronted by strategic policy makers, suitable funding, and redesign of STEM curricula.

Ways of Addressing Challenges in the Classroom

Educators often use inter-disciplinary instruction and collaborative projects among peers in order to tackle with challenges and obstacles. Participants state that collaboration offers shared resources and strategies. Inter-disciplinary instruction is based on STEM seminars and workshops. A notable challenge among educators is the time constraints, motivating many to incorporate STEM principles into current subjects instead of treating STEM as an independent subject. Some educators devote personal availability and funding provision to guarantee learners obtain experiential learning, with some pursuing third-party investment, supporters, or funding opportunities to obtain required materials. Moreover, some include recycling and cost-effective materials to make up for insufficient funding, while others rely on tech-based incorporation and Web-based tools to elevate their lessons.

Bridging Gaps Through Teacher Training, Resources and Policy Reform

Based on the findings, it is necessary to improve STEM-focused professional growth disciplines, and advanced accessibility to resources to gain successful STEM incorporation in the educational context. Participants note the necessity of hands-on sessions, targeted workshops, and support to effectively integrate STEM education into their teaching practice. Educators also suggest reduced class sizes, enhanced tech tools, and renovated spaces; to confront the setbacks they face in everyday teaching practice. These factors are related to a better funding by policy makers and stakeholders, so that STEM education results in enhanced educational achievements and academic success. Participants stress the importance of these structured interventions in alignment to boosting their competence as STEM instructors.

In addition to institutional changes, educators stress the importance of networks that promote collaboration, as well as peer mentoring that help improve the educators' professional development. It is important to have a network to exchange opinions, express ideas, and share the feelings reflecting on classroom experiences. This leads to bridging the gap that exists among theoretical elements, practice, and results of STEM implementation. Flexibility in curricula is also a topic in which educators are very interested in. Traditional curricula are an obstacle for teachers who want to integrate STEM approaches, tailor new content with hands-on activities, and incorporate real-world issues, like climate change, artificial intelligence, and active citizenship. Finally, participants state that STEM approach can serve as a mean of equity and inclusion, that enable all students to learn in a meaningful and productive way.

DISCUSSION

STEM as a Facilitator for Student Engagement and Success

STEM–focused curricula has been proved to play key role for students' engagement, enthusiasm, and academic success. STEM approach offers a learning experience to all students, regardless of their learning profile and cultural background (Holmes et al., 2022). A large number of scientific research has shown that learners who take part in STEM activities that include problem solving, project-based learning, experimental inquiry and collaborative learning have positively changed their attitude towards school procedures (Margot & Kettler, 2020; Thibaut, Ceuppens, De Loof, et al., 2018; Wang, Moore, Roehrig & Park, 2011). Especially, students who struggle with traditional teaching methods tend to get more excited about hands-on, activity-based STEM projects. This hods true because STEM approach offers alternative ways of access to knowledge and is adapted to the individual needs and learning profiles of the students.

The experiential nature of STEM activities leads to deeper understanding through hands-on activities, like model construction, robotics, experiments and ICT. Students are motivated to develop high value skills, like critical and analytical thinking, collaboration and problem-solving skills (Chiu, Price & Ovrahim, 2025; Li, Wang & Xiao, 2020). Educators also observe that students with low self-esteem or limited engagement for the lesson tend to have an elevated curiosity in thematical units related to science, technology and engineering. This leads to a better preparation for the demands of the modern labor market and the professions of the future.

Moreover, the integration of STEM curricula contributes to inclusive learning and equity because they offer differentiated ways of learning (Mohr-Schroeder, Cavalcanti, & Blyman, 2020). Besides, this approach is aligned with the principles of universal design for learning (UDL) (Schreffler, Vasquez III, Chini & James, 2019; Davies, Schelly & Spooner, 2021). STEM framework promotes a learning environment that strengthens all students regardless of their skills, cultural background, interests or learning profile, and leads to self-regulation and preparation for 21st century skills.

Teacher Training and Institutional Support

Successful integration of STEM approach depends on the quality of educators' training in a large scale. Educators' training and lack of institutional support come in the first place of factors that influence STEM's success. Lack of systematic and targeted professional development, in accordance to insufficient support from educational structures represents a key barrier to the effective incorporation of STEM in daily instructional routines (Spyropoulou, Mathiopoulos & Kameas, 2025; El-Deghaidy, Mansour, Alzaghal & Alhammad, 2021). In this research, participants mention the need for structured training and access to updated materials. When there is inadequate institutional support, educators are forced to make use of their own time and money to finance STEM activities for their students. They seek supplies, or look for external funding, that may lead to professional burnout and cause STEM initiatives to be unsustainable. According to the findings of the present research, these setbacks can be confronted with an all-inclusive reform-driven approach, that needs curriculum modifications, professional growth, and support framework from the state.

It further highlights that there must be a wholistic reform-with curriculum modifications, professional growth programs, and state funding to ensure universal access to STEM education while alleviating the burden on the educators. Institutional empowerment is not limited to provide supplies, but extends to the building of collaborative culture, teacher recognition and empowerment.

Having supportive networks and expert-led coaching play a pivotal role in educators' enforcement. Providing equal access in professional development opportunities is necessary for the promotion of educational justice and qualitative teaching. Institutional empowerment for educators improves teaching effectiveness and contributes to the development of an education system that is aligned with contemporary societal and labor market needs. Besides, according to literature review, lack of institutional support often leads educators to personally bear the cost of incorporating STEM activities, whether in terms of time or financial resources (Nesterenko, Mytsyk, Petryk, Kovachov & Suchikova, 2024; Spyropoulou et al., 2025; Dong, Wang & Yang, 2020; El-Deghaidy et al., 2021; ALI Research Staff.,

2023). It is crucial to increase investment in materials and infrastructure (European Commission Joint Research Centre, 2024), and overcome institutional limitations and resource shortages (Park et al., 2020; Ejiwale, 2013).

Challenges Hindering STEM Education

STEM application in school environments often meets obstacles and faces diverse challenges that influence the quality and sustainability of related teaching practices. According to the findings of the research, a lot of educators mention they are held back by a lack of time (77 mentions), they do not have enough resources (60 mentions), and there is limited training on STEM-related approaches (48 mentions). The close schedules and traditional curricula do not provide room for experiential and project-based teaching. This results in seeing STEM practices as a part of an existing course, for which there is a limited committed time. Due to limited training and lack of time, educators prefer reverting to incorporating separate STEM elements into traditional curricula, decreasing the cohesion and interdisciplinarity of STEM approach (Thibaut, Ceuppens, De Loof, et al., 2018; Margot, & Kettler, 2019; Dare, Ellis, & Roehrig, 2018; Park, Byun, & Sim, 2020). The financial constraints and technological frameworks aggravate obstacles, restricting learning environments from preparing academic settings with robotics equipment, programming software, and experimental equipment. In addition, learners' hesitation to STEM activities (referenced 9 times) points to the necessity for plans to improve involvement and illustrate STEM's relevance to real-world applications. The findings of this research are aligned to others research outcomes, that agree on improving activities in the basis on connecting them to real-world problems (Mohr-Schroeder, Cavalcanti, & Blyman, 2020; Honey et al., 2014). Lack of contextual relevance in STEM education and unfamiliarity on behalf of students result in disengagement, especially when learning fail to prove sufficient scaffolding or incentives (Labster, 2023; Perry, 2022; Harvard Business Publishing Education, 2023).

Global Collaboration and Recognition Through STEM Initiatives

The participation of teachers and students in international STEM initiatives, like Erasmus+, eTwinning and global educational initiatives, has proved to be a crucial factor that enhances learning experience and personal development, because they promote exchange of ideas, multicultural collaborations and a holistic approach of knowledge and skills development that exceeds the limited barriers of isolated learning subjects. International STEM competitions, virtual online meetings via educational platforms and collaborative projects, lead students to gain experience in practices and develop skills that reinforce their self-confidence, preparing them in a globalized demanding world. The identity of the participants of the research is connected to members of such educational communities, the Scientix and eTwinning communities. The questionnaire was shared among the educators in the platform of Scientix ambassadors, as well as in the European School Education Platform, and more concisely, as a post in eTwinning community forum. These educators state that STEM initiatives enhance cognitive competences as well as 21st century skills, like soft skills, interpersonal skills and leadership abilities. Taking part in STEM projects in international level improves the capability of students to take initiatives, to solve problems in real-world structures and collaborative and communication skills. Learners work with peers from other schools and countries, in multi-language and multi-cultural environments. This framework improves their ability to become active citizens of the world. International acknowledgement through the sharing of collaborative projects and awards and recognition that derives from STEM activities is a powerful motivation for students to be more engaged and focused on learning. At the same time, educators seek innovative methods and strategies that augment their personal learning network and the ability to design and implement innovative and inclusive collaborative initiatives. Several reports support the outcomes of the research which stress the successful influence of STEM instruction to pupils problem-solving skills and leadership expertise that prepare them as future innovators (Chiu et al., 2025; Li et al., 2020; Margot & Kettler, 2020). Global STEM projects foster leadership and real-world problem-solving (Chiu et al., 2025), help students to develop critical thinking and collaborative skills (Margot & Kettler, 2019), and enhances innovation and leadership readiness (Li, Wang & Xiao, 2020; Geesa, Stith & Teague, 2021; Mohr-Schroeder, Cavalcanti & Blyman, 2020). Finally, STEM instructional strategies promote problem-solving and innovation skills for students (Thibaut et al., 2018), help them grow their analytical and leadership skills (Dare et al., 2018), and enhance their engagement and leadership potential (Wang et al., 2011; Labster, 2023).

Overcoming Challenges

The research findings evidently show the positive impact of STEM teaching on students' active engagement and development of their learning outcomes. Of specific interest is the contribution of the STEM approach to experiential learning, interdisciplinary teaching, and worldwide collaboration. Students warmly welcome activities that integrate science, technology, engineering, and mathematics—especially when these are associated with actual problems, and allow them to experiment, collaborate, and learn 21st-century competencies.

However, STEM integration often meets challenges. According to the participants' views in the present research, educators lack time and resources. Time plays a key-role to tight traditional curricula that are not designed for STEM initiatives. The shortage of materials, resources and supplies is also another problem stated by educators that prevent them from incorporating STEM practices in their everyday teaching. Institutional support is another issue for educators, a factor that hinders STEM sustainability in teaching. Absence or limited access to training and professional development in STEM practices and instruction is a challenge that educators face. The majority of them state that they need to be instructed on STEM issues and in innovative STEM practices. Finally, the participants report that they would like to have more support from the state, and the policy makers about STEM education. However, apart from all the challenges and the setbacks, according to the findings of the research, educators show a remarkable adaptability, because they devote personal time and sources in a creative and innovative way. They seek partnerships in global educational communities, like Scientix and eTwinning platforms for collaborative projects, and to develop their personal learning network, where they share good practices.

The relation between schools and community, as well as with international partnerships and collaborations, solidifies STEM culture, and functions as catalysts for the improvement of educational practices and learning achievements. The effective use of ICT tools and digital platforms, and the incorporation of global topics like climate change, sustainability, and artificial intelligence in everyday teaching, respond to the needs of students. Literature review supports these findings (Gao, Li, Shen, & Sun, 2020; Fazio, 2024; DeCoito, 2016; Purzer, Moore, & Baker, 2015; Zhao & Gearhart, 2021; Caprile, Palmen, Sanz, & Dente, 2015).

Institutional support and stakeholders' advocacy, sufficient and planned fundings, educators' continuous training, and reformation of curricula according to new educational trends of the 21st century needs and challenges, can transform educational paradigm, improve equity in educational access in knowledge, and get students prepared to be active, responsible and innovative citizens. Numerous empirical studies strongly corroborate these findings, and support the need of a well-planned and curricula-design planning for a STEM-based education. This alignment between current research and observed outcomes not only validates the effectiveness of the pedagogical strategies employed but also underscores the urgency of institutional support for their sustained implementation (National Academy of Engineering & National Research Council, 2014; Sanders, 2009; Bryan, Moore, Johnson, & Roehrig, 2015).

CONCLUSION

This research has examined the outcomes in academic achievements, the challenges, and the significance of STEM education in varied educational settings, based on the insights of European educators, mainly ambassadors of Scientix, the STEM European community, highlighting three significant conclusions. Firstly, STEM approach empowers students' engagement, and academic achievements, especially within learners facing challenges in traditional subjects. Hands-on and cross-disciplinary strategies initiate critical thinking, and commitment in STEM future careers. Secondly, teachers face multiple challenges in STEM incorporation, like time constraints, lack of assets, and limited professional development. Thirdly, European communities, such as Erasmus, eTwinning and Scientix alliances, serve as a catalyst on supporting STEM instructions, offering teachers and students prospects for progress, partnerships, and worldwide acknowledgment.

Moreover, the findings of this research underscores specific deficiencies which require deeper investigation. While qualitative insights reveal the beneficial impacts of STEM framework, there is limited quantitative data evaluating prolonged scholarly progress outside student involvement. In addition, the research lacks in-depth investigation on the academic growth of diverse instructional strategies, making it uncertain which strategies lead to optimal outcomes in varied academic environments. Extended study is required in order to investigate how cultural and financial disparities have an important impact on STEM application in schools.

Ultimately, future research should focus on quantifying long-term results of STEM education by studying academic achievements, and competency growth through the years, with specific and measurable criteria. Likewise, comparative studies measuring the efficacy of different STEM instructional approaches may deliver empirical observations for educators and policymakers. Extending research in area-based disparities and fairness in STEM education will facilitate inclusiveness in STEM learning opportunities. Addressing these issues will strengthen the basis of STEM education's framework, and allow educators, schools, and policy-makers to make progress for continuous innovation in knowledge and skills acquisition.

REFERENCES

Aires, N. (2000). Comparisons between conditional Poisson sampling and Pareto sampling designs. *Journal of Statistical Planning and Inference*, Volume 88, Issue 1. Pages 133-147. ISSN 0378-3758. DOI: 10.1016/S0378-3758(99)00205-0

ALI Research Staff. (2023). The Challenges of STEM Education: Barriers to Participation. *Accelerate Learning*. https://blog.acceleratelearning.com/the-challenges-of-stem-education-barriers-to-participation

Ary, D., Jacobs, L. C., Irvine, C. K., & Walker, D. A. (2018). *Introduction to research in education* (10th ed.). Cengage Learning.

Bal, A. P., & Bedir, S. G. (2021). EXAMINING TEACHERS' VIEWS ON STEM EDUCATION. *European Journal of Education Studies*, *8*(3).

Bartram, B. (2019). Using questionnaires. In Lambert, M. (Ed.), *Practical research methods in education: An early researcher's critical guide* (pp. 11–30). Routledge., DOI: 10.4324/9781351188395-1

Becker, K., & Park, K. (2011). Effects of integrative approaches among STEM subjects on students' learning: A meta-analysis. *Journal of STEM Education: Innovations and Research*, *12*(5/6), 23–37.

Bihu, R. (2020). Questionnaire survey methodology in educational and social science studies. *European American Journal, 8*(2), 45–60. https://eajournals.org/wp-content/uploads/Questionnaire-Survey-Methodology-in-Educational-and-Social-Science-Studies.pdf

Bryan, L. A., Moore, T. J., Johnson, C. C., & Roehrig, G. H. (2015). *STEM road map: A framework for integrated STEM education.* National Science Teachers Association Press.

Caprile, M., Palmen, R., Sanz, P., & Dente, G. (2015). *Encouraging STEM studies: Labour market situation and comparison of practices targeted at young people in different Member States.* European Parliament.

Chiu, A., Price, C. A., & Ovrahim, E. (2025). Supporting youth STEM engagement through international collaboration. *International Journal of STEM Education*, *9*(1), 1–15. DOI: 10.1186/s40594-025-00456-9

Chiu, T. K. F., Li, Y., Ding, M., Hallström, J., & Koretsky, M. D. (2025). A decade of research contributions and emerging trends in the International Journal of STEM Education. *International Journal of STEM Education, 12*(1), 12. Advance online publication. DOI: 10.1186/s40594-025-00533-7

Cohen, L., Manion, L., & Morrison, K. (2018). *Research methods in education* (8th ed.). Routledge., DOI: 10.4324/9781315456539

Creswell, J. W. (2015). *Research design: Qualitative, quantitative, and mixed methods approach* (4th ed.). Pearson Education.

Dare, E. A., Ellis, J. A., & Roehrig, G. H. (2018). Understanding science teachers' implementations of integrated STEM curricula through a phenomenological multiple case study. *International Journal of STEM Education, 5*(4), 4. Advance online publication. DOI: 10.1186/s40594-018-0101-z PMID: 30631694

Davies, P. L., Schelly, C. L., & Spooner, C. L. (2021). Promoting inclusive STEM classrooms through Universal Design for Learning: A case study in undergraduate engineering. *Journal of Postsecondary Education and Disability, 34*(2), 123–138.

DeCoito, I. (2016). STEM education in Canada: A knowledge synthesis. *Canadian Journal of Science, Mathematics and Technology Education = Revue Canadienne de l'Enseignement des Sciences, des Mathématiques et de la Technologie, 16*(2), 121–143. DOI: 10.1080/14926156.2016.1166297

Dong, Y., Wang, Y., & Yang, L. (2020). Barriers to STEM education in secondary schools: A comparative study. *International Journal of STEM Education, 7*(1), 1–15. DOI: 10.1186/s40594-020-00210-x

Ejiwale, J. A. (2013). Barriers to successful implementation of STEM education. *Journal of Education and Learning, 7*(2), 63–74. DOI: 10.5539/jel.v7n2p63

El-Deghaidy, H., Mansour, N., Alzaghal, M., & Alhammad, F. (2021). STEM education and teacher professional development: A systematic review. *Research in Science & Technological Education, 39*(1), 1–24. DOI: 10.1080/02635143.2020.1788316

Elliott, M. R., & Valliant, R. (2017). Inference for Nonprobability Samples. *Statistical Science, 32*(2), 249–264. DOI: 10.1214/16-STS598

English, L. D. (2016). STEM education K–12: Perspectives on integration. *International Journal of STEM Education, 3*(3), 3. Advance online publication. DOI: 10.1186/s40594-016-0036-1

European Commission Joint Research Centre. (2024). STEM education: Report highlights need for more policy efforts and research. *European Education Area.* https://education.ec.europa.eu/news/stem-education-report-highlights-need-for-more-policy-efforts-and-research

European Schoolnet. (2025). *Scientix (official website).* Retrieved from https://www.scientix.eu/

Fazio, X. (2024). STEM education: International perspectives in STEM education. In *Global Perspectives on STEM Education* (pp. 93–108). Springer., DOI: 10.1007/978-3-031-60676-2_6

Fraenkel, J. R., Wallen, N. E., & Hyun, H. H. (2019). *How to design and evaluate research in education* (10th ed.). McGraw-Hill Education.

Gall, M. D., Gall, J. P., & Borg, W. R. (2015). *Applying educational research: How to read, do, and use research to solve problems of practice* (7th ed.). Pearson.

Gao, X., Li, P., Shen, J., & Sun, H. (2020). Reviewing assessment of student learning in interdisciplinary STEM education. *International Journal of STEM Education, 7*(24), 24. Advance online publication. DOI: 10.1186/s40594-020-00225-4

Geesa, R. L., Stith, K. M., & Teague, G. M. (2021). Integrative STEM education and leadership for student success. In *The Palgrave Handbook of Educational Leadership and Management Discourse* (pp. 1–20). Springer., DOI: 10.1007/978-3-030-39666-4_36-1

Grafström, A. (2010). On unequal probability sampling designs. Thesis for: PhD. Advisor: Lennart Bondesson. Retrieved from https://www.researchgate.net/publication/240924161_On_unequal_probability_sampling_designs

Harvard Business Publishing Education. (2023). Why your students are disengaged. *Inspiring Minds.* https://hbsp.harvard.edu/inspiring-minds/why-your-students-are-disengaged

Holmes, K., Berger, N., Mackenzie, E., Attard, C., & Ryan, V. (2022). The impact of place-based contextualized curriculum on student engagement and motivation in STEM education. *Frontiers in Education.* https://www.frontiersin.org/research-topics/14933

Honey, M., Pearson, G., & Schweingruber, H. (Eds.). (2014). *STEM integration in K–12 education: Status, prospects, and an agenda for research.* National Academies Press., DOI: 10.17226/18612

Johnson, B., & Christensen, L. (2017). *Educational research: Quantitative, qualitative, and mixed approaches* (6th ed.). SAGE Publications.

Kafyulilo, A. C., & Fisser, P. (2015). Teachers' perceptions of the use of ICT in education: A survey study. *International Journal of Education and Development using ICT, 11*(1), 55–70.

Kelley, T. R., & Knowles, J. G. (2016). A conceptual framework for integrated STEM education. *International Journal of STEM Education, 3*(11), 11. Advance online publication. DOI: 10.1186/s40594-016-0046-z

Labster. (2023). From disengagement to discovery: Transforming STEM education. *Labster Guides.* https://www.labster.com/guides/from-disengagement-to-discovery-transforming-stem-education

Li, Y., Wang, K., & Xiao, Y. (2020). Global STEM education: A review of international collaboration and student outcomes. *Journal of Science Education and Technology, 29*(4), 567–580. DOI: 10.1007/s10956-020-09876-3

Li, Y., Wang, K., Xiao, Y., & Froyd, J. E. (2020). Research and trends in STEM education: A systematic review of journal publications. *International Journal of STEM Education, 7*(1), 11. Advance online publication. DOI: 10.1186/s40594-020-00207-6

Lodico, M. G., Spaulding, D. T., & Voegtle, K. H. (2019). *Methods in educational research: From theory to practice* (4th ed.). Wiley.

Margot, K., & Kettler, T. (2020). Teachers' perception of STEM integration and education: A systematic literature review. *International Journal of STEM Education, 7*, 11.

Margot, K. C., & Kettler, T. (2019). Teachers' perception of STEM integration and education: A systematic literature review. *International Journal of STEM Education, 6*(1), 2. DOI: 10.1186/s40594-018-0151-2

Mohr-Schroeder, M. J., Cavalcanti, M., & Blyman, K. (2020). Equity and access in STEM: Inclusive strategies for teaching and learning. *International Journal of STEM Education, 7*(42). Advance online publication. DOI: 10.1186/s40594-020-00241-4

Molina-Ascanio, M., ... (2023). Innovative STEM teaching: The latest trends in STEM education. *Scientix.* https://www.scientix.eu/documents/10137/121801/Molina_Ascanio_2023_et_al_Innovative-STEM-Final-Ready-for-publication_compressed.pdf

Muijs, D. (2021). *Doing quantitative research in education with SPSS* (2nd ed.). SAGE Publications.

Nadelson, L. S., & Seifert, A. (2017). Integrated STEM defined: Contexts, challenges, and the future. *The Journal of Educational Research, 110*(3), 221–223. DOI: 10.1080/00220671.2017.1289775

National Academy of Engineering & National Research Council. (2014). *STEM integration in K–12 education: Status, prospects, and an agenda for research.* National Academies Press., DOI: 10.17226/18612

National Science Foundation. (2024). *U.S. STEM Workforce: Size, Growth, and Employment.* Retrieved from ncses.nsf.gov/pubs/nsb20245/u-s-stem-workforce-size-growth-and-employment

Nesterenko, M., Mytsyk, H., Petryk, K., Kovachov, S., & Suchikova, Y. (2024). From resistance to acceptance: The role of higher education in the integration of STEM education for sustainable development. *Journal for STEM Education Research.* Advance online publication. DOI: 10.1007/s41979-024-00141-0

Oldfield, M. (2016). *Unequal sample sizes and the use of larger control groups pertaining to power of a study.* Ministry of Defense, UK. DOI: 10.6084/m9.figshare.23988477

Papagiannopoulou, T., & Vaiopoulou, J. (2024). Teachers' attitudes towards STEM education: Exploring the role of their readiness via a structural equation model. *European Journal of Investigation in Health, Psychology and Education, 14*(11), 2850–2864. DOI: 10.3390/ejihpe14110187 PMID: 39590024

Park, H., Byun, S. Y., & Sim, J. (2020). Teachers' perceptions and practices of STEM education in Korea. *Asia-Pacific Journal of Teacher Education, 48*(2), 179–197. DOI: 10.1080/1359866X.2019.1574602

Perry, M. (2022). Student engagement: No learning without it. *MIT Teaching Systems Lab.* https://dspace.mit.edu/handle/1721.1/147885

Purzer, Ş., Moore, R., & Baker, D. (2015). Engineering design in the science classroom: STEM integration through design-based learning. *Science Education International, 26*(3), 217–229.

Rauteda, K. R. (2025). Quantitative research in education: Philosophy, uses, and limitations. [JMRD]. *Journal of Multidisciplinary Research, 2*(1), 1–11. DOI: 10.56916/jmrd.v2i1.993

Sanders, M. (2009). STEM, STEM education, STEMmania. *Technology Teacher, 68*(4), 20–26.

Schreffler, J., Vasquez, E.III, Chini, J., & James, W. (2019). Universal Design for Learning in postsecondary STEM education for students with disabilities: A systematic literature review. *International Journal of STEM Education*, *6*(8), 8. Advance online publication. DOI: 10.1186/s40594-019-0161-8

Schulz, K., & Grimes, D. (2002). Unequal group sizes in randomized trials: Guarding against guessing. *Lancet*, *359*(9310), 966–970. DOI: 10.1016/S0140-6736(02)08029-7 PMID: 11918933

Scientix. (n.d.). Scientix: The community for science education in Europe. Retrieved from https://www.scientix.eu/

Shahali, E. H. M., & Halim, L. (2024). The influence of science teachers' beliefs, attitudes, self-efficacy and school context on integrated STEM teaching practices. *International Journal of Science and Mathematics Education*, *22*(4), 787–807. DOI: 10.1007/s10763-023-10403-9

Spyropoulou, N., Mathiopoulos, K., & Kameas, A. (2025). "We believe in STEAM education, but we need support": In-service teachers' voices on the realities of STEAM implementation. *Education Sciences*, *15*(10), 1300. DOI: 10.3390/educsci15101300

Taylor, L., Dai, H. M., Ng, H., Playfoot, D., & Rose, S. (2025). Editorial: Improving quantitative research in higher education learning and teaching. *Journal of University Teaching & Learning Practice*, *22*(2). Advance online publication. DOI: 10.53761/jc59jm21

Thibaut, L., Ceuppens, S., De Loof, H., De Meester, J., Goovaerts, L., Struyf, A., Boeve-de Pauw, J., Dehaene, W., Deprez, J., De Cock, M., Hellinckx, L., Knipprath, H., Langie, G., Struyven, K., Van de Velde, D., Van Petegem, P., & Depaepe, F. (2018). Integrated STEM education: A systematic review of instructional practices in secondary education. *European Journal of STEM Education*, *3*(1). Advance online publication. DOI: 10.20897/ejsteme/85525

Vaiopoulou, J., Papagiannopoulou, T., & Stamovlasis, D. (2023). Attitudes towards STEM education: Nonlinear effects of teachers' readiness and the crucial role of affective conditions. *Frontiers in Education*, *8*, 1244678. Advance online publication. DOI: 10.3389/feduc.2023.1244678

Wang, H., Moore, T. J., Roehrig, G. H., & Park, M. S. (2011). STEM integration: Teacher perceptions and practice. *Journal of Pre-College Engineering Education Research*, *1*(2), 1–13. DOI: 10.7771/2157-9288.1068

Winkler, C. E., & Wofford, A. M. (2024). Trends and motivations in critical quantitative educational research: A multimethod examination across higher education scholarship and author perspectives. *Research in Higher Education, 65*(7), 1368–1394. DOI: 10.1007/s11162-024-09802-w

Zhao, Y., & Gearhart, M. (2021). Designing STEM curriculum for global competence: Lessons from international programs. *Journal of Curriculum Studies, 53*(5), 645–662. DOI: 10.1080/00220272.2021.1910457

Chapter 10
Hybrid Pedagogies for STEAM Teacher Education:
Integrating Games, Digital Tools, and Creative Practices in Portugal

Pedro Neves Rito
http://orcid.org/0000-0002-4507-0323
Polytechnic Institute of Viseu, Portugal

ABSTRACT

This chapter explores the integration of STEAM methodologies in Portuguese teacher training programs, emphasizing the pedagogical potential of hybrid approaches that combine digital and analog tools. Drawing on policy frameworks, it examines how accessible platforms such as Scratch, GeoGebra, and Arduino IDE, together with recyclable materials and educational board games, foster inclusive, creative, and practical learning experiences. Case studies from higher education institutions in Portugal demonstrate how structured training empowers educators with the confidence and skills necessary to implement interdisciplinary and student-centered learning. The chapter highlights the impact of these practices on teachers and students, noting increased engagement, collaboration, and equity in classrooms. It also addresses infrastructure, teacher preparation, and sustainability challenges, offering strategic recommendations for future training. This work contributes to the literature on equitable and effective STEAM education by implementing hybrid pedagogies.

DOI: 10.4018/979-8-2600-1568-1.ch010

INTRODUCTION

The concept of Science, Technology, Engineering, Arts, and Mathematics (STEAM) emerged as an integrative approach that connects science, technology, engineering, arts, and mathematics within a coherent curricular framework, emphasizing interdisciplinary problem-solving and creativity, as proposed by Yakman (2008). More recent reviews have documented how STEAM initiatives support creativity, digital competence, and innovation across various educational levels, followed by appropriate references.

STEAM education, an interdisciplinary approach that integrates STEAM, has increasingly been recognized as vital for preparing students to navigate the complex challenges of the 21st century. It fosters critical thinking, problem-solving, creativity, collaboration, and technological fluency, all essential competencies for contemporary and future job markets (Commission, 2020; OECD, 2024). Teacher training programs, therefore, play a crucial role in embedding these skills and methodologies in educational practice, shaping the educators who will implement innovative pedagogies in classrooms worldwide (Correia et al., 2024; Costa et al., 2022).

Globally, STEAM has become a cornerstone of educational reform, driven by international organizations and educational policy frameworks emphasizing its importance for sustainable development and societal advancement (OECD, 2024). Reports from organizations like the United Nations Educational, Scientific and Cultural Organization (UNESCO) and the European Commission (EC) highlight the urgent need to reform teacher education to integrate STEAM pedagogies, aligning educational outcomes with global economic and technological shifts (Commission, 2020; UNESCO, 2025). Countries like Finland, Australia, and the United States have pioneered comprehensive STEAM integration into teacher training programs, showcasing significant improvements in student engagement and achievement across disciplinary boundaries (Herro et al., 2018).

Current literature suggests that STEAM education is no longer understood as simply attaching artistic subjects to technical curricula. Instead, it is increasingly framed as a transdisciplinary approach intended to address complex problems situated in authentic contexts. From early childhood education to higher education, STEAM is presented as a way to cultivate creativity, support innovation, and strengthen digital competence through learning experiences that integrate knowledge, practices, and values across disciplines. This shift also implies a rethinking of how learners participate in knowledge construction, moving from passive reception to active engagement with authentic challenges that require interpretation, design, and decision-making (Chappell et al., 2025; Mullick et al., 2025; Thoma et al., 2023).

A notable feature of the current STEAM landscape is the emphasis on inclusive and adaptive pedagogies. In early childhood settings, researchers have proposed the Inclusive STEAM Pedagogy framework, which promotes a continuous cycle of planning, action, and reflection (Mullick et al., 2025; Thoma et al., 2023). Rather than relying on rigid instruction, this approach prioritizes responsiveness to diverse learning needs and utilizes play-based learning to sustain engagement, curiosity, and foundational skill development. In primary education, inclusion is reinforced through frameworks such as Universal Design for Learning and Connectivism (UDLC). These perspectives aim to reduce barriers to participation and encourage collaboration, ensuring that STEAM activities are accessible to students with diverse abilities, backgrounds, and learning profiles. In this sense, inclusion is not treated as an add-on, but as a guiding principle that shapes task design, interaction, and assessment.

In higher education, the integration of project-based learning within STEAM contexts is frequently described as effective, particularly when learning is connected to societal issues and professional practice (García-Llamas et al., 2025). The Road STEAMer framework, for example, highlights characteristics such as equity, disciplinary interrelationships, and explicit connections to real contexts (Chappell et al., 2025). It is often used to support engagement with wicked problems, including the climate emergency, where solutions require both technical reasoning and human-centered judgment. Collectively, these approaches portray STEAM as a field defined by methodologies that flatten disciplinary hierarchies, connect learning to meaningful contexts, and position students as active agents capable of contributing to change.

The implications for creativity and innovation are central to this literature. The integration of the Arts into STEM is widely described as a catalyst for creative thinking because it encourages learners to combine convergent reasoning with divergent exploration (García-Llamas et al., 2025). For example, in engineering competitions, such as iSTEAM PowerTech, the inclusion of artistic elements has been linked to improvements in creative thinking and aesthetic literacy. Importantly, art in these activities is not merely decorative (Mao & Hong, 2025). Physical properties associated with artistic additions, including weight, balance, and symmetry, can directly influence the mechanical performance of an engineered artifact. As a result, students must engage in systematic experimentation and iterative design, using creative choices that also carry functional consequences.

Innovation in STEAM is also increasingly associated with contextual understanding, which refers to the ability to connect scientific knowledge with sociocultural values, human-centered design principles, and historical perspectives (Liu & Wu, 2025). Research indicates that when students examine the context of a problem, for instance, through perspective taking, engagement with community needs, or analysis of local history, they are more likely to propose solutions that are distinctive and culturally relevant (Mao & Hong, 2025; Vedrenne-Gutiérrez et al., 2024). This emphasis aligns with entrepreneurship education in higher education, where entrepreneurial mindsets and intentions are promoted as drivers of innovation, knowledge mobilization, and technology transfer (Anubhav et al., 2024).

STEAM is likewise presented as a key pathway for developing digital competence, often bridging everyday technology use and the more specialized skills demanded in academic and professional environments. In medical education, the use of learning analytics within STEAM-oriented learning has been reported to enhance students' self-perception of digital competencies, including information literacy, digital content creation, and digital problem-solving (Oliva-Córdova et al., 2025). These tools can support autonomous learning while enabling more personalized pedagogical interventions informed by evidence of learner activity and progress. In primary education, digital competence is strengthened through activities that utilize devices and programming resources, such as robotics and artificial intelligence, as well as activities that do not require devices, like logic-based games (Thoma et al., 2023). Together, these experiences can enhance computational thinking, including logical reasoning and algorithmic thinking.

In Portugal, the integration of STEAM methodologies in teacher training programs has gained notable momentum in recent years, influenced by both international trends and national educational policies. Portuguese education authorities increasingly emphasize curricular flexibility, interdisciplinarity, and digital transition as essential components of educational innovation (Wastiau et al., 2024). Initiatives such as the "*Perfil dos Alunos à Saída da Escolaridade Obrigatória e Aprendizagens Essenciais*" explicitly advocate for STEAM education as a means of cultivating 21st-century competencies among Portuguese students, prompting corresponding adjustments in teacher preparation programs (Costa et al., 2022; Wastiau et al., 2024).

Recent trends significantly influencing the integration of STEAM in teacher training include the increasing availability and incorporation of accessible digital and analog tools. Digital platforms like Scratch, GeoGebra, and Arduino IDE, which are open-source and free, provide educators and trainees with versatile resources to facilitate interactive and creative learning experiences (Correia & Martins, 2024). Simultaneously, there is a growing appreciation for analog materials such as educational board games, recyclable materials, and simple electronics, which effectively complement digital tools, promoting hands-on experimentation and practical learning experiences (Correia et al., 2024; Costa et al., 2022).

Moreover, combining analog and digital elements, hybrid learning approaches are becoming increasingly popular and are recognized for enhancing student engagement and deepening learning outcomes. This integration encourages teachers to adopt more dynamic, inclusive pedagogies, fostering environments where students construct knowledge through practical and meaningful experiences (Correia & Martins, 2024).

Equity and accessibility have also become pivotal trends influencing STEAM integration. Using freely available digital and analog resources ensures that STEAM education can be implemented equitably, irrespective of institutional or socioeconomic barriers (Wastiau et al., 2024). By reducing reliance on costly proprietary technologies, teacher training programs in Portugal empower future educators to implement equitable, engaging, and effective pedagogies across diverse classroom contexts. In the context of creative interdisciplinary work, creativity, collaboration, and equity can be understood as tightly connected rather than separate goals. The review by Moirano et al. (2020) portrays creative interdisciplinary cooperation as a shared and active construction of competent knowledge, in which a variety of expertise is fused through a co-creative combination process to generate new knowledge that is accurate, functional, and usable in context. At the same time, the authors highlight that diversity can trigger collaboration problems that are not merely technical, but also social and relational, including jargon-based communication barriers, protection of intellectual turf, subgroup formation that leads to exclusion and distrust, and interpersonal conflict that can erode team relationships.

From this perspective, equity is not limited to who is present in the team; it also concerns how participation and influence are distributed during the work. The review therefore emphasizes the importance of deliberate leadership, management, and facilitation practices that enable teams to integrate ideas, orient and promote discussion, and ensure a balanced voice for everyone throughout the entire process, thereby preventing the silencing of unique knowledge and the marginalization of boundary-related frictions (Moirano et al., 2020).

In other words, equitable collaboration becomes a practical condition for creativity because it fosters trust, reduces exclusion, and enables the synthesis of differences into coherent outcomes, rather than allowing misunderstandings, competing agendas, or communication gaps to diminish the creative potential of interdisciplinarity.

This document explores these global and national contexts, examining how STEAM education has been integrated into teacher training in Portugal and identifying key factors influencing its successful implementation. Through this exploration, the text aims to highlight best practices, challenges, and future opportunities for embedding robust and inclusive STEAM methodologies into teacher education programs.

CONCEPTUAL FRAMEWORK AND METHODOLOGY

In this chapter, hybrid learning is understood as the deliberate integration of face-to-face and online learning activities within a single course or programme, where digital environments complement and extend in-person interactions (Correia & Martins, 2024; Kučera & Haffner, 2025; Ortega-Arranz et al., 2024). Recent reviews in higher education have highlighted the potential of hybrid formats to increase flexibility and accessibility for diverse student populations, while also revealing persistent challenges related to technological infrastructure, institutional readiness, and the need for sustained professional development among teaching staff (Anubhav et al., 2024; García-Llamas et al., 2025).

STEAM education is an interdisciplinary educational approach that integrates science, technology, engineering, arts, and mathematics (Yakman, 2008). This methodology aims to enhance critical thinking, creativity, collaboration, and problem-solving skills by blending these disciplines into cohesive and interactive learning experiences (Herro et al., 2018). Unlike traditional methods, STEAM promotes real-world applications, encouraging students to engage actively and meaningfully with content through hands-on projects and interdisciplinary tasks (Costa et al., 2022).

Hybrid Learning in Higher Education and Teacher Education

Hybrid learning, as being a central concept of this study, combines digital and analog resources to create dynamic educational experiences. Hybrid approaches leverage the strengths of digital tools - such as online simulations, coding platforms, and virtual labs - and analog tools, including physical manipulatives, board games, and recyclable materials. By integrating these two types of resources, hybrid learning fosters deeper engagement, inclusivity, and practical comprehension of complex concepts (Correia & Martins, 2024; Correia et al., 2024; Kučera & Haffner, 2025). In higher education, hybrid learning environments combine in-person classroom participation with online learning in a coordinated way, often allowing students on campus and those remote to engage simultaneously through digital platforms. This model aims to combine the flexibility and accessibility associated with online learning with the social interaction and immediacy of classroom teaching, creating a more adaptable learning experience that can cater to diverse student needs. At the same time, research highlights that hybrid formats introduce practical and pedagogical challenges, including technical disruptions, time management demands, communication and collaboration difficulties, and added complexity in assessment and feedback. For hybrid learning to be effective, it typically requires strong technological integration, intentional instructional design, active engagement strategies, and sustained support for instructors, allowing teaching practices to be adjusted to the realities of learning across physical and virtual spaces (Gudoniene et al., 2025).

Within this conceptual framework, inclusive education emphasizes equitable access to educational resources and opportunities, catering to diverse student needs and contexts. This approach seeks to eliminate barriers associated with socioeconomic status, disabilities, or cultural backgrounds, ensuring that all students receive quality educational experiences. Therefore, Inclusivity in STEAM education involves carefully selecting and integrating universally accessible resources and methodologies to provide equal opportunities for meaningful learning across varied educational settings (OECD, 2024; UNESCO, 2025).

Portuguese STEAM or STEM Teacher Education

The methodological foundation of this study involves analyzing specific teacher training programs implemented in Portugal that integrate STEAM (or STEM) approaches. These programs, typically offered within master's degree courses in teacher education, professional development workshops, and continuing education initiatives, provide practical training in effectively using digital and analog tools. Participants include pre-service and in-service teachers from various educational levels, ensuring a comprehensive understanding of STEAM implementation across educational contexts (Costa et al., 2022; Wastiau et al., 2024).

The training programs analyzed in this study incorporate a diverse range of resources, prioritizing tools that are accessible, adaptable, and pedagogically effective. The platforms chosen are based on their open-source nature, widespread community support, extensive online resources, adaptability across education levels, and proven ability to enhance student engagement and understanding of complex STEAM concepts (Correia et al., 2024; García-Llamas et al., 2025).

Analog tools integrated into these training programs include recyclable materials, educational board games, basic electronics components, and traditional art supplies. The selection criteria for these analog resources focused on their cost-effectiveness, availability, potential for hands-on experiential learning, and ease of integration into interdisciplinary STEAM projects. Educational board games, in particular, were highlighted due to their ability to foster strategic thinking, collaboration, and creative problem-solving in an engaging, playful context (Costa et al., 2022).

Criteria for selecting digital and analog tools included their potential to support inclusive education by being affordable or freely available, thus addressing socioeconomic barriers and promoting equity. Tools were also evaluated based on their ease of use, adaptability to diverse classroom settings, and alignment with curricular objectives outlined in national educational policies such as Portugal's Digital Transition Strategy and curricular flexibility frameworks (Wastiau et al., 2024).

This conceptual framework and methodological approach provide the basis for examining how STEAM education, supported by hybrid learning methodologies and inclusive practices, can be effectively integrated into teacher training programs. By evaluating teachers' practical experiences in Portugal, this study seeks to contribute valuable insights into best practices and inform future educational policies and training strategies.

The Portuguese initiatives examined here can be characterised as hybrid learning environments, since they combine synchronous face to face workshops with asynchronous online tasks and collaborative work mediated by digital platforms.

DIGITAL AND ANALOG TOOLS IN STEAM EDUCATION

Integrating digital and analog tools within STEAM education enhances educational outcomes by fostering creativity, critical thinking, and practical problem-solving skills. In recent years, research has underscored the value of accessible and flexible tools in providing equitable and engaging learning experiences for diverse student populations (Chevalier et al., 2020; Lavicza et al., 2022).

Open-source digital tools have become particularly prominent due to their accessibility, adaptability, and supportive online communities. Scratch, developed by MIT, allows students to learn programming through visual block-based coding, promoting computational thinking and creativity (Molina-Ayuso et al., 2022; Suriyaarachchi et al., 2022; Yadav et al., 2017). GeoGebra supports interactive learning in mathematics, offering dynamic, visual representations of mathematical concepts that facilitate student understanding and exploration (Romero Albaladejo & García López, 2024). Tinkercad provides a user-friendly, browser-based 3D modeling and design platform, enabling students to engage in interactive design processes fundamental to engineering education (Hain & Motaref, 2020). Arduino IDE empowers learners to engage deeply with electronics and programming by enabling hands-on experimentation and creating interactive projects, thus bridging theoretical knowledge with practical applications (Bedoya-Cano et al., 2025).

While digital resources offer significant benefits, analog tools play a vital role in STEAM education by providing tangible, hands-on experiences that reinforce learning. Materials such as recyclable resources, basic electronics components, and educational board games foster an experiential learning environment that encourages active participation and collaborative problem-solving (Boltsi et al., 2024). Recyclable materials, easily accessible and cost-effective, stimulate creativity and resourcefulness, encouraging students to innovate sustainably (Larkin, 2015). Educational board games, in particular, are praised for their ability to develop strategic thinking, teamwork, and critical reasoning skills through interactive and playful contexts, making complex STEAM concepts more approachable and engaging (Noda et al., 2019).

Research emphasizes the complementary nature of digital and analog tools within educational frameworks, highlighting that their combined use often results in richer learning experiences than their applications (Lavicza et al., 2022; Romero Albaladejo & García López, 2024). For example, integrating analog construction activities with digital simulations can deepen students' conceptual understanding by allowing them to visualize, manipulate, and test theoretical concepts practically. Studies show that blending digital and analog methodologies fosters a more comprehensive understanding and retention of STEAM-related concepts as students actively engage cognitive and motor skills in learning processes (Noda et al., 2019).

Moreover, the hybrid approach encourages inclusivity by accommodating diverse learning styles and needs. While digital tools can provide adaptable and personalized learning paths for students with various abilities, analog resources facilitate group collaboration and tactile learning experiences beneficial for kinesthetic learners. These tools help educators create inclusive, differentiated, and compelling STEAM learning environments that cater comprehensively to student diversity.

In conclusion, integrating digital and analog resources in STEAM education provides robust pedagogical advantages. The strategic use of accessible open-source digital platforms combined with hands-on analog activities represents an effective approach to fostering inclusive, engaging, and practical STEAM learning experiences. This chapter further explores specific examples and analyzes their effectiveness within contemporary educational contexts.

HYBRID LEARNING: CASE STUDIES FROM PORTUGAL

Hybrid learning is an educational approach combining digital and analog resources to enrich learning experiences. By integrating both tools, educators can offer diverse, engaging, and inclusive learning opportunities that cater to different student needs and learning styles (Costa et al., 2022). In STEAM education, hybrid learning methodologies are particularly beneficial, promoting hands-on exploration alongside digital innovation, thus fostering deeper conceptual understanding and practical problem-solving skills (Thi To Khuyen et al., 2020).

Digital and Analog Integration in Portuguese Education: Key Initiatives Shaping Teacher Training

Several Portuguese initiatives such as: "*Escola Digital*" (Coppi et al., 2025; Meirinhos, 2024); "*Laboratórios Digitais (LED)*" (Sousa, 2023); "Erasmus+ ICT Training" (Alves & Escorel, 2024); or "Portugal Digital Academy" (Correia & Henriques, 2025), demonstrate effective digital and analog tool integration within teacher training programs.

The "*Escola Digital*" project, launched by the Portuguese Government, represents a profound reform in public education aimed at fostering the digital transition across primary and secondary schools. By 2026, the initiative will have solidified its impact through three fundamental pillars: (1) the widespread distribution of laptops and mobile connectivity for students and teachers; (2) the continuous digital training of educators through structured professional development programs, and (3) the creation of digital educational resources and dematerialized textbooks. This strategic investment is not merely about modernizing the physical infrastructure of schools but also about democratizing access to technology, tackling social exclusion, and equipping younger generations with the critical digital skills required by the contemporary labor market. By integrating technological tools into everyday pedagogical practices, the project aims to transform learning methods, making them more interactive, personalized, and resilient to the challenges of an increasingly globalized world.

A key initiative within Portugal's Recovery and Resilience Plan (RRP) is the Digital Education Labs (LED), scheduled for completion by 2026, are innovative learning spaces established in schools to modernize the educational landscape. These labs provide students in the 2nd and 3rd cycles of basic education and secondary school with access to cutting-edge equipment, including robotics, electronics, and multimedia art tools. The primary goal is to foster STEM skills and active learning methodologies, encouraging students to engage in collaborative, hands-on projects that integrate computational thinking and creativity. As of 2026, these laboratories serve as vital hubs for digital inclusion, ensuring that the younger generation is equipped with the technical and critical skills necessary to thrive in a digital-first global economy.

The Erasmus+ ICT training projects in Funchal, Madeira, are expected to establish themselves by 2026 as premier hubs for the professional development of European educators, focusing on the practical integration of Information and Communication Technologies in school settings. These initiatives offer structured courses that range from foundational digital literacy to advanced applications of Artificial Intelligence and gamification tools in the classroom. By leveraging Funchal's unique setting, the program combines technical training with cultural exchange, empowering teachers to create more inclusive and dynamic learning environments that are fully equipped to address contemporary digital challenges.

Another project founded by de RRP, the Portugal Digital Academy (*"Academia Portugal Digital"*), a cornerstone of the national Digital Transition Action Plan, aims to establish itself by 2026 as the leading platform for upskilling and digital empowerment of the Portuguese population. This initiative provides self-assessment tools based on the European Digital Competence Framework (DigComp), enabling citizens and professionals to identify skill gaps and access personalized, free training pathways. By integrating a broad network of partners and educational resources, the project aims to democratize technological literacy, bridge the digital divide, and enhance the competitiveness of the national workforce, preparing the country for the demands of an increasingly automated and data-driven global economy.

Integration Examples of Analog and Digital Methods

Several of the Portuguese initiatives like the training sessions frequently incorporate open-source digital platforms alongside tangible materials like recyclable resources and basic electronics (Costa et al., 2022). One notable example involves teachers guiding students in constructing robots using recyclable materials and programming them via Arduino IDE. This integration allows participants to experience a tangible manifestation of abstract digital concepts, significantly enhancing comprehension and retention (Thi To Khuyen et al., 2020).

Educational board games have also been effectively paired with digital simulations. In workshops conducted by teacher training centers in Portugal, participants used board games to introduce strategic and critical thinking, complemented by digital tools to simulate real-world scientific scenarios. This approach successfully encouraged deeper engagement and enhanced collaborative skills among trainees (Correia & Martins, 2024).

Another initiative involved integrating outdoor analog activities with digital tools, such as mobile applications, for environmental data collection. Teachers trained in these hybrid approaches reported higher student motivation and a better understanding of ecological concepts through hands-on experiences combined with immediate digital feedback and data analysis.

Some Portuguese schools have also experimented with hybrid projects involving students creating physical art installations enhanced with digital projections or augmented reality, demonstrating STEAM concepts creatively and interactively. Such projects provided authentic interdisciplinary experiences that effectively engaged students and enriched their understanding (Thi To Khuyen et al., 2020).

Analysis of Portuguese Teacher Training Initiatives

The Portuguese Ministry of Education's initiatives, such as the Digital Transition Strategy, have significantly supported the adoption of hybrid learning methods in teacher training programs (Wastiau et al., 2024). Programs like "*Escola Digital*" equipped schools with digital devices and effectively trained educators to integrate digital and analog resources into their teaching practice. Workshops under this program offered comprehensive training sessions focusing on implementing hybrid methodologies to promote equity and inclusive education

Higher education in Portugal has also seen relevant initiatives, including a teacher training program developed by the Polytechnic Institute of Santarem that serves as a model of effective hybrid learning practices. This postgraduate certificate program, titled "STEAM Education", systematically trained educators in integrating digital tools (such as programming platforms and digital simulations) with analog activities (including physical manipulatives and educational games). Trainees participated in structured projects, blending digital and physical experiences to design practical classroom interventions. Feedback from participants underscored enhanced confidence and skill in implementing interdisciplinary and inclusive STEAM practice (Correia et al., 2024; Santarém, 2023).

Other Portuguese universities and polytechnics, such as the Polytechnic Institute of Porto and Polytechnic Institute of Cávado and Ave, have similarly implemented hybrid learning training programs. These initiatives typically involve collaborative workshops where educators develop interdisciplinary projects combining digital simulations and analog experimentation, resulting in notable increases in teacher enthusiasm and classroom innovation (Costa et al., 2022).

Impact on Teacher Practices

Empirical evidence from these training initiatives illustrates substantial shifts in teaching practices. Teachers reported increased pedagogical confidence, highlighting improved abilities in facilitating interdisciplinary and inclusive learning environments. These educators subsequently applied hybrid methodologies in their classrooms, emphasizing active learning and student-centered approaches (Costa et al., 2022; Thi To Khuyen et al., 2020).

Research suggests that teacher training interventions have significantly influenced classroom dynamics, prompting educators to transition from traditional instructional methods to more innovative, engaging pedagogies. Educators noted that incorporating hybrid learning strategies improved their ability to address diverse student needs, creating more equitable learning opportunities (Correia & Martins, 2024).

Impact on Student Engagement

Students whose teachers participated in hybrid learning training demonstrated increased engagement, motivation, and overall academic performance. Studies indicated higher levels of student participation and improved collaborative skills due to the dynamic nature of hybrid educational practices (Correia & Martins, 2024). Specifically, students engaged more actively in classroom activities that blended digital and analog elements, displaying enhanced creativity, problem-solving abilities, and enthusiasm for learning (Correia et al., 2024).

Teachers also reported positive outcomes regarding students' emotional and social development. Combining digital and analog resources fostered a supportive and inclusive classroom environment, allowing students of various abilities to contribute meaningfully. These inclusive practices were particularly beneficial in reducing educational disparities and promoting equitable learning experiences (Wastiau et al., 2024).

This hybrid learning methods implemented in Portuguese teacher training initiatives greatly benefit educators and students. By integrating digital and analog resources, these programs effectively enhanced teacher confidence, transformed pedagogical practices, and significantly increased student engagement. Future training initiatives should continue emphasizing hybrid methodologies, considering their profound impact on creating inclusive, innovative, and equitable educational experiences.

DISCUSSION: EQUITY, ACCESSIBILITY, AND SUSTAINABILITY

This section examines the Portuguese case studies in relation to broader debates on equity, accessibility, and sustainability in STEAM and hybrid learning. It identifies key challenges and opportunities for future teacher education.

Equity, Accessibility, And Sustainability

Teacher preparation for STEAM education faces fundamental challenges in understanding and implementing integrated approaches. Research indicates that many practitioners interpret STEAM as merely a series of activities rather than a holistic educational philosophy. This misconception stems from the inherent complexity of integrating multiple disciplines, which challenges traditional subject-specific teaching models. Teachers report significant difficulties with cross-disciplinary collaboration, often struggling to arrange adequate time for collaborative planning or independent development of relevant activities.

Integrating STEAM education in teacher training presents numerous opportunities to foster equitable and inclusive learning environments. However, this integration also faces considerable challenges that must be acknowledged and addressed to achieve sustainable implementation. This section examines the role of free resources in promoting equitable education, identifies barriers to effective implementation, and discusses strategies to overcome these challenges in the context of Portuguese educational initiatives.

Role of Free Resources in Promoting Equitable Education

Free and open-source resources play a critical role in democratizing education by offering equitable access to educational tools, irrespective of socioeconomic background. Digital platforms open source, as well as open-source hardware like

Arduino, have significantly reduced financial barriers, providing schools and teachers in economically disadvantaged contexts with robust educational tools (OECD, 2024; Romero Albaladejo & García López, 2024). These resources enable educators to deliver interactive and engaging curricula without incurring substantial costs, thus bridging socioeconomic divides and promoting inclusivity in STEAM education.

Analog resources, including recyclable materials and educational board games, reinforce equity by being affordable, accessible, and adaptable. Recyclable materials encourage sustainable practices and creativity, enabling students to innovate using readily available resources. Educational board games provide interactive and collaborative learning opportunities, enhancing critical thinking and teamwork without significant financial investment (Reinholz et al., 2021).

Portuguese teacher training programs increasingly leverage these free resources to ensure inclusive access to high-quality STEAM education. Programs such as "*Escola Digital*" demonstrate how equipping schools with open-source digital tools and training teachers to utilize low-cost analog materials significantly promotes educational equity (Wastiau et al., 2024).

Barriers to Effective Implementation

Despite these benefits, several barriers hinder the effective implementation of STEAM education using free resources. Among these are technological infrastructure limitations, resistance to pedagogical change, insufficient teacher training, and sustainability concerns.

Technological infrastructure remains a significant challenge, especially in rural and economically disadvantaged areas. Inconsistent internet connectivity and limited availability of devices restrict the effective use of digital tools, compromising the quality and continuity of STEAM education (Wastiau et al., 2024). This digital divide exacerbates educational inequalities, necessitating targeted interventions to improve infrastructure.

Another critical barrier is resistance to pedagogical change among educators accustomed to traditional teaching methods. Teachers may feel inadequately prepared or reluctant to adopt new methodologies involving digital and analog tools. Effective professional development and ongoing support are necessary to overcome this inertia and foster a positive shift toward innovative STEAM pedagogies (Costa et al., 2022).

Practical implementation barriers significantly impact STEAM education adoption. Teachers consistently report pacing, time management challenges, and struggling to cover required content while implementing integrated STEAM activities. These timing issues are compounded by insufficient planning periods and the demanding nature of coordinating multiple subject areas within single lessons.

Resource limitations present another substantial obstacle. Limited access to appropriate materials can hinder the success of the STEAM program, as these programs typically require resources spanning multiple disciplinary areas beyond what traditional single-subject classes demand. Budget constraints often prevent adequate material provision for all students, creating equity concerns and implementation challenges.

The availability of quality curriculum resources remains problematic. Many educators report a lack of STEAM-specific lesson plans and teaching materials, requiring additional preparation time that teachers may not have. This resource gap forces educators to develop materials independently, often without adequate training or support for creating practical integrated activities.

Moreover, insufficient training in integrating digital and analog resources constitutes another major hurdle. Teachers frequently express uncertainty about effectively combining these resources, resulting in inconsistent and suboptimal classroom implementation. Comprehensive training programs emphasizing hands-on, practical applications and peer collaboration can significantly mitigate this challenge (Correia et al., 2024).

Sustainability of STEAM Initiatives

Ensuring the long-term sustainability of STEAM education initiatives is another considerable challenge. Initial enthusiasm and funding for pilot projects often diminish over time, jeopardizing their continuity. Sustainable implementation requires consistent financial, institutional, and community support, which can be challenging to maintain (Correia & Martins, 2024; OECD, 2024).

Current teacher preparation programs often fail to address the unique demands of STEAM education. Traditional preparation models focus on single disciplines, creating a disconnect with the integrative requirements of STEAM teaching. This preparation gap necessitates extensive professional development efforts that many school systems struggle to provide consistently.

Teacher workload and resource maintenance further threaten sustainability. Managing hybrid learning environments demands significant preparation and adaptability from educators, increasing their workload and potentially leading to burnout without adequate institutional support. Continuous professional development, structured support systems, and resource-sharing networks are critical to maintaining educator enthusiasm and reducing burnout risk (Thi To Khuyen et al., 2020).

Strategies for Overcoming Challenges

Addressing these challenges requires multifaceted strategies involving policy, infrastructure development, professional training, and community engagement. Policy interventions, such as Portugal's Digital Transition Strategy, demonstrate governmental commitment to providing schools with the necessary technological infrastructure and support. Continued digital connectivity and educational technology investments are essential for sustainable STEAM implementation (Wastiau et al., 2024).

Professional development programs must prioritize practical training and ongoing support, equipping teachers with the skills and confidence necessary to integrate free resources effectively. Structured peer collaboration and mentorship programs can enhance teachers' professional growth, encourage innovation, and foster a supportive community (Carvalhais & Azevedo, 2024; Costa et al., 2022; Terçariol et al., 2024).

Community engagement and partnerships with local organizations and industries can also bolster sustainability. These collaborations can provide financial support, expertise, and additional resources, ensuring the ongoing viability of STEAM initiatives. Schools that establish strong community ties can sustain and expand their educational programs more effectively, benefiting both students and educators (Wannapiroon & Pimdee, 2022).

Digital platforms and online learning environments offer scalable solutions for STEAM teacher preparation. Self-paced online courses provide flexibility for working educators while maintaining quality standards through structured curricula. These platforms can deliver content efficiently while allowing teachers to progress according to their schedules and learning needs (Lavicza et al., 2022).

Hybrid delivery models combining online and face-to-face components show particular effectiveness. Research indicates that teachers appreciate the flexibility of hybrid approaches while valuing the community-building aspects of in-person interactions. (Singh et al., 2021). This combination allows for efficient content delivery while maintaining the collaborative elements essential for STEAM learning.

Virtual reality and simulation technologies present emerging opportunities for teacher training in STEAM contexts. These tools can provide immersive experiences that help teachers understand complex interdisciplinary concepts and practice implementation strategies in safe, controlled environments (Leavy et al., 2023).

Promoting equity and accessibility through free resources in STEAM education represents a significant opportunity to address educational disparities. However, realizing these opportunities requires recognizing and overcoming substantial implementation barriers. By investing in infrastructure, providing comprehensive teacher training, and fostering strong community partnerships, Portugal can ensure the effective, sustainable integration of STEAM education, ultimately enhancing educational equity and student outcomes.

CONCLUSION

Effective implementation of STEAM education requires comprehensive and systemic support that extends well beyond the preparation of individual teachers. School administrators must receive targeted training to effectively support STEAM initiatives, which includes understanding the necessary resources, scheduling logistics, and appropriate evaluation strategies. Administrative backing is a pivotal factor in determining teachers' success in implementing STEAM methodologies.

The alignment of educational policies at both district and state levels plays a crucial role in facilitating the adoption of STEAM education. When curriculum standards and assessment frameworks endorse integrated instructional approaches, educators are afforded greater flexibility to apply STEAM strategies in their classrooms. Such alignment helps to minimize the conflict between innovative pedagogies and traditional accountability measures.

Developing professional learning communities (PLCs) within schools provides ongoing, peer-supported structures essential to sustained STEAM implementation. These collaborative environments enable educators to exchange experiences, collaboratively address challenges, and maintain the momentum of innovative instructional practices well beyond initial training sessions.

As STEAM-focused teacher training programs become more widespread, ensuring the consistency and quality of these initiatives grows increasingly important. Using research-based frameworks for evaluating professional development programs ensures that such efforts lead to measurable improvements in teaching practices and student learning outcomes.

Feedback loops between training initiatives and classroom applications offer critical data for continuous program refinement. When training providers systematically gather data on participant outcomes and the challenges encountered during implementation, they can adapt their models to better align with teachers' evolving needs.

Longitudinal studies tracking teacher training participants provide valuable insights into the long-term sustainability of STEAM implementation. Identifying which elements of training programs lead to enduring changes in instructional practice contributes to the design of more effective future professional development initiatives.

While integrating STEAM into teacher education presents notable challenges, it also offers considerable opportunities for innovation and growth. Educators often face substantial barriers, including limited pedagogical training, inadequate resources, and lack of systemic support. However, emerging models of professional development show promise in addressing and overcoming these obstacles. Achieving success requires a holistic strategy that attends to individual educator development and the broader structural conditions that shape implementation.

The most impactful STEAM teacher training programs provide ongoing, collaborative support that blends theoretical foundations with practical, hands-on experience. Delivery models that offer flexibility to accommodate teachers' schedules and professional responsibilities have shown particular potential, as have those that connect training content to real-world contexts and community-based partnerships. The field would greatly benefit from continued empirical research on effective training models, increased investment in high-quality professional development, and educational policies promoting integrated learning approaches. Existing evidence underscores that, with adequate support and training, educators can effectively implement STEAM strategies that enhance student engagement and prepare learners for the demands of a rapidly evolving 21st-century world.

ACKNOWLEDGMENT

This work is funded by National Funds through the FCT - Foundation for Science and Technology, I.P., within the scope of the project Refª UIDB/05507/2020 and DOI identifier https://doi.org/10.54499/UIDB/05507/2020. Furthermore, we would like to thank the Centre for Studies in Education and Innovation (Ci&DEI) and the Polytechnic of Viseu for their support.

REFERENCES

Alves, D., & Escorel, V. (2024). From Erasmus to European education area and a case study *16th International Conference on Education and New Learning Technologies*, Spain, Palma. DOI: 10.21125/edulearn.2024.1800

Anubhav, K., Dwivedi, A. K., & Aashish, K. (2024). Entrepreneurship education in higher education (2002–2022): A technology-empowered systematic literature review. *International Journal of Management Education*, *22*(3), 100993. DOI: 10.1016/j.ijme.2024.100993

Bedoya-Cano, O., Marín-Marín, J.-A., & López-Belmonte, J. (2025). Integrating Arduino and Artificial Intelligence in STEM Education. In (pp. 149-165). https://doi.org/DOI: 10.1007/978-3-031-82915-4_7

Boltsi, A., Kalovrektis, K., Xenakis, A., Chatzimisios, P., & Chaikalis, C. (2024). Digital Tools, Technologies, and Learning Methodologies for Education 4.0 Frameworks: A STEM Oriented Survey. *IEEE Access : Practical Innovations, Open Solutions*, *12*, 12883–12901. DOI: 10.1109/ACCESS.2024.3355282

Carvalhais, L., & Azevedo, P. (2024). Digital Teacher Training in the Portuguese National Plan for Digital Development at Schools: A Case Study. *Technology. Knowledge and Learning*, *29*(3), 1579–1595. DOI: 10.1007/s10758-024-09760-3

Chappell, K., Hetherington, L., Juillard, S., Aguirre, C., & Duca, E. (2025). A framework for effective STEAM education: Pedagogy for responding to wicked problems. *International Journal of Educational Research Open*, *9*, 100474. DOI: 10.1016/j.ijedro.2025.100474

Chevalier, M., Giang, C., Piatti, A., & Mondada, F. (2020). Fostering computational thinking through educational robotics: A model for creative computational problem solving. *International Journal of STEM Education*, *7*(1), 39. DOI: 10.1186/s40594-020-00238-z

Commission, E. (2020). *Education and training monitor 2020 – Teaching and learning in a digital age.* https://education.ec.europa.eu/about-eea/education-and-training-monitor

Coppi, M., Fialho, I., & Gomes, S. (2025). Capacitação digital em Portugal. *Educação Sociedade & Culturas*, •••, 1–25. DOI: 10.24840/esc.vi70.982

Correia, J. D., & Henriques, S. (2025). *Assessing Digital and Info-Communication Competencies in Higher Education: A Blended Approach for e-Learning Environments* Perspectives and Trends in Education and Technology, Volume 2, Cham.

Correia, M., & Martins, C. (2024). *Primary pre-service teachers' understanding of STEAM education through lesson planning* The 15th Conference of the European Science Education Research Association (ESERA), Cappadocia, Türkiye. http://hdl.handle.net/10400.15/4955

Correia, M., Ribeirinha, T., Beirante, D., Santos, R., Ramos, L., Dias, I. S., Luís, H., Catela, D., Galinha, S., Arrais, A., Portelada, A., Pinto, P., Simões, V., Ferreira, R., Franco, S., & Martins, M. C. (2024). Outdoor STEAM Education: Opportunities and Challenges. *Education Sciences*, *14*(7), 688. Advance online publication. DOI: 10.3390/educsci14070688

Costa, M., Domingos, A., Teodoro, V., & Vinhas, É. (2022). Teacher Professional Development in STEM Education: An Integrated Approach with Real-World Scenarios in Portugal. *Mathematics*, *10*(21), 3944. https://www.mdpi.com/2227-7390/10/21/3944. DOI: 10.3390/math10213944

García-Llamas, P., Taboada, A., Sanz-Chumillas, P., Lopes Pereira, L., & Baelo Álvarez, R. (2025). Breaking barriers in STEAM education: Analyzing competence acquisition through project-based learning in a European context. *International Journal of Educational Research Open*, *8*, 100449. DOI: 10.1016/j.ijedro.2025.100449

Gudoniene, D., Staneviciene, E., Huet, I., Dickel, J., Dieng, D., Degroote, J., Rocio, V., Butkiene, R., & Casanova, D. (2025). Hybrid Teaching and Learning in Higher Education: A Systematic Literature Review. *Sustainability (Basel)*, *17*(2), 756. DOI: 10.3390/su17020756

Hain, A., & Motaref, S. (2020). Implementing Interactive 3-D Models in an Entry-level Engineering Course to Enhance Students'. *Visualization*. Advance online publication. DOI: 10.18260/1-2--34782

Herro, D., Quigley, C., & Jacques, L. A. (2018). Examining technology integration in middle school STEAM units. *Technology, Pedagogy and Education*, *27*(4), 485–498. DOI: 10.1080/1475939X.2018.1514322

Kučera, E., & Haffner, O. (2025). Competency-Based Hybrid Learning: A Modern Approach to Teaching Programming and Digital Technologies Subjects. *IEEE Access : Practical Innovations, Open Solutions, 13*, 54892–54919. DOI: 10.1109/ACCESS.2025.3555333

Larkin, T. L. (2015). Creativity in STEM education: Reshaping the creative project. 1184-1189. https://doi.org/DOI: 10.1109/ICL.2015.7318203

Lavicza, Z., Weinhandl, R., Prodromou, T., Anđić, B., Lieban, D., Hohenwarter, M., Fenyvesi, K., Brownell, C., & Diego-Mantecón, J. M. (2022). Developing and Evaluating Educational Innovations for STEAM Education in Rapidly Changing Digital Technology Environments. *Sustainability (Basel), 14*(12), 7237. Advance online publication. DOI: 10.3390/su14127237

Leavy, A., Dick, L., Meletiou-Mavrotheris, M., Paparistodemou, E., & Stylianou, E. (2023). The prevalence and use of emerging technologies in STEAM education: A systematic review of the literature. *Journal of Computer Assisted Learning, 39*(4), 1061–1082. DOI: 10.1111/jcal.12806

Liu, C.-Y., & Wu, C.-J. (2025). Extracting the actions of contextual understanding in STEAM research: Direction for STEAM course design. *Thinking Skills and Creativity, 56*, 101770. DOI: 10.1016/j.tsc.2025.101770

Mao, Q., & Hong, J.-C. (2025). An exploration of the value of artwork in an integrated STEAM competition. *Thinking Skills and Creativity, 57*, 101857. DOI: 10.1016/j.tsc.2025.101857

Meirinhos, M. F. A. (2024). *Escola Digital: rumo à escola de competências*. Pimenta Cultural., DOI: 10.31560/pimentacultural/978-85-7221-249-6

Moirano, R., Sánchez, M. A., & Štěpánek, L. (2020). Creative interdisciplinary collaboration: A systematic literature review. *Thinking Skills and Creativity, 35*, 100626. DOI: 10.1016/j.tsc.2019.100626

Molina-Ayuso, Á., Adamuz-Povedano, N., Bracho-López, R., & Torralbo-Rodríguez, M. (2022). Introduction to Computational Thinking with Scratch for Teacher Training for Spanish Primary School Teachers in Mathematics. *Education Sciences, 12*(12), 899. DOI: 10.3390/educsci12120899

Mullick, J., Wang, Q., Vlcek, S., & Sikder, S. (2025). "The possibility of meeting the needs of all children": A framework for enhancing inclusive STEAM pedagogy in early childhood settings. *International Journal of Educational Research, 133*, 102705. DOI: 10.1016/j.ijer.2025.102705

Noda, S., Shirotsuki, K., & Nakao, M. (2019). The effectiveness of intervention with board games: A systematic review. *BioPsychoSocial Medicine*, *13*(1), 22. DOI: 10.1186/s13030-019-0164-1 PMID: 31641371

OECD. T. O. f. E. C.-o. a. D. (2024). *Future of Education and Skills 2030/2040*. Retrieved 25/05/2025 from https://www.oecd.org/

Oliva-Córdova, L. M., Tohom, M. F. V., Salazar de la Cruz, R. C., & Martín-Núñez, J. L. (2025). Application of learning analytics in medical education: Enhancing student digital competences within the STEAM framework. *International Journal of Educational Research Open*, *9*, 100511. https://doi.org/doi.org/10.1016/j.ijedro.2025.100511. DOI: 10.1016/j.ijedro.2025.100511

Ortega-Arranz, A., Amarasinghe, I., Martínez-Monés, A., Asensio-Pérez, J. I., Dimitriadis, Y., Corrales-Astorgano, M., & Hernández-Leo, D. (2024). Collaborative activities in hybrid learning environments: Exploring teacher orchestration load and students' perceptions. *Computers & Education*, *219*, 105105. DOI: 10.1016/j.compedu.2024.105105

Reinholz, D. L., White, I., & Andrews, T. (2021). Change theory in STEM higher education: A systematic review. *International Journal of STEM Education*, *8*(1), 37. DOI: 10.1186/s40594-021-00291-2

Romero Albaladejo, I. M., & García López, M. (2024). Mathematical attitudes transformation when introducing GeoGebra in the secondary classroom. *Education and Information Technologies*, *29*(8), 10277–10302. DOI: 10.1007/s10639-023-12085-w

Santarém, I. P. (2023). *Pós-graduação em Educação STEAM*. Retrieved 23-5-2025 from https://www.ipsantarem.pt/eses/pgest/

Singh, J., Evans, E., Reed, A., Karch, L., Qualey, K., Singh, L., & Wiersma, H. (2021). Online, Hybrid, and Face-to-Face Learning Through the Eyes of Faculty, Students, Administrators, and Instructional Designers: Lessons Learned and Directions for the Post-Vaccine and Post-Pandemic/COVID-19 World. *Journal of Educational Technology Systems*, *50*(3), 301–326. DOI: 10.1177/00472395211063754

Sousa, M. R. (2023). *Lei das Grandes Opções para 2023 -2026*. Diário da República Retrieved from https://files.diariodarepublica.pt/1s/2023/08/14900/0000300113.pdf

Suriyaarachchi, H., Denny, P., & Nanayakkara, S. (2022). Scratch and Sense: Using Real-Time Sensor Data to Motivate Students Learning Scratch *SIGCSE 2022: Proceedings of the 53rd ACM Technical Symposium on Computer Science Education*, Providence, RI, USA. https://doi.org/DOI: 10.1145/3478431.3499316

Terçariol, A. A. L., Bioto, P. A., Melaré Vieira Barros, D., Caeiro, L., & Barnabé, J. (2024). Educação STEAM: Formação, percepções e práticas sob olhares de Brasil e Portugal. *Dialogia*, (50). Advance online publication. DOI: 10.5585/50.2024.27833

Thi To Khuyen, N., Van Bien, N., Lin, P.-L., Lin, J., & Chang, C.-Y. (2020). Measuring Teachers' Perceptions to Sustain STEM Education Development. *Sustainability (Basel)*, *12*(4), 1531. Advance online publication. DOI: 10.3390/su12041531

Thoma, R., Farassopoulos, N., & Lousta, C. (2023). Teaching STEAM through universal design for learning in early years of primary education: Plugged-in and unplugged activities with emphasis on connectivism learning theory. *Teaching and Teacher Education*, *132*, 104210. DOI: 10.1016/j.tate.2023.104210

UNESCO. (2025). *Framework for the implementation of Education for Sustainable Development (ESD) beyond 2019.* https://unesdoc.unesco.org/ark:/48223/pf0000370215

Vedrenne-Gutiérrez, F., López-Suero, C. C., De Hoyos-Bermea, A., Mora-Flores, L. P., Monroy-Fraustro, D., Orozco-Castillo, M. F., Martínez-Velasco, J. F., & Altamirano-Bustamante, M. M. (2024). The axiological foundations of innovation in STEM education – A systematic review and ethical meta-analysis. *Heliyon*, *10*(12), e32381. DOI: 10.1016/j.heliyon.2024.e32381 PMID: 38994089

Wannapiroon, N., & Pimdee, P. (2022). Thai undergraduate science, technology, engineering, arts, and math (STEAM) creative thinking and innovation skill development: A conceptual model using a digital virtual classroom learning environment. *Education and Information Technologies*, *27*(4), 5689–5716. DOI: 10.1007/s10639-021-10849-w PMID: 35068986

Wastiau, P., Looney, J., & Laanpere, M. (2024, 1-06-2024). *Portugal's digital transition strategy for education. System change case studies series.* Retrieved 14-04-2025 from https://erte.dge.mec.pt

Yadav, A., Stephenson, C., & Hong, H. (2017). Computational thinking for teacher education. *Communications of the ACM*, *60*(4), 55–62. DOI: 10.1145/2994591

Yakman, G. (2008). STEAM Education: an overview of creating a model of integrative education.

Chapter 11
From Analysis to Urban Project With an Eco-Social Approach:
ECOLAB Reference Project Laboratory as a Teaching Methodology Applied to the Guadalmedina River

Rubén Mora-Esteban
Independent Researcher, Spain

Francisco Conejo Arrabal
http://orcid.org/0000-0001-7180-2893
Independent Researcher, Spain

Jorge Asencio-Juncal
http://orcid.org/0000-0001-9037-6869
Escuela Técnica Superior de Arquitectura, Universidad de Málaga, Spain

Nuria Nebot Gómez de Salazar
http://orcid.org/0000-0001-6187-0972
Independent Researcher, Spain

ABSTRACT

This work presents an educational experience conducted within the context of the second-year Urban Planning 1 course at the School of Architecture in Málaga. Students are introduced to a public space project, for which they must consider

DOI: 10.4018/979-8-2600-1568-1.ch011

ecological and social aspects. The difficulty the students encountered in transitioning from analysis and diagnosis to project implementation led the teachers to implement the ECOLAB Reference Project Laboratory teaching methodology, which provides resources and tools to facilitate critical and argumentative project implementation. The Guadalmedina river area becomes an open-air classroom where students can explore and learn about local issues and the consequences of meeting or not meeting ecological and social criteria for citizens and the environment.

INTRODUCTION

In the context of the current climate emergency, teaching architecture and urban planning presents an urgent challenge: training professionals who can design more sustainable and socially inclusive cities. Many authors emphasise the importance of rethinking higher education to encourage critical thinking and transformative action in response to the climate crisis (De Manuel Jerez & Donadei, 2020; Luque Pulgar, 2023). Traditionally dominated by transmissive teaching models, the university environment is seeing a growing demand for active methodologies that connect learning with real-world societal and environmental issues (Kayser, 2023). In response to this demand, we present an innovative teaching approach for the "Urban Planning I" module of the "Fundamentals of Architecture" degree at the University of Málaga (academic year 2024–25). This approach is based on project-based learning (PBL) and focuses on a highly relevant local case study: the Guadalmedina river as it flows through Málaga city.

Urban Planning I is a second-year course designed for students encountering urban issues and challenges for the first time. Through the examination of local urban issues, the course provides a framework for the critical analysis of cities within the context of the climate crisis. The course explores methodologies to address urban analysis and strategies from a complexity perspective (Parcerisa Bundó & Rubert de Ventós, 2014), with a focus on understanding the multiple factors in which social and environmental aspects play a fundamental role. Students develop their skills by initiating a public space project that incorporates social and ecological sustainability criteria.

Through the development of various teaching activities, students must conduct an urban analysis and diagnosis of a specific local environment and its issues (Phase 1). This will enable them to propose strategies for improving and transforming these environments, integrating social and ecological aspects (Phase 2). In recent years, students have struggled to translate their knowledge of urban analysis and diagnosis into specific project proposals.

To address this issue, the teaching team has implemented a teaching activity called the 'Eco-social Reference Projects Laboratory' (ECO-LAB), which is an applied research workshop on international reference projects with sustainability criteria. As shown in Figure 1, the ECO-LAB workshop aims to facilitate the transition for students from the analysis and diagnosis phase to the proposal phase of sustainable urban design.

Figure 1. Eco-social reference projects laboratory' (ECO-LAB) as an applied research workshop on international reference projects with sustainability criteria

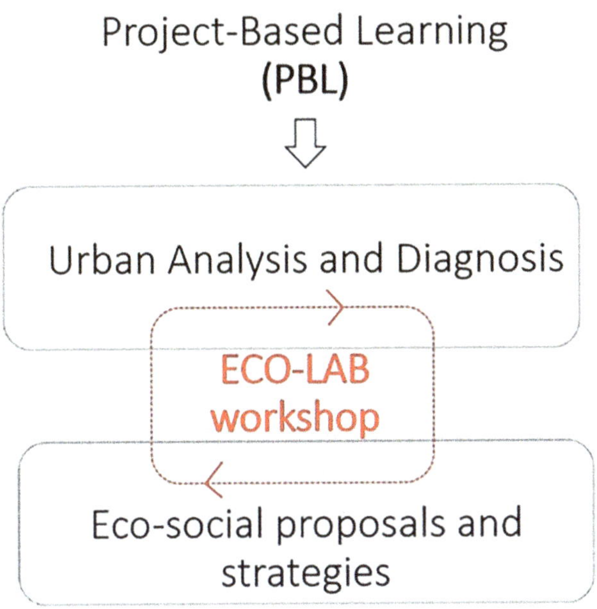

The general framework for the different planned teaching activities is based on a project-based learning (PBL) methodology, using a real-life case study of the Guadalmedina river. This river runs from north to south through the city of Málaga for six kilometres, passing through 16 neighbourhoods adjacent to the river until it flows into the sea. This urban river is usually dry for most of the year because of a dam at the start of its urban section. It is a complex scenario where environmental challenges such as water management and flood risk, as well as a lack of river ecosystem, converge with social and urban challenges such as disconnection between neighbourhoods and degraded spaces. There are also opportunities for the transformation of public spaces. Due to these characteristics, the Guadalmedina river area has been proposed as an ideal teaching laboratory in which students can apply approaches to urban eco-social regeneration. The aim of the course project focused on this area is to connect academic learning with a real-life context, thereby enhancing student motivation and meaningful learning.

This paper presents the teaching experience of the Urban Planning I course. It describes the course's general pedagogical approach based on problem-based learning (PBL), its methodological development in stages and the 'Eco-social Reference Projects Laboratory' workshop. It also presents some results obtained. It emphasises the pedagogical aspects (the implementation of PBL and active learning), the urban aspects (the problems and potential of the Guadalmedina river in the city) and the eco-social aspects (the integration of environmental and social considerations into urban projects). Theoretical bases and related experiences are referenced throughout the text, and the achievements and lessons learned from this pedagogical experience are analysed.

URBAN-ECOSOCIAL CONTEXT OF THE GUADALMEDINA RIVER

The central element of this teaching experience is the Guadalmedina river, a seasonal Mediterranean river that runs from north to south through the urban area of Málaga. Historically, its bed has remained dry for most of the year, carrying large amounts of water only during periods of heavy rainfall. This has turned the Guadalmedina into an urban void of sorts: a concrete channel that not only protects the city from frequent flooding but also acts as a physical barrier, dividing the urban fabric into east and west. For decades, the dry riverbed has been perceived as an eyesore and a degraded space, unused and disconnected from the daily lives of Málaga's residents. Consequently, the neighbourhoods adjacent to the river have suffered relative marginalisation and disconnection from each other due to this territorial fracture.

Various solutions have been proposed by local authorities to integrate this river axis into the city, although there have even been proposals to divert it on several occasions (Asencio-Juncal, 2023). One of the most controversial plans was the well-known Guadalmedina Plan, which was first promoted in 2000. This plan involved covering and vaulting the urban section of the river in order to build a large avenue and new urban spaces on top of it (Wikipedia, n.d.). Supporters of the plan argued that it would close the urban gap, provide space for facilities and green areas, improve north-south mobility, and reduce the risk of flooding by channelling the river's flow (tunnels were planned to divert the water, etc.).

However, large sections of the public, as well as experts and environmental groups, opposed the plan, arguing that it would result in the permanent loss of an important part of the city's identity and that it contradicted modern principles of restoring urban rivers to their natural state (Herrera et al., 2009). Indeed, the European Union's Water Framework Directive prioritises the renaturalisation of surface water bodies unless there are safety or health imperatives (European Parliament & Council of the European Union, 2000; Fernández-Garrido, 2017).

In line with this paradigm shift, alternative proposals have emerged that focus on the renaturalisation of the Guadalmedina river, i.e. restoring it as a living river with permanent ecological flow and riparian vegetation, as well as public spaces on its banks that would act as green corridors within the city (Mora-Esteban et al., 2025). This eco-social vision involves transforming the riverbed into a river park and ecological corridor, providing environmental value in the form of ecological connectivity, increased biodiversity, urban heat mitigation and flood absorption, as well as social value in the form of spaces for leisure, sports and citizen gatherings, and fostering cohesion between neighbourhoods that were previously isolated by the river's physical barrier.

Today, the debate on the future of the Guadalmedina river is ongoing, making it a prime example of the challenges associated with sustainable urban regeneration. The Spanish government's National Strategy for Green Infrastructure, Ecological Connectivity and Restoration emphasises the importance of integrating nature-based solutions into urban environments (Ministry for Ecological Transition and Demographic Challenge, 2021). Malaga has the opportunity to put these principles into practice with the Guadalmedina, whether through riverbed naturalisation projects, the creation of linear parks or hybrid interventions that combine hydraulic safety with green public spaces. Furthermore, any action taken on the river must consider the participation of the local population and their needs to ensure eco-social regeneration—that is, regeneration that is both ecological and socially inclusive.

Within this framework, the Guadalmedina river and its surrounding neighbourhoods have been chosen as the real-life setting in which Urban Planning I students can develop proposals to improve a public space. The area's multidimensional complexity—in terms of hydrology, the environment, urban planning, society and history—makes it an ideal open-air classroom in which to apply knowledge of sustainable urban planning.

PEDAGOGICAL APPROACH: PROJECT-BASED LEARNING (PBL)

Project-Based Learning (PBL) was adopted as the methodological foundation of the teaching approach, with the aim of overcoming the limitations of traditional teaching methods in urban planning education. PBL is an active pedagogical strategy in which students acquire knowledge and skills by planning and executing real or simulated projects. They work together to solve complex problems (Chandia-Jaure & Godoy-Donoso, 2019).

This approach contrasts with conventional transmissive pedagogy, in which teachers present theoretical content for students to memorise. In PBL, however, students take the lead in their own learning, constructing knowledge based on practical experience, enquiry and critical reflection. This philosophy aligns with the views of educators such as Paulo Freire, who advocated for a liberating education in which learners cease to be passive recipients and instead become active agents who question, engage in dialogue and produce knowledge (Freire, 1970).

In the case of Urban Planning I, the adoption of PBL was a response to the need to engage students with real-world problems — in this instance, how to intervene in the Guadalmedina area — and to give them the tools necessary to generate creative and sustainable proposals. Porlán (2017) argues that to improve university teaching, we must break with the unidirectional model and promote participatory dynamics, in which students learn by doing in cooperation with their peers and under the guidance of teaching staff acting as facilitators.

These ideas were applied in the design of a teaching sequence in which the teachers took on the roles of guides and mediators. They encouraged students to research examples of international best practices through the "Laboratory" activity, draw their own conclusions, and apply the knowledge gained to design decisions based on social and environmental sustainability criteria. This active methodology also aimed to empower students by making them aware of their ability to address real urban issues within the university setting.

A key aspect of the approach was establishing connections between the classroom and the real world. Several studies have shown that learning becomes more meaningful when it is linked to authentic and local contexts (Chandia-Jaure & Godoy-Donoso, 2019; Nebot-Gómez de Salazar et al., 2025). Working in the Guadalmedina area, an environment familiar to the students with an impact on their own city, increased their commitment and understanding of the social and environmental relevance of their proposals for improvement. Similarly, the methodology fostered teamwork and interpersonal skills: students had to collaborate in groups, negotiate ideas, communicate results, and collectively build knowledge, all of which are essential professional skills.

Note that the ABP approach to architecture does not start from scratch, since the traditional project method used in architecture schools already involves learning through design. However, the innovation here was the deliberate structuring of the learning process into clear stages, incorporating research from external sources and the synthesis of strategies before tackling the final design. This made the preliminary phase of strategic ideation, which is often vague in conventional project workshops, more systematic.

Additionally, formative assessment tools such as interim presentations and group self-assessment, as well as collaborative resources like sharing strategies on collective boards, were introduced to enrich the experience beyond project criticism. In summary, the pedagogical approach combined the theoretical foundations of active education with project-based practice to create a dynamic, participatory learning environment connected to the eco-social reality of Málaga.

OBJECTIVES OF THE TEACHING EXPERIENCE

The teaching experience with PBL in Urban Planning I pursues a series of pedagogical and educational objectives, designed to address identified shortcomings and enhance skills among students. Specifically, the following objectives are established:

- **Encourage critical thinking** among students (and teachers) of Urban Planning in the face of the challenges posed by the climate crisis, promoting a reflective and questioning attitude towards the current urban model and its eco-social implications. The aim is for future architects/urban planners to develop sensitivity and judgement in the face of real problems, in line with the idea of educating transformative critical thinking (De Manuel Jerez & Donadei, 2020).
- **Generate a non-transmissive pedagogy** that transforms the learning dynamic into an active, participatory and collaborative process (Porlán, 2017). Rather than passively receiving information, students must act as active agents who construct their own knowledge through experience, reflection, and dialogue. Breaking with the traditional lecture format is key to achieving this objective, as it involves students in their learning in an autonomous and collective manner.
- **Foster the connection between learning and the real world** by integrating practical experiences and relevant contexts into the educational process. In this case, this involves linking the subject to the urban reality of Málaga (the Guadalmedina River and its surroundings), ensuring that the knowledge acquired has a tangible application and enabling students to learn from their surroundings. This objective acknowledges that learning is more meaningful when it relates to situations that are relevant to students (Luque Pulgar, 2023).
- **Learn from the experiences** and success stories of other sustainable urban projects that can be applied in different contexts. The aim is to broaden your horizons beyond the local case and familiarise yourself with global innova-

tions in urban design (Chandia-Jaure & Godoy-Donoso, 2019). These references serve to both inspire you and provide concrete examples of effective design strategies.

- **Provide students with a "toolbox"** for public space projects, consisting of a list of specific strategies and design actions based on social and ecological sustainability criteria. The aim is that, after the training process, each student will have a repertoire of ideas, criteria, and technical and formal solutions that they can apply to their projects to make them more sustainable. This includes strategies for green urban design, such as green infrastructure and sustainable drainage, as well as strategies for social inclusion, such as participatory design and universal accessibility. Other strategies include those for sustainable mobility and climate resilience. By the end of the course, students will have developed a set of strategies that they can use to guide their projects and future professional activities.

These objectives guided the planning and execution of the PBL experience, ensuring that each designed activity contributed to at least one of them. The methodology implemented in phases and how these goals were articulated in the development of the teaching project are detailed below.

METHODOLOGY AND RESULTS OF THE TEACHING ACTIVITIES

Approach to the Context and Local Issues for Urban Analysis and Diagnosis

To help students understand the context and its problems, the course included several practical in situ activities. For instance, guided tours were organised with local experts, including members of community groups who have studied and worked on the Guadalmedina river. During these visits, students explored the riverbed and its surroundings, identifying issues such as accessibility problems, areas of pollution or litter, and areas with excessive sunlight and no shade. They also noted areas with potential for new uses.

In collaboration with the ONCE Foundation, the Atolmi association for people with disabilities, and the Málaga Accesible development group, a universal accessibility workshop was held to assess the difficulties and opportunities of integrating the river into the city from the perspective of people with reduced mobility. This hands-on approach to the environment, combined with interaction with local experts, strengthened the connection between the subject matter and the local reality, promoting precisely the kind of real-world link sought by active teaching methods.

Before conducting the urban diagnosis, the students carried out preliminary analyses of the site. These analyses focused on various physical, social, and environmental aspects. They made urban cartographies, socio-spatial analyses of the surrounding neighbourhoods and the historical evolution of the river among other studies. These analyses formed part of the initial phases of the course. Building on this contextual knowledge, the next stage was to implement a PBL methodology to guide students in generating proposals for the eco-social regeneration of the Guadalmedina area.

"Eco-social Reference Projects Laboratory" ECO-LAB, or Applied Research Workshop on Sustainability Projects

Methodologically, the teaching experience was implemented during the first two weeks of the last exercise of the course, in which students had to make a proposal for improving a public space based on sustainability criteria. The work plan was structured in four key stages, following the principles of Project-Based Learning. Each stage involved various participatory activities and required the interaction of different agents (teachers, students and even external agents in some cases). The phases of the process are described below:

Phase 1: Collective identification of the sustainability criteria for urban spaces

This stage took the form of a practical class session designed as a guided brainstorming exercise. The teachers introduced some key sustainability concepts in the design of public spaces using visual examples and questions. The students were then invited to identify and state the sustainable design criteria relevant to the intervention in urban spaces, either as a whole class or organised into teams.

This collaborative process resulted in an initial list of criteria and strategies that the students felt would be relevant for improving a public space such as the Guadalmedina river. Proposals included expanding green spaces and increasing biodiversity, improving connectivity for pedestrians and cyclists between neighbourhoods, restoring water features to the urban landscape, creating community facilities on the riverbanks, ensuring universal accessibility and strengthening the cultural identity associated with the river.

Each idea was briefly discussed, clarifying concepts (e.g., what is meant by green infrastructure or social inclusion) and grouping them into preliminary categories. This phase allowed us to build a shared conceptual framework on urban sustainability based on the students' own contributions. It also served to identify prior knowledge and possible gaps, which the teachers were able to address by clarifying doubts or providing references (Higueras, 2013) on sustainable urban design criteria.

Phase 2: Selection of relevant reference projects

Building on the sustainability criteria that had already been discussed, the case study exploration phase began. Previously, the teaching staff conducted a survey to ascertain which types of public space aroused the most interest or were considered the most relevant for in-depth analysis. The results showed a particular interest in river parks, urban green corridors, multifunctional squares, and soft mobility environments, to name a few. Based on these preferences, the teaching team compiled a list of exemplary urban projects (national and international) incorporating sustainability strategies that could be transferred to the Guadalmedina context.

Notable cases included the renaturalisation of the Cheonggyecheon River in Seoul, initiatives to 'daylight' underground rivers in European cities, the conversion of infrastructure into green spaces (such as New York's High Line) and urban parks designed to manage rainwater. There were also local examples of participatory interventions in degraded spaces. Each group of students chose (or was assigned) one of these projects to analyse in depth.

The selection aimed to cover various approaches and scales so that the class as a whole would explore various strategies. This phase incorporated a research component, whereby students had to consult bibliographies, publications and graphic materials on the selected cases. This developed their skills in searching for and analysing architectural and urban planning information.

Phase 3. Detailed Analysis of the Selected Projects

Once a reference project had been assigned to each team, they had one week to perform a detailed analysis. Each group of four or five students studied different aspects of their case study, aiming to extract applicable lessons. The issues analysed included urban form and space design (organisation, dimensions and scales), the technical solutions employed (vegetation, drainage systems, street furniture and sustainable materials), the objectives of the intervention (renaturation, social cohesion and sustainable mobility) and the challenges faced and how they were addressed.

To document the analysis, the groups produced drawings or diagrams illustrating the main design operations, infographic containing key data and descriptive sheets outlining the strategies that had been identified. For instance, the group analysing the Cheonggyecheon River project in Seoul highlighted actions such as removing infrastructure to reveal the river again, creating retention basins, introducing native flora along the riverbanks and developing pedestrian paths to reconnect neighbourhoods. Another group working on a coastal park in Spain emphasised the importance of citizen participation and the inclusion of cultural facilities in order to revitalise the area.

The analysis aimed to understand why the projects were successful and what effects they generated, rather than simply describing them. In this way, the students developed a well-informed repertoire of sustainable urban intervention strategies based on real-world examples.

Phase 4: Presentation of the results and collective synthesis of the strategies

Following the individual analytical work of each group, the knowledge generated was shared in order to take advantage of it collaboratively. Phase 4 was divided into two complementary sub-stages:

- **Phase 4.1: Presentation of the results in group dynamics.** Each team presented their case study in sessions organised by working tables, with four or five groups working on related projects grouped together. The presentations included posters or slides summarising the key aspects of the project, particularly the design strategies identified. For around an hour, each table held a discussion, moderated by the teachers. After each presentation, the other groups asked questions or made comments. This approach enabled students to learn from various examples and compare different approaches while encouraging oral expression and critical debate.
- **Phase 4.2: Collaborative extraction of specific strategies and actions.** Building on the information already shared, a collective synthesis phase followed. Based on the initial criteria established in the previous phase and supported by teachers, recurring patterns were identified, resulting in the formulation of five general strategies for sustainable urban design:
    - (A) Socio-community activation: promotion of cultural and leisure activities and strengthening of social ties.
    - (B) Green infrastructure and renaturalisation: incorporation of vegetation, water and nature-based solutions.
    - (C) Mobility and sustainable connectivity: prioritising pedestrians, cyclists and public transport users.
    - (D) Inclusion and universal accessibility: ensuring safe, comfortable and accessible design for all.
    - (E) Heritage, identity and cultural landscape: enhancement of history, local identity and landscape.

Each roundtable analysed one of these strategies, developing a list of specific actions based on the analysed projects or new proposals applicable to the Guadalmedina case. For example, under Strategy A, ideas such as multipurpose facilities (cultural kiosks and sports areas), event programming on the river (fairs and markets) and community urban gardens emerged. Under strategy B, the proposals included the planting of riverside forests and the creation of wetlands for water purification and natural shading. All the proposals were compiled in a collective repository of ideas and validated and organised with the teaching staff. The final result of this phase was a matrix of strategies and specific actions to serve as a consultation tool for the next stage of the project.

Applying Lessons Learned to the Guadalmedina River Project

In the final stage of the course, students must propose ways to improve a public space in their working environment, bearing in mind eco-social criteria. With this objective in mind, they transitioned from the abstract realm of references to the specific case of the Guadalmedina river. Each student, already working individually on a project to improve a section or area of the assigned urban environment, had to apply the relevant strategies and actions collected to their proposal.

To this end, they were given access to a repository of strategies resulting from the previous phase, which they could use as an open “toolbox.” The students analysed which of these strategies best addressed the specific issues and opportunities of their section of the river. For instance, a group working on a peripheral section with vulnerable communities and a lack of meeting spaces nearby decided to prioritise the socio-community activation strategy. They proposed squares and neighbourhood facilities in their design, combined with vegetation to create a green infrastructure and pleasant environments.

Other students, focusing on the mouth of the river next to the historic centre, placed more emphasis on the strategy of heritage identity and landscape, integrating interpretative tours on the history of the port and the city, while implementing sustainable drainage solutions for occasional flooding (green infrastructure strategy). In this way, each student project was shaped by a clear theoretical-practical underpinning: the proposals did not emerge from spontaneous occurrences, but were informed by real references and guided by validated strategies.

In this phase, the teachers’ work consisted of providing project tutorials to ensure that students applied the lessons learned in a coherent way, avoiding the superficial copying of a benchmark without adapting it to the local context, for example. Note that the repository of strategies was not a set of fixed instructions, but rather a flexible starting point. Students could devise new, specific actions as long as they aligned with one of the agreed general strategies. By the end of this phase, each student had developed at least one intervention strategy for the selected public space that incorporated social and environmental sustainability criteria as shown in Figure 2.

Figure 2. Proposal for neighbourhood improvement through the socio-community activation strategy. Student: Helena López Muñoz. Teachers of the subject

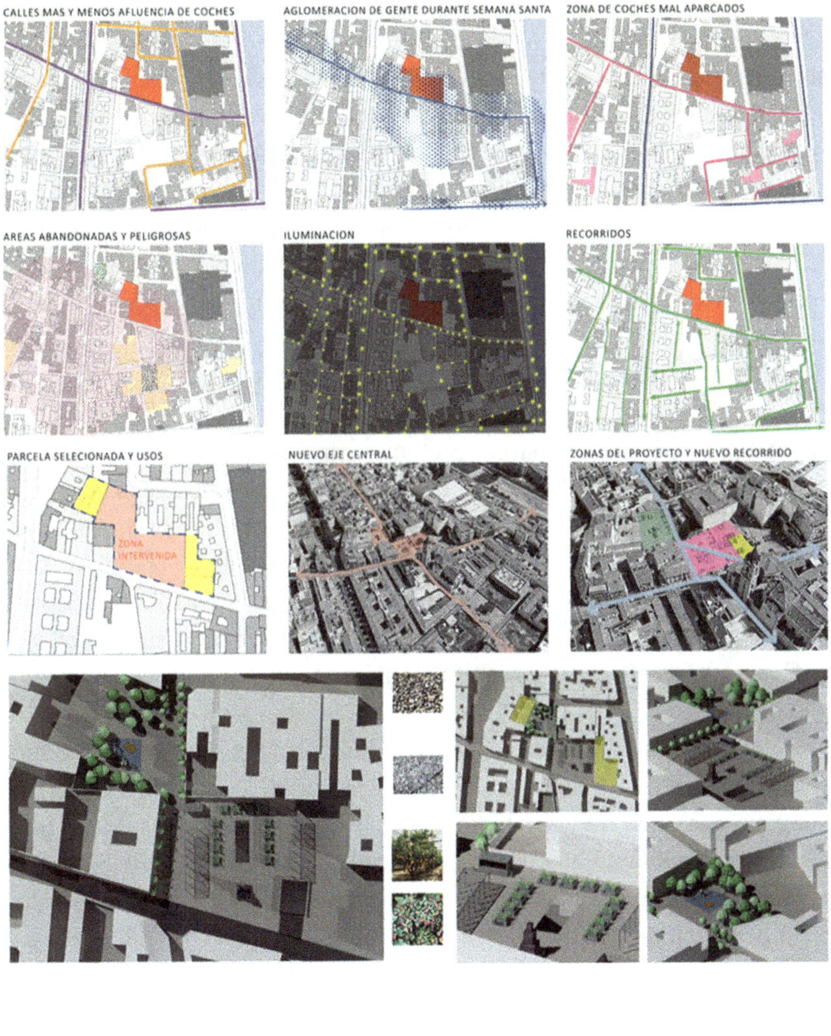

In summary, this phased methodology has successfully articulated a comprehensive PBA process, from identifying local issues and analysing the urban working environment (Phase 1) to investigating existing solutions and achieving a collective creative synthesis (Phase 2: Reference Project Laboratory), culminating in the practical application of these principles to a local project (Phase 3). This intense initial period of work laid a solid foundation for the subsequent exercise in proposing improvements to the environments. This exercise was much more enriching, as it empowered and equipped students with the conceptual and technical tools necessary for designing public spaces that apply sustainability criteria.

IMPLICATIONS AND DISCUSSION

The results show that using the Guadalmedina area as a teaching laboratory through PBL was highly beneficial. Key competences were strengthened in the students (critical thinking, teamwork, sustainable design, theory-practice connection) and creative contributions to a real urban problem were produced. The discussion suggests that this methodology is replicable and can be adapted to other urban contexts and related subjects, provided there is adequate planning and a teaching vocation towards innovation and eco-social responsibility.

Implications on the Student Learning Process

Implementing this project-based teaching approach has had some positive outcomes in terms of both the learning process and the students' final results. First, the primary objective of enhancing students' ability to develop project ideas based on sustainable principles has been accomplished. Compared to previous courses, the teaching staff observed that after the applied research workshop on eco-social projects, students approached their design proposals for the Guadalmedina with greater fluency and creativity, integrating environmental and social considerations from the outset.

The initial intervention proposals that resulted from the project showed superior quality and coherence: students were able to articulate concrete strategies drawn from the repository and translate them into relevant spatial actions. Many projects, for example, incorporated green infrastructure solutions such as flood parks, rain gardens and riparian woodlands to improve climate resilience while providing living spaces. Others emphasised pedestrian and cyclist connectivity by designing walkways or continuous riverside paths that linked previously isolated neighbourhoods.

Attention to the social dimension was also evident, with community facilities, spaces for cultural and sporting activities, and strategies for citizen participation forming part of several proposals. This reflects the students' understanding that the regeneration of the river should benefit and involve the local population. Overall, the Guadalmedina lab produced rich, multi-dimensional project ideas, demonstrating that the students had internalised the eco-social vision throughout the process.

These qualitative results are supported by the feedback obtained through an activity evaluation questionnaire that was distributed to the students. In this anonymous, voluntary questionnaire, more than 80% of participants stated that the analysis of reference projects and the synthesis of strategies were useful or very useful for their own urban project. Many commented that, without these preliminary phases, they would not have known where to start designing or would have resorted to conventional, non-innovative solutions. A significant proportion also valued the collaborative work positively, with many stating that learning from their peers by examining different case studies had broadened their understanding of the possibilities for public spaces.

As for the methodology itself, most found it more motivating than a traditional theoretical class, as it actively involved them; they highlighted that working on a real problem in their city made them feel that what they learned had tangible relevance, agreeing with Nebot-Gómez de Salazar et al.'s (2025) when they pointed out the importance of contextualising the teaching of urban planning in the real climate emergency. Of course, there were also limitations mentioned: some students noted that the intense pace of the first weeks was demanding and that coordinating in a group was not always easy, but in general they recognised these challenges as part of collaborative learning.

Implications for Teachers and Societal Transfer

From the teachers' perspective, the experience provided valuable insights into innovative teaching methods. It was found that active pedagogical approaches such as PBL can increase student engagement and performance, but they require careful planning and effort from the teaching team. In this case, preparing materials such as project references and surveys, and organising group activities, and coordinating several teachers to moderate the work tables simultaneously meant a considerable workload. Nevertheless, the teachers involved agreed that it was very worthwhile: the class was filled with creative energy, the students took more responsibility for their learning, and the teacher's role was enriched by becoming a facilitator who learns alongside their students.

In line with Freire's (1970) proposals for dialogical education, this horizontality generated an atmosphere of trust and openness in the classroom. Additionally, the experience enabled teachers to update the subject content by incorporating contemporary debates on green infrastructure, citizen participation, and climate change mitigation —the topics that are often marginalised in traditional curricula. In other words, teaching was aligned with the real-world challenges that future architects will face, helping to reduce the gap between academia and professional practice. Medina (2024) highlights the importance of adapting university teaching to meet current social demands, a concept that this experience exemplifies.

One notable aspect was the beneficial impact of using the Guadalmedina area as a case study on both learning and the collective understanding of this urban space. As it was a local issue, disseminating the results internally (through open presentations and an exhibition of student project panels) attracted the attention of other students, professors, and even external stakeholders invited to the final reviews. This created opportunities for dialogue between the university and the city, enabling students' innovative ideas on river regeneration to contribute to the public conversation. In this sense, the experience aligned with teaching innovation initiatives that emphasise collaboration with social entities and the associative fabric, similar to those described by González-Vera, Nebot-Gómez de Salazar and Asencio-Juncal (2023) in the context of urban planning education.

Although there was no formal collaboration with associations during the development of the project (beyond the occasional visit by experts to assess universal accessibility), the foundations were laid for future editions in which citizens could be more directly involved, for example through opinion surveys of neighbours about the river, public presentations or exhibitions of student proposals.

Academic Evaluation and Limitations of Teaching Experience

In terms of academic assessment, the learning outcomes were evident in both the grades and the project evaluation rubrics. Students who actively participated in the initial PBL phases tended to submit projects that were more complete and well-justified, scoring higher on criteria such as 'integration of environmental criteria' and 'urban design innovation'. This suggests that PBL enhances the educational experience and contributes to more objective academic performance. However, it should be recognised that it is complex to isolate the specific contribution of the methodology to the grades, given that multiple factors are involved. Nevertheless, the observed correlation is consistent with the qualitative impressions: students emerged from the process stronger.

Finally, from a critical perspective, it is important to discuss the limitations and outstanding issues that arose from this experience. One practical limitation was time: while it was useful to concentrate the PBL in the first few weeks for launching the project, it also implied an intense level of dedication that may have overwhelmed some students. Some traditional theoretical content was sacrificed to make room for these activities, raising the question of how to balance both facets of the curriculum by integrating improvement cycles without neglecting essential content (Porlán & Villarejo-Ramos, 2024).

Furthermore, while the experience focused on design strategies, it could be expanded in future to incorporate deeper participatory management aspects. For example, citizen consultation processes could be simulated, or collaboration with local authorities could be established to define criteria. This would further enrich the eco-social dimension of learning by making students aware of not only what to design but also how to implement urban transformations within institutional and community contexts.

CONCLUSION

The above experience highlights the value of reorienting urban planning education towards active, contextual pedagogical models, particularly in the face of global challenges such as the climate emergency, which require new professional skills. By focusing on the real-life case study of the eco-social regeneration of the Guadalmedina river and using project-based learning as a methodology, an educational environment was created in which theory and practice were meaningfully intertwined. Students acquired technical knowledge of the sustainable design of public spaces and developed a deep understanding of the social and environmental implications of their proposals. In other words, they learned urbanism by practising it in a real context, with the complexity and responsibility that this entails.

The main conclusions are as follows: (1) Using real case studies and references enriched the ideation process, helping students to translate the abstract concept of sustainability into concrete project solutions. (2) Collaboration and the collective construction of knowledge through group dynamics, discussions and joint synthesis fostered communication, teamwork and peer learning skills among the students, demonstrating that the classroom can function as a small community of practice. (3) Applying the learned strategies to the Guadalmedina case validated the approach: students generated viable and creative proposals, demonstrating a qualitative leap compared to traditional methods where design was often approached without this prior knowledge. (4) The experience reinforced the idea that urban education can and should contribute to eco-social transformation by training professionals who are more aware of and capable of dealing with these issues. In this way, the university can find solutions for sustainable cities in the future (Luque Pulgar, 2023).

In operational terms, this experience demonstrates that PBL methodologies can be implemented in architecture courses with large groups, provided there is clear instructional design and active engagement from teaching staff. It also highlights the advantage of selecting specific local issues or sites as the main learning focus, as this boosts student motivation and the relevance of their reflections. The Guadalmedina proved to be an effective catalyst for learning, and other cities or environments could fulfil a similar role in different academic contexts.

Finally, it should be noted that teaching innovation is an ongoing process. This initial exploration of PBL in Urban Planning has paved the way for enhancements in future iterations, such as refining the selection of case studies, incorporating student feedback to refine the dynamics, and intensifying interaction with external stakeholders (institutions and communities) to further enhance the realism of the project. Each iteration will enable the balance between theoretical content, practical work, and social participation to be fine-tuned in pursuit of a truly integrative urbanism pedagogy. At a time when universities are seeking to train professionals capable of adapting our cities to climate change and social justice demands, experiences such as this demonstrate a fruitful approach: transforming the classroom into an environment that goes beyond traditional teaching.

ACKNOWLEDGMENT

This work has been developed within the framework of the Permanent Network for Training and Innovation in the Classroom (Improvement Groups of Historical Sciences and Architecture -NOVEL24) of the University of Malaga. We would like to thank the ONCE Foundation, the ATOLMI association and the Malaga Accessible Development Association for their participation in the teaching experience described above. Also, the guided visit to the Guadalmedina river environment carried out by Mr. Juan Antonio Gómez Negrillo.

REFERENCES

Asencio-Juncal, J. (2023). Redefining the relationship between nature and the city: the rivers Guadalmedina in Málaga and Genil in Granada. *L'industria delle costruzioni. Gestione delle risorse idriche e rigenerazione urbana*, (493), 43-49.

Chandia-Jaure, R., & Godoy-Donoso, D. (2019). Agua y ciudadanía: Estrategia didáctica para la formación en contextos de cambio climático. En D. García-Escudero & B. Bardí i Milà (Eds.), *JIDA'19. VII Jornadas sobre Innovación Docente en Arquitectura* (pp. 533–543). Iniciativa Digital Politècnica, UPC. https://doi.org/DOI: 10.5821/jida.2019.8373

De Manuel Jerez, E., & Donadei, M. (2020). El papel de la universidad para educar al pensamiento crítico frente a los retos del cambio climático. En M. Fernández-Villa et al. (Eds.), *V CIED: Desafíos al desarrollo: procesos de cambio hacia la justicia global* (pp. 1976–1993). HEGOA (UPV/EHU).

European Parliament and Council of the European Union. (2000). *Directive 2000/60/EC of the European Parliament and of the Council of 23 October 2000 establishing a framework for Community action in the field of water policy. Official Journal of the European Communities, L 327*, 1–73. https://eur-lex.europa.eu/legal-content/EN/TXT/?uri=CELEX:32000L0060

Fernández-Garrido, R. (2017). *Regenerating Málaga: Guadalmedina and SOHO*. Paper presented at the COTMA VII Congress, Málaga. https://fernandez-garrido.com/wp-content/uploads/2017/10/REGENERANDO-M%C3%81LAGA-GUADALMEDINA-Y-SOHO-Fern%C3%A1ndez-Garrido-Rafael.pdf

Freire, P. (1970). *Pedagogía del oprimido*. Siglo XXI Editores.

González-Vera, V. M., Nebot-Gómez de Salazar, N., & Asencio-Juncal, J. (2023). Experiencia de innovación docente en la enseñanza del urbanismo: análisis y diagnóstico de entornos urbanos en colaboración con entidades sociales y tejido asociativo. In Pinilla Gómez, M., & Cruz Carvajal, S. (Eds.), *Estudios de innovación docente como punto de encuentro en ciencias humanísticas y sociales* (pp. 753–773). Editorial Dykinson.

Herrera, T., Blanco, F. and Puche, P. (2009). El río Grande de Málaga: la movilización social y la investigación científica como base de su defensa. *Ríos con vida AEMS*, (83), 24-27.

Higueras, E. (2013). *Desarrollo urbano sostenible y criterios de diseño urbano para ordenaciones residenciales*. [Online monograph]. https://lc.cx/DY7-Sv

Kayser, B. (2023, May 14). Más vocación ante la emergencia climática. *El País*. https://elpais.com

Luque Pulgar, E. (2023). *Docentes ante la crisis climática: Retos transformadores*. Universidad Nacional de Educación a Distancia (UNED). https://doi.org/DOI: 10.5944/educxx1.29427

Ministry for the Ecological Transition and the Demographic Challenge. (2021). *National strategy for green infrastructure, ecological connectivity and restoration: The need to integrate nature-based solutions in urban environments*. https://www.miteco.gob.es/es/biodiversidad/temas/ecosistemas-y-conectividad/conectividad/estrategiainfraestructuraverde.aspx

Mora-Esteban, R., Conejo-Arrabal, F., Romero-Martínez, J. M., & Nebot-Gómez de Salazar, N. (2025). Problems and restoration strategies of urban Mediterranean rivers in Spain: Guadalmedina River as a potential ecological corridor in the green-blue infrastructure of Malaga, Spain. *TeMA – Journal of Land Use, Mobility and Environment, 1*. https://doi.org/DOI: 10.6093/1970-9870/11115

Nebot-Gómez de Salazar, N., Asencio-Juncal, J., Chamizo-Nieto, F. J., & Jiménez-Morales, E. (2025). The climate emergency from the perspective of urban planning: A teaching experience at the bachelor's degree in architecture (Universidad de Málaga, Spain). In *Challenges of educational innovation in contemporary society* (pp. 205–224). IGI Global., DOI: 10.4018/979-8-3373-0705-3.ch010

Parcerisa Bundó, J., & Rubert de Ventós, M. (2014). *La ciudad no es una hoja en blanco*. Ediciones LUB. DOI: 10.5821/ebook-9788469702284

Porlán, R. (2017). *Enseñanza universitaria: cómo mejorarla*. Ed. Morata.

Porlán, R., & Villarejo-Ramos, A. F. (Coords.). (2024). *Ciclos de mejora en el aula. Curso 2022-23: Experiencias de Innovación Docente de la Universidad de Sevilla*. Universidad de Sevilla.

Various Authors. (2011). *Guadalmedina: An invisible river*. Rizoma Foundation.

Wikipedia. (n.d.). *Plan Guadalmedina*. In *Wikipedia, The Free Encyclopedia*. Retrieved June 10, 2025, from https://es.wikipedia.org/wiki/Plan_Guadalmedina

KEY TERMS AND DEFINITIONS

Climate Emergency: A situation in which urgent action is required to reduce or halt climate change and avoid potentially irreversible environmental damage resulting from this process.

Critical Thinking: ability to analyse information thoroughly and objectively. It implies access to contrasted information and sources, and interpretation of the data in an argued way.

Eco-Social Transition: the design and transformation of cities must incorporate environmental and ecological criteria in addition to being socially just and inclusive cities.

Guadalmedina River: river that runs through the city of Malaga until it flows into the sea. It is conceived as a learning environment for architecture students on how to implement ecological and social factors in urban environments and watercourses.

Learning Based Project Methodologies: PBL is an active pedagogical strategy in which students acquire knowledge and skills by planning and executing real or simulated projects.

Public Space: places of collective use, open and accessible to all citizens, where different types of activities (cultural, social, economic) take place and where personal relations, conflicts and public life of the citizens take place.

Sustainable Cities: We refer to sustainable cities mainly from an environmental and socially inclusive point of view. Sustainable cities offer healthy urban environments for people, accessibility to natural spaces and green areas, as well as comfortable meeting places that promote interpersonal relationships.

Urban Project: Proposal to transform a public space to solve certain problems such as the lack of climatic comfort, universal accessibility, or the urban degradation of certain public spaces. The need to incorporate ecological and social conditions in improvement or intervention projects is raised.

Chapter 12
Universal Design Learning Applied Through Gamification in Higher Education:
An Experience From Two Gamification Innovations Implemented in the Course 'Sociology of Education'

Karla Berrens
http://orcid.org/0000-0003-0270-5154
CRIT Research Group, GIDASRES, CR Polis, University of Barcelona, Spain

Marina Elias
http://orcid.org/0000-0002-8268-4965
GIDASRES, CR Polis, University of Barcelona, Spain

ABSTRACT

This article is based on two gamification innovations developed at the Faculty of Education of the University of Barcelona. They were implemented on the subject "Sociology of Education". During the 2023–2024 academic year, the project "Effects on Learning through Gamification as a Tool for Summative Assessment in the Sociology Course of the Primary Education Degree" invited students to use Wooclap for one of the course's summative assessments and to gamify the theoretical content. In the 2024–2025 academic year, the project "Fylki: strategic project, Education faculty" was implemented. It involved a board game designed to allow

DOI: 10.4018/979-8-2600-1568-1.ch012

students to revisit key concepts addressed in the course through play, such as social structure, equality, justice, and equity. The objectives of the research projects were, through play, to generate an environment allowing students with diverse learning needs to engage with course content and take responsibility for their learning.

INTRODUCTION

This article analyses the results from two gamification research projects developed at two degrees from the Faculty of Education of the University of Barcelona (UB). The degrees are the BA in Primary Education (GEP) and the BA in Childhood education (GEI). The innovation projects were implemented on the subject "Sociology of Education, social changes, educational changes and multiculturality" that both degrees share. It is a theoretical subject that lasts one semester, students take it in the first semester of year 1. The topic "Sociology of education: social changes, educational changes and multiculturality" ('sociology of education' from here onwards) is a theoretical subject that students undertake in the first semester of the first year of both GEI and GEP degrees, and students find it dense. The innovation projects were implemented for an academic year each, during two consecutive years. During the 2023–2024 academic year, the project titled "Effects on Learning through Gamification as a Tool for Summative Assessment in the Sociology Course of the Primary Education Degree" (2023PMD-UB/033), recognized as a teaching innovation by UB's RIMDA, was launched. In this project, students were made familiar with the Wooclap platform. This is a gamification platform designed for educational purposes. The project was an innovation action based on gamifying the second assessment, second of the four summative assessments the course has. However, course content was also partially gamified to increase the digital literacy students had with this tool and to learn it well before the assessment. Using Wooclap encouraged active student participation and enhanced motivation toward the subject matter. During the 2024–2025 academic year, a second gamification project was implemented with the Faculty of Education's RIMDAE initiative, "Fylki: strategic project, Education faculty" (2024PEDC-EDU/001). This gamification involved creating a large board game designed to allow students to personally experience social inequality and injustice. Through play, students revisited key concepts addressed in the course, such as social structure, roles, norms, equality, justice, and equity. This gamified approach fostered a deeper understanding of concepts otherwise rather difficult to digest for first year students. The objectives of the research projects were, through play, to generate an environment allowing students with diverse learning needs to engage with course content and take responsibility for their learning. This chapter examines, through an exploration of both innovation research projects, the benefits gamification has for students' motivation and learning. It makes an argument for the application of UDL in our teaching to avoid leaving students behind.

BACKGROUND

Gamification is importing elements that are native to games into other contexts (originally not playful) contexts to generate a playful environment (Deterding et al., 2011; de-Marcos et al., 2014; Dominguez et al., 2013; Giannetto, Chao, & Fontana, 2013; Goehle, 2013; Hanus & Fox, 2015; Mekler et al., 2013; Muntean, 2011; O'Donovan et al., 2013; Prince, 2013; Pedreira et al., 2014; Watson, Hancock, & Mandryk, 2013). Gamification in the classroom fosters an engagement of different classroom power dynamics, shifting power from the teacher to the students, thus increasing participation (Fernández-Veláquez et al., 2025). Gamifying education is a key element in cultivating motivation and making students aware of their agency with regards to their own learning. They are put in a position where, through engaging with the games, they are taking responsibility for their own learning. Gamifying this subject increase motivation and changes the perception students have over the materials, it becomes part of their game. As Li et al. (2023) points out, gamification strengthens learners' conceptual understanding and learning can become positive. In addition, in higher education gamification enhances academic achievement, increases attentional focus, fosters a sense of satisfaction, and as previously mentioned, increases motivation (Alshammari, 2020).

The games "provide encouragement through very short-term goals, so that the player can fail and try again until they succeed" (O'Donovan, Gain, & Marais, 2013, p. 242), this in turn enhances the interplay between intrinsic and extrinsic motivation (Muntean, 2011, p. 326)

When gamification is used with and for students with diverse learning (ADHD for example), gamification or 'serious games' have been proven to be a key tool to enhance motivation, effort, and attention. In addition, it also helps build competencies such as mental agility, stimulate understanding, reflexive engagement, and strategic reasoning (García Redondo et al. 2019). With gamification in higher education, an important part is finding the right game. When there is a good fit between game and topic, they expand motivation and can expand concentration duration for students with attention and hyperactivity. Universal design for learning (UDL) is an educational approach promoting the creation of flexible and accessible learning environments, able to cater to students' diversity. Their aim is to eliminate learning barriers to learning by offering multiple means of representation, expression, and engagement. In this context, gamification is an ideal complementary strategy, incorporating gaming elements to increase students' motivation, active implication and heighten a sense of belonging in their own learning process. Integrating gamification within the UDL's framework, learning is personalised enabling each student to meaningfully participate according to their interests, abilities and needs. This combination facilitates the creation of inclusive educational experiences promoting both the development of competencies and student autonomy and engagement in flexible learning environments. Thus, combining these two approaches supports not only equitable participation but also the development of competencies through more meaningful motivating educational experiences (Briones Suárez, Montero Ramírez, Caranqui Pintag & Ramirez Melendres, 2024).

Moreover, when approaching gamification for evaluation, we strive to provide an evaluation that will be as accessible for all students (with and without diverse learning) as possible. Finding a format that is more appealing and engages students is also a way to foster students' agency and their own responsibility towards their own learning. Recent advances in inclusive education have highlighted the necessity to find assessment methods tailored to include students with diverse learnings (Jadán-Guerrero et al., 2023; Li et al., 2023). In this context, gamification facilitates a progression in content, from basic to advanced, thereby supporting collaborative learning, fostering students' agency and autonomy, and enhancing attention to diversity.

TEACHING INNOVATIONS

The First Innovation: Using Technology for UDL

Wooclap's Platform

The first innovation (wooclap) had four objectives: to motivate students in their learning through gamification of the evaluation contents; to foster an evaluation methodology dynamic and adapted to students with diversity; to enhance digital literacy in the framework of an integrated formation; to engage students in their learning agency and responsibility.

This innovation was implemented in the GEI degree program. There were 11 class groups in the first year, and it was implemented in one of them. There was a total of 55 students enrolled in the group, 1 of them had chosen the single-test assessment mode and 2 of them did not come to class often and as such, they did not take part in this evaluation. Hence the project had 52 participants to the project, 19 men and 33 women, aged between 18 and 27.

Sociology of Education is a first year, first term subject. The way it is currently organised, the subject has four evaluations throughout the semester (each has a different weight in the overall grade, the first 20%, the second and third a 25%

each, the final exam 20% and a 10% of participation in class). For this project, we changed the second evaluation from an essay format towards a gamified evaluation using the program wooclap. Therefore, there was a first evaluation in October, the gamified evaluation in November, a third evaluation in December and the final exam in January, concluding the semester at the beginning of February with the final grades. We will focus on the second evaluation and the second objective of the project in this paper.

Wooclap is a platform enabling the gamification of course materials; you can also create interactive presentations. Wooclap presents the option to evaluate comprehension through several kinds of questions to evaluate comprehension and more open-ended ones to gather information or comments.

1. **Wooclap options to evaluate comprehension:**
   . Test type.
   . Open question.
   . Label an image.
   . Complete a puzzle.
   . Search in an image.
   . Term combination.
   . Fill in the blanks.
   . Guess a number.
   . Sort.
   . Script concordance.
   . Conceptual concordance.
2. **Wooclap options to gather comments:**
   . Structure.
   . Survey.
   . Word cloud.
   . Brainstorm.
   . Value.
   . Priorities.

Wooclap's gamified evaluation was individual. The teaching staff prepared 4 different models to avoid cheating in class and each student had a unique code to access the platform and start the evaluation. It consisted of seven questions. At the beginning of the evaluation students were instructed there were seven questions, one of them being longer and encouraged to read over all the questions and then start the evaluation. The structure of the evaluation was a combination of several kinds of questions, having one of them as an open-ended question with no word limit. Wooclap presents one question at a time. Once that question is resolved or, if you prefer to leave it for later, you can scroll through the other ones. But there is only one question at any given time per screen. This methodology reduces the angst many students with ADHD have when presented with an exam paper that has several questions regarding where to start. Having one question per screen increases concentration, decreases anxiety, and allows students to pace themselves. It reduces the fatigue generated by convergence insufficiency that many people having ADHD have (Granet et al. 2005). Last but not least, wooclap's gamified evaluation is individual, therefore it allows the teacher to notice students that are falling behind, not working enough or have difficulties; this is particularly important since a big proportion of evaluated coursework in the degree is done in groups.

Students were given a pre-survey gathering of academic-social information as well as previous digital literacy. Once the gamification finalised, they were given a post-survey gathering information and feedback on the gamification of the assessment and the course content. This will be expanded in the next section, solutions, and recommendations.

The Second Innovation: Going Analogical for UDL

Fylki's Game

The aim of the game was to dive into theoretical aspects of the course such as social structure, meritocracy, poverty, and family structure. These concepts were previously explained during the course. We find our students often have difficulty understanding poverty and vulnerability situations, mostly when they affect infants. The game enables students to experience, through play, what does it mean to live in privileged or vulnerability situations, to have or to lack resources (economical for example) or any other element that has been introduced in the game (privilege, health, food, schooling). To play, groups had to be composed of a minimum of 8 people, creating 4 villages and having a minimum of 2 people per village. The game is designed to accommodate large groups, making it well-suited for first-year classes in the GEI and GEP programs, where group sizes can reach up to 50 students. It allows for the simultaneous participation of up to 48–50 students, organized into villages of 7 participants each, with the possibility of running two games at the same time. A full session of 90 minutes is used for the activity. Setup takes approximately 15–20 minutes, which includes watching a short introductory video, explaining the game rules, organising teams, and solving the first enigma. The gameplay itself typically lasts around 45 minutes, depending on the number of villages involved. The final 10 minutes are reserved for reflection. During this time, students are encouraged to connect the elements of the game to the course's theoretical content. This reflective phase is crucial, as it helps translate the experiential learning from the game into academic language, deepening students' understanding of the sociological concepts covered in class.

SOLUTIONS AND RECOMMENDATIONS

Digital and Analogical Gamifications' Results

We have presented two teaching innovations through the gamification of course content. In this section, we are going to focus on the results and recommendations that come from our experiences.

For the first gamification, students replied to a post-survey questionnaire to evaluate the experience of innovation. Under the question "*Using wooclap for assessment is a good idea*", 100% of the respondents agreed. The question "*I felt calm with the relationship between number of questions and time to reply*" had 100% of students agreeing, some stating "I *could read questions slowly*", "*I was comfortable and feeling safe with the proportion of questions and time*". This data demonstrates that the rhythm the gamification brought was received positively by all students. It enabled them to take their time in the assessment and that was very well-valued.

Finally, for the question specifically addressing students with diverse learning "*I have diverse learning (for example, ADHD, dyslexia, TEA, etc). Wooclap is a tool ...*", students had to put an X on either "*positive because..*", "*negative because...*" or "*neutral because...*" and complete the sentence. All students except 1(who marked neutral), selected "positive" and the reasons they stated were "*the question format is concrete, short and schematic", "I have dyslexia, this formats is good for me because questions are shorter and clearer", "it allows different kinds of response and a fast correction in the majority of questions", "I have ADHD and this is a good tool, it's good for me", "it is visual and has feedback", "more freedom" (anonymous respondents, POST-SURVEY PRI).* Therefore, after examining the post-survey, the importance of the gamification of assessment for students with diverse needs is notorious. This kind of evaluation enabled students to approach it with confidence and lessening evaluation anxiety and having questions they stated were clear. They were shorter and more specific; there was one per page, thus lessening spatial anxiety for people with ADHD and dyslexia. The nature of wooclap's activities (except for the open-ended question) is a concise instruction and requires an action-based specific answer thus becoming a positive tool to encourage focus, motivation and a calmer response to a test situation.

The second innovation was applied to several contexts. The first application was within the teaching innovation project's training session framework. This became a pilot session for the board game. The instructor of the course on teaching innovation and classmates from the same group participated in the implementation of the game, collected comments, and later compiled them into various suggestions. A joint session to share evaluations was held. The result of this session were some improvements in the game's design such as lessening the teacher's implication to encourage students' autonomy, improving the introductory video, having a larger game board, and the suggestion of having two parallel groups to play simultaneously to reduce the number of students in one given game. When there are 50 people participating in one game, attention gets lost, as happened in this training session. Therefore, enabling two board games to have two simultaneous games was a positive change, particularly for Higher Education as groups are very large in the first year.

This gamification was also tested in primary school with 'year six' students. In this case, several elements were adapted to make it easier for the students, but overall, the game achieved the same objectives. The result was positive engagement by students and by the teacher. The opening of a space following the game, where students could enquire about the notions developed in the games, allowed teachers to explain complex concepts to primary school children. For the students, having this space after the experience of having played, eased getting a better understanding of complex concepts.

In Higher Education, students easily perceive the topics the game works with such as family structure, social structure, vulnerability some families have, birth injustice (being born in a family with resources or not), Matthew effect...In the initial setup, at the start of the game, students are faced with some initial texts where some of these concepts appear. These are concepts that are explained in the first block of the course "sociology of education" for GEI and GEP degrees. Through the game, we can encourage reflection on the power of decisions and how those change depending on the context; for example, vulnerability situations do not encourage the best possible rational decision-making. Being in the comfort of a privileged situation (like the Gná village) or with a specific problematic like extreme poverty (Seren village), the proximity to illegality or addition of a next of kin (Urd village) or the distinctive factor of having a family member with a profession serving the community (such as a teacher, doctors...etc) are some of the characterisations students experience through the game. This aspect is key because it makes theoretical concepts, often difficult to understand for first year students, accessible. Learning through experiencing the concepts also invites the students to gain a new perspective and a different understanding of these concepts, varying a lot to what could be achieved by regular teaching methods.

Gamifying the evaluation resulted in generating an evaluation that generated less anxiety and was more accessible to a variety of learning styles. Then, through an experiential approach, dense theoretical concepts can be made accessible and through play, understood. Therefore, overall, the findings from both gamifications indicated that the methodologies employed increase comprehension among all students, including those with diverse learning profiles.

FUTURE RESEARCH DIRECTIONS

For these projects, we already have future research planned. This coming year we are going to expand the gamification to more groups in both GEI and GEP degrees. We will design pre and post implementation surveys for both gamifications to gather data focusing specifically on diverse learning needs and the effects both gamifications have on theoretical comprehension and overall improvement of results.

Future research in the intersection between gamification and UDL could incorporate generative artificial intelligence into gamification. Future research could investigate a teaching experience using generative artificial intelligence tools to customise the course for different kinds of learning diversity and encourage students to test different styles and use the one that is a better fit for them.

CONCLUSION

The objective of this chapter was to examine, through an exploration of both innovation research projects, the benefits gamification has for students' motivation and learning. In this chapter, we have explained the experience of implementing two teaching innovations in the Faculty of Education at the University of Barcelona. Both innovations were implemented in the degrees GEI and GEP and in the subject "sociology of education". The findings indicate that gamification does increase motivation and comprehension of a difficult theoretical topic. Students are more motivated through play; may that be a digital platform or a large board game. Complicated topics are made more accessible through play, and students become involved in their own learning, taking responsibility for it and feeling they are part of the learning experience. Our analysis reveals that a tool such as wooclap makes learning more accessible and, through having only one question per page, increases attentional focus and enhances a sense of academic achievement, lessening anxiety and providing a calmer platform from which to approach the evaluation (Alshammari, 2020). We have also seen how a board game can increase students' awareness of complicated issues that can only be dealt with theoretically during the course. Gamifying those concepts means making them easier for students to understand through play and through a defined role play where students will experience the results of having some of the situations defined in each of the game's villages. Thus, by making learning experiential, we are also providing a different platform from which students can learn, one where learning differences may not be as defining.

Hence, gamifying the course contents and evaluation resulted in the creation of a space where the learning process, the exchange of knowledge was not done vertically but it was horizontal, and students as teachers, were all elements exchanging knowledge, sharing a praxis. This change in the classroom learning dynamics invites diversity to become an asset instead of an issue, because the more diverse the classroom is, the richer the game becomes. This was more visible in the board game than in the digital gamification and it is a platform that invites everybody to build on diversity and difference to enrich the learning environment and foster conceptual sharing. Therefore, incorporating gamification in our teaching methods is applying an element of Universal design learning that is key, inclusion. This, in turn, will help make the process of teaching and learning more equitable and not leave anyone behind. When we play, we are a team, we advance as a team, we overcome as a team, the more varied the team is, the more skills it has. Having classrooms with diverse learning students is not an issue to overcome, it's a richness to explore and no student is left behind.

ACKNOWLEDGMENT

We want to thank RIMDA, UB as this research was supported by RIMDA, funding the project 2023PMD-UB/033, and Education Faculty to promote and fund RIMDAE, institutional project to improve the innovative education 2024PEDC-EDU/001.

REFERENCES

Alshammari, M. T. (2020). Evaluation of gamification in e-learning systems for elementary school students. *TEM Journal, 9*(2), 806. https://doi.org/ [DOI]DOI: 10.18421/TEM92-51

Briones Suárez, K. B., Montero Ramírez, I. S., Caranqui Pintag, M. A., & Ramirez Melendres, R. M.Karen Belén Briones SuárezIrwing Stalin Montero RamírezMartha Alicia Caranqui PintagRoxana Mabel Ramirez Melendres. (2024). Gamificación y DUA: Creando entornos de aprendizaje inclusivos. *Revista Imaginario Social*, *7*(4). Advance online publication. DOI: 10.59155/is.v7i4.252

de-Marcos, L., Domínguez, A., Saenz-de-Navarrete, J., & Pagés, C. (2014). An empirical study comparing gamification and social networking on e-learning. *Computers & Education*, *75*, 82–91. DOI: 10.1016/j.compedu.2014.01.012

Deterding, S., Dixon, D., Khaled, R., & Nacke, L. (2011). From game design elements to gamefulness: defining "gamification". *MindTrek '11: Proceedings of the 15th International Academic MindTrek Conference: Envisioning Future Media Environments* doi/DOI: 10.1145/2181037.2181040

Domínguez, A., Saenz-de-Navarrete, J., de-Marcos, L., Fernández-Sanz, L., Pagés, C., & Martínez-Herráiz, J. J. (2013). Gamifying learning experiences: Practical implications and outcomes. *Computers & Education*, *63*, 380–392. DOI: 10.1016/j.compedu.2012.12.020

Fernández-Velásquez, J. D. R., López-Regalado, O., & Fernández-Hurtado, G. A. (2025). Educational dualism in action: Systematic review of gamification and flipped classrooms' effects on young learners. *Contemporary Educational Technology*, *17*(1), 557. DOI: 10.30935/cedtech/15749

García-Redondo, P., García, T., Areces, D., Núñez, J. C., & Rodríguez, C. (2019). Serious Games and Their Effect Improving Attention in Students with Learning Disabilities. *International Journal of Environmental Research and Public Health*, *16*(14), 2480. DOI: 10.3390/ijerph16142480 PMID: 31336804

Giannetto, D., Chao, J., & Fontana, A. (2013). Gamification in a Social Learning Environment. *Issues in Informing Science and Information Technology*, *10*, 1–13. DOI: 10.28945/1806

Goehle, G. (2013). Gamification and Web-based Homework. *PRIMUS (Terre Haute, Ind.)*, *23*(3), 234–246. DOI: 10.1080/10511970.2012.736451

Granet, D. B., Gomi, C. F., Ventura, R., & Miller-Scholte, A. (2005). The Relationship between Convergence Insufficiency and ADHD. *Strabismus*, *13*(4), 163–168. DOI: 10.1080/09273970500455436 PMID: 16361187

Hanus, M. D.,&Fox, J. (2015). Assessing the effects of gamification in the classroom: A longitudinal study on intrinsic motivation, social comparison, satisfaction, effort, and academic performance. *Computers & Education, 80,* 152 161. https://doi.org/ DOI: 10.1016/j.compedu.2014.08.019

Jadán-Guerrero, J., Avilés-Castillo, F., Buele, J., & Palacios-Navarro, G. (2023). Gamification in Inclusive Education for Children with Disabilities: Global Trends and Approaches - A Bibliometric Review. In Gervasi, O. (Eds.), Lecture Notes in Computer Science: Vol. 14104. *Computational Science and Its Applications – ICCSA 2023 Workshops. ICCSA 2023*. Springer., DOI: 10.1007/978-3-031-37105-9_31

Li, Q., Yin, X., Yin, W., Dong, X., & Li, Q. (2023). Evaluation of gamification techniques in learning abilities for higher school students using FAHP and EDAS methods. *Soft Computing*, •••, 1–19. Advance online publication. DOI: 10.1007/s00500-023-08179-9 PMID: 37362302

Mekler, E.D., Bruhlmann, F., Opwis, K. Tuch, A.N. (2013). Disassembling gamification: the effects of points and meaning on user motivation and performance. *CHI EA '13: CHI '13 Extended Abstracts on Human Factors in Computing Systems*, 1137 – 1142. Doi/DOI: 10.1145/2468356.2468559

Muntean, C. I. (2011). Raising engagement in e-learning through gamification», *Proceedings 6th International Conference on Virtual Learning ICVL*, pp. 323-329.

O'Donovan, S., Gain, J., & Marais, P. (2013) A case study in the gamification of a university-level games development course. In *Proceedings of the South African Institute for Computer Scientists and Information Technologists Conference* (SAICSIT '13). Association for Computing Machinery, New York, NY, USA, pp.242–251. DOI: 10.1145/2513456.2513469

Pedreira, O., Garcia, F., Brisaboa, N., & Piattini, M. (2014). Gamification in software engineering - A systematic mapping. *Information and Software Technology*. Advance online publication. DOI: 10.1016/j.infsof.2014.08.007

Prince, J. D. (2013). Gamification. *Journal of Electronic Resources in Medical Libraries, 10*(3), 162–169. DOI: 10.1080/15424065.2013.820539

Watson, D., Hancock, M., & Mandryk, R. (2013). Gamifying behaviour that leads tolearning. *Proceedings of the First International Conference on gameful design, research, and applications*, pp. 87 - 90. DOI: 10.1145/2583008.2583021

ADDITIONAL READING

Annetta, L., Minogue, J., Holmes, S., & Cheng, M.-T. (2009). Investigating the impact of video games on high school students' engagement and learning about genetics. *Computers & Education, 53*(1), 74–85. DOI: 10.1016/j.compedu.2008.12.020

Barata, G., Gama, S., Jorge, J., & Gonçalves, D. (2013). Improving participation and learning with gamification. In *Proceedings of the First International Conference on Gameful Design, Research, and Applications (Gamification '13)* (pp. 10–17). Association for Computing Machinery. https://doi.org/DOI: 10.1145/2583008.2583010

Batson, L., & Feinberg, S. (2006). Game designs that enhance motivation and learning for teenagers. *Electronic Journal for the Integration of Technology in Education, 5*, 34–43.

Chans, G. M., & Portuguez Castro, M. (2021). Gamification as a strategy to increase motivation and engagement in higher education chemistry students. *Computers, 10*(10), 132. DOI: 10.3390/computers10100132

Kapp, K. M. (2012). *The Gamification of Learning and Instruction: Game-based Methods and Strategies for Training and Education*. Pfeiffer.

Lister, M. (2015). Gamification: The effect on student motivation and performance at the post-secondary level. *Issues and Trends in Educational Technology, 3*(2). University of Arizona Libraries. Retrieved May 27, 2024, from https://www.learntechlib.org/p/171075/

Lovett, B. J., & Nelson, J. M. (2021). Systematic review: Educational accommodations for children and adolescents with attention-deficit/hyperactivity disorder. *Journal of the American Academy of Child and Adolescent Psychiatry, 60*(4), 448–457. DOI: 10.1016/j.jaac.2020.07.891 PMID: 32745597

O'Donovan, S., Gain, J., & Marais, P. (2013). A case study in the gamification of a university-level games development course. *Proceedings of the South African Institute for Computer Scientists and Information Technologists Conference, (SAICSIT'13)*, 242 - 251. DOI: 10.1145/2513456.2513469

Teixes, F. (2015). *Gamificación: fundamentos y aplicaciones*. Editorial UOC.

Vickers, M. Z. (2010). *Accommodating college students with learning disabilities: ADD, ADHD, and dyslexia*. Pope Center Series on Higher Education Policy.

KEY TERMS AND DEFINITIONS

Agency: the capacity of students to take ownership of their learning process, make decisions, and act with autonomy and responsibility in educational settings.

Diverse Learning Needs: a range of cognitive, emotional, or physical differences among students (e.g., ADHD, dyslexia, autism) that require varied instructional strategies to ensure equitable access to learning.

Experiential Learning: a learning process through which students gain knowledge and skills by engaging in direct experiences and reflecting on them, often used in gamified or role-play scenarios.

Gamification: the application of game elements and principles in non-game contexts—such as education—to foster engagement, motivation, and active participation in learning.

Inclusive Education: an approach that ensures all students, regardless of their abilities or backgrounds, have equal access to quality education and meaningful participation in learning activities.

Motivation: a psychological factor that drives students to engage with learning tasks. Gamification is used to enhance both intrinsic and extrinsic motivation in educational contexts.

Summative Assessment: an evaluation method used to measure student learning at the end of an instructional unit, often contributing to final grades. In this context, it was gamified to enhance accessibility and reduce anxiety.

Universal Design for Learning (UDL): an educational framework aimed at creating flexible and inclusive learning environments by offering multiple means of representation, expression, and engagement to accommodate diverse learners.

Chapter 13
Gamification Learning for Urban Educational Challenges:
A Mixed-Methods Quasi-Experimental Study in PGDM Programs

Senthil Kumar A. V.
http://orcid.org/0000-0002-8587-7017
Nehru Institute of Information Technology and Management, India

Revati Ramrao Rautrao
http://orcid.org/0000-0001-7803-8699
Dr D.Y. Patil B-School, India

Sanjayan Thottapattunjalil Suseelan
GVM's Dr. Dada Vaidya College of Education, Ponda, India

Nagakishore Bhavanam S.
http://orcid.org/0000-0003-3798-6945
Mangalayatan University, Jabalpur, India

Sambasiva Rao K. R. S.
http://orcid.org/0000-0002-0061-8754
Dr. RVR NRI Institute of Technology (Deemed to be) University, India

Nasir Ahmad Ganaie
http://orcid.org/0000-0001-6781-834X
Department of Political Science, School of Social Sciences, University of Kashmir, Srinagar, India

ABSTRACT

This study sees the new Gamification strategies used in the Post Graduate Diploma (PGDM) programs to solve urban educational challenges. The study uses a semi-professional approach with mixed methods to investigate how well the urban management improves the learning strategy for student engagement, knowledge retention,

DOI: 10.4018/979-8-2600-1568-1.ch013

and skill development. According to its unique design, the research uses a mixture of quantitative and qualitative data collection methods such as study, performance reviews, focus groups and intensive interviews with coaches and students. According to the results, gamification improves the results of learning because it improves participants' motivation, accelerates their problems to solve problems, and helps them understand complex urban problems. The report's conclusions have ramifications for curriculum improvement, educational strategies, and the creation of customised gamification solutions for management packages with a city concentration.

INTRODUCTION

Improvement in student engagement, inspiration becomes more important when it comes to changing the higher education scenario, especially for the Post Graduate Diploma in Management (PGDM) programs. Urban students' diverse learning requirements, which are quickly influenced by the digital environment and experienced learning preferences, are often not sufficiently addressed by traditional educational techniques. Close this difference, Gamification-Non-Gaming references include deliberate sports aspects, such as playing technique. Gamification encourages students' involvement, group learning, and internal motivation by using functions such as leads, points, brands, and fiction challenges (Nguyen-Viet et al., 2024).

Due to its complexity, diversity and resource restrictions, urban education provides both special opportunities and difficulties for innovative teaching. In this connection, it presents a viable way to reconsider gamification, how the course is distributed, how the assessment is held, and how students and instructors interact (Alenezi, 2023). Although there is a tax of research that shows that the gamified learning environment can increase cognitive and emotional results, some empirical tests are still done in PGDM programs. Further research is necessary to guarantee gamification in urban school training and an inclusive and reference-sensitive use of shareholding-focused design thinking.

This study observed how to influence the results of learning and student engagement in PGDM programs located in the urban educational environment. By combining shareholding instructional methods with gamification principles, it tries to create an ideological structure that leads to both theory and behaviour. This study is grounded in mixed-methods inquiry, combining quantitative analysis of learner performance with qualitative insights from faculty and student experiences (Qudsi, 2024). Through this approach, the study seeks to advance scholarly understanding of gamification as a catalyst for educational transformation in urban India.

A. BACKGROUND AND CONTEXT

The integration of gamification into postgraduate management education reflects a change in basic assumptions in pedagogical design, particularly within the urban academic ecosystems. As PGDM programs evolve to meet the demands of digitally native learners, traditional didactic methods increasingly reveal limitations in fostering sustained engagement, critical thinking, and participatory learning. Urban institutions, often characterised by diverse student demographics and competitive academic environments, necessitate innovative instructional strategies that resonate with learners' cognitive and motivational profiles. Gamification—defined as the application of game-based mechanics in non-game contexts offers a dynamic framework for reconfiguring classroom interactions, assessment modalities, and curriculum delivery. Its relevance is amplified in urban settings where students navigate complex socio-academic pressures and require adaptive, immersive learning experiences. Despite its growing prominence in the global education discourse, empirical research on gamification within Indian PGDM programs remains nascent. This study situates gamification within the broader context of equity-centred design thinking, aiming to explore its potential to democratize learning, enhance academic performance, and cultivate reflective practice (Slamet, 2024). By examining its application in urban postgraduate classrooms, this research contributes to a nuanced understanding of how gamified interventions can recalibrate educational outcomes and foster inclusive, learner-centric environments in management education.

Overview of Urban Educational Challenges

Urban education in India is characterised by a complex interplay of demographic diversity, infrastructural constraints, and pedagogical fragmentation. Metropolitan classrooms often host students from varied linguistic, socioeconomic, and cultural backgrounds, creating a dynamic yet challenging learning environment. Despite their proximity to technological hubs and policy innovation, urban institutions frequently grapple with overcrowded classrooms, uneven access to digital resources, and limited faculty–student interaction. The rapid expansion of private educational providers has further intensified competition, often prioritising performance metrics over holistic learning. Moreover, urban learners face heightened academic pressure, fragmented attention spans, and reduced intrinsic motivation factors exacerbated by rigid curricula and conventional teaching methods. These challenges are not in accordance with industry standards due to insufficient teaching preparation and a lack of integration of experiential learning and industry standards (Anderle et al., 2025). Equity still has differences, especially for first-generation students, who often find it difficult to meet institutional needs. Educational innovation is necessary to solve these complex problems that include inclusive, flexible and reference sensitive. When strategically embedded within urban PGDM programs, gamification offers a promising avenue for reconfiguring learning environments, fostering engagement, and democratising access to quality education through participatory and reflective modalities.

Introduction to Gamification in Learning

Gamification has emerged as a pedagogical innovation that redefines learner engagement by embedding game-based elements into educational environments. Rather than trivialising academic rigour, gamification strategically harnesses motivational dynamics—such as goal orientation, feedback loops, and incremental challenges—to cultivate sustained cognitive involvement. In management education, particularly in PGDM programs, gamification offers a framework to transform passive learning into active knowledge construction. It aligns with constructivist principles, enabling learners to navigate complex concepts through experiential tasks, scenario-based simulations, and collaborative problem-solving. The integration of mechanics such as point systems, badges, and narrative progression fosters a sense of achievement and autonomy, which is critical for adult learners in urban academic settings (Jun & Lucas, 2024). Gamification supports differentiated instruction by accommodating diverse learning styles and promoting inclusive participation. Its application transcends mere entertainment and functions as a scaffold for critical thinking, ethical reasoning, and reflective practice. Despite its global adoption, contextual adaptation of gamification in Indian postgraduate classrooms remains underexplored. This study posits that gamification is not a peripheral tool but a central pedagogical strategy capable of recalibrating curriculum delivery, enhancing learner agency, and contributing to the democratisation of education in urban management institutions.

Brief Explanation of PGDM Programs

Post Graduate Diploma in Management (PGDM) programs represent a dynamic and industry-responsive alternative to traditional university-affiliated business degrees in India. Offered primarily by autonomous institutions approved by the All-India Council for Technical Education (AICTE), PGDM curricula are designed to be agile, interdisciplinary, and aligned with evolving market demands. Unlike conventional MBA programs that often follow rigid university frameworks, PGDM courses benefit from curricular flexibility, allowing institutions to integrate contemporary themes such as digital transformation, sustainability, and entrepreneurial innovation. PGDM institutions often collaborate with industry partners to co-design modules and ensure relevance and employability. In urban educational contexts, PGDM programs cater to a diverse student body navigating competitive academic and professional landscapes. Emphasis on soft skills, global exposure, and technology-enabled learning further distinguishes PGDM offerings (Amish, 2024). As management education undergoes a change in basic assumptions, PGDM programs are increasingly positioned as incubators of future-ready professionals who are equipped to address complex business challenges through innovation, adaptability, and ethical leadership. Their modular structure and outcome-based design make them ideal platforms for integrating gamified pedagogies and equity-centred learning strategies.

B. RESEARCH PROBLEM AND SIGNIFICANCE

Despite the increasing digitisation of education and proliferation of learner-centred pedagogies, PGDM programs in urban India continue to rely heavily on conventional instructional models that inadequately address student engagement, motivation, and retention. The absence of adaptive, experiential frameworks has resulted in a pedagogical disconnect, particularly among urban learners navigating competitive academic environments and diverse cognitive profiles. Gamification, though widely recognised for its potential to enhance learning outcomes, remains underutilised and insufficiently theorised within the context of postgraduate management education. Existing studies often lack contextual specificity and fail to account for the socio-academic complexities of urban institutions. This study addresses a critical gap by investigating how gamification can be strategically embedded into PGDM curricula to foster inclusive, participatory, and outcome-driven learning.(Reis Da Silva, 2024). It seeks to develop a conceptual framework that integrates game-based mechanics with equity-centred design thinking, thereby offering a novel lens to reimagine curriculum delivery. The significance of this study lies in its potential to inform policy, guide institutional innovation, and contribute to scholarly discourse on pedagogical transformation. By situating gamification within the urban educational milieu, this study advances a nuanced understanding of its role in democratizing access, enhancing learner agency, and recalibrating management education for the digital age (Reis Da Silva, 2024).

Importance of Addressing Urban Educational Challenges

There is a need to accept urban education difficulties to promote egalitarian, flexible and future learning ecosystems. Despite being at the intersection of policy change and technology innovation, urban institutions often meet systemic inequalities that interfere with inclusive educational development. Reference -sensitive intervention is necessary to solve congested classes, dissatisfied infrastructure and educational challenges caused by socio-economic differences. Urban students usually attract cognitive overload, less attention and increased screen requirements, which are worse than exceptionally low opportunities for strict courses and practical learning. These circumstances eliminate the cycles of academic boycott by unevenly affecting the first generation and marginalised students (Mallén-Lacambra & Mamas, 2025). Addressing these problems is important for the democratisation of high-quality education and is not a simple, practical idea. Innovative academics with revolutionary ability to assess the distribution of courses, improvement in the student agency and promote participation include gamification, mixed teaching, and shareholder-focused design. By prioritising urban educational reforms, schools can produce graduates who are flexible, introspective, and socially affected and who can successfully interact with the international environment. Additionally, it leads to dealing with these issues for more common development purposes such as civilian empowerment, economic inclusion, and social mobility. The purpose of this project is to reconsider Urban PGDM education through inclusive, attractive, and purposeful academic contours, using gamification as a catalyst technique within the improvement agenda (Maryana et al., 2024).

Potential Benefits of Gamification in PGDM Programs

For Post Graduate Diploma in Management (PGDM) programs, Gamification provides a revolutionary learning method that improves educational results and dedication in many ways. Teachers can create a learning environment for partnerships that encourage sports-based elements such as adaptive challenges, scoring systems and colleague-based leadership boards, such as internal inspiration and teamwork. By enabling students to contact complex management concepts through interactive simulation and landscape-based activities, this approach overcomes traditional training and bridges the difference between theoretical abstraction and practical implementation. Giving students latitude to make their own decisions in risk-free situations that repeat the business issues of the real world promotes cognitive agility, strategic thinking, and reflective practice (Maryana et al., 2024). Students can monitor their progress and change their real-time approach to personal learning paths, and in addition to quick response loops, which encourage even more self-regulated learning. In addition, the technical interface for gamification complements the necessary digital abilities in modern business ecology systems, which improves students' preparations for dynamic, computer-driven work settings. Gamification provides a scalable and inclusive paradigm in urban PGDM references to learning, promoting the connection and improvement of educational results through innovation and shareholding-focused design, where students are prominent and academic pressure is reduced (Li et al., 2022).

C. RESEARCH OBJECTIVES AND QUESTIONS

The educational ability of Gamification in the Post Graduate Diploma in Management (PGDM) programs is the subject of this study, which focuses on urban education. The evaluation of the effect of incorporating sports-based components was the main goal of the leadership board, adaptive challenges and premium system student motivation, engagement, and academic achievement. This study is trying to evaluate how well these mechanisms are working to improve the understanding of complex leadership persons and promote participation by involving them in course design. A secondary goal is to study the importance of false business scenarios to promote important thinking, moral logic, and strategic decision-making among PGDM students. The study has observed how the accelerated response system affects self-regulated learning and reflection activities to support unique academic routes. In addition, it considers how much the technical skills and flexibility of the students have improved, so that they can sew digitally for several job environments. The study questions aim to address the quantitative and qualitative aspects of simplification effects, including the implications of learning, their impact on the development of students and practical management techniques. The project aims to provide a relevant overview of the Gamified course for continuing education.

Primary Research Objectives

This study examines educational intervals in urban PGDM programs and examines how digital natives improve leadership training for students. The main goal is to increase the students' inspiration, engagement, and educational success by incorporating a sports-based strategy. Custom tasks, incentive plans, realistic situations, and immediate response are examples of independent variables. All examples of engagement, performance, inspiration, important thinking, decision, and digital preparations are examples of variables. Digital infrastructure, institutional environment, and teacher demographics are considered as variables. According to the hypothesis, compared to students in traditional environments, individuals who meet the Gamified Learning environment will show a strong understanding of engagement, a better understanding of complex business ideas and employment in the digital industry. A versatile perspective on the effect of gamification on management education is given by this mixed methodological approach.

Research Questions

A series of research questions centred on detecting the educational efficiency of gamification in urban PGDM programs acts as a compass of studies. This is the first to check the effect of involving gaming-based components in management education on how students are motivated and engaged, such as leadership boards, reward systems and customised challenges are met. Second, it examines how much better understanding and storage of complex business concepts are achieved using gamified learning settings, unlike traditional teaching techniques. Third, it seems that the syllabus that includes simulated real-world conditions helps students to strengthen their critical thinking, moral logic, and strategic decision-making skills. Fourth, it considers how self-regulated learning and contemplative academic behaviour are promoted by immediate reaction methods. Fifth, it looks at methods that affect students' readiness to trade ecosystems that interact with digital means, especially in relation to technical flow and adaptive abilities. The final goal of the study is to evaluate how gamification affects different student profiles in urban PGDM settings to provide more knowledge of its scalability and inclusion. Together, these inquiries guide the construction of an ideological structure that presents Gamification as a playing strategy in education.

To carry out the theoretical structures that emphasize this study, a conceptual structure was designed to portray the conditions that have been enclosed between Gamification input and student results in PGDM education, in PGDM education. (Figure 1).

Figure 1. Conceptual framework of gamified pedagogy in PGDM education

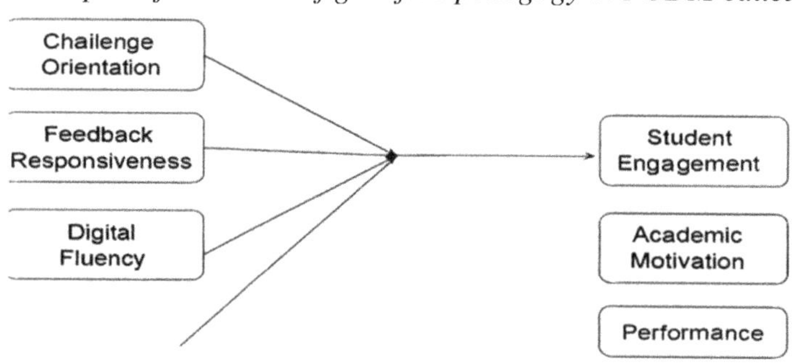

This structure shows how gamification creates - challenge orientation, feedback responsibilities, digital flow, and Game works - Impact student results, such as students' involvement, academic motivation, and performance. Customised et al. (2011), with modifications for PGDM reference.

D. LITERATURE REVIEW

a. Urban Educational Challenges

The diverse environment of urban education in India is influenced by the expectations of the student, the inequality of the infrastructure and demographic inequality. Educational models that are unable to effectively represent the living reality of urban students, package classrooms and uneven access to digital resources are all questions that often meet metropolitan institutions that comply with the two scholarly debates. Studies by Kumar (2021) and Sharma (2023) underscore the disconnection between curriculum design and the socio-cultural diversity of urban student populations, resulting in diminished engagement and academic alienation (Sharma, 2023). Urban students often also experience cognitive fragmentation because of digital stimuli, competitive pressure, and a lack of personal training. According to research, structural injustice is making institutional norms difficult for students in excluded communities and first-generation students to navigate and receive educational assistance. Even when political frameworks support technology and competent and diverse education, urban areas use these outlines differently. According to recent studies, instructional regions are required through experienced, flexible, and student-centred approaches. As proposed by Singh and Mehta (2022), because gamification encourages inspiration, participation, and reflective commitment, it provides an approach to the prevention of urban learning settings. However, there are still some empirical studies unique to PGDM conditions, such as a concentrated probe into how gamification can help with the complexity of urban education.

Overview of Current Issues in Urban Education

Systemic complications that interfere with similar teaching results and institutional results are becoming increasingly widespread in India's urban education system. Lower instructional quality and limited educational assistance are caused by congested classes, infrastructure with limited resources and dissatisfied policy implementation. These difficulties get worse than socio-economic inequality because children of disadvantaged families often do not have access to digital resources, educational material, or safe teaching places. Professional burnout and lower wages are the main causes of teacher turnover, which reduces institutional morale and instructional continuity. During infection for remote and hybrid learning, the digital distinction that is activated has highlighted deep differences in technical access and digital literacy (Shaikh & Ali, 2025). In addition, the cultural diversity of urban classes requires an instructional structure that includes all languages and cultures. Because of a lack of infrastructure, no questions about mental health affected by academic and urban stresses are well handled. Standardised evaluation procedures often reduce experience and general learning, limit the extent of the course and hinder innovation. Both physical and psychosocial factors compromise the integrity of the learning environment. Parental engagement is constrained by economic precarity and linguistic barriers, thus weakening home–school collaboration. A multi-interest strategy is required that includes political changes, participation in society and creative academics to solve these interconnected problems and promote inclusive, flexible, and student-centric urban education systems (Weidl & Erling, 2025).

Factors Contributing to Urban Educational Challenges

The persistence of educational disparities in urban settings is shaped by a constellation of interrelated structural, socio-economic, and pedagogical factors. Overcrowded classrooms and under-resourced institutions compromise instructional quality, limiting opportunities for differentiated learning and individualised support. Socioeconomic stratification further impedes equitable access, with students from marginalised communities often lacking digital infrastructure, academic scaffolding, and psychosocial stability. Teacher attrition, which is driven by professional fatigue, limited career progression, and inadequate remuneration, disrupts pedagogical continuity and institutional coherence. Technological asymmetries—exacerbated during remote learning transitions—have widened achievement gaps, revealing uneven digital literacy and access across urban student populations (Chikwe et al., 2024). The cultural plurality of metropolitan classrooms demands responsive and inclusive teaching strategies, yet curricular rigidity often fails to accommodate linguistic and cognitive diversity. Mental health vulnerabilities, rooted in urban stressors and socio-environmental precarity, remain insufficiently addressed due to limited counselling frameworks. Standardised assessment regimes prioritise performance metrics over holistic development, narrowing the curricular scope and stifling creativity. Both physical and emotional factors undermine the integrity of the learning environments (Mouboua et al., 2024). Parental engagement is constrained by economic precarity, time poverty, and linguistic barriers. These multifactorial challenges necessitate systemic reform and pedagogical innovation to foster inclusive, resilient, and learner-centred urban education ecosystems.

Existing Approaches to Address Urban Educational Problems

Contemporary efforts to mitigate urban educational challenges have evolved through a blend of policy reform, pedagogical innovation, and community engagement. Governments and educational institutions have initiated infrastructure upgrades, digital inclusion programs, and targeted funding to alleviate resource constraints and overcrowding. Equity-focused interventions, such as midday meal schemes, scholarship initiatives, and inclusive enrolment drives, aim to reduce socioeconomic barriers and promote access. Teacher retention strategies increasingly emphasise professional development, mentorship models, and performance-linked incentives to combat burnout and attrition. Bridge the digital divide, urban schools have adopted blended learning platforms, mobile-based content delivery, and public–private partnerships for device distribution (Eden et al., 2024). Culturally responsive pedagogy is gaining traction, with curricula being adapted to reflect linguistic diversity and local contexts. Mental health support is integrated through school-based counselling, peer mentoring, and trauma-informed teaching practices. Assessment reforms advocate competency-based evaluation over rote testing, encouraging holistic learning. Safety protocols, including surveillance systems and psychosocial safety audits, are institutionalised to ensure secure learning environments. Parental engagement is fostered by multilingual communication tools, flexible meeting schedules, and community liaisons. These approaches collectively underscore the need for systemic, inclusive, and context-sensitive strategies to transform urban education into a resilient learner-centric domain.

b. Gamification in Education

Gamification in education signifies a transformative shift from conventional instructional paradigms toward learner-centric, experience-driven pedagogy. By embedding game mechanics such as point systems, adaptive challenges, narrative progression, and peer-based competition, educators can cultivate immersive learning environments that stimulate intrinsic motivation and sustained engagement. This approach aligns with constructivist and experiential learning theories, enabling students to interact with content through simulated scenarios that mirror real-world complexity. The integration of digital platforms and interactive technologies further enhances the scalability and responsiveness of gamified instruction, accommodating diverse cognitive styles and fostering inclusive participation. Immediate feedback loops and personalised progression pathways empower learners to monitor their academic trajectory, recalibrate strategies, and develop metacognitive awareness (Qudsi, 2024). Beyond performance enhancement, gamification nurtures critical thinking, ethical reasoning, and collaborative problem-solving—skills that are essential for navigating dynamic professional landscapes. The emerging literature underscores its potential to democratize education by bridging engagement gaps and promoting equity in urban classrooms. As institutions adapt to the demands of digital transformation and learner diversity, gamification offers a robust framework for reimaging curriculum delivery, assessment modalities, and pedagogical relationships. Its judicious implementation within PGDM programs can catalyse educational innovation and prepare students for complex, interconnected global challenges (Foreman-Brown et al., 2022).

Definition and Principles of Gamification

Gamification is defined as the strategic incorporation of game-design elements into non-game contexts to enhance user engagement, motivation, and cognitive investment. In educational settings, it functions as a pedagogical catalyst that transforms routine learning activities into dynamic, purposeful experiences (M. Li et al., 2023). Central to gamification are principles such as goal setting, progress visualisation, immediate feedback, reward mechanisms, and social interactivity, all of which activate intrinsic psychological drivers such as autonomy, mastery, and relatedness. Unlike superficial point-based systems, effective gamification integrates narrative arcs, adaptive challenges, and collaborative tasks that foster deeper learning and sustained participation. It emphasises the balance between extrinsic incentives (e.g., badges, scores) and intrinsic rewards (e.g., self-efficacy, curiosity), thereby promoting long-term behavioural change and academic resilience. This approach is inherently flexible, allowing for contextual adaptation across disciplines and learner profiles. As digital technologies evolve, gamification increasingly leverages analytics, personalisation algorithms, and immersive interfaces to tailor learning pathways and optimise outcomes. Ethical implementation remains paramount, ensuring that gamified environments uphold inclusivity, transparency, and learner autonomy (Wulan et al., 2024). Within PGDM programs, gamification offers a robust framework for reimaging curriculum delivery, enhancing managerial competencies, and preparing students for complex, data-driven professional ecosystems.

Applications of Gamification in Various Educational Contexts

Gamification has emerged as a versatile pedagogical strategy with cross-disciplinary applicability across educational levels, from foundational schooling to advanced professional training. In primary education, gamified modules often incorporate interactive quests and level-based progression to reinforce numeracy and literacy skills, fostering early cognitive engagement and enthusiasm for learning. Secondary institutions leverage role-play simulations and narrative-driven challenges to deepen conceptual understanding in subjects such as history, science, and civics, enabling students to embody historical actors or solve real-world dilemmas. At the tertiary level, universities increasingly adopt augmented and virtual reality platforms to gamify complex domains such as molecular biology, engineering design, and environmental systems, facilitating immersive exploration and spatial reasoning. Language acquisition platforms use gamified structures—daily streaks, achievement badges, and peer competition—to promote consistency and fluency. In professional development and executive education, gamification manifests through scenario-based simulations and decision-making games that mirror industry challenges, enhancing strategic thinking and leadership competencies (Lee et al., 2023). Across contexts, gamification activates intrinsic motivation, supports differentiated instruction, and fosters self-regulated learning through immediate feedback and adaptive pathways. Its capacity to personalise learning, cultivate engagement, and scaffold higher-order thinking positions gamification as a transformative tool in contemporary education systems.

Benefits and Limitations of Gamification in Learning

Gamification in education offers a dynamic approach to learning, transforming traditional methods into interactive experiences. By incorporating game-like elements, educators can spark curiosity and motivation among students. This approach taps into the natural human inclination for competition and achievement, making learning more enjoyable and engaging. Students may find themselves more willing to tackle challenging subjects when presented in a gamified format, leading to increased participation and effort. However, gamification is not without its limitations. The focus on external rewards might overshadow the intrinsic value of learning, potentially creating a dependency on incentives. Some students may become overly competitive, losing sight of collaborative learning opportunities. Additionally, designing effective gamified systems requires considerable time and resources, which may not be feasible for all educational institutions (Lee et al., 2023). There's also a risk of oversimplifying complex subjects to fit game mechanics, potentially compromising the depth of understanding. Balancing entertainment with educational value remains a challenge, as it ensures that gamification benefits all learning styles equally. Despite these challenges, gamification can be a powerful tool to enhance educational outcomes and student engagement (Qudsi, 2024).

c. PGDM Programs and Innovative Learning Approaches

PGDM programs are evolving to meet the dynamic needs of the business world through the incorporation of innovative learning approaches. These programs emphasise experiential learning, integrating real-world case studies, industry projects, and simulations to bridge the gap between theory and practice. The use of online modules and traditional classes allows for mixed teaching models, so students can interact with courses at their own pace. Students can now focus on topics that are most relevant to their goals, thanks to the increasing popularity of individual learning routes based on the skills and professional goals of each student. By learning how to group projects and colleagues, a cooperative teaching environment improves communication and collaboration skills. State-of-the-art technology, such as virtual reality and artificial intelligence, is used to improve decision-making ability and offer attractive educational opportunities. Innovation and start-up culture are promoted by entrepreneurship incubators of PGDM programs. Students' approaches are expanded by global risk through exchange programs, international cooperation, and virtual cross-cultural initiatives. The exam is replaced with continuous evaluation techniques, such as project-based assessments and a portfolio, which encourage the development of broader skills. These advanced approaches, PGDM programs teach students to become flexible, visionary leaders, who are constantly equipped to challenge business problems in the global environment (Crogman et al., 2025).

Overview of PGDM programs

Living with the changing business atmosphere, PGDM programs have changed significantly. Improve the actual skills of students; these programs are now a high priority with experiential learning, including business participation and real-world projects. A more interdisciplinary approach is now ideal in the course, and it combines classic business courses with advanced subjects such as technological progress, stability, and data analysis. While the counselling program guides professionals in the industry, it allows students to adapt their education to fulfil some job aspirations. Students were able to build important decision-making skills by simulating complex business scenarios using advanced technology (Bohari et al., 2024). Focus on developing soft skills, such as emotional intelligence and pairing, to equip graduates for leadership relationships in a variety of surroundings. The incubation centres and start-up initiatives promote entrepreneurship by promoting creative thinking. Virtual exchange programs and multinational cooperation promote global perspectives. Methods for continuous evaluation, such as colleagues' review and project-based assessments, guarantee full skill development. These PGDM programs produce adaptable, progressive individuals who can manage the challenges in a modern business environment (Konak et al., 2024).

Current Teaching Methods in PGDM Programs

The Post Graduate Diploma in Management (PGDM) program uses its current teaching strategies for the needs of a rapidly changing business environment. Today, these courses focus on firsthand learning and the use of industrial projects, case studies, and simulation, which is to bridge the information difference between theory and behaviour. Mixing online modules with traditional classroom education offers flexibility and mixed methods for individual teaching routes (Brennan et al.,

2023). Because modern commercial concerns are linked, interdisciplinary courses are becoming increasingly popular. Technical knowledge is expanded with a focus on developing soft skills such as communication, management, and emotional intelligence. Industry partnerships facilitate guest lectures, internships, and mentorship programs, thus providing students with real-world insights. Data-driven decision-making and digital literacy are integrated across the curriculum to prepare students for technology-driven workplaces. Collaborative learning through group projects and peer-to-peer interactions fosters teamwork and networking skills. Continuous assessment methods, including presentations, reports, and practical applications, are replacing the traditional exam-centric evaluations (Aldhilan et al., 2024).

Integration of Innovative Learning Approaches in Management Education

Management education is undergoing a transformative shift and is embracing innovative learning approaches to prepare future leaders for the complexities of the modern business landscape. By integrating experiential learning, cross-disciplinary collaboration, and technology-enhanced methodologies, institutions foster a more dynamic and engaging educational environment. Case-based learning, simulations, and real-world projects are increasingly employed to bridge the gap between theory and practice, enabling students to develop critical thinking and critical thinking skills in authentic contexts. Flipped classrooms and blended learning models are revolutionising traditional lecture-based instruction, encouraging active participation and self-directed learning. Furthermore, the incorporation of design thinking principles and entrepreneurial mindsets into curricula is nurturing creativity and innovation among management students. Global virtual teams and international immersion programs are expanding cultural awareness and fostering adaptability in an interconnected world. As management education evolves, emphasis on emotional intelligence, ethical decision-making, and sustainable business practices is growing, preparing graduates to navigate complex organisational challenges (Hsu & Wu, 2023). This comprehensive approach to management education is to cultivate well-rounded professionals equipped with the diverse skill set required to lead an ever-changing business ecosystem.

This table synthesises key thematic clusters, constructs, representative studies, and methodological trends relevant to gamified pedagogy in urban PGDM programs.

Table 1. Structured literature review on gamification in PGDM education

Thematic Cluster	Key Constructs	Representative Studies	Methodological Notes
Gamification Theory & Models	Game elements, motivation, self-determination, flow theory	Deterding et al. (2011); Deci & Ryan (1985); Kapp (2012)	Conceptual frameworks are foundational for pedagogical design.
Pedagogical Impact	Learner autonomy, engagement, performance, retention	Hamari et al. (2014); Su & Cheng (2015); Toda et al. (2021)	Quantitative surveys; experimental designs
Urban Higher Education Contexts	Digital readiness, equity, and institutional constraints	Mahapatra & Sharma (2020); Singh & Rao (2019)	Contextual studies: urban student diversity
Mixed-Methods in EdTech Research	Triangulation, SEM, thematic coding, NVivo, survey design	Creswell & Plano Clark (2017); Hair et al. (2019)	Integration of qualitative and quantitative techniques
Management Education Challenges	Curriculum alignment, faculty readiness, and gamification barriers	Jain & Bansal (2021); Kumar & Mehta (2023)	Case studies; policy-oriented recommendations

E. METHODOLOGY

This study adopted a mixed-methods research design to comprehensively investigate the pedagogical impact of gamification in urban PGDM programs. This approach integrates both quantitative and qualitative techniques to ensure methodological triangulation and contextual depth. A systematic literature review was initially conducted to construct a theoretical foundation and identify the key constructs relevant to gamified learning, student engagement, and academic performance. A structured examination tool that included both reference-specific elements and standardised scores was created based on these comments that fit the goals of the study. A stratified random sample selection of 500 PGDM students from several metropolitan universities was conducted through an online survey, which guaranteed educational and cultural diversity. Educationists and twenty business experts participated in semi-structured interviews to gather complex attitudes towards the difficulties of simplification in leadership education and the benefits. Descriptive statistics, exploratory factor analysis, and structural equation modelling were used to evaluate quantitative data to evaluate hypotheses and analyse quantitative data to detect variable correlations. Identifying new patterns, theme coding and ongoing evaluation were used on qualitative data. Member confirmation, pilot samples and data trial all work to strengthen validity and addiction. Strict compliance. The oral guidelines were maintained, including informed consent, oblivion, and data protection. A complete and versatile examination of the researcher with this integrated technique is possible.

a. Research Design

This study saw the educational effects of gamification in urban PGDM programs using a convergence mixed-method approach. The study guaranteed analytical depth and triangulated validity by combining quantitative measures and qualitative conclusions. A systematic study that measures academic performance and engagement levels was given to a layered selection of PGDM students at different metropolitan universities to obtain quantitative data. Reference -specific construction that corresponded to the ideological study structure was included in the instrument. In addition, semi-composed interviews provided qualitative insight into design, implementation and perceived effect from teachers and industry experts. This two-dimensional strategy improved the depth of explanation and addiction. Strict compliance with moral principles was maintained, including informed permission, oblivion, and data protection. The design facilitates a versatile understanding of how gamification promotes skills development, student commitment, and course distribution.

Data Collection Procedures

In the quantitative phase, a structured online survey is administered to a stratified sample of 500 PGDM students across urban institutions. The survey captured pre- and post-intervention data on student engagement, academic performance, and perceptions of gamified learning environments. Participants were divided into intervention and control groups, with the former exposed to gamified instructional modules over six weeks. Ensure consistency, standardised instructions and digital consent forms were provided before participation. In the qualitative phase, semi-structured interviews and focus group discussions were conducted with twenty academic and industrial experts. These sessions were audio-recorded, transcribed verbatim, and anonymised to maintain confidentiality. Data collection instruments were pilot-evaluated and refined based on expert feedback to enhance clarity and contextual relevance.

Data Analysis

Quantitative data were analysed using SPSS and AMOS software, employing descriptive statistics, reliability testing (Cronbach's alpha), exploratory factor analysis, and structural equation modelling (SEM) to examine the relationships among variables and test hypotheses. Pre- and post-intervention comparisons were conducted using paired t-tests and ANOVA to assess the impact of gamification. Qualitative data were analysed through thematic coding using NVivo, following a constant comparative method to identify recurring patterns, emergent themes, and contextual insights. The triangulation of findings across data sources enhanced validity, while member checking and peer debriefing ensured interpretive accuracy.

Overview of Study Timeline and Phases

This study captures the changing dynamics of Gamification in Urban PGDM education. This study is conducted in three parts. With full literature analysis, the construction of an ideological structure was discovered, and the instrument verification through special consultation and pilot test was conducted during the study process. This phase performs theoretical and functional groundwork for further research. The quasi-experimental design was operated in the intervention phase, where participants were divided into intervention and control groups. Over the course of six weeks, the gamified teaching module was placed, and data was collected at various times to track behaviour change, performance, and commitment. Guarantee continuity and temporary sensitivity to the data, the structured questionnaire and observation logs were used. The analysis steps synthesise the data together using qualitative theme analysis and using strict statistical methods such as ANOVA and structural equation modelling. By facilitating the triangle of the data, this integrated technique makes it possible to identify relevant insights and causal patterns. Under the timeline, the repetition response facilitates recent problems. By ensuring consistency, depth and adaptability, the phased structure eventually increases to a strong amount of data that supports the reassessment of educational practices in continuing education.

b. Participants and Sampling

The study was employed in a stable targeted test survey of five hundred students registered in the Metropolitan PGDM programs in various institutional contexts. Maintain relevance and demographic diversity. Stratification was based on educational performance, institutional type, and geographical location. People with different experiences in digital and Gamified learning settings were made possible by the method of this sample. Twenty professionals in academia and business were also chosen specifically for the qualitative phase because of their efficiency in experienced learning, course design, and directive innovation. In the context of Urban Management Education, the study aims to capture both empirical trends and explanatory insight, assisted by a double-level test method, making the representation easier.

Description of Target Population

The aim of the study was a demographic study of adult students from students for students in urban and rural areas in India, at the ages of 18 to 65 years. The group offers a representative cross-section of modern urban students, as it represents a wide range of socio-economic origins, educational paths, and career goals. In PGDM programs, participants who have previously been aware of the environment with digital learning are given preference in the inclusion criteria, which guarantees a basic understanding of technology water education. The conclusions are more culturally relevant because the Court has a balanced representation in gender identity, language groups, and geographical connections. Evaluate the uneven effects of gamification, the levels of educational preparedness to participants, digital literacy and experience with experienced academics differ. This study is trying to produce insights into local educational dynamics and generalisation by capturing this variability. In addition, population design considers the institutional variation in private management schools, university-decorated programs, and independent institutions, which makes the extent of the analysis broader. The chosen cohort provides a sturdy base to check the educational efficiency of Gamification in the complex, the real educational ecosystem, despite the obstacles in the non-detection test.

Sampling Method and Criteria

This study adopted a stratified random sampling technique to ensure demographic diversity and contextual relevance within the target population of adult learners aged eighteen to -65 years. The participants were selected from urban and peri-urban regions across India, representing a wide array of socioeconomic strata, educational qualifications, and professional affiliations. Stratification is based on institutional type (autonomous, affiliated, private), geographic location, and academic standing to capture the heterogeneity in learning environments and digital exposure. Inclusion criteria required a minimum of five years of engagement with digital technologies, ensuring baseline familiarity with online platforms and gamified interfaces. The sample was balanced across gender identities and includes individuals from varied linguistic, cultural, and regional backgrounds. Further stratification considers participants' digital literacy levels and prior experience with technology-mediated instruction. This comprehensive sampling framework was designed to capture a broad spectrum of learner experiences, pedagogical interactions, and institutional contexts. This study enhances its analytical depth and relevance by incorporating individuals with differing degrees of technological proficiency and academic preparedness. While acknowledging limitations in external generalizability, the sampling method supports robust internal validity and facilitates nuanced exploration of gamification's pedagogical impact in postgraduate management education.

Demographic Information

The demographic profile of the study participants reflects a diverse and representative cross-section of urban postgraduate management learners in India. The sample comprised 500 PGDM students aged 21-35 years, with a mean age of 26.4 years. The gender distribution was balanced, including male, female, and non-binary individuals, ensuring inclusivity and relevance to contemporary educational discourse. Participants hailed from metropolitan and tier-two urban centres, representing varied linguistic, cultural, and regional backgrounds. Socioeconomic diversity was evident, with students from lower-middle, middle, and upper-middle income groups, enabling comparative analysis across financial strata. Educational backgrounds spanned commerce, engineering, humanities, and science disciplines, contributing to a multidimensional understanding of learner engagement. Digital literacy levels ranged from moderate to advanced, with all participants having prior exposure to technology-mediated instruction. Additionally, stratification based on academic performance and institutional type (autonomous, affiliated, private) allowed for a nuanced exploration of gamification's impact across learning environments. This demographic composition enhances the study's analytical depth, supports internal validity, and aligns with its objective to examine gamified pedagogy within complex, real-world educational ecosystems.

c. Data Collection Methods

This study employed a multi-phase data collection strategy aligned with its mixed-methods quasi-experimental design. Quantitative data were gathered using a structured online survey administered to a stratified sample of 500 PGDM students across urban management institutions. The survey instrument comprised validated scales measuring student engagement, academic motivation, and perceived learning outcomes, alongside context-specific items related to gamification constructs. Data were collected at two intervals, pre- and post-intervention, allowing for a comparative analysis of changes resulting from the gamified instructional modules. Ensure consistency and minimise response bias, standardised instructions and digital consent protocols were embedded within the survey platform.

Qualitative data collection was conducted concurrently through semi-structured interviews and focus group discussions with twenty academic and industrial experts. These sessions explored experiential insights into gamification design, implementation challenges, and pedagogical efficacy. Interviews were audio-recorded, transcribed verbatim, and anonymised to uphold ethical standards. Field notes and reflective memos were maintained to capture non-verbal cues and contextual nuances. The dual-mode data collection approach enabled methodological triangulation, enhancing the depth, validity, and interpretive richness of the findings. This comprehensive strategy ensured that both empirical trends and experiential narratives were systematically captured to inform the analytical framework of the study.

Quantitative Data Collection Tools and Procedures

The quantitative string of this research used a strictly designed study equipment to measure the perception of student engagement, academic motivation, and gamified instructions. This combined valid scales - such as students' engagement involvement (SEI) and academic motivational scale (AMS) - challenge the goals targeted to elements targeted to gaming structures such as accountability, response, and digital flow. Effectively managed a stratified selection of 500 PGDM students in urban institutions, capturing the survey data from before and after the intervention of six weeks. Built-in consent was secured through protocols and standardised instructions. The reliability was confirmed through the pilot sample (Cronbach's alpha > 0.80), and the construct generation was established through search factor analysis. The automated check -protected data integrity. This strong process adjusted longitudinal analysis and statistical modelling with semi-practical design and academic goals for the study.

d. Data Analysis Techniques

This study used descriptive figures to shorten the main matrix as mean, median, mode and standard deviation. Statistical technology, including hypothesis tests and confidence intervals, supports extensive generalisation. Data visualisation tools were used to expose tools, plots and graph trends, relationships, and patterns, which increase interpretation and analytical clarity in the dataset.

Data Analysis Techniques

1. Descriptive Statistics

Understand the basic pattern of student engagement, descriptive figures were obtained using a selection of twenty students with PGDM. Measures such as average, mode and standard deviation were calculated to summarise the central trend and variability. This matrix provides basic insight into the learned behaviour before subordinate analysis.

Table 2. Engagement scores

Statistic	Value
Mean	84.5
Median	84.5
Mode	94
Standard Deviation	5.92

This table indicates high and consistent levels of score grouping in the mid-eighties.

The histogram represents the frequency distribution of visual commitment points, highlights concentrations around the 80-90 area and has a slightly positive slant due to high outliers.

Figure 2. Distribution of student engagement scores

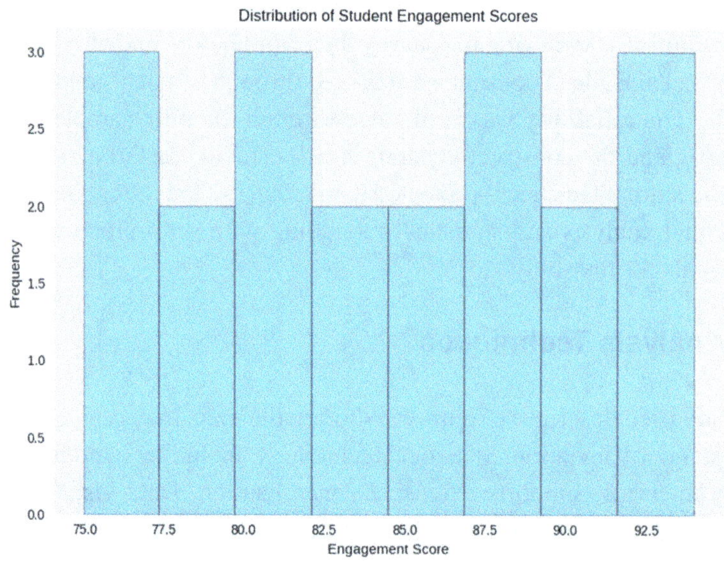

2. *Inferential Statistics*

Subordinated statistical techniques were used to investigate the effect of Gamified Instructional Strategy on students' involvement and academic results. The linked sample T-scripts were held to compare the score before and after intervention in the experimental group, and assessed the statistical importance of the changes seen. In addition, one-way ANOVA was used to evaluate the difference in institutional types and educational performance states. The confidence interval and the P values were calculated to determine the reliability and generality of the findings. These methods enabled the identification of the meaningful pattern beyond the hypothesis test and descriptive subpoena, and supported the cause of the semi-user structure.

3. Correlation Analysis

Pearson's correlation coefficient was used to detect the relationship between the most important variables, including student engagement, digital flow, response responsibility, and academic motivation. The analysis revealed moderate to strong positive correlations between gamification structures and student results, suggesting that extended interaction and challenge orientation are associated with elevated levels of engagement. Scattered plots and correlations were generated to imagine these associations and to increase the stress of explanation. This analytical layer provided empirical anchoring for the conceptual structure and later informed structural modelling.

4. Regression Analysis

Many regression analyses were used to investigate the forecast conditions between gamification structures and student learning outcomes. Independent variable challenge orientation, response responsibility and digital currents were, while dependent variables were academic motivation and engagement points. Ensure statistical validity, the model was evaluated for multiculturalism, symmetry, and generality of residue. Adjusted R^2 values indicated the ratio of the variance explained by the predictions, where standardised beta coefficients reveal the relative power of the effect of each variable. The analysis demonstrated that response is an important predictor for accountability and digital flow involvement, suggesting that an interactive and adaptive learning environment improves students' participation and motivation.

5. Structural Equation Modelling (SEM)

Validate the conceptual framework and assess latent constructs. Structural Equation Modelling was conducted using AMOS software. The SEM approach enabled the simultaneous analysis of multiple interrelated variables, integrating both measurement and structural components. Confirmatory Factor Analysis (CFA) was first performed to establish the construct validity and reliability. Fit indices such as CFI, RMSEA, and χ^2/df were evaluated to determine model adequacy. The final model confirmed the significant pathways between gamification elements and academic outcomes, supporting the hypothesised relationships. SEM provided a robust analytical lens for testing theoretical assumptions and uncovering the complex mediating effects within the pedagogical ecosystem.

RESULTS

Quantitative Findings

Descriptive statistics revealed a high baseline level of student engagement (M = 84.5, SD = 5.92), with post-intervention scores showing a significant increase (M = 89.3, SD = 4.87; $p < 0.01$). Paired sample t-tests confirmed the efficacy of the gamified modules in enhancing academic motivation and digital fluency. One-way ANOVA indicated significant differences in engagement across institutional types (F (2,497) = 4.62, $p < 0.05$), with autonomous institutions showing the highest gains. Regression analysis identified feedback responsiveness ($\beta = 0.42$, $p < 0.001$) and digital fluency ($\beta = 0.36$, $p < 0.01$) as strong predictors of engagement. Structural Equation Modelling validated the conceptual framework, with fit indices (CFI = 0.94, RMSEA = 0.05) supporting model adequacy.

Qualitative Insights

A thematic analysis of expert interviews and focus group discussions yielded five salient themes that illuminate the pedagogical dynamics of gamification in PGDM education. First, gamification has emerged as a catalyst for fostering learner autonomy, promoting self-directed engagement and intrinsic motivation. Second, institutional readiness varied, with some environments embracing innovation and others exhibiting structural resistance. Thirdly, educational adaptation to industry expectations underlined the relevance of experiential learning to prepare students for challenges in the real world. Fourth, digital fatigue and cognitive addiction appeared as unexpected results, especially for high-intensity modules. In the fifth vulnerable access and participation, equity, technical infrastructure, and inequalities in the preparation of the student. Participants emphasised the value of adaptive response and challenge-based tasks to maintain a constant meaningful commitment and strengthen the ability of gamification as a transformative instructional strategy in various academic ecosystems.

Integration of Findings

Quantitative analysis detected significant reforms in student engagement and education motivation, such as after a gamified intervention. Descriptive figures indicated that the average engagement points increased from 84.5 to 89.3, suggesting more stability in low standard deviations. The linked sample t-tests the statistically significant benefit (p <0.01), while ANOVA emphasised the institutional difference in responsibility for Gamified educational. Visual representation - including histograms and regression plots - met the distribution of main variables such as feedback response and digital fluency.

Qualitative conclusions, experts obtained from interviews and thematic analysis of focus groups, emphasised the five-emergent theme: the student's autonomy, institutional adaptability, cognitive additions, equity in access and educational device. Illustrative quotes emphasised the transformative ability of gamification, and held a participant in mind, "Gamified modules felt the students as fellow producers, not just the recipients." The pattern showed that adaptive response and challenge-based tasks promoted deep involvement in contexts. Integration of quantitative and qualitative consequences demonstrated strong convergence around the effectiveness of gaming, while diversion emphasised relevant obstacles such as digital fatigue and infrastructural boundaries. The approach to mixed levels enriched the explanatory structure and provided supplementary insights that address research questions. This triangulated evidence base supports the development of scalable, equity-centred gamification models in postgraduate management education.

Table 3. Distribution of qualitative codes across emergent themes

Theme	Code Frequency	Representative Quote
Learner Autonomy	42	"Gamified tasks helped me take control of my own learning pace."
Institutional Readiness	35	"Faculty training and tech support were crucial for successful implementation."
Pedagogical Alignment	39	"Gamification worked best when aligned with course objectives and assessments."
Digital Fatigue	28	"Too many digital tasks made me feel overwhelmed and disengaged."
Equity in Access	31	"Not all students had equal access to devices or stable internet during gamified modules."

Table 3 presents the frequency and distribution of coded responses across the five emergent themes, highlighting both the prevalence and illustrative quotes.

Figure 3. Simplified gamification implementation framework

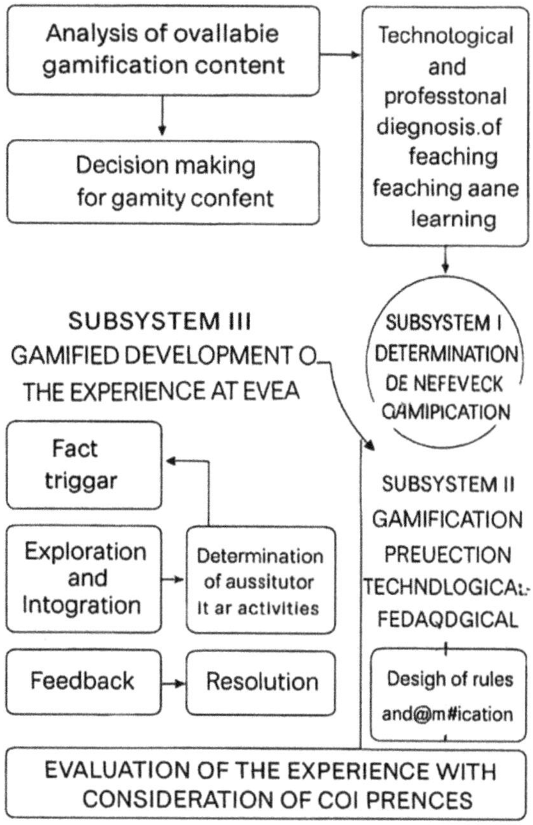

This flowchart outlines the structured process for implementing gamification in PGDM education, including decision-making, pedagogical projection, experiential development, and evaluation. It was developed by the author based on the synthesis of gamification design literature and pedagogical diagnostics.

This paper outlines a structured approach to gamification in higher education, including pedagogical diagnostics, content analysis, and experiential design, which are remarkably like the subsystems illustrated.

DISCUSSION

a. Interpretation of Findings

The study's findings offer compelling evidence that gamification significantly enhances student engagement, academic motivation, and digital fluency in urban PGDM programs. The observed increase in post-intervention engagement scores aligned directly with the research questions, confirming that structured gamified modules foster deeper learner involvement. These results resonate with the existing literature, particularly the studies by Deterding et al. (2011) and Hamari et al. (2014), which underscore the motivational affordances of game-based learning environments. However, this study extends prior work by situating gamification within postgraduate management education in the Indian context, revealing nuanced institutional and learner-level dynamics. Theoretical implications are substantial: The findings validate self-determination theory (Deci & Ryan, 1985) by demonstrating how autonomy-supportive gamified tasks enhance intrinsic motivation. Moreover, the integration of challenge orientation and adaptive feedback supports constructivist learning principles, suggesting that gamification can serve as a scaffold for experiential and reflective learning. Divergences in institutional readiness and digital fatigue highlight the need for context-sensitive implementation strategies. Overall, this study contributes to pedagogical theory by offering an empirically grounded framework for gamification that balances cognitive engagement, technological adaptability, and equity in access, advancing the discourse on learner-centred innovation in higher education.

b. Implications for Practice

The findings from the study emphasised the game-based learning in the form of a viable educational strategy to strengthen the students' involvement and inspiration in PGDM programs. Practical applications include challenge-based modules, adaptive response systems, and integration of digital brands to promote autonomy and performance. Solving urban educational challenges, like infrastructure Inequalities and digital fatigue, institutions should use scalable, reference-sensitive Gamification models supported by faculty training and inclusive design. This innovation can find the interval for engagement, especially in weird classes. In addition, the strategic use of gamification management education adapts to the expectations of the industry, agrees, and technology, cutting new graduates. At a broader level, such pedagogical reforms contribute to urban development by promoting equitable access to quality education and fostering innovation-driven human capital in metropolitan economies.

LIMITATIONS AND FUTURE RESEARCH DIRECTIONS

While the study offers valuable insights into the pedagogical impact of gamification, certain limitations warrant acknowledgement. Although methodologically sound, the quasi-experimental design restricts causal generalisation beyond the sampled PGDM institutions. Additionally, reliance on self-reported data may introduce response bias, and digital infrastructure disparities could affect intervention fidelity. Future research should explore longitudinal designs to assess sustained learning outcomes and behavioural shifts. Expanding the study across diverse geographic regions and academic disciplines would enhance its external validity. Moreover, integrating adaptive AI-driven gamification tools and examining their efficacy across learner profiles is a promising avenue. Replication studies with randomised control trials could further validate the framework and inform scalable, equity-centred innovations in postgraduate management education.

CONCLUSION

This study advances theoretical understanding by empirically validating gamification as a pedagogical enhancer within urban postgraduate management education. This contributes to the literature by situating gamification in the framework of self-determination theory and constructivist learning, demonstrating how adaptive feedback and challenge-based modules foster autonomy, competence, and relatedness. Practically, the findings offer actionable insights for educators and curriculum designers seeking to integrate game-based strategies into PGDM programs. Policymakers are urged to support infrastructure development and faculty training to ensure equitable access and sustainable implementation. This study's significance lies in its capacity to bridge pedagogical innovation with urban educational reform, addressing learner diversity, digital engagement, and industry alignment. As urban institutions grapple with evolving learner expectations and technological disruptions, gamification has emerged as a strategic tool for fostering inclusive, future-ready education. Stakeholders—including academic leaders, accreditation bodies, and edtech developers collaboratively design scalable gamification frameworks that prioritise learner agency, contextual relevance, and ethical integration. Future initiatives should focus on longitudinal impact assessment, cross-disciplinary adaptation, and AI-enhanced personalisation to deepen gamification's transformative potential in higher education ecosystems.

RECOMMENDATIONS

Based on the findings of this study, several action-rich recommendations have been proposed to increase the integration of gamification into PGDM programs and solve urban educational challenges. First, institutions should invest in faculty development programs that endow teachers with educational and technical competencies, which are necessary to design and implement the Gamified learning environment. Second, course planners must be built into the main modules to promote learned autonomy and continuous commitment, adaptive reaction mechanisms, and digital brands in the main modules. Third, decision makers should prefer similar access to digital infrastructure and ensure that gamification does not increase existing inequalities in urban education. Fourth, institutional management should use the reference-sensitive framework with industry expectations and student diversity. For the fifth, academics, collaborative partnerships between Edtech companies and industry interests should be encouraged to scale scalable, morally founded Gamification models. Finally, future initiatives should include longitudinal monitoring and AI-enhanced individualisation to limit gaming-fitted pedagogies and assess their continuous impact on student results. These recommendations aim to promote inclusive, innovative management education that responds to the developed requirements of urban learners and makes meaningful contributions to the development of human capital in metropolitan settings.

FUTURE DIRECTIONS

Based on the empirical and theoretical contributions of this study, future research should pursue a longitudinal study to assess the continuous effect of Gamification on teaching results in different academic cycles. Expanding the scope of involvement of interdisciplinary colleagues, such as engineering science, law and social sciences, will increase generality and expose domain-specific educational shades. Comparative studies in rural and semi-urban institutions, infrastructure and cultural variables can affect gamification efficacy. In addition, the integration of AI-driven personalisation and adaptive teaching analysis presents a promising limit in the gamified module, which enables real-time reaction and differential instructions. Future inquiries should also check the intersection of Gamification with equity frameworks, find out how the inclusive design can reduce digital division and promote participation. A mixed-method design that involves dramatological elements can gain deep insight into learned identification, motivation, and resistance in the confined environment. In addition, policy-oriented research can evaluate institutional preparedness, financing models and management structures required for scalable implementation. The replication study using randomised control tests will further validate the frame and refine the cause. Overall, the purpose of these directions is to pursue a transformative, reference-sensitive paradigm for Gamified Education, which corresponds to students' needs, technological innovations, and permanent urban development.

REFERENCES

Aldhilan, D., Afzal, A., & Rafiq, S. (2024). The innovative pedagogical approaches & challenges in the early childhood education: insights from Saudi Arabia. *Gomal University Journal of Research, 42*(2), 159–176. DOI: 10.51380/gujr-40-02-03

Alenezi, A. (2023). Teacher perspectives on AI-driven gamification: impact on student motivation, engagement, and learning outcomes. *Information Technologies and Learning Tools, 97*(5), 138–148. DOI: 10.33407/itlt.v97i5.5437

Amish, M. (2024). Enhancing Workplace Skills through Work-Based Learning in Engineering Education. *International Journal of Innovative Science and Research Technology (IJISRT)*, 1983–1990. DOI: 10.38124/ijisrt/IJISRT24JUL1276

Anderle, F., Cattoni, A., Venuti, P., & Pasqualotto, A. (2025). Exploring the impact and acceptability of gamified tools to address educational needs in decoding and writing skills: A pilot study. *Research in Developmental Disabilities, 160*, 104967. DOI: 10.1016/j.ridd.2025.104967 PMID: 40086126

Bohari, A., Jiang, L., Udang, L. N., Wider, W., Lajuma, S., & Tanucan, J. C. M. (2024). Transformational leadership's role in shaping Education 4.0 within higher education. *Journal of Infrastructure, Policy, and Development, 8*(8), 4900. DOI: 10.24294/jipd.v8i8.4900

Brennan, A., McAvoy, J., Dempsey, M., O'Leary, S., O'Dea, M., & Prendergast, M. (2023). How COVID-19 impacted soft skills development: The views of software engineering students. *Cogent Education, 10*(1), 2171621. Advance online publication. DOI: 10.1080/2331186X.2023.2171621

Chikwe, C., Ediae, A., Ajuwon, O., & Dagunduro, A. (2024). Sociological barriers to equitable digital learning: A data-driven approach. *Comprehensive Research and Reviews in Multidisciplinary Studies, 2*(1), 027–034. DOI: 10.57219/crrms.2024.2.1.0038

Crogman, H. T., Cano, V. D., Pacheco, E., Boroon, R., & Sonawane, R. B. (2025). Virtual Reality, Augmented Reality, and Mixed Reality in Experiential Learning: Transforming Educational Paradigms. *Education Sciences, 15*(3), 303. DOI: 10.3390/educsci15030303

Eden, C., Adeniyi, I., & Chisom, O.Chima Abimbola EdenOnyebuchi Nneamaka ChisomIdowu Sulaimon Adeniyi. (2024). Parent and community involvement in education: strengthening partnerships for social improvement. *International Journal of Applied Research in Social Sciences, 6*(3), 372–382. DOI: 10.51594/ijarss.v6i3.894

Foreman-Brown, G., Fitzpatrick, E., & Twyford, K. (2022). Reimagining teacher identity in the post-COVID-19 university: Becoming digitally savvy, reflective in practice, collaborative, and relational. *Educational and Developmental Psychologist, 40*(1), 18–26. DOI: 10.1080/20590776.2022.2079406

Hsu, C.-Y., & Wu, T.-T. (2023). *Applications of Business Simulation Games in Flipped Classrooms to Facilitate Student Engagement and Higher-Order Thinking Skills for Sustainable Learning Practices*. MDPI AG. DOI: 10.20944/preprints202311.0082.v1

Jun, M., & Lucas, T. (2024). Gamification elements and their impacts on education: A review. *Multidisciplinary Reviews, 8*(5), 2025155. DOI: 10.31893/multirev.2025155

Konak, A., Kulturel-Konak, S., Schneider, D. R., & Mehta, K. (2024). Enhancing student learning in innovation competitions and programs. *European Journal of Engineering Education, 50*(2), 360–380. DOI: 10.1080/03043797.2024.2394945

Lee, J. Y., Woo, J., & Pyon, C. U. (2023). Digital Twin for Math Education: A Study on the Utilisation of Games and Gamification for University Mathematics Education. *Electronics (Basel), 12*(15), 3207. DOI: 10.3390/electronics12153207

Li, M., Ma, S., & Shi, Y. (2023). Examining the effectiveness of gamification as a tool promoting teaching and learning in educational settings: A meta-analysis. *Frontiers in Psychology, 14*, 1253549. Advance online publication. DOI: 10.3389/fpsyg.2023.1253549 PMID: 37876838

Li, X., Chu, S. K. W., Xia, Q., & Yang, Y. (2022). Using Gamification to Facilitate Students' Self-Regulation in E-Learning: A Case Study on Students' L2 English Learning. *Sustainability (Basel), 14*(12), 7008. DOI: 10.3390/su14127008

Mallén-Lacambra, C., & Mamas, C. (2025). Ethics of Care: A Theoretical Underpinning for Relational Inclusivity. *Teoría de la Educación. Teoría de la Educación, 37*(2), 99–124. DOI: 10.14201/teri.32183

Maryana, M., Rahmi, H., & Halim, C. (2024). The Impact of Gamification on Student Engagement and Learning Outcomes in Mathematics Education. *International Journal of Business, Law, and Education, 5*(2), 1697–1608. DOI: 10.56442/ijble.v5i2.682

Mouboua, P., Atobatele, F., & Akintayo, O.Patricia Diane MouboauFadeke Adeola AtobateleOlateju Temitope Akintayo. (2024). Cross-cultural competence in global HRD: Strategies for developing an inclusive and diverse workforce. *International Journal of Science and Research Archive, 12*(1), 103–113. DOI: 10.30574/ijsra.2024.12.1.0765

Nguyen-Viet, B., Nguyen-Duy, C., & Nguyen-Viet, B. (2024). How does gamification affect learning effectiveness? The mediating roles of engagement, satisfaction, and intrinsic motivation. *Interactive Learning Environments, 33*(3), 2635–2653. DOI: 10.1080/10494820.2024.2414356

Qudsi, H. (2024). Gamification in education: boosting student engagement and learning outcomes. *ShodhKosh: Journal of Visual and Performing Arts, 5*(4). Advance online publication. DOI: 10.29121/shodhkosh.v5.i4.2024.2542

Reis Da Silva, T. M. H. (2024). *Gamification as a Pedagogical Tool in Geriatric Nursing*. Igi Global. DOI: 10.4018/979-8-3693-8322-3.ch005

Shaikh, M. S., & Ali, S. I. (2025). *Revolutionising the Impact of Education Using Advanced Online Tools*. Igi Global. DOI: 10.4018/979-8-3693-8593-7.ch028

Sharma, P. (2023). Pedagogical Practices in the Technology-Intervened Indian Education System. *Indian Journal of Social Science and Literature, 3*(2), 1–9. DOI: 10.54105/ijssl.K1632.123223

Slamet, J. (2024). Empowering Slow Learners: Gamification's Impact on Students' Engagement and Academic Performance in an LMS for Undergraduate Students. *International Journal of Information and Education Technology (IJIET), 14*(2), 193–203. DOI: 10.18178/ijiet.2024.14.2.2040

Weidl, M., & Erling, E. J. (2025). Exploring Multilingualism to Inform Linguistically and Culturally Responsive English Language Education. *Education Sciences, 15*(6), 763. DOI: 10.3390/educsci15060763

Wulan, D. R., Rohman, T., Nainggolan, D. M., Fiyul, A. Y., & Hidayat, Y. (2024). Exploring the Benefits and Challenges of Gamification in Enhancing Student Learning Outcomes. *Global International Journal of Innovative Research, 2*(7), 1657–1674. DOI: 10.59613/global.v2i7.238

Compilation of References

Aires, N. (2000). Comparisons between conditional Poisson sampling and Pareto sampling designs. *Journal of Statistical Planning and Inference*, Volume 88, Issue 1. Pages 133-147. ISSN 0378-3758. DOI: 10.1016/S0378-3758(99)00205-0

Alalawi, K., Athauda, R., & Chiong, R. (2025). An Extended Learning Analytics Framework Integrating Machine Learning and Pedagogical Approaches for Student Performance Prediction and Intervention. *International Journal of Artificial Intelligence in Education*, *35*(3), 1239–1287. DOI: 10.1007/s40593-024-00429-7

Al-Azawei, A., Serenelli, F., & Lundqvist, K. (2016). Universal Design for Learning (UDL): A content analysis of peer reviewed journals from 2012 to 2015. *The Journal of Scholarship of Teaching and Learning*, *16*(3), 39–56. DOI: 10.14434/josotl.v16i3.19295

Al-Bahrani, A., Patel, D., & Sheridan, B. (2015). Engaging students using social media: The students' perspective. *International Review of Economics Education*, *19*, 36–50. DOI: 10.1016/j.iree.2015.06.001

Aldhilan, D., Afzal, A., & Rafiq, S. (2024). The innovative pedagogical approaches & challenges in the early childhood education: insights from Saudi Arabia. *Gomal University Journal of Research*, *42*(2), 159–176. DOI: 10.51380/gujr-40-02-03

Aleca, O. E., & Mihai, F. (2025). The Role of Digital Infrastructure and Skills in Enhancing Labor Productivity: Insights from Industry 4.0 in the European Union. *Systems*, *13*(2), 113. Advance online publication. DOI: 10.3390/systems13020113

Alenezi, A. (2023). Teacher perspectives on AI-driven gamification: impact on student motivation, engagement, and learning outcomes. *Information Technologies and Learning Tools*, *97*(5), 138–148. DOI: 10.33407/itlt.v97i5.5437

ALI Research Staff. (2023). The Challenges of STEM Education: Barriers to Participation. *Accelerate Learning*. https://blog.acceleratelearning.com/the-challenges-of-stem-education-barriers-to-participation

Allen, L. K., & Kendeou, P. (2024). ED-AI Lit: An interdisciplinary framework for AI literacy in education. *Policy Insights from the Behavioral and Brain Sciences, 11*(1), 3–10. DOI: 10.1177/23727322231220339

Allison, J., Hwang, G. J., Mayer, R. E., Pellas, N., Karnalim, O., de Freitas, S., Ng, O.-L., Huang, Y.-M., Hooshyar, D., Seidman, R. H., Al-Emran, M., Mikropoulos, T. A., Schroeder, N. L., Roscoe, R. D., & Sanusi, I. (2025). From generative AI to extended reality: Multidisciplinary perspectives on the challenges, opportunities, and future of educational computing. *Journal of Educational Computing Research, 63*(6), 1327–1363. DOI: 10.1177/07356331251359964

Al-Shaikhli, D. (2023). The effect of the tracking technology on students' perceptions of their continuing intention to use a learning management system. *Education and Information Technologies, 28*(1), 343–371. ProQuest Central; Social Science Premium Collection. DOI: 10.1007/s10639-022-11156-8

Alshammari, M. T. (2020). Evaluation of gamification in e-learning systems for elementary school students. *TEM Journal, 9*(2), 806. https://doi.org/ [DOI]DOI: 10.18421/TEM92-51

Al-Shanfari, L., Abdullah, S., Fstnassi, T., & Al-Kharusi, S. (2023). Instructors' Perceptions of Intelligent Tutoring Systems and Their Implications for Studying Computer Programming in Omani Higher Education Institutions. *International Journal of Membrane Science and Technology, 10*(2), 947–967. *Scopus.* Advance online publication. DOI: 10.15379/ijmst.v10i2.1395

Alves, D., & Escorel, V. (2024). From Erasmus to European education area and a case study *16th International Conference on Education and New Learning Technologies*, Spain, Palma. DOI: 10.21125/edulearn.2024.1800

Amanbay, M. (2023, April 4). *The ethics of AI-generated art. SSRN.* https://ssrn.com/abstract=4551467

Amish, M. (2024). Enhancing Workplace Skills through Work-Based Learning in Engineering Education. *International Journal of Innovative Science and Research Technology (IJISRT)*, 1983–1990. DOI: 10.38124/ijisrt/IJISRT24JUL1276

Anderle, F., Cattoni, A., Venuti, P., & Pasqualotto, A. (2025). Exploring the impact and acceptability of gamified tools to address educational needs in decoding and writing skills: A pilot study. *Research in Developmental Disabilities, 160*, 104967. DOI: 10.1016/j.ridd.2025.104967 PMID: 40086126

Andhika, A., Aldila, A. S., Supriyono, L. A., Previana, C. N., & Habibie, D. R. (2024). The Effectiveness of Adaptive Learning Systems Integrated with LMS in Higher Education. *Jurnal KomtekInfo*, 49–56. DOI: 10.35134/komtekinfo.v11i2.505

Andrade, H. L., & Valtcheva, A. (2009). Promoting learning and achievement through self-assessment. *Theory into Practice, 48*(1), 12–19. DOI: 10.1080/00405840802577544

Annamalah, S., Aravindan, K. L., & Ahmed, S. (2025). Driving open innovation in SMEs: The role of organizational and strategic dynamics. *Journal of Innovation and Entrepreneurship, 14*(1), 119. Advance online publication. DOI: 10.1186/s13731-025-00588-4

Anubhav, K., Dwivedi, A. K., & Aashish, K. (2024). Entrepreneurship education in higher education (2002–2022): A technology-empowered systematic literature review. *International Journal of Management Education, 22*(3), 100993. DOI: 10.1016/j.ijme.2024.100993

Apoki, U. C., Ali Hussein, A. M., Humam K Majeed Al-Chalabi, Costin Badica, & Mocanu, M. L. (2022). The Role of Pedagogical Agents in Personalised Adaptive Learning: A Review. *Sustainability, 14*(11), 6442. ProQuest Central. DOI: 10.3390/su14116442

Arancibia, M. L., Cabero, J., & Marín, V. (2020). Creencias sobre la enseñanza y uso de las tecnologías de la información y la comunicación (TIC) en docentes de educación superior. *Formación Universitaria, 13*(3), 89–100. Advance online publication. DOI: 10.4067/S0718-50062020000300089

Arsovic, B., & Stefanovic, N. (2020). E-learning based on the adaptive learning model: Case study in Serbia. *Sadhana, 45*(1), 266. DOI: 10.1007/s12046-020-01499-8

Ary, D., Jacobs, L. C., Irvine, C. K., & Walker, D. A. (2018). *Introduction to research in education* (10th ed.). Cengage Learning.

Asencio-Juncal, J. (2023). Redefining the relationship between nature and the city: the rivers Guadalmedina in Málaga and Genil in Granada. *L'industria delle costruzioni. Gestione delle risorse idriche e rigenerazione urbana*, (493), 43-49.

Baba, K., El Faddouli, N.-E., & Cheimanoff, N. (2024). Mobile-Optimized AI-Driven Personalized Learning: A Case Study at Mohammed VI Polytechnic University. *International Journal of Interactive Mobile Technologies, 18*(4), 81–96. *Scopus.* Advance online publication. DOI: 10.3991/ijim.v18i04.46547

Bal, A. P., & Bedir, S. G. (2021). EXAMINING TEACHERS' VIEWS ON STEM EDUCATION. *European Journal of Education Studies, 8*(3).

Bandura, A. (1997). Self-efficacy: The exercise of control. *The Freeman.*

Barragán-Moreno, S. P., & Guzmán-Rincón, A. (2025). Digital divide as an explanatory variable for dropout in higher education. *International Journal of Educational Technology in Higher Education*, *22*(1), 60. Advance online publication. DOI: 10.1186/s41239-025-00550-0

Barrera, D. F., & Devechi, C. P. V. (2024). Platformization of Brazilian Public Higher Education: Implications for the educational project. *Edutec*, *87*, 101–114.

Barrett, H. (2007). Researching electronic portfolios and learner engagement: The REFLECT Initiative. *Journal of Adolescent & Adult Literacy*, *50*(6), 436–449. DOI: 10.1598/JAAL.50.6.2

Barrot, J. S. (2021). Scientific Mapping of Social Media in Education: A Decade of Exponential Growth. *Journal of Educational Computing Research*, *59*(4), 645–668. DOI: 10.1177/0735633120972010

Bartram, B. (2019). Using questionnaires. In Lambert, M. (Ed.), *Practical research methods in education: An early researcher's critical guide* (pp. 11–30). Routledge., DOI: 10.4324/9781351188395-1

Basilio, S. G. (2025). Knowledge Production and Intellectual Property: A Perspective on Scientific Publications in the Capitalist System. *TripleC*, *23*(1), 94–109. DOI: 10.31269/triplec.v23i1.1520

Becker, K., & Park, K. (2011). Effects of integrative approaches among STEM subjects on students' learning: A meta-analysis. *Journal of STEM Education: Innovations and Research*, *12*(5/6), 23–37.

Bedoya-Cano, O., Marín-Marín, J.-A., & López-Belmonte, J. (2025). Integrating Arduino and Artificial Intelligence in STEM Education. In (pp. 149-165). https://doi.org/DOI: 10.1007/978-3-031-82915-4_7

Berrill, D., & Addison, E. (2010). 'Professional learning portfolios' for teachers: A site for understanding, improving practice and leadership. *Professional Development in Education*, *36*(4), 639–665.

Bhambri, P., & Kant, S. (2025a, February 1-2). A taxonomy of bias in machine learning: Classification, sources, and implications for ethical AI [Paper presentation]. Lincoln-SPAST Global Sustainability Programme (SGS-24), 1st International Conference of L-GPR Program, Lincoln University College, Malaysia. SPAST Proceedings, 1(2). https://spast.org/techrep/article/view/5387/724

Bhambri, P., & Kant, S. (2025b, April 26-27). Ethical AI systems: A comprehensive framework for bias mitigation and fairness in machine learning [Paper presentation]. Lincoln-SPAST Global Sustainability Programme (SGS-24), 2nd International Conference of L-GPR Program, Lincoln University College, Malaysia. SPAST Proceedings, 1(2). https://spast.org/techrep/article/view/5385/698

Bhambri, P., & Khang, A. (2024a). The human-machine nexus with art-making generative AIs. In Hai-Jew, S. (Ed.), *Making art with generative AI tools* (pp. 73–85). IGI Global., DOI: 10.4018/979-8-3693-1950-5.ch004

Bhambri, P., & Khang, A. (2024b). Machine learning advancements in E-health: Transforming digital healthcare. In *Medical robotics and AI-assisted diagnostics for a high-tech healthcare industry* (pp. 174–194). IGI Global., DOI: 10.4018/979-8-3693-2105-8.ch012

Bhambri, P., & Khang, A. (2025). Edge computing for enhancing efficiency and sustainability in green transportation systems. In Khang, A. (Ed.), *Driving green transportation system through artificial intelligence and automation* (pp. 43–65). Springer., DOI: 10.1007/978-3-031-72617-0_3

Bhambri, P., & Rani, S. (2025). Advancements in educational technology: Navigating the landscape of user experience in Web 3.0. In Pelet, J.-É. (Ed.), *Architecting the digital future: Platforms, design, and application* (pp. 365–396). IGI Global., DOI: 10.4018/979-8-3693-2973-3.ch014

Bicharra García, A. C. (2020). Ética e Inteligência Artificial. *Computação Brasil*, (43), 14–22. DOI: 10.5753/compbr.2020.43.1791

Bihu, R. (2020). Questionnaire survey methodology in educational and social science studies. *European American Journal, 8*(2), 45–60. https://eajournals.org/wp-content/uploads/Questionnaire-Survey-Methodology-in-Educational-and-Social-Science-Studies.pdf

Bohari, A., Jiang, L., Udang, L. N., Wider, W., Lajuma, S., & Tanucan, J. C. M. (2024). Transformational leadership's role in shaping Education 4.0 within higher education. *Journal of Infrastructure, Policy, and Development, 8*(8), 4900. DOI: 10.24294/jipd.v8i8.4900

Boltsi, A., Kalovrektis, K., Xenakis, A., Chatzimisios, P., & Chaikalis, C. (2024). Digital Tools, Technologies, and Learning Methodologies for Education 4.0 Frameworks: A STEM Oriented Survey. *IEEE Access : Practical Innovations, Open Solutions, 12*, 12883–12901. DOI: 10.1109/ACCESS.2024.3355282

Bostrom, N. (2014). *Superintelligence: Paths, Dangers, Strategies*. Oxford University Press.

Bottega, J. A., Kich, V. A., de Jesus, J. C., Steinmetz, R., Kolling, A. H., Bedin Grando, R. B., da Silva Guerra, R. S., & Tello Gamarra, D. F. T. (2023). Jubileo: An Immersive Simulation Framework for Social Robot Design. *Journal of Intelligent & Robotic Systems*, *109*(4), 91. Advance online publication. DOI: 10.1007/s10846-023-01991-3

Brennan, A., McAvoy, J., Dempsey, M., O'Leary, S., O'Dea, M., & Prendergast, M. (2023). How COVID-19 impacted soft skills development: The views of software engineering students. *Cogent Education*, *10*(1), 2171621. Advance online publication. DOI: 10.1080/2331186X.2023.2171621

Briceño Caballero, M. M. (2024). Percepciones de la integridad en la docencia universitaria: Perspectiva del alumnado. *Praxis Educativa (Santa Rosa)*, *19*, 1–20. Advance online publication. DOI: 10.5212/PraxEduc.v.19.22859.004

Briones Suárez, K. B., Montero Ramírez, I. S., Caranqui Pintag, M. A., & Ramirez Melendres, R. M.Karen Belén Briones SuárezIrwing Stalin Montero RamírezMartha Alicia Caranqui PintagRoxana Mabel Ramirez Melendres. (2024). Gamificación y DUA: Creando entornos de aprendizaje inclusivos. *Revista Imaginario Social*, *7*(4). Advance online publication. DOI: 10.59155/is.v7i4.252

Bryan, L. A., Moore, T. J., Johnson, C. C., & Roehrig, G. H. (2015). *STEM road map: A framework for integrated STEM education*. National Science Teachers Association Press.

Bryant, L. H., & Chittum, J. R. (2013). E-portfolio effectiveness: A broad synthesis of research findings. *International Journal of E-Portfolio*, *3*(2), 111–131.

Butson, R., & Spronken-Smith, R. (2024). AI and its implications for research in higher education: A critical dialogue. *Higher Education Research & Development*, *43*(3), 563–577. DOI: 10.1080/07294360.2023.2280200

Buzzetto, M. (2010). Assessing the efficacy and effectiveness of an e-portfolio used for summative assessment. *Interdisciplinary Journal of E-Learning and Learning Objects*, *6*, 61–85.

Cabero, J. (2016). ¿Qué debemos aprender de las pasadas investigaciones en Tecnología Educativa? *Revista Interuniversitaria de Investigación en Tecnología Educativa*, *0*, 23–33. DOI: 10.6018/riite/2016/256741

Camacho Marín, R. J., & Semanate Zapata, R. D. (2023). Percepciones de los docentes sobre la implementación de tecnología en el aula. *Revista Ciencia y Descubrimiento, 1*(3). Advance online publication. DOI: 10.70577/c0gcrz88RCD

Caprile, M., Palmen, R., Sanz, P., & Dente, G. (2015). *Encouraging STEM studies: Labour market situation and comparison of practices targeted at young people in different Member States.* European Parliament.

Carvalhais, L., & Azevedo, P. (2024). Digital Teacher Training in the Portuguese National Plan for Digital Development at Schools: A Case Study. *Technology. Knowledge and Learning, 29*(3), 1579–1595. DOI: 10.1007/s10758-024-09760-3

CAST. (2018). *Universal Design for Learning guidelines version 2.2.* CAST.

Chandia-Jaure, R., & Godoy-Donoso, D. (2019). Agua y ciudadanía: Estrategia didáctica para la formación en contextos de cambio climático. En D. García-Escudero & B. Bardí i Milà (Eds.), *JIDA'19. VII Jornadas sobre Innovación Docente en Arquitectura* (pp. 533–543). Iniciativa Digital Politècnica, UPC. https://doi.org/DOI: 10.5821/jida.2019.8373

Chappell, K., Hetherington, L., Juillard, S., Aguirre, C., & Duca, E. (2025). A framework for effective STEAM education: Pedagogy for responding to wicked problems. *International Journal of Educational Research Open, 9*, 100474. DOI: 10.1016/j.ijedro.2025.100474

Cheng, J., & Qian, J. (2025). Exploring the key factors influencing tourists' intention to use mobile AR educational applications from the perspective of structural equation modeling. *NPJ Heritage Science, 13*(1), 119. Advance online publication. DOI: 10.1038/s40494-025-01575-4

Chen, J. J. (2025). From Turing's conception of machine intelligence to the evolution of AI in early childhood education: Conceptual, empirical, and practical insights. AI. *Brain and Child, 1*(1), 1. DOI: 10.1007/s44436-025-00002-6

Chevalier, M., Giang, C., Piatti, A., & Mondada, F. (2020). Fostering computational thinking through educational robotics: A model for creative computational problem solving. *International Journal of STEM Education, 7*(1), 39. DOI: 10.1186/s40594-020-00238-z

Chikwe, C., Ediae, A., Ajuwon, O., & Dagunduro, A. (2024). Sociological barriers to equitable digital learning: A data-driven approach. *Comprehensive Research and Reviews in Multidisciplinary Studies, 2*(1), 027–034. DOI: 10.57219/crrms.2024.2.1.0038

Chiu, A., Price, C. A., & Ovrahim, E. (2025). Supporting youth STEM engagement through international collaboration. *International Journal of STEM Education, 9*(1), 1–15. DOI: 10.1186/s40594-025-00456-9

Chiu, T. K. (2024). Future research recommendations for transforming higher education with generative AI. *Computers and Education: Artificial Intelligence, 6*, 100197. DOI: 10.1016/j.caeai.2023.100197

Chiu, T. K. F., Li, Y., Ding, M., Hallström, J., & Koretsky, M. D. (2025). A decade of research contributions and emerging trends in the International Journal of STEM Education. *International Journal of STEM Education, 12*(1), 12. Advance online publication. DOI: 10.1186/s40594-025-00533-7

Cianciolo, A. T., & Regehr, G. (2023). The Case for Feedback-in-Practice as a Topic of Educational Scholarship. *Academic Medicine : Journal of the Association of American Medical Colleges, 98*(3), 317–321. DOI: 10.1097/ACM.0000000000005013 PMID: 36222528

Cohen, L., Manion, L., & Morrison, K. (2017). *Research Methods in Education* (8th ed.). Routledge., DOI: 10.4324/9781315456539

Commission, E. (2020). *Education and training monitor 2020 – Teaching and learning in a digital age.* https://education.ec.europa.eu/about-eea/education-and-training-monitor

Conde, M. Á., Rodríguez-Sedano, F. J., Rodríguez Lera, F. J., Gutiérrez-Fernández, A., & Guerrero-Higueras, Á. M. (2021). WhatsApp or Telegram. Which is the Best Instant Messaging Tool for the Interaction in Teamwork? In Zaphiris, P., & Ioannou, A. (Eds.), *Learning and Collaboration Technologies: New Challenges and Learning Experiences* (pp. 239–249). Springer., DOI: 10.1007/978-3-030-77889-7_16

Coppi, M., Fialho, I., & Gomes, S. (2025). Capacitação digital em Portugal. *Educação Sociedade & Culturas*, •••, 1–25. DOI: 10.24840/esc.vi70.982

Correia, J. D., & Henriques, S. (2025). *Assessing Digital and Info-Communication Competencies in Higher Education: A Blended Approach for e-Learning Environments* Perspectives and Trends in Education and Technology, Volume 2, Cham.

Correia, M., & Martins, C. (2024). *Primary pre-service teachers' understanding of STEAM education through lesson planning* The 15th Conference of the European Science Education Research Association (ESERA), Cappadocia, Türkiye. http://hdl.handle.net/10400.15/4955

Correia, M., Ribeirinha, T., Beirante, D., Santos, R., Ramos, L., Dias, I. S., Luís, H., Catela, D., Galinha, S., Arrais, A., Portelada, A., Pinto, P., Simões, V., Ferreira, R., Franco, S., & Martins, M. C. (2024). Outdoor STEAM Education: Opportunities and Challenges. *Education Sciences, 14*(7), 688. Advance online publication. DOI: 10.3390/educsci14070688

Costa, M., Domingos, A., Teodoro, V., & Vinhas, É. (2022). Teacher Professional Development in STEM Education: An Integrated Approach with Real-World Scenarios in Portugal. *Mathematics, 10*(21), 3944. https://www.mdpi.com/2227-7390/10/21/3944. DOI: 10.3390/math10213944

Creely, E., & Blannin, J. (2025). Creative partnerships with generative AI. Possibilities for education and beyond. *Thinking Skills and Creativity, 56*, 101727. DOI: 10.1016/j.tsc.2024.101727

Creswell, J. W. (2015). *Research design: Qualitative, quantitative, and mixed methods approach* (4th ed.). Pearson Education.

Creswell, J. W., & Poth, C. N. (2018). *Qualitative inquiry and research design: Choosing among five approaches* (4th ed.). Sage Publications.

Crogman, H. T., Cano, V. D., Pacheco, E., Boroon, R., & Sonawane, R. B. (2025). Virtual Reality, Augmented Reality, and Mixed Reality in Experiential Learning: Transforming Educational Paradigms. *Education Sciences, 15*(3), 303. DOI: 10.3390/educsci15030303

Dare, E. A., Ellis, J. A., & Roehrig, G. H. (2018). Understanding science teachers' implementations of integrated STEM curricula through a phenomenological multiple case study. *International Journal of STEM Education, 5*(4), 4. Advance online publication. DOI: 10.1186/s40594-018-0101-z PMID: 30631694

Davies, P. L., Schelly, C. L., & Spooner, C. L. (2021). Promoting inclusive STEM classrooms through Universal Design for Learning: A case study in undergraduate engineering. *Journal of Postsecondary Education and Disability, 34*(2), 123–138.

Dávila Morán, R. C., & Agüero Corzo, E. C. (2023). Desafíos éticos de la inteligencia artificial: Implicaciones para la sociedad y la economía. *Revista Conrado, 19*(94), 137–144. DOI: 10.52575/rc.v19i94.3326

Davis, M. H., & Ponnamperuma, G. G. (2005). Portfolio assessment. *Journal of Veterinary Medical Education, 32*(3), 279–284. DOI: 10.3138/jvme.32.3.279 PMID: 16261482

De Manuel Jerez, E., & Donadei, M. (2020). El papel de la universidad para educar al pensamiento crítico frente a los retos del cambio climático. En M. Fernández-Villa et al. (Eds.), *V CIED: Desafíos al desarrollo: procesos de cambio hacia la justicia global* (pp. 1976–1993). HEGOA (UPV/EHU).

DeCoito, I. (2016). STEM education in Canada: A knowledge synthesis. *Canadian Journal of Science, Mathematics and Technology Education = Revue Canadienne de l'Enseignement des Sciences, des Mathématiques et de la Technologie, 16*(2), 121–143. DOI: 10.1080/14926156.2016.1166297

de-Marcos, L., Domínguez, A., Saenz-de-Navarrete, J., & Pagés, C. (2014). An empirical study comparing gamification and social networking on e-learning. *Computers & Education, 75*, 82–91. DOI: 10.1016/j.compedu.2014.01.012

Deneen, C., & Shroff, R. H. (2014). Empowering students through e-portfolio assessment: Interrelationships among feedback, self-regulated learning and e-portfolio use. *Assessment & Evaluation in Higher Education, 39*(7), 1–17.

Desimone, L. M. (2009). Improving impact studies of teachers' professional development: Toward better conceptualizations and measures. *Educational Researcher, 38*(3), 181–199. DOI: 10.3102/0013189X08331140

Deterding, S., Dixon, D., Khaled, R., & Nacke, L. (2011). From game design elements to gamefulness: defining "gamification". *MindTrek '11: Proceedings of the 15th International Academic MindTrek Conference: Envisioning Future Media Environments* doi/DOI: 10.1145/2181037.2181040

Domínguez, A., Saenz-de-Navarrete, J., de-Marcos, L., Fernández-Sanz, L., Pagés, C., & Martínez-Herráiz, J. J. (2013). Gamifying learning experiences: Practical implications and outcomes. *Computers & Education, 63*, 380–392. DOI: 10.1016/j.compedu.2012.12.020

Dong, Y., Wang, Y., & Yang, L. (2020). Barriers to STEM education in secondary schools: A comparative study. *International Journal of STEM Education, 7*(1), 1–15. DOI: 10.1186/s40594-020-00210-x

Dorfsman, M. I. (2012). La profesión docente en contextos de cambio: el docente global en la sociedad de la información. *Revista de Educación a Distancia - Docencia Universitaria en la Sociedad del Conocimiento*, 6, 1-23. https://www.um.es/ead/reddusc/6/marcelo_dusc6.pdf

Du Plooy, E., Casteleijn, D., & Franzsen, D. (2024). Personalized adaptive learning in higher education: A scoping review of key characteristics and impact on academic performance and engagement. *Heliyon*, *10*(21), e39630. DOI: 10.1016/j.heliyon.2024.e39630 PMID: 39524879

Durango, I., Gallud, J. A., & Penichet, V. M. R. (2025). The data dance: Choreographing seamless partnerships between humans, data, and GenAI. *International Journal of Data Science and Analytics*, *20*(4), 3613–3640. DOI: 10.1007/s41060-024-00684-w

Durnell, E., Howell, R. T., Okabe-Miyamoto, K., & Zizi, M. (2025). From mistrust to confidence: How NeuroTech improves privacy for mistrusted digital environments in a formerly incarcerated population. *Computers in Human Behavior*, *173*, 108794. Advance online publication. DOI: 10.1016/j.chb.2025.108794

Eden, C., Adeniyi, I., & Chisom, O.Chima Abimbola EdenOnyebuchi Nneamaka ChisomIdowu Sulaimon Adeniyi. (2024). Parent and community involvement in education: strengthening partnerships for social improvement. *International Journal of Applied Research in Social Sciences*, *6*(3), 372–382. DOI: 10.51594/ijarss.v6i3.894

Ejiwale, J. A. (2013). Barriers to successful implementation of STEM education. *Journal of Education and Learning*, *7*(2), 63–74. DOI: 10.5539/jel.v7n2p63

Elamin, M. O. I. (2024). AI through the ages: Unlocking key opportunities and navigating challenges in the history and future of artificial intelligence. *International Journal of Religion*, *5*(12), 1152–1166. DOI: 10.61707/tarzcj89

El-Deghaidy, H., Mansour, N., Alzaghal, M., & Alhammad, F. (2021). STEM education and teacher professional development: A systematic review. *Research in Science & Technological Education*, *39*(1), 1–24. DOI: 10.1080/02635143.2020.1788316

Elliott, M. R., & Valliant, R. (2017). Inference for Nonprobability Samples. *Statistical Science*, *32*(2), 249–264. DOI: 10.1214/16-STS598

El-Sabagh, H. A. (2021). Adaptive e-learning environment based on learning styles and its impact on the development of students' engagement: Revista de Universidad y Sociedad del Conocimiento. *International Journal of Educational Technology in Higher Education, 18*(1). ProQuest Central; Social Science Premium Collection. DOI: 10.1186/s41239-021-00289-4

English, L. D. (2016). STEM education K–12: Perspectives on integration. *International Journal of STEM Education*, *3*(3), 3. Advance online publication. DOI: 10.1186/s40594-016-0036-1

Ertmer, P. A. (2005). Teacher pedagogical beliefs: The final frontier in our quest for technology integration? *Educational Technology Research and Development, 53*(4), 25–39. DOI: 10.1007/BF02504683

Ertmer, P. A., & Ottenbreit-Leftwich, A. T. (2010). Teacher technology change: How knowledge, confidence, beliefs, and culture intersect. *Journal of Research on Technology in Education, 42*(3), 255–284. DOI: 10.1080/15391523.2010.10782551

Essa, S. G., Celik, T., & Human-Hendricks, N. E. (2023). Personalized Adaptive Learning Technologies Based on Machine Learning Techniques to Identify Learning Styles: A Systematic Literature Review. *IEEE Access : Practical Innovations, Open Solutions, 11*, 48392–48409. DOI: 10.1109/ACCESS.2023.3276439

European Commission Joint Research Centre. (2024). STEM education: Report highlights need for more policy efforts and research. *European Education Area.* https://education.ec.europa.eu/news/stem-education-report-highlights-need-for-more-policy-efforts-and-research

European Parliament and Council of the European Union. (2000). *Directive 2000/60/EC of the European Parliament and of the Council of 23 October 2000 establishing a framework for Community action in the field of water policy. Official Journal of the European Communities, L 327*, 1–73. https://eur-lex.europa.eu/legal-content/EN/TXT/?uri=CELEX:32000L0060

European Schoolnet. (2025). *Scientix (official website).* Retrieved from https://www.scientix.eu/

Evenstein Sigalov, S., & Cohen, A. (2025). Leveraging Wikipedia for educational innovation: A higher education course model for enhancing students' competencies and collaborative knowledge creation. *International Journal of Educational Technology in Higher Education, 22*(1), 27. Advance online publication. DOI: 10.1186/s41239-025-00518-0

Fazio, X. (2024). STEM education: International perspectives in STEM education. In *Global Perspectives on STEM Education* (pp. 93–108). Springer., DOI: 10.1007/978-3-031-60676-2_6

Feng, W., Lai, X., Zhang, X., Fan, X., & Du, Y. (2025). Research on the construction and application of intelligent tutoring system for english teaching based on generative pre-training model. *Systems and Soft Computing, 7*, 200232. Advance online publication. DOI: 10.1016/j.sasc.2025.200232

Fernández-Garrido, R. (2017). *Regenerating Málaga: Guadalmedina and SOHO*. Paper presented at the COTMA VII Congress, Málaga. https://fernandez-garrido.com/wp-content/uploads/2017/10/REGENERANDO-M%C3%81LAGA-GUADALMEDINA-Y-SOHO-Fern%C3%A1ndez-Garrido-Rafael.pdf

Fernández-Velásquez, J. D. R., López-Regalado, O., & Fernández-Hurtado, G. A. (2025). Educational dualism in action: Systematic review of gamification and flipped classrooms' effects on young learners. *Contemporary Educational Technology, 17*(1), 557. DOI: 10.30935/cedtech/15749

Fitrah, M., Sofroniou, A., Setiawan, C., Widihastuti, W., Yarmanetti, N., Jaya, M. P. S., Panuntun, J. G., Arfaton, A., Beteno, S., & Susianti, I. (2025). The Impact of Integrated Project-Based Learning and Flipped Classroom on Students' Computational Thinking Skills: Embedded Mixed Methods. *Education Sciences, 15*(4), 448. Advance online publication. DOI: 10.3390/educsci15040448

Foreman-Brown, G., Fitzpatrick, E., & Twyford, K. (2022). Reimagining teacher identity in the post-COVID-19 university: Becoming digitally savvy, reflective in practice, collaborative, and relational. *Educational and Developmental Psychologist, 40*(1), 18–26. DOI: 10.1080/20590776.2022.2079406

Fossey, E., Harvey, C., McDermott, F., & Davidson, L. (2002). Understanding and evaluating qualitative research. *The Australian and New Zealand Journal of Psychiatry, 36*(6), 717–732. DOI: 10.1046/j.1440-1614.2002.01100.x PMID: 12406114

Fraenkel, J. R., Wallen, N. E., & Hyun, H. H. (2019). *How to design and evaluate research in education* (10th ed.). McGraw-Hill Education.

Freire, E., Enrique, E., Nagua, C., & Xavier, D. (2020). La ética en las investigaciones educativas. *Revista Universidad y Sociedad, 12*(4), 333-340. Epub 02 de agosto de 2020. Retrieved from 21th October 2025. http://scielo.sld.cu/scielo.php?script=sci_arttext&pid=S2218-36202020000400333&lng=es&tlng=es

Freire, P. (1970). *Pedagogía del oprimido*. Siglo XXI Editores.

Fromm, Y. M., Rasch, J., & Ifenthaler, D. (2025). Technology-enhanced personalized learning environments based on prior knowledge in continuing education: An experimental study. *Smart Learning Environments, 12*(1), 54. Advance online publication. DOI: 10.1186/s40561-025-00407-z

Fullan, M., & Langworthy, M. (2014). *A rich seam: How new pedagogies find deep learning*. Pearson.

Gall, M. D., Gall, J. P., & Borg, W. R. (2015). *Applying educational research: How to read, do, and use research to solve problems of practice* (7th ed.). Pearson.

Gao, X., Li, P., Shen, J., & Sun, H. (2020). Reviewing assessment of student learning in interdisciplinary STEM education. *International Journal of STEM Education, 7*(24), 24. Advance online publication. DOI: 10.1186/s40594-020-00225-4

García-Llamas, P., Taboada, A., Sanz-Chumillas, P., Lopes Pereira, L., & Baelo Álvarez, R. (2025). Breaking barriers in STEAM education: Analyzing competence acquisition through project-based learning in a European context. *International Journal of Educational Research Open*, *8*, 100449. DOI: 10.1016/j.ijedro.2025.100449

García-Redondo, P., García, T., Areces, D., Núñez, J. C., & Rodríguez, C. (2019). Serious Games and Their Effect Improving Attention in Students with Learning Disabilities. *International Journal of Environmental Research and Public Health, 16*(14), 2480. DOI: 10.3390/ijerph16142480 PMID: 31336804

Gârdan, I. P., Manu, M. B., Gârdan, D. A., Negoi ă, L. D. L., Pa tiu, C. A., Ghi ă, E., & Zaharia, A. (2025). Adopting AI in education: Optimizing human resource management considering teacher perceptions. *Frontiers in Education, 10*, 1488147. DOI: 10.3389/feduc.2025.1488147

Garzón, J., Burgos, D., & Tlili, A. (2025). Advantages and challenges associated with mobile learning in education: A systematic literature review. *Journal of Computers in Education, 12*(4), 1173–1205. DOI: 10.1007/s40692-024-00342-x

Geesa, R. L., Stith, K. M., & Teague, G. M. (2021). Integrative STEM education and leadership for student success. In *The Palgrave Handbook of Educational Leadership and Management Discourse* (pp. 1–20). Springer., DOI: 10.1007/978-3-030-39666-4_36-1

Ghitis, T., & Alba, A. (2019). Percepciones de futuros docentes sobre el uso de tecnología en educación inicial. *Revista Electrónica de Investigación Educativa, 21*(e23), 1–12. DOI: 10.24320/redie.2019.21.e23.2034

Giannetto, D., Chao, J., & Fontana, A. (2013). Gamification in a Social Learning Environment. *Issues in Informing Science and Information Technology*, *10*, 1–13. DOI: 10.28945/1806

Gibson, D., & Barrett, H. (2003). Directions in electronic portfolio development. *Canadian Journal of Learning and Technology*, *31*(3), 1–15.

Gnambs, T., & Hawrot, A. (2025). The development of social, gender, and migration-related disparities in digital competencies during adolescence. *Computers in Human Behavior*, *173*, 108800. Advance online publication. DOI: 10.1016/j.chb.2025.108800

Goehle, G. (2013). Gamification and Web-based Homework. *PRIMUS (Terre Haute, Ind.)*, *23*(3), 234–246. DOI: 10.1080/10511970.2012.736451

Gómez-Marí, I., Lacruz-Pérez, I., & Sanz-Cervera, P. (2023). Percepciones y actitudes del profesorado hacia el uso de la tecnología como herramienta inclusiva. *REIDOCREA*, *12*(8), 86–97. DOI: 10.30827/Digibug.81000

González Fernández, M. O., Romero-López, M. A., Sgreccia, N. F., & Latorre Medina, M. J. (2025). Marcos normativos para una IA ética y confiable en la educación superior: Estado de la cuestión. *RIED-Revista Iberoamericana de Educación a Distancia*, *28*(2). Advance online publication. DOI: 10.5944/ried.28.2.43511

González, L. A., Neyem, A., Contreras-McKay, I., & Molina, D. (2022). Improving learning experiences in software engineering capstone courses using artificial intelligence virtual assistants. *Computer Applications in Engineering Education, 30*(5), 1370–1389. *Scopus.* Advance online publication. DOI: 10.1002/cae.22526

González-Vera, V. M., Nebot-Gómez de Salazar, N., & Asencio-Juncal, J. (2023). Experiencia de innovación docente en la enseñanza del urbanismo: análisis y diagnóstico de entornos urbanos en colaboración con entidades sociales y tejido asociativo. In Pinilla Gómez, M., & Cruz Carvajal, S. (Eds.), *Estudios de innovación docente como punto de encuentro en ciencias humanísticas y sociales* (pp. 753–773). Editorial Dykinson.

Grafström, A. (2010). On unequal probability sampling designs. Thesis for: PhD. Advisor: Lennart Bondesson. Retrieved from https://www.researchgate.net/publication/240924161_On_unequal_probability_sampling_designs

Granet, D. B., Gomi, C. F., Ventura, R., & Miller-Scholte, A. (2005). The Relationship between Convergence Insufficiency and ADHD. *Strabismus*, *13*(4), 163–168. DOI: 10.1080/09273970500455436 PMID: 16361187

Grant, M. M. (2019). Difficulties in defining mobile learning: Analysis, design characteristics, and implications. *Educational Technology Research and Development*, *67*(2), 361–388. DOI: 10.1007/s11423-018-09641-4

Guardiola Jiménez, P. F. (2014). *Mis publicaciones de sociología*. https://www.um.es/docencia/pguardio/

Gudoniene, D., Staneviciene, E., Huet, I., Dickel, J., Dieng, D., Degroote, J., Rocio, V., Butkiene, R., & Casanova, D. (2025). Hybrid Teaching and Learning in Higher Education: A Systematic Literature Review. *Sustainability (Basel)*, *17*(2), 756. DOI: 10.3390/su17020756

Guerra, V. E. B., O'Brien, M. I. Z., Bajaña, V. P. M., Villacrés, E. B. R., Pacheco, M. de J. N., Rodríguez, N. E. C., & Zúñiga, W. W. B. (2024). Percepciones y experiencias de docentes universitarios sobre la inteligencia artificial: Transformación, ética y desafíos en el uso académico por estudiantes. *LATAM Revista Latinoamericana de Ciencias Sociales y Humanidades, 5*(6), Article 6. DOI: 10.56712/latam.v5i6.3204

Hain, A., & Motaref, S. (2020). Implementing Interactive 3-D Models in an Entry-level Engineering Course to Enhance Students'. *Visualization*. Advance online publication. DOI: 10.18260/1-2--34782

Hakkal, S., & Ait Lahcen, A. A. (2025). Leveraging graph neural network for learner performance prediction. *Expert Systems with Applications*, *293*, 128724. Advance online publication. DOI: 10.1016/j.eswa.2025.128724

Hallam, G., & Creagh, T. (2010). E-portfolios for the trades: Can they work? *Education + Training*, *52*(6/7), 500–513.

Hanus, M. D.,&Fox, J. (2015). Assessing the effects of gamification in the classroom: A longitudinal study on intrinsic motivation, social comparison, satisfaction, effort, and academic performance. *Computers & Education, 80,* 152 161. https://doi.org/ DOI: 10.1016/j.compedu.2014.08.019

Harati, S., Perez, L., Molowny-Horas, R., & Pontius, R. G.Jr. (2021). Validating models of one-way land change: An example case of forest insect disturbance. *Landscape Ecology*, *36*(10), 2919–2935. DOI: 10.1007/s10980-021-01272-0

Harvard Business Publishing Education. (2023). Why your students are disengaged. *Inspiring Minds.* https://hbsp.harvard.edu/inspiring-minds/why-your-students-are-disengaged

Hattie, J. (2012). *Visible learning for teachers: Maximizing impact on learning.* Routledge. DOI: 10.4324/9780203181522

Heafner, T. L., & Fitchett, P. G. (2015). Principals' and teachers' reports of instructional time allocations in third grade abstract. *Journal of International Social Studies*, *5*(1), 81–100.

Hellín, C. J., Calles-Esteban, F., Valledor, A., Gómez, J., Otón-Tortosa, S., & Tayebi, A. (2023). Enhancing Student Motivation and Engagement through a Gamified Learning Environment. *Sustainability (Basel)*, *15*(19), 19. Advance online publication. DOI: 10.3390/su151914119

Hernández-Falagán, D. (2020). Pedagogía colaborativa y redes sociales. Diseñar en cuarentena. In Bardí i Milà, B., & García-Escudero, D. (Eds.), *VIII Jornadas sobre Innovación Docente en Arquitectura (JIDA'20)* (pp. 186–197). Iniciativa Digital Politècnica Oficina de Publicacions Acadèmiques Digitals de la UPC, Publicaciones y Divulgación Científica de la Universidad de Málaga., DOI: 10.5821/jida.2020.9336

Herrera, T., Blanco, F. and Puche, P. (2009). El río Grande de Málaga: la movilización social y la investigación científica como base de su defensa. *Ríos con vida AEMS*, (83), 24-27.

Herro, D., Quigley, C., & Jacques, L. A. (2018). Examining technology integration in middle school STEAM units. *Technology, Pedagogy and Education*, *27*(4), 485–498. DOI: 10.1080/1475939X.2018.1514322

Higueras, E. (2013). *Desarrollo urbano sostenible y criterios de diseño urbano para ordenaciones residenciales*. [Online monograph]. https://lc.cx/DY7-Sv

Holmes, K., Berger, N., Mackenzie, E., Attard, C., & Ryan, V. (2022). The impact of place-based contextualized curriculum on student engagement and motivation in STEM education. *Frontiers in Education.* https://www.frontiersin.org/research-topics/14933

Honey, M., Pearson, G., & Schweingruber, H. (Eds.). (2014). *STEM integration in K–12 education: Status, prospects, and an agenda for research.* National Academies Press., DOI: 10.17226/18612

Hsu, C.-Y., & Wu, T.-T. (2023). *Applications of Business Simulation Games in Flipped Classrooms to Facilitate Student Engagement and Higher-Order Thinking Skills for Sustainable Learning Practices.* MDPI AG. DOI: 10.20944/preprints202311.0082.v1

Huang, X., & Qiao, C. (2024). Enhancing computational thinking skills through artificial intelligence education at a STEAM high school. *Science & Education*, *33*(2), 383–403. DOI: 10.1007/s11191-022-00392-6

Hu, Y. (2025). Creating interactive AI learning environments: Integrating interdisciplinary approaches and Taoist art principles. *Interactive Learning Environments*, *33*(6), 1–20. DOI: 10.1080/10494820.2025.2454442

Iksan, Z. H., & Saufian, S. M. (2017). Mobile Learning: Innovation in Teaching and Learning Using Telegram. *International Journal of Pedagogy and Teacher Education*, *1*(1), 19–26. DOI: 10.20961/ijpte.v1i1.5120

Inan, F. A., & Lowther, D. L. (2010). Factors affecting technology integration in K-12 classrooms: A path model. *Educational Technology Research and Development*, *58*(2), 137–154. DOI: 10.1007/s11423-009-9132-y

Iqbal, J., Asgarova, V., Hashmi, Z. F., Ngajie, B. N., Asghar, M. Z., & Järvenoja, H. (2025). Exploring faculty experiences with generative artificial intelligence tools integration in second language curricula in Chinese higher education. *Discover Computing*, *28*(1), 128. Advance online publication. DOI: 10.1007/s10791-025-09655-6

Iqbal, M. Z., Alradhi, H. I., Alhumaidi, A. A., Alshaikh, K. H., AlObaid, A. M., Alhashim, M. T., & AlSheikh, M. H. (2020). Telegram as a Tool to Supplement Online Medical Education During COVID-19 Crisis. *Acta Informatica Medica*, *28*(2), 94–97. DOI: 10.5455/aim.2020.28.94-97 PMID: 32742059

Jadán-Guerrero, J., Avilés-Castillo, F., Buele, J., & Palacios-Navarro, G. (2023). Gamification in Inclusive Education for Children with Disabilities: Global Trends and Approaches - A Bibliometric Review. In Gervasi, O. (Eds.), Lecture Notes in Computer Science: Vol. 14104. *Computational Science and Its Applications – ICCSA 2023 Workshops. ICCSA 2023*. Springer., DOI: 10.1007/978-3-031-37105-9_31

Jain, K., & Raghuram, J. N. V. (2024). Unlocking potential: The impact of AI on education technology. *Multidisciplinary Reviews*, *7*(3), 2024049–2024049. DOI: 10.31893/multirev.2024049

Jiang, B., Cheng, T., Tsou, M.-H., Zhu, D., & Ye, X. (2025). Advancing translational human dynamics research: Bridging space, mind, and computational urban science in the era of GeoAI. *Computational Urban Science*, *5*(1), 12. Advance online publication. DOI: 10.1007/s43762-025-00171-3

Johnson, B., & Christensen, L. (2017). *Educational research: Quantitative, qualitative, and mixed approaches* (6th ed.). SAGE Publications.

Jordan, K. (2023). How can messaging apps, WhatsApp and SMS be used to support learning? A scoping review. *Technology, Pedagogy and Education*, *32*(3), 275–288. DOI: 10.1080/1475939X.2023.2201590

Jun, M., & Lucas, T. (2024). Gamification elements and their impacts on education: A review. *Multidisciplinary Reviews*, *8*(5), 2025155. DOI: 10.31893/multirev.2025155

Kafyulilo, A. C., & Fisser, P. (2015). Teachers' perceptions of the use of ICT in education: A survey study. *International Journal of Education and Development using ICT, 11*(1), 55–70.

Kamali, J., Alpat, M. F., & Bozkurt, A. (2024). AI ethics as a complex and multifaceted challenge: Decoding educators' AI ethics alignment through the lens of activity theory. *International Journal of Educational Technology in Higher Education*, *21*(1), 62. DOI: 10.1186/s41239-024-00496-9

Kassens, A. L. (2014). Tweeting Your Way to Improved #Writing, #Reflection, and #Community. *The Journal of Economic Education, 45*(2), 101–109. DOI: 10.1080/00220485.2014.889937

Katonane Gyonyoru, K. I., & Katona, J. (2024). Student Perceptions of AI-Enhanced Adaptive Learning Systems: A Pilot Survey. *2024 IEEE 7th International Conference and Workshop Óbuda on Electrical and Power Engineering (CANDO-EPE)*, 93–98. DOI: 10.1109/CANDO-EPE65072.2024.10772884

Kayser, B. (2023, May 14). Más vocación ante la emergencia climática. *El País*. https://elpais.com

Kayyali, M. (2024). Future possibilities and challenges of AI in education. In *Transforming education with generative AI: Prompt engineering and synthetic content creation* (pp. 118–137). IGI Global Scientific Publishing. DOI: 10.4018/979-8-3693-1351-0.ch006

Kelley, T. R., & Knowles, J. G. (2016). A conceptual framework for integrated STEM education. *International Journal of STEM Education, 3*(11), 11. Advance online publication. DOI: 10.1186/s40594-016-0046-z

Kernstock, P., Harms, C., Hein, A., & Krcmar, H. (2025). Establishing and governing data ecosystems at the crossroads of centralization and decentralization. *Electronic Markets, 35*(1), 71. Advance online publication. DOI: 10.1007/s12525-025-00810-x

Khogali, H. O., & Mekid, S. (2024). Perception and Ethical Challenges for the Future of AI as Encountered by Surveyed New Engineers. *Societies (Basel, Switzerland), 14*(12), 271. DOI: 10.3390/soc14120271

Kistaubayev, Y., Liébana-Cabanillas, F., Shaikh, A. A., Mutanov, G., Ussatova, O., & Shinbayeva, A. (2025). Enhancing Transparency and Trust in Higher Education Institutions via Blockchain: A Conceptual Model Utilizing the Ethereum Consortium Approach. *Sustainability (Basel), 17*(20), 9350. Advance online publication. DOI: 10.3390/su17209350

Koehler, M. J., & Mishra, P. (2009). What is technological pedagogical content knowledge (TPACK)? *Contemporary Issues in Technology & Teacher Education, 9*(1), 60–70.

Koh, J., Cowling, M., Jha, M., & Sim, K. N. (2022). Collaborating with AI for better student-teacher reconnection. *ASCILITE Publications*, e22126–e22126. DOI: 10.14742/apubs.2022.126

Konak, A., Kulturel-Konak, S., Schneider, D. R., & Mehta, K. (2024). Enhancing student learning in innovation competitions and programs. *European Journal of Engineering Education, 50*(2), 360–380. DOI: 10.1080/03043797.2024.2394945

Kong, S. C., & Hu, W. (2025). A study of developing administrative Staff's conceptual understanding of generative artificial intelligence through professional Development: Evaluation of a course using tests, surveys and thematic analysis of reflective writings. *Computers and Education: Artificial Intelligence, 9*, 100444. Advance online publication. DOI: 10.1016/j.caeai.2025.100444

Koole, M. L. (2009). A Model for Framing Mobile Learning. In Ally, M. (Ed.), *Mobile Learning: Transforming the Delivery of Education and Training* (pp. 25–47). AU Press., DOI: 10.15215/aupress/9781897425435.01

Kovan Mzwri, & Turcsányi-Szabo, M. (2025). The Impact of Prompt Engineering and a Generative AI-Driven Tool on Autonomous Learning: A Case Study. *Education Sciences, 15*(2), 199. ProQuest Central; Social Science Premium Collection. DOI: 10.3390/educsci15020199

Kozma, R. B. (2003). Technology and classroom practices: An international study. *Journal of Research on Technology in Education, 36*(1), 1–14. DOI: 10.1080/15391523.2003.10782399

Kučera, E., & Haffner, O. (2025). Competency-Based Hybrid Learning: A Modern Approach to Teaching Programming and Digital Technologies Subjects. *IEEE Access : Practical Innovations, Open Solutions, 13*, 54892–54919. DOI: 10.1109/ACCESS.2025.3555333

Kyslova, M. A., Semerikov, S. O., & Slovak, K. I. (2025). Mobile learning evolution: A decade of developments (2014-2023). *Educational Technology Quarterly, 2025*(2), 186–208. DOI: 10.55056/etq.25

Labster. (2023). From disengagement to discovery: Transforming STEM education. *Labster Guides*. https://www.labster.com/guides/from-disengagement-to-discovery-transforming-stem-education

Lam, B. H. (2023). E-portfolios, assessment and data ethics in higher education. *Assessment & Evaluation in Higher Education, 48*(3), 1–16.

Lamberti, P. M., Bombaerts, G., & IJsselsteijn, W. (2025). Mind the gap: Bridging the divide between computer scientists and ethicists in shaping moral machines. *Ethics and Information Technology, 27*(1), 2. DOI: 10.1007/s10676-024-09806-1

Larkin, T. L. (2015). Creativity in STEM education: Reshaping the creative project. 1184-1189. https://doi.org/DOI: 10.1109/ICL.2015.7318203

Lavicza, Z., Weinhandl, R., Prodromou, T., Anđić, B., Lieban, D., Hohenwarter, M., Fenyvesi, K., Brownell, C., & Diego-Mantecón, J. M. (2022). Developing and Evaluating Educational Innovations for STEAM Education in Rapidly Changing Digital Technology Environments. *Sustainability (Basel), 14*(12), 7237. Advance online publication. DOI: 10.3390/su14127237

Ldokova, G., Frumina, S., & Alwaely, S. A. (2025). Taking into account students' psychotypes and using their neuropsychological maps when implementing digital educational technologies within the Metaverse. *Smart Learning Environments, 12*(1), 15. Advance online publication. DOI: 10.1186/s40561-024-00344-3

Leavy, A., Dick, L., Meletiou-Mavrotheris, M., Paparistodemou, E., & Stylianou, E. (2023). The prevalence and use of emerging technologies in STEAM education: A systematic review of the literature. *Journal of Computer Assisted Learning, 39*(4), 1061–1082. DOI: 10.1111/jcal.12806

Lee, C. E. (2020). Facebook Use in Malaysian Higher Education Classroom. In Tatnall, A. (Ed.), *Encyclopedia of Education and Information Technologies* (pp. 751–758). Springer., DOI: 10.1007/978-3-030-10576-1_141

Lee, J. Y., Woo, J., & Pyon, C. U. (2023). Digital Twin for Math Education: A Study on the Utilisation of Games and Gamification for University Mathematics Education. *Electronics (Basel), 12*(15), 3207. DOI: 10.3390/electronics12153207

Levin, I., Semenov, A. L., & Gorsky, M. (2025). Smart Learning in the 21st Century: Advancing Constructionism Across Three Digital Epochs. *Education Sciences, 15*(1), 45. Advance online publication. DOI: 10.3390/educsci15010045

Li, J. (2025). Enhancing learning through an adaptive web-based educational search framework integrating natural language processing and machine learning techniques. *Discover Computing, 28*(1), 213. Advance online publication. DOI: 10.1007/s10791-025-09732-w

Li, M., Ma, S., & Shi, Y. (2023). Examining the effectiveness of gamification as a tool promoting teaching and learning in educational settings: A meta-analysis. *Frontiers in Psychology, 14*, 1253549. Advance online publication. DOI: 10.3389/fpsyg.2023.1253549 PMID: 37876838

Lim, L., Lim, S. H., & Lim, R. W. Y. (2022). Measuring Learner Satisfaction of an Adaptive Learning System. *Behavioral Sciences (Basel, Switzerland), 12*(8), 264. Advance online publication. DOI: 10.3390/bs12080264 PMID: 36004835

Lindholst, A. C., Eriksen, T. B., & Knudsen, S. V. (2024). Danish school pupils' perception of their learning outcomes from participating in computer-based adaptive tests: A pressure for just clicking something? *Scandinavian Journal of Educational Research*, *68*(6), 1186–1202. DOI: 10.1080/00313831.2023.2228823

Ling, H.-C., & Chiang, H.-S. (2022). Learning Performance in Adaptive Learning Systems: A Case Study of Web Programming Learning Recommendations. *Frontiers in Psychology*, *13*, 770637. Advance online publication. DOI: 10.3389/fpsyg.2022.770637 PMID: 35153951

Lintz, J. (2025). Exploring the impacts of artificial intelligence interventions on providers' practices: Perspectives from a rural medical center. *Journal of Medical Artificial Intelligence*, *8*, 39. Advance online publication. DOI: 10.21037/jmai-24-422

Li, Q., Yin, X., Yin, W., Dong, X., & Li, Q. (2023). Evaluation of gamification techniques in learning abilities for higher school students using FAHP and EDAS methods. *Soft Computing*, •••, 1–19. Advance online publication. DOI: 10.1007/s00500-023-08179-9 PMID: 37362302

Liu, C.-Y., & Wu, C.-J. (2025). Extracting the actions of contextual understanding in STEAM research: Direction for STEAM course design. *Thinking Skills and Creativity*, *56*, 101770. DOI: 10.1016/j.tsc.2025.101770

Liu, R., Wu, Y., Zhao, K., Zhou, Z., Gao, X., Lin, X., Zhang, X., Chen, X., & Lu, G. (2025). Online Resource Provisioning and Batch Scheduling for AIoT Inference Serving in an XPU Edge Cloud. *IEEE Transactions on Emerging Topics in Computing*, *13*(1), 234–249. DOI: 10.1109/TETC.2024.3403874

Li, X., Chu, S. K. W., Xia, Q., & Yang, Y. (2022). Using Gamification to Facilitate Students' Self-Regulation in E-Learning: A Case Study on Students' L2 English Learning. *Sustainability (Basel)*, *14*(12), 7008. DOI: 10.3390/su14127008

Li, Y., Wang, K., & Xiao, Y. (2020). Global STEM education: A review of international collaboration and student outcomes. *Journal of Science Education and Technology*, *29*(4), 567–580. DOI: 10.1007/s10956-020-09876-3

Li, Y., Wang, K., Xiao, Y., & Froyd, J. E. (2020). Research and trends in STEM education: A systematic review of journal publications. *International Journal of STEM Education*, *7*(1), 11. Advance online publication. DOI: 10.1186/s40594-020-00207-6

Lobanova, A., Hrabovets, I., Prykhodko, O., Karytka, V., Kalashnikova, L., & Chernous, L. (2024). Artificial intelligence in teaching social disciplines: Opportunities and challenges of tools. *Educational Technology Quarterly*, *2024*(4), 360–377. DOI: 10.55056/etq.813

Lodico, M. G., Spaulding, D. T., & Voegtle, K. H. (2019). *Methods in educational research: From theory to practice* (4th ed.). Wiley.

Lorenzo, G., & Ittelson, J. (2005). *An overview of e-portfolios*. Educause Learning Initiative.

Luque Pulgar, E. (2023). *Docentes ante la crisis climática: Retos transformadores*. Universidad Nacional de Educación a Distancia (UNED). https://doi.org/DOI: 10.5944/educxx1.29427

Madshaven, J. M., Omlin, C. W. P., & Spanos, A. (2025). Making Historical Consciousness Come Alive: Abstract Concepts, Artificial Intelligence, and Implicit Game-Based Learning. *Education Sciences*, *15*(9), 1128. Advance online publication. DOI: 10.3390/educsci15091128

Maimaiti, G., & Hew, K. F. (2025). Gamified self-regulated learning improves EFL Reading comprehension, motivation, self-regulation skills and process patterns: Quasi-experiment with process mining. *The Internet and Higher Education*, *67*, 101042. Advance online publication. DOI: 10.1016/j.iheduc.2025.101042

Majjate, H., Bellarhmouch, Y., Jeghal, A., Yahyaouy, A., Tairi, H., & Zidani, K. A. (2025). Assessing the impact of ethical aspects of recommendation systems on student trust and engagement in E-learning platforms: A multifaceted investigation. *Education and Information Technologies*, *30*(3), 3953–3977. DOI: 10.1007/s10639-024-12979-3

Maldonado, C. E. (2024b). *Inteligencia artificial y ética*. Ediciones desde abajo.

Maldonado, C. E. (2024a). El problema de la ética: El convivio. Ética e Inteligencia Artificial. *Revista Iberoamericana de Complejidad y Ciencias Económicas*, *2*(2), 31–48. DOI: 10.48168/ricce.v2n2p31

Mallén-Lacambra, C., & Mamas, C. (2025). Ethics of Care: A Theoretical Underpinning for Relational Inclusivity. *Teoría de la Educación. Teoría de la Educación*, *37*(2), 99–124. DOI: 10.14201/teri.32183

Manca, S. (2020). Snapping, pinning, liking or texting: Investigating social media in higher education beyond Facebook. *The Internet and Higher Education*, *44*, 100707. DOI: 10.1016/j.iheduc.2019.100707

Mao, Q., & Hong, J.-C. (2025). An exploration of the value of artwork in an integrated STEAM competition. *Thinking Skills and Creativity*, *57*, 101857. DOI: 10.1016/j.tsc.2025.101857

Margot, K., & Kettler, T. (2020). Teachers' perception of STEM integration and education: A systematic literature review. *International Journal of STEM Education, 7*, 11.

Marín García, S. (2019). *Ética e inteligencia artificial.* Cuadernos de la Cátedra CaixaBank de Responsabilidad Social Corporativa, No. 42. IESE Business School. https://dx.doi.org/DOI: 10.15581/018.ST-522

Maryana, M., Rahmi, H., & Halim, C. (2024). The Impact of Gamification on Student Engagement and Learning Outcomes in Mathematics Education. *International Journal of Business, Law, and Education, 5*(2), 1697–1608. DOI: 10.56442/ijble.v5i2.682

Matos Lopes, R. (2017). Facebook in educational research: A bibliometric analysis. *Scientometrics, 111*(3), 1591–1621. DOI: 10.1007/s11192-017-2294-1

Md Yusof, N., & Abdullah, A. (2025). The efficacy of Telegram Messenger as a tool for enhancing argumentative writing among students in open and distance learning. *Asian Association of Open Universities Journal, 20*(1), 4–16. DOI: 10.1108/AAOUJ-07-2022-0091

Meirinhos, M. F. A. (2024). *Escola Digital: rumo à escola de competências.* Pimenta Cultural., DOI: 10.31560/pimentacultural/978-85-7221-249-6

Mekler, E.D., Bruhlmann, F., Opwis, K. Tuch, A.N. (2013). Disassembling gamification: the effects of points and meaning on user motivation and performance. *CHI EA '13: CHI '13 Extended Abstracts on Human Factors in Computing Systems*, 1137 – 1142. Doi/DOI: 10.1145/2468356.2468559

Ministry for the Ecological Transition and the Demographic Challenge. (2021). *National strategy for green infrastructure, ecological connectivity and restoration: The need to integrate nature-based solutions in urban environments.* https://www.miteco.gob.es/es/biodiversidad/temas/ecosistemas-y-conectividad/conectividad/estrategiainfraestructuraverde.aspx

Mirata, V., Hirt, F., Bergamin, P., & Van Der Westhuizen, C. (2020). Challenges and contexts in establishing adaptive learning in higher education: Findings from a Delphi study. *International Journal of Educational Technology in Higher Education, 17*(1), 32. DOI: 10.1186/s41239-020-00209-y

Mishra, P., & Koehler, M. J. (2006). Technological pedagogical content knowledge: A framework for teacher knowledge. *Teachers College Record, 108*(6), 1017–1054. DOI: 10.1111/j.1467-9620.2006.00684.x

Moemeke, C. D. (2024). Artificial intelligence and machine learning in enhancing science learning experiences: Exploring possibilities and concerns. *NIU Journal of Educational Research, 10*(2), 59–72.

Mohr-Schroeder, M. J., Cavalcanti, M., & Blyman, K. (2020). Equity and access in STEM: Inclusive strategies for teaching and learning. *International Journal of STEM Education, 7*(42). Advance online publication. DOI: 10.1186/s40594-020-00241-4

Moirano, R., Sánchez, M. A., & Štěpánek, L. (2020). Creative interdisciplinary collaboration: A systematic literature review. *Thinking Skills and Creativity, 35*, 100626. DOI: 10.1016/j.tsc.2019.100626

Molina-Ascanio, M., ... (2023). Innovative STEM teaching: The latest trends in STEM education. *Scientix.* https://www.scientix.eu/documents/10137/121801/Molina_Ascanio_2023_et_al_Innovative-STEM-Final-Ready-for-publication_compressed.pdf

Molina-Ayuso, Á., Adamuz-Povedano, N., Bracho-López, R., & Torralbo-Rodríguez, M. (2022). Introduction to Computational Thinking with Scratch for Teacher Training for Spanish Primary School Teachers in Mathematics. *Education Sciences, 12*(12), 899. DOI: 10.3390/educsci12120899

Mora-Esteban, R., Conejo-Arrabal, F., Romero-Martínez, J. M., & Nebot-Gómez de Salazar, N. (2025). Problems and restoration strategies of urban Mediterranean rivers in Spain: Guadalmedina River as a potential ecological corridor in the green-blue infrastructure of Malaga, Spain. *TeMA – Journal of Land Use, Mobility and Environment, 1.* https://doi.org/DOI: 10.6093/1970-9870/11115

Morán-Ortega, S.-A., Ruiz-Tirado, S.-G., Simental-López, L.-M., & Tirado-López, A.-B. (2024). Barreras de la Inteligencia Artificial generativa en estudiantes de educación superior. Percepción docente. *Revista De Investigación En Tecnologías De La Información, 12*(25), 26–37. DOI: 10.36825/RITI.12.25.003

Mouboua, P., Atobatele, F., & Akintayo, O.Patricia Diane MoubouaFadeke Adeola AtobateleOlateju Temitope Akintayo. (2024). Cross-cultural competence in global HRD: Strategies for developing an inclusive and diverse workforce. *International Journal of Science and Research Archive, 12*(1), 103–113. DOI: 10.30574/ijsra.2024.12.1.0765

Muijs, D. (2021). *Doing quantitative research in education with SPSS* (2nd ed.). SAGE Publications.

Mukhamadiyeva, S., & Hernández-Torrano, D. (2024). Adaptive Learning to Maximize Gifted Education: Teacher Perceptions, Practices, and Experiences. *Journal of Advanced Academics, 35*(4), 652–670. DOI: 10.1177/1932202X241253166

Mullick, J., Wang, Q., Vlcek, S., & Sikder, S. (2025). "The possibility of meeting the needs of all children": A framework for enhancing inclusive STEAM pedagogy in early childhood settings. *International Journal of Educational Research, 133*, 102705. DOI: 10.1016/j.ijer.2025.102705

Muntean, C. I. (2011). Raising engagement in e-learning through gamification», *Proceedings 6th International Conference on Virtual Learning ICVL*, pp. 323-329.

Nadelson, L. S., & Seifert, A. (2017). Integrated STEM defined: Contexts, challenges, and the future. *The Journal of Educational Research, 110*(3), 221–223. DOI: 10.1080/00220671.2017.1289775

National Science Foundation. (2024). *U.S. STEM Workforce: Size, Growth, and Employment*. Retrieved from ncses.nsf.gov/pubs/nsb20245/u-s-stem-workforce-size-growth-and-employment

Nebot-Gómez de Salazar, N., Asencio-Juncal, J., Chamizo-Nieto, F. J., & Jiménez-Morales, E. (2025). The climate emergency from the perspective of urban planning: A teaching experience at the bachelor's degree in architecture (Universidad de Málaga, Spain). In *Challenges of educational innovation in contemporary society* (pp. 205–224). IGI Global., DOI: 10.4018/979-8-3373-0705-3.ch010

Neisser, U. (1981). *Cognición y realidad: principios e implicaciones de la psicología cognitiva*. Marova.

Nesterenko, M., Mytsyk, H., Petryk, K., Kovachov, S., & Suchikova, Y. (2024). From resistance to acceptance: The role of higher education in the integration of STEM education for sustainable development. *Journal for STEM Education Research*. Advance online publication. DOI: 10.1007/s41979-024-00141-0

Ng, D. T. K., Su, J., Leung, J. K. L., & Chu, S. K. W. (2024). Artificial intelligence (AI) literacy education in secondary schools: A review. *Interactive Learning Environments, 32*(10), 6204–6224. DOI: 10.1080/10494820.2023.2255228

Nguyen-Viet, B., Nguyen-Duy, C., & Nguyen-Viet, B. (2024). How does gamification affect learning effectiveness? The mediating roles of engagement, satisfaction, and intrinsic motivation. *Interactive Learning Environments, 33*(3), 2635–2653. DOI: 10.1080/10494820.2024.2414356

Ng, W., Nicholas, H., Loke, S., & Torabi, T. (2010). Designing Effective Pedagogical Systems for Teaching and Learning with Mobile and Ubiquitous Devices. In Gogh, T. T. (Ed.), *Multiplatform E-Learning Systems and Technologies: Mobile Devices for Ubiquitous ICT-Based Education* (pp. 42–56). IGI Global., DOI: 10.4018/978-1-60566-703-4.ch003

Nicolau-Corbacho, A., Verdú-Vázquez, A., & Gil-López, T. (2019). Incorporación del *blended learning* al taller de proyectos arquitectónicos. In García-Escudero, D., & Bardí i Milà, B. (Eds.), *VII Jornadas sobre Innovación Docente en Arquitectura (JIDA'19)* (pp. 648–662). Iniciativa Digital Politècnica Oficina de Publicacions Acadèmiques Digitals de la UPC., DOI: 10.5821/jida.2019.8391

Nishat, A. (2025). Rethinking Intelligence: An Interdisciplinary Framework for AI Research. *Pioneer Research Journal of Computing Science*, *2*(2), 162–169.

Noda, S., Shirotsuki, K., & Nakao, M. (2019). The effectiveness of intervention with board games: A systematic review. *BioPsychoSocial Medicine*, *13*(1), 22. DOI: 10.1186/s13030-019-0164-1 PMID: 31641371

Nogués-Pedregal, A. M., & Carmona-Zubiri, D. (2024). Twitter as an instructional tool for critical thinking and creativity in Higher Education. In *10th International Conference on Higher Education Advances (HEAd'24)* (pp. 186–193). Universitat Politecnica de València. https://doi.org/DOI: 10.4995/HEAd24.2024.17272

Nowrozy, R., & Jam, D. (2024). Embracing the generative AI revolution: advancing tertiary education in cybersecurity with GPT. arXiv preprint arXiv:2403.11402.

Núñez, L., Conde, S., Ávila, J., & Mirabent, M. (2015). Implicaciones, uso y resultados de las TIC en educación primaria. Estudio cualitativo de un caso. *Edutec. Revista Electrónica de Tecnología Educativa*, 53, 1-17. https://dx.doi.DOI: 10.21556/edutec.2015.53.581

O'Donovan, S., Gain, J., & Marais, P. (2013) A case study in the gamification of a university-level games development course. In *Proceedings of the South African Institute for Computer Scientists and Information Technologists Conference* (SAICSIT '13). Association for Computing Machinery, New York, NY, USA, pp.242–251. DOI: 10.1145/2513456.2513469

OECD. (2020). *Digital education outlook 2020: Delivering digital skills*. OECD Publishing.

OECD. T. O. f. E. C.-o. a. D. (2024). *Future of Education and Skills 2030/2040*. Retrieved 25/05/2025 from https://www.oecd.org/

Oldfield, M. (2016). *Unequal sample sizes and the use of larger control groups pertaining to power of a study.* Ministry of Defense, UK. DOI: 10.6084/m9.figshare.23988477

Oliva-Córdova, L. M., Tohom, M. F. V., Salazar de la Cruz, R. C., & Martín-Núñez, J. L. (2025). Application of learning analytics in medical education: Enhancing student digital competences within the STEAM framework. *International Journal of Educational Research Open, 9,* 100511. https://doi.org/doi.org/10.1016/j.ijedro.2025.100511. DOI: 10.1016/j.ijedro.2025.100511

Organization for Economic Co-operation and Development [OECD] (2026). *OECD Digital Education Outlook 2026: Exploring Effective Uses of Generative AI in Education.* OECD Publishing. https://doi.org/DOI: 10.1787/062a7394-en

Ortega-Arranz, A., Amarasinghe, I., Martínez-Monés, A., Asensio-Pérez, J. I., Dimitriadis, Y., Corrales-Astorgano, M., & Hernández-Leo, D. (2024). Collaborative activities in hybrid learning environments: Exploring teacher orchestration load and students' perceptions. *Computers & Education, 219,* 105105. DOI: 10.1016/j.compedu.2024.105105

Ortiz, É. R. C., & Cruz, D. del P. P., Ortiz, D. M. C., Sánchez, M. F. P., & Sánchez, L. F. C. (2025). Integración de la Inteligencia Artificial en la Educación: Desafíos y Oportunidades para el Aprendizaje Personalizado. *Polo del Conocimiento, 10*(2), 2. Advance online publication. DOI: 10.23857/pc.v10i2.8879

Panjaburee, P., Komalawardhana, N., & Ingkavara, T. (2022). Acceptance of personalized e-learning systems: A case study of concept-effect relationship approach on science, technology, and mathematics courses. *Journal of Computers in Education, 9*(4), 681–705. ProQuest Central; Social Science Premium Collection. DOI: 10.1007/s40692-021-00216-6

Papagiannopoulou, T., & Vaiopoulou, J. (2024). Teachers' attitudes towards STEM education: Exploring the role of their readiness via a structural equation model. *European Journal of Investigation in Health, Psychology and Education, 14*(11), 2850–2864. DOI: 10.3390/ejihpe14110187 PMID: 39590024

Papamitsiou, Z., Pappas, I. O., Sharma, K., & Giannakos, M. N. (2020). Utilizing Multimodal Data Through fsQCA to Explain Engagement in Adaptive Learning. *IEEE Transactions on Learning Technologies, 13*(4), 689–703. DOI: 10.1109/TLT.2020.3020499

Parcerisa Bundó, J., & Rubert de Ventós, M. (2014). *La ciudad no es una hoja en blanco.* Ediciones LUB. DOI: 10.5821/ebook-9788469702284

Parker, J. L., Richard, V. M., Acabá, A., Escoffier, S., Flaherty, S., Jablonka, S., & Becker, K. P. (2025). Negotiating meaning with machines: AI's role in doctoral writing pedagogy. *International Journal of Artificial Intelligence in Education, 35*(3), 1218–1238. DOI: 10.1007/s40593-024-00425-x

Park, H., Byun, S. Y., & Sim, J. (2020). Teachers' perceptions and practices of STEM education in Korea. *Asia-Pacific Journal of Teacher Education, 48*(2), 179–197. DOI: 10.1080/1359866X.2019.1574602

Passey, D. (2019). Technology-enhanced learning: Rethinking the term, the concept and its theoretical background. *British Journal of Educational Technology, 50*(3), 972–986. DOI: 10.1111/bjet.12783

Patel, N. S., & Indurkhya, N. (Eds.). (2025). *The Rise of Intelligent Machines: A Multi-disciplinary Perspective from Industry and Impact on Higher Education.* CRC Press.

Pathak, V., Jena, B., & Kalra, S. (2013). Qualitative research. *Perspectives in Clinical Research, 4*(3), 192–197. DOI: 10.4103/2229-3485.115389 PMID: 24010063

Pedreira, O., Garcia, F., Brisaboa, N., & Piattini, M. (2014). Gamification in software engineering - A systematic mapping. *Information and Software Technology.* Advance online publication. DOI: 10.1016/j.infsof.2014.08.007

Perry, M. (2022). Student engagement: No learning without it. *MIT Teaching Systems Lab.* https://dspace.mit.edu/handle/1721.1/147885

Peters, M. A., Jackson, L., Papastephanou, M., Jandrić, P., Lazaroiu, G., Evers, C. W., Cope, B., Kalantzis, M., Araya, D., Tesar, M., Mika, C., Chen, L., Wang, C., Sturm, S., Rider, S., & Fuller, S. (2024). AI and the future of humanity: ChatGPT-4, philosophy and education–Critical responses. *Educational Philosophy and Theory, 56*(9), 828–862. DOI: 10.1080/00131857.2023.2213437

Polyzos, N. (2007). *Assessment in contemporary school settings.* Grigoris Publications. [In Greek]

Porlán, R., & Villarejo-Ramos, A. F. (Coords.). (2024). *Ciclos de mejora en el aula. Curso 2022-23: Experiencias de Innovación Docente de la Universidad de Sevilla.* Universidad de Sevilla.

Porlán, R. (2017). *Enseñanza universitaria: cómo mejorarla.* Ed. Morata.

Prensky, M. (2001). Digital natives, digital immigrants part 2: Do they really think differently? *On the Horizon, 9*(6), 1–6. DOI: 10.1108/10748120110424843

Prince, J. D. (2013). Gamification. *Journal of Electronic Resources in Medical Libraries, 10*(3), 162–169. DOI: 10.1080/15424065.2013.820539

Przegalinska, A., & Triantoro, T. (2024). *Converging minds: The creative potential of collaborative AI.* CRC Press. DOI: 10.1201/9781032656618

Purzer, Ş., Moore, R., & Baker, D. (2015). Engineering design in the science classroom: STEM integration through design-based learning. *Science Education International, 26*(3), 217–229.

Qudsi, H. (2024). Gamification in education: boosting student engagement and learning outcomes. *ShodhKosh: Journal of Visual and Performing Arts, 5*(4). Advance online publication. DOI: 10.29121/shodhkosh.v5.i4.2024.2542

Radianti, J., Majchrzak, T. A., Fromm, J., & Wohlgenannt, I. (2020). A systematic review of immersive virtual reality applications for higher education: Design elements, lessons learned, and research agenda. *Computers & Education, 147*, 103778. DOI: 10.1016/j.compedu.2019.103778

Rahman, S., Ramakrishnan, T., & Ngamassi, L. (2020). Impact of social media use on student satisfaction in Higher Education. *Higher Education Quarterly, 74*(3), 304–319. DOI: 10.1111/hequ.12228

Rampin, R., & Rampin, V. (2021). Taguette: Open-source qualitative data analysis. *Journal of Open Source Software, 6*(68), 3522. DOI: 10.21105/joss.03522

Rana, R., & Bhambri, P. (2024a). Artificial Intelligence and Internet of Things (IoT) facilitated digital twin for Industry 4.0 application domains. In Rani, S., Bhambri, P., Kumar, S., Pareek, P. K., & Elngar, A. A. (Eds.), *AI-driven digital twin and Industry 4.0* (pp. 168–181). CRC Press., DOI: 10.1201/9781003395416-11

Rana, R., & Bhambri, P. (2024b). Generative AI in web application development: Enhancing user experience and performance. In Shah, I. A., & Jhanjhi, N. Z. (Eds.), *Generative AI for web engineering models* (pp. 471–486). IGI Global., DOI: 10.4018/979-8-3693-3703-5.ch021

Rani, S., Kataria, A., Bhambri, P., Pareek, P. K., & Puri, V. (2024). Artificial intelligence in personalized health services for better patient care. In Gupta, S. K., Karras, D. A., & Natarajan, R. (Eds.), *Revolutionizing healthcare: AI integration with IoT for enhanced patient outcomes* (pp. 89–108). Springer., DOI: 10.1007/978-3-031-65022-2_6

Rauteda, K. R. (2025). Quantitative research in education: Philosophy, uses, and limitations. [JMRD]. *Journal of Multidisciplinary Research, 2*(1), 1–11. DOI: 10.56916/jmrd.v2i1.993

Reinholz, D. L., White, I., & Andrews, T. (2021). Change theory in STEM higher education: A systematic review. *International Journal of STEM Education, 8*(1), 37. DOI: 10.1186/s40594-021-00291-2

Reis Da Silva, T. M. H. (2024). *Gamification as a Pedagogical Tool in Geriatric Nursing*. Igi Global. DOI: 10.4018/979-8-3693-8322-3.ch005

Ren, Y., Shang, J., Zhang, M., Xu, X., & Geng, Z. (2025). Federated learning with local–global collaboration for predicting acute coronary syndrome. *Chemometrics and Intelligent Laboratory Systems*, *267*, 105515. Advance online publication. DOI: 10.1016/j.chemolab.2025.105515

Roe, J., Perkins, M., & Furze, L. (2025). Reflecting Reality, Amplifying Bias? Using Metaphors to Teach Critical AI Literacy. *Journal of Interactive Media in Education, 2025*(1). DOI: 10.5334/jime.961

Romero Albaladejo, I. M., & García López, M. (2024). Mathematical attitudes transformation when introducing GeoGebra in the secondary classroom. *Education and Information Technologies*, *29*(8), 10277–10302. DOI: 10.1007/s10639-023-12085-w

Rong, J., Terzidis, K., & Ding, J. (2024). Kids AI Design Thinking Education for Creativity Development. *Archives of Design Research*, *37*(3), 119–133. DOI: 10.15187/adr.2024.07.37.3.119

Sahayu, W., Triyono, S., & Ungu, N. K. (2026). Digital Technology in Differentiated English Language Teaching: A Systematic Review with Bibliometric Insights. *Indonesian Journal of Science and Technology*, *11*(1), 167–188. DOI: 10.17509/ijost.v11i2.89685

Sajja, R., Sermet, Y., Cikmaz, M., Cwiertny, D., & Demir, I. (2024). Artificial Intelligence-Enabled Intelligent Assistant for Personalized and Adaptive Learning in Higher Education. *Information (Basel)*, *15*(10), 596. DOI: 10.3390/info15100596

Saladino, M., Marín Suelves, D., & San Martín Alonso, Á. (2020). Percepción docente del aprendizaje mediado tecnológicamente en aulas italianas. *Revista Interuniversitaria de Formación del Profesorado*, *34*(3), 175–194. DOI: 10.47553/rifop.v34i3.80593

Sana, J. K., Rahman, M. S., & Rahman, M. S. (2025). Privacy-preserving customer churn prediction model in the context of telecommunication industry. *Engineering Applications of Artificial Intelligence*, *162*, 112514. Advance online publication. DOI: 10.1016/j.engappai.2025.112514

Sanders, M. (2009). STEM, STEM education, STEMmania. *Technology Teacher*, *68*(4), 20–26.

Sangodiah, A., Wei, W. C., Ayob, A. N. B., Jalil, N. B. A., Subramaniam, C. R. S. P. R., & Lirong, G. (2023). Machine Learning Clustering Analysis Towards Educator's Readiness to Adopt Augmented Reality as a Teaching Tool. *Mendel, 29*(2), 147–154. DOI: 10.13164/mendel.2023.2.147

Santarém, I. P. (2023). *Pós-graduação em Educação STEAM*. Retrieved 23-5-2025 from https://www.ipsantarem.pt/eses/pgest/

Sayed, W. S., Noeman, A. M., Abdellatif, A., Abdelrazek, M., Badawy, M. G., Hamed, A., & El-Tantawy, S. (2023). AI-based adaptive personalized content presentation and exercises navigation for an effective and engaging E-learning platform. *Multimedia Tools and Applications, 82*(3), 3303–3333. ProQuest Central. DOI: 10.1007/s11042-022-13076-8

Schreffler, J., Vasquez, E.III, Chini, J., & James, W. (2019). Universal Design for Learning in postsecondary STEM education for students with disabilities: A systematic literature review. *International Journal of STEM Education*, *6*(8), 8. Advance online publication. DOI: 10.1186/s40594-019-0161-8

Schulz, K., & Grimes, D. (2002). Unequal group sizes in randomized trials: Guarding against guessing. *Lancet*, *359*(9310), 966–970. DOI: 10.1016/S0140-6736(02)08029-7 PMID: 11918933

Scientix. (n.d.). Scientix: The community for science education in Europe. Retrieved from https://www.scientix.eu/

Selwyn, N. (2012). *Education and technology: Key issues and debates*. Bloomsbury Academic.

Shahali, E. H. M., & Halim, L. (2024). The influence of science teachers' beliefs, attitudes, self-efficacy and school context on integrated STEM teaching practices. *International Journal of Science and Mathematics Education*, *22*(4), 787–807. DOI: 10.1007/s10763-023-10403-9

Shaikh, M. S., & Ali, S. I. (2025). *Revolutionising the Impact of Education Using Advanced Online Tools*. Igi Global. DOI: 10.4018/979-8-3693-8593-7.ch028

Sharma, P. (2023). Pedagogical Practices in the Technology-Intervened Indian Education System. *Indian Journal of Social Science and Literature*, *3*(2), 1–9. DOI: 10.54105/ijssl.K1632.123223

Shvartz, E., Zur, O., Attal, L., Nujeidat, Z., Plopsky, G., & Bahir, D. (2025). GPT-4o vs. residency exams in ophthalmology—A performance analysis. *Journal of Medical Artificial Intelligence*, *8*, 48. Advance online publication. DOI: 10.21037/jmai-24-269

Sidorkin, A. M. (2025). Extended executive cognition, a learning outcome for the AI age. *Computers and Education Open, 9*, 100294. Advance online publication. DOI: 10.1016/j.caeo.2025.100294

Silvera, L., & Reyes Alvarado, S. (2023). Análisis de los Códigos de Ética de las Universidades en Panamá. *Sapientia, 14*(3), 26–39. DOI: 10.54138/27107566.465

Simões, J. M., & Caldeira, W. (2024). Ethics concerns in the use of computer-generated images for human communication. *Journal of Ethics in Higher Education*, (4), 169–192. DOI: 10.26034/fr.jehe.2024.5962

Singh, J., Evans, E., Reed, A., Karch, L., Qualey, K., Singh, L., & Wiersma, H. (2021). Online, Hybrid, and Face-to-Face Learning Through the Eyes of Faculty, Students, Administrators, and Instructional Designers: Lessons Learned and Directions for the Post-Vaccine and Post-Pandemic/COVID-19 World. *Journal of Educational Technology Systems, 50*(3), 301–326. DOI: 10.1177/00472395211063754

Slamet, J. (2024). Empowering Slow Learners: Gamification's Impact on Students' Engagement and Academic Performance in an LMS for Undergraduate Students. *International Journal of Information and Education Technology (IJIET), 14*(2), 193–203. DOI: 10.18178/ijiet.2024.14.2.2040

Sousa, M. R. (2023). *Lei das Grandes Opções para 2023 -2026*. Diário da República Retrieved from https://files.diariodarepublica.pt/1s/2023/08/14900/0000300113.pdf

Sousa, N. M. T. (2025). Academic libraries as hubs of artificial intelligence competency. *Discover Artificial Intelligence, 5*(1), 221. Advance online publication. DOI: 10.1007/s44163-025-00490-8

Souto, M. E. V. C., Fernandes, A. C., Silva, A. B. S., de Freitas Ribeiro, L. H., & de Medeiros Fernandes, T. A. A. (2025). A multi-model longitudinal assessment of ChatGPT performance on medical residency examinations. *Frontiers in Artificial Intelligence, 8*, 1614874. Advance online publication. DOI: 10.3389/frai.2025.1614874 PMID: 40918587

Spyropoulou, N., Mathiopoulos, K., & Kameas, A. (2025). "We believe in STEAM education, but we need support": In-service teachers' voices on the realities of STEAM implementation. *Education Sciences, 15*(10), 1300. DOI: 10.3390/educsci15101300

Stark, L., & Crawford, K. (2019). The work of art in the age of artificial intelligence: What artists can teach us about the ethics of data practice. *Surveillance & Society, 17*(3/4), 442-455. https://dx.doi.DOI: 10.24908/ss.v17i3/4.10821

Stolpe, K., & Hallström, J. (2024). Artificial intelligence literacy for technology education. *Computers and Education Open, 6*, 100159. DOI: 10.1016/j.caeo.2024.100159

Storozhyk, M. (2024). Philosophy of future: Analytical overview of interaction between education, science, and artificial intelligence in the context of contemporary challenges. *Futurity Philosophy*, *3*(1), 23–47.

Suriyaarachchi, H., Denny, P., & Nanayakkara, S. (2022). Scratch and Sense: Using Real-Time Sensor Data to Motivate Students Learning Scratch *SIGCSE 2022: Proceedings of the 53rd ACM Technical Symposium on Computer Science Education*, Providence, RI, USA. https://doi.org/DOI: 10.1145/3478431.3499316

Taylor, L., Dai, H. M., Ng, H., Playfoot, D., & Rose, S. (2025). Editorial: Improving quantitative research in higher education learning and teaching. *Journal of University Teaching & Learning Practice*, *22*(2). Advance online publication. DOI: 10.53761/jc59jm21

Tello, I., & Cascales, A. (2015). Las TIC y las necesidades específicas de apoyo educativo: Análisis de las competencias TIC en los docentes. *Revista Iberoamericana de Educación a Distancia*, *18*(2), 355–383. DOI: 10.5944/ried.18.2.13536

Tenorio-Sepúlveda, G. C., Arguelles, A. J., Hernández-López, R., & Ramirez-Montoya, M. S. (2025). DIGITAL ESCAPE ROOMS TO DEVELOP COMPUTATIONAL THINKING: LEARNING ANALYTICS IN SCIENCE CLUB. *Journal of Information Technology Education*, *24*, 025. Advance online publication. DOI: 10.28945/5604

Terán Torres, H. (2023). *La implementación de la Inteligencia Artificial en la enseñanza de la programación: Un estudio sobre el uso ético de ChatGPT en el aula. Encuentro Internacional de Educación en Ingeniería*. EIEI ACOFI., DOI: 10.26507/paper.2768

Terçariol, A. A. L., Bioto, P. A., Melaré Vieira Barros, D., Caeiro, L., & Barnabé, J. (2024). Educação STEAM: Formação, percepções e práticas sob olhares de Brasil e Portugal. *Dialogia*, (50). Advance online publication. DOI: 10.5585/50.2024.27833

Thi To Khuyen, N., Van Bien, N., Lin, P.-L., Lin, J., & Chang, C.-Y. (2020). Measuring Teachers' Perceptions to Sustain STEM Education Development. *Sustainability (Basel)*, *12*(4), 1531. Advance online publication. DOI: 10.3390/su12041531

Thibaut, L., Ceuppens, S., De Loof, H., De Meester, J., Goovaerts, L., Struyf, A., Boeve-de Pauw, J., Dehaene, W., Deprez, J., De Cock, M., Hellinckx, L., Knipprath, H., Langie, G., Struyven, K., Van de Velde, D., Van Petegem, P., & Depaepe, F. (2018). Integrated STEM education: A systematic review of instructional practices in secondary education. *European Journal of STEM Education*, *3*(1). Advance online publication. DOI: 10.20897/ejsteme/85525

Thoma, R., Farassopoulos, N., & Lousta, C. (2023). Teaching STEAM through universal design for learning in early years of primary education: Plugged-in and unplugged activities with emphasis on connectivism learning theory. *Teaching and Teacher Education, 132*, 104210. DOI: 10.1016/j.tate.2023.104210

Tijjani, K. S., Levent, Y. S., & Levent, T. (2025). Smart Cities in the Global Context: Geographical Analyses of Regional Differentiations. *Systems, 13*(4), 296. Advance online publication. DOI: 10.3390/systems13040296

Tirado-Morueta, R. J., & Aguaded-Gómez, J. I. (2014). Influencias de las creencias del profesorado sobre el uso de la tecnología en el aula. *Review of Education*, (363), 230–255. DOI: 10.4438/1988-592X-RE-2012-363-179

Tondeur, J., van Braak, J., Ertmer, P. A., & Ottenbreit-Leftwich, A. (2017). Understanding the relationship between teachers' pedagogical beliefs and technology use in education: A systematic review of qualitative evidence. *Educational Technology Research and Development, 65*(3), 555–575. DOI: 10.1007/s11423-016-9481-2

Tong, Y. (2024). Integration of artificial intelligence into the general education curriculum: Importance, approaches, challenges, and a conceptual framework for liberal arts universities. In INTED2024 Proceedings (pp. 7582-7589). IATED.

Troussas Christos, Chrysafiadi Konstantina, & Virvou, M. (2021). Personalized tutoring through a stereotype student model incorporating a hybrid learning style instrument. *Education and Information Technologies, 26*(2), 2295–2307. ProQuest Central; Social Science Premium Collection. DOI: 10.1007/s10639-020-10366-2

Tschannen-Moran, M., & Hoy, A. W. (2001). Teacher efficacy: Capturing an elusive construct. *Teaching and Teacher Education, 17*(7), 783–805. DOI: 10.1016/S0742-051X(01)00036-1

Tudor, C., Florescu, M., Polychronidou, P., Stamatiou, P., Vlachos, V., & Kasabali, K. (2025). Cloud Adoption in the Digital Era: An Interpretable Machine Learning Analysis of National Readiness and Structural Disparities Across the EU. *Applied Sciences (Basel, Switzerland), 15*(14), 8019. Advance online publication. DOI: 10.3390/app15148019

UNESCO. (2008). Estándares de competencias en TIC para docentes. Retrieved from www.oei.es/historico/tic/UNESCOEstandaresDocentes.pdf

UNESCO. (2021). *Recomendación sobre la ética de la inteligencia artificial.* Organización de las Naciones Unidas para la Educación, la Ciencia y la Cultura. Retrieved from https://www.unesco.org/es/artificial-intelligence/recommendation-ethics

UNESCO. (2022). *Reimagining our futures together: A new social contract for education.* UNESCO Publishing.

UNESCO. (2025). *Framework for the implementation of Education for Sustainable Development (ESD) beyond 2019.* https://unesdoc.unesco.org/ark:/48223/pf0000370215

Vaiopoulou, J., Papagiannopoulou, T., & Stamovlasis, D. (2023). Attitudes towards STEM education: Nonlinear effects of teachers' readiness and the crucial role of affective conditions. *Frontiers in Education, 8*, 1244678. Advance online publication. DOI: 10.3389/feduc.2023.1244678

Various Authors. (2011). *Guadalmedina: An invisible river.* Rizoma Foundation.

Vatankhah, S., Bamshad, V., Arici, H. E., & Duan, Y. (2024). Ethical implementation of artificial intelligence in the service industries. *Service Industries Journal, 44*(9-10), 661–685. DOI: 10.1080/02642069.2024.2359077

Vavoula, G., & Sharples, M. (2002). KLeOS: A Personal, Mobile, Knowledge and Learning Organisation System. In M. Milrad, U. Hoppe, & Kinshuk (Eds.), *Proceedings of the IEEE International Workshop on Wireless and Mobile Technologies in Education (WMTE 2002)* (pp. 152–156). IEEE. https://doi.org/DOI: 10.1109/WMTE.2002.1039239

Vedrenne-Gutiérrez, F., López-Suero, C. C., De Hoyos-Bermea, A., Mora-Flores, L. P., Monroy-Fraustro, D., Orozco-Castillo, M. F., Martínez-Velasco, J. F., & Altamirano-Bustamante, M. M. (2024). The axiological foundations of innovation in STEM education – A systematic review and ethical meta-analysis. *Heliyon, 10*(12), e32381. DOI: 10.1016/j.heliyon.2024.e32381 PMID: 38994089

Vergara León, M. J. (2012). *Percepción de docentes y estudiantes sobre el currículo de estudios de una universidad privada de Lima* [Tesis de maestría, Universidad San Ignacio de Loyola]. Repositorio USIL. https://repositorio.usil.edu.pe/handle/20.500.14005/1348

Waldeck, J. H. (2007). Answering the Question: Student Perceptions of Personalized Education and the Construct's Relationship to Learning Outcomes. *Communication Education, 56*(4), 409–432. DOI: 10.1080/03634520701400090

Wang, H., Moore, T. J., Roehrig, G. H., & Park, M. S. (2011). STEM integration: Teacher perceptions and practice. *Journal of Pre-College Engineering Education Research, 1*(2), 1–13. DOI: 10.7771/2157-9288.1068

Wang, M., Zhu, J., Hwang, G.-J., Chang, S.-C., Yang, Q.-F., & Zhang, D. (2025). Boosting Student Engagement in STEM: Integrating Large Language Model-Based Virtual Agents Into Alternate Reality Games. *Journal of Computer Assisted Learning*, *41*(6), e70139. Advance online publication. DOI: 10.1111/jcal.70139

Wannapiroon, N., & Pimdee, P. (2022). Thai undergraduate science, technology, engineering, arts, and math (STEAM) creative thinking and innovation skill development: A conceptual model using a digital virtual classroom learning environment. *Education and Information Technologies*, *27*(4), 5689–5716. DOI: 10.1007/s10639-021-10849-w PMID: 35068986

Wastiau, P., Looney, J., & Laanpere, M. (2024, 1-06-2024). *Portugal's digital transition strategy for education. System change case studies series.* Retrieved 14-04-2025 from https://erte.dge.mec.pt

Watson, D., Hancock, M., & Mandryk, R. (2013). Gamifying behaviour that leads tolearning. *Proceedings of the First International Conference on gameful design, research, and applications*, pp. 87 - 90. DOI: 10.1145/2583008.2583021

Weidl, M., & Erling, E. J. (2025). Exploring Multilingualism to Inform Linguistically and Culturally Responsive English Language Education. *Education Sciences*, *15*(6), 763. DOI: 10.3390/educsci15060763

Wikipedia. (n.d.). *Plan Guadalmedina.* In *Wikipedia, The Free Encyclopedia.* Retrieved June 10, 2025, from https://es.wikipedia.org/wiki/Plan_Guadalmedina

Winkler, C. E., & Wofford, A. M. (2024). Trends and motivations in critical quantitative educational research: A multimethod examination across higher education scholarship and author perspectives. *Research in Higher Education*, *65*(7), 1368–1394. DOI: 10.1007/s11162-024-09802-w

Wulan, D. R., Rohman, T., Nainggolan, D. M., Fiyul, A. Y., & Hidayat, Y. (2024). Exploring the Benefits and Challenges of Gamification in Enhancing Student Learning Outcomes. *Global International Journal of Innovative Research*, *2*(7), 1657–1674. DOI: 10.59613/global.v2i7.238

Xie, X., & Lu, C. (2025). Bridging the Digital Gradient: How Digital Literacy and Information Perception Shape Innovation and Entrepreneurship Across Urban, County and Township Students. *Sustainability (Basel)*, *17*(22), 9942. Advance online publication. DOI: 10.3390/su17229942

Xi, L., Zhang, Y., & Wang, Q. (2026). Investigating the effects of an LLM-based Socratic conversational agent on students' academic performance and reflective thinking in higher education. *Computers & Education, 241*, 105494. Advance online publication. DOI: 10.1016/j.compedu.2025.105494

Yadav, A., Stephenson, C., & Hong, H. (2017). Computational thinking for teacher education. *Communications of the ACM, 60*(4), 55–62. DOI: 10.1145/2994591

Yakman, G. (2008). STEAM Education: an overview of creating a model of integrative education.

Yıldız, T. (2025). The minds we make: A philosophical inquiry into theory of mind and artificial intelligence. *Integrative Psychological & Behavioral Science, 59*(1), 10. DOI: 10.1007/s12124-024-09876-2 PMID: 39743649

Yinka, A. R., & Queendarline, N. N. (2018). Telegram as a social media tool for teaching and learning in tertiary institutions. *International Journal of Multidisciplinary Research and Development, 5*(7), 95–98.

Zahra, S. T., Bibi, E., & Younus, Z. (2025). Artificial Intelligence (AI) and Human Mind: Struggles and Strengths in the Education Sector. In Artificial Intelligence and Human Agency in Education: Volume One: The Nexus Between AI and Human Agency in Educational Contexts (pp. 265-289). Springer Nature Singapore.

Zhang, X. (2025). Research on the application of big data learning recommendation model driven by knowledge graph algorithm in educational information platform optimization. *Systems and Soft Computing, 7*, 200298. Advance online publication. DOI: 10.1016/j.sasc.2025.200298

Zhao, Y., & Gearhart, M. (2021). Designing STEM curriculum for global competence: Lessons from international programs. *Journal of Curriculum Studies, 53*(5), 645–662. DOI: 10.1080/00220272.2021.1910457

Zhou, T., Liu, K., Li, X., Jiang, N., & Chunguo, C. (2026). Joint Data Compression, Secure Multi-Part Collaborative Task Offloading and Resource Assignment in Ultra-Dense Networks. *IEEE Transactions on Network Science and Engineering, 13*, 278–295. DOI: 10.1109/TNSE.2025.3582977

Zhu, W., Wei, L., & Qin, Y. (2025). Artificial Intelligence in Education (AIEd): Publication Patterns, Keywords, and Research Focuses. *Information (Basel), 16*(9), 725. Advance online publication. DOI: 10.3390/info16090725

Zichichi, M., Ferretti, S., D'Angelo, G., & Rodríguez-Doncel, V. (2022). Data governance through a multi-DLT architecture in view of the GDPR. *Cluster Computing, 25*(6), 4515–4542. DOI: 10.1007/s10586-022-03691-3

Zimmerman, B. J. (2002). Becoming a self-regulated learner: An overview. *Theory into Practice*, *41*(2), 64–70. DOI: 10.1207/s15430421tip4102_2

Zourmpakis, A.-I., Kalogiannakis, M., & Papadakis, S. (2023). Adaptive Gamification in Science Education: An Analysis of the Impact of Implementation and Adapted Game Elements on Students' Motivation. *Computers*, *12*(7), 7. Advance online publication. DOI: 10.3390/computers12070143

About the Contributors

Antonio Cortijo Ocaña is a distinguished professor at the University of California Santa Barbara. He is the author of over 60 books and monographs ranging from studies on classical culture to humanism, economic history, political theory, and religious persecution in the medieval and early modern period. He has also translated numerous Catalan works into English, from medieval classics to contemporary philosophers and poets. In addition, many of his publications are multidisciplinary and bridge the fields of humanities and applied psychology and education. He has received numerous awards and grants during his career. He is a member of the Royal Academy of Good Letters (Barcelona) and co-director of the Center for Medieval Studies (UCSB). Finally, he is the founder and director of the journal eHumanista

Javier Fernández-Molina is a lecturer in the Department of Innovation and Didactic Training at the University of Alicante (Spain), where he contributes to undergraduate and postgraduate teacher education. His research lies at the intersection of CLIL, digital innovation in language education, and English literacy development, with particular emphasis on phonetics, pronunciation, and phonics in early and primary education. He has engaged in international research and teaching collaborations across Europe, the United States, and Asia, and has participated in transnational initiatives such as Transform4Europe. He is a member of the ACQUA and ELEI_UA research groups and has published in peer-reviewed journals and edited volumes in the areas of language education and educational technology.

***

Senthil Kumar A.V. is working as a Professor and Director, PG and Research Department of Computer Applications, Hindusthan College of Arts & Science, Coimbatore, Tamilnadu. To his credit he has industrial experience for five years and teaching experience of 29 years. He has also received his Doctor of Science (D.Sc in Computer Science). He has to his credit 84 Book Chapters, 234 papers in International and National Journals, 85 papers in International Conferences in International and National Conferences, and edited 18 books and 3 Text books. He is as Associate Editor of IEEE Access. He is an Editor-in-Chief for many journals and Key Member for India, Machine Intelligence Research Lab (MIR Labs). He is an Editorial Board Member and Reviewer for various International Journals. He is also a Committee member for various International Conferences. He has guided 16 Ph.D scholars and guiding 3 Ph. D scholars now.

Jorge Asencio-Juncal is PhD in Tourism (2021) University of Malaga, Architect (2007) and Technical Architect (2001), University of Granada. Master degree in Landscaping, Gardening and Public Space (2013) and Master degree in Urban Planning (2016), University of Granada. Associate lecturer (Adjunct Professor) in the ETS of Architecture of Malaga, Urban Planning and Territorial Planning Area, since 2010. Participating in several national research projects and educational innovation projects, currently researching in the HUM_969-UTOPIìA group (Urbanism, Tourism, Landscape and Architectural Innovation). He has lectured at different national and international universities, having publications on topics related to landscape and heritage, land planning and urban projects. He has participated as a coordinator and teacher in several courses, workshops and conferences related to urban planning and landscape. He has coordinated various university programs for Development Cooperation, within the International Volunteering Program for Development Cooperation at the University of Malaga. He combines teaching and researching works with the free exercise of the profession, focusing his activity mainly on urban projects, gardening, landscape and public space projects, either for private clients or for public administrations. He has developed part of his activity in the Urban Planning Area of the City Hall of Granada. Also as a support technician of the Vice-Rectorate of Heritage, Infrastructure and Equipment at the University of Granada. Since 2008 he is a foundational partner of CampoAbierto, an architecture, landscape, design and research platform, where he currently develops his professional activity.

Karla Berrens is a tenure-track lecturer at the Sociology department, a researcher in Creativity, Innovation and Urban Transformation Research Group (CRIT-UB), also ascribed to POLIS research center: Art, City and Society (CR-Polis-UB) and a member of the Aural Diversity research network. Karla is also a member of GIDASRES interdisciplinary teaching innovation research group and GID-CIVITAS a sociology teaching innovation group. Her research career focuses on urban research, approaching the city through interdisciplinary lenses. She is a specialist in hybrid research methodologies and sensory studies, with a particular focus on space, place and the cartographies of the senses. Her research line on Sociology of Education focusses on students with diverse learning approaches and gamification in Higher Education.

Pankaj Bhambri is an accomplished Associate Professor in the Department of Information Technology at Guru Nanak Dev Engineering College, Ludhiana, with over 21 years of teaching and research experience. Recognized as a Top 2% Scientist by Stanford University and Elsevier, his expertise spans Artificial Intelligence, Machine Learning, the Internet of Things, and Cloud Computing. A prolific researcher, he has authored numerous patents, published extensively in Scopus and SCIE-indexed journals, and edited several influential books with international publishers like CRC Press and Springer. Dr. Bhambri is also an active academic leader, guiding Ph.D. candidates, serving on technical committees for international conferences, and currently pursuing a Post Doctorate Fellowship at Lincoln University College, Malaysia.

S Nagakishore Bhavanam having 16 years of Experience in Teaching and Research. In which 12 Years of Administrative experience as Registrar, Mangalayatan University Jabalpur (MUJ), Jabalpur, Madhya Pradesh, Assistant Director, IQAC, Acharya Nagarjuna University (ANU), Coordinator, Rankings, ANU, Head of the Department, ECE, University College of Engineering & Technology, ANU and many more positions at Acharya Nagarjuna University, Guntur, Andhra Pradesh. So far Published 190 research & review articles, 30 Patents are Published and 2 Innovation and 11 Design Patent grants were secured from National & International (UK & Canada) Level. Contributed 11 Text Books, 23 Book chapters in Electronics and Computer Science Engineering field and received 12 awards. Seven (07) doctorate degrees are awarded under my supervision. During my administrative experience more than 60 State level, National, International level Seminars/ Conferences/Workshops are organized. More than 150 ranks received by ANU and 57 ranks received by Mangalayatan University, Jabalpur under my supervision. Delivered more than 70 lectures as resource person/speaker at reputed organizations, Universities.

Francisco José Chamizo-Nieto is Architect (2016), Master in Teaching, specialty Drawing, Image and Plastic Arts (2017), and Doctor (2023) in the Interuniversity PhD Program City, Territory and Sustainable Planning. Collaborator in the Emerging Technologies for Citizenship Chair (UMA - Malaga City Council; 2018-2019). Member of the research group HUM-969 Urbanism, Tourism, Landscape and Architectural Innovation (UTOPIA), and the Institute Habitat, Territory and

Digitization (iHTD) of the University of Malaga. His PhD has been financed through a competitive predoctoral contract supported by the Spanish Ministry of Universities (FPU19/02468) at the University of Malaga in the Department of Art and Architecture (Area of Urban Planning). He has also obtained three other grants in competitive public calls, allowing him to undertake multidisciplinary research through two predoctocal (2021; 2022) and one postdoctoral (2024) international research stays at the University of Lisbon. He is currently a substitute teaching tutor at the University of Seville in the Department of Urban and Regional Planning (2025-present), combining research and teaching duties.

Marina Elias Andreu is an associate professor at the Department of Sociology of the University of Barcelona specialized in sociology of education. She is a researcher in Creativity, Innovation and Urban Transformation Research Group (CRIT-UB), also ascribed to POLIS research center: Art, City and Society (CR-Polis-UB). Marina is the coordinator of GIDASRES interdisciplinary teaching innovation research group and member of GID-CIVITAS a sociology teaching innovation group. Her research focuses on education inequalities in the education field. This includes analysis on transitions and trajectories of students to post-compulsory education, students' profiles in terms of motivations, strategies to study, engagement through inequalities as social background, ethnic differentiation, gender, and other life conditions. Her research projects have permitted the development of policy recommendations and orientations to secondary education and higher education institutions.

Jorge Fernández Herrero has a PhD in Educational Innovation from the University of Alicante and a degree in Architecture. Currently, he is Assistant Professor at the Department of Didactics and School Organization, Department of General Didactics and Specific Didactics. Author of articles published in national and international journals and several book chapters, he focuses on the following lines of research: use of creativity and information and communication technologies as educational tools, with special sensitivity to students with autism spectrum disorder (ASD). His most recent publications are: The first steps for adapting an artificial intelligence emotion expression recognition software for emotional management in the educational context (2023); Creative group activities for the improvement of social and emotional competencies of youth with ASD (2022); Gender and territory in the vicious circle of school failure (2022); Virtual drawing as a previous educational intervention in autism spectrum disorder: A case study (2021); An immersive virtual reality educational intervention on people with autism spectrum disorders (ASD) for the development of communication skills and problem-solving (2019); Transition to College for Students with Autism Spectrum

Disorder: Needs and Facilitation Strategies. Is Virtual Reality a Useful Tool in the Transition Process?(2019); A Bibliometric Study on the Use of Virtual Reality (VR) as an Educational Tool for High-Functioning Autism Spectrum Disorder (ASD) Children (2018); He has also presented papers in relevant national and international congresses, seminars and conferences, within this same field of research. He is also part of the Interdisciplinary Research Group in University Teaching-Education and Information and Communication Technologies/Inclusive Education, currently collaborating in projects of excellence in Educational Research at regional level and having previously participated in sustainability projects at national level.

Nasir Ahmad Ganaie holds a PhD (2019) in Political Science from the Central University of Hyderabad, India. He currently serves as a Post-Doctoral Fellow at the Department of Political Science, School of Social Sciences, University of Kashmir. His scholarly expertise encompasses a broad spectrum of critical areas, including public policy, e-governance, digitalization, comparative politics, conflict resolution, identity politics, separatism, terrorism, and the evolving dynamics of new-age militancy. He particularly specializes in conflict studies, counter-terrorism operations, armed insurgency, cyber terrorism and radicalization. In recognition of his outstanding research contributions, he has been honoured with several prestigious awards, including the Global Goodwill Ambassadorship for Peace (2017), Excellent Researcher Award (2018), Best Young Researcher Award (2018), and Performance Excellence Award (2019).

Maximiliano Merino Suárez is an Occupational Therapist, holds a Master's degree in Occupational Therapy with a specialization in Physical Health, and is a PhD candidate in Technologies Applied to Knowledge at the University of Alicante, Spain. He also has postgraduate training in artificial intelligence applications in healthcare, learning assessment, research ethics, clinical epidemiology, and research methodology. He currently serves as a university academic and program director in higher education, with extensive experience in teaching, academic management, clinical simulation, curriculum evaluation, and quality assurance. He has led and participated in research, educational innovation, and community engagement projects, including initiatives focused on tele-assistance for older adults, digital learning, and competency-based assessment. His research interests include artificial intelligence applied to education and health, adaptive learning systems in higher education, psychoeducational and emotional variables in university students, and learning assessment. He has presented his work at national and international conferences and has published in peer-reviewed journals in the fields of occupational therapy and health education.

Claudia Prieto-Latorre is an Assistant Professor of Economics at the Department of Applied Economics at the University of Malaga. She holds a PhD in Economics from the same University. Her research interests lie in the Economics of Education in areas such as school peer effects and sources of educational inequalities. In particular, she is interested in quantifying how peer and school compositional effects can impact educational and societal outcomes. She has published 14 peer-reviewed articles in journals such as Socioeconomic Planning Sciences, the American Educational Research Journal, and Applied Economic Analysis, among others. She has also presented her research at various reputable international conferences. She regularly lectures in Statistics and Econometrics at undergraduate and graduate level at the University of Malaga.

Revati Rautrao is a scholar, HR expert, and educator with 20+ years of experience, known for her research in sustainability, AI in education, and women's empowerment.

Pedro Rito has a doctorate in Information Technologies and Systems (from the University of Minho), a master's degree in Multimédia in Education (from the University of Aveiro), and a degree in Computer Engineering from the Instituto Superior de Engenharia de Coimbra. He has been a Professor at the School of Education at the Polytechnic Institute of Viseu since 2007, where he has worked on curricular units such as web programming, creative programming, microcontroller programming, and the use of sensors, as well as ICT training for pre-school and primary school teachers. He is interested in the adoption and diffusion of technologies, creative programming and the development of creative applications, the design and development of video games, and the design and implementation of tangible interfaces. He is a member of the CI&DEI Research Group.

KRS Sambasiva Rao, presently as Vice-Chancellor of Mangalayatan University at Jabalpur, Madhya Pradesh, and formerly Vice-Chancellor of Mizoram Central University during 2017-2022 and Rector (Pro-Vice Chancellor) and Vice-Chancellor (i/c) of Acharya Nagarjuna University during 2014-2017. He did D.Sc. in Biotechnology from Berhampur University, in the field of Microbial Biotechnology; Ph.D. in Zoology from Sri Venkateswara University, in the field of Toxicology and Physiology; PhD. in Pharmaceutical Science from Andhra University, on Dosage formulation and Drug delivery systems. Prof.Rao had Post Graduation in M.Sc. Zoology, M.Sc. Psychology, M.Sc. Information Technology, MBA Big Data Analytics and MA Sociology. Prof. Rao earlier worked as a Professor of Zoology and Biotechnology at Acharya Nagarjuna University over 29 years during 1988 to 2017, and worked in the areas of Aquaculture Biotechnology, Microbial Biotechnology and

Molecular Biology. Prof. Rao published over 275 research papers in various national and international journals and filed eight patents and edited/authored 20 books.

Dini Sari is an Information Technology professional with a strong interest in developing intelligent systems based on Artificial Intelligence (AI) and the Internet of Things (IoT). With a solid academic background and professional experience in digital technology environments, she actively explores the integration of AI and IoT to create innovative solutions that support automation, operational efficiency, and digital transformation. Dini is frequently involved in research related to intelligent analytics, sensor data processing, and the development of connected system architectures. Her dedication to research and technology drives her commitment to continuously expanding her expertise and contributing to the advancement of industries based on digital innovation.

Binastya Anggara Sekti has been a lecturer at the Faculty of Computer Science, Esa Unggul University, Jakarta, since 2016. He is actively involved in the Artificial Intelligence and Information Security Study Group. He holds a Bachelor's degree in Informatics Engineering from the Bandung Institute of Technology and a Master's degree in Information Systems Management from Trisakti University, Jakarta. Prior to entering academia, he accumulated over 25 years of professional experience as an IT practitioner in various companies across Jakarta. His work focused on developing data centers for internet service providers and delivering IT solutions for the manufacturing and oil & gas sectors. His research interests include artificial intelligence, cybersecurity, and the development of IT infrastructure.

Sanjayan T.S has been working as an assistant professor in Rd.He delivered almost 61 Distinguished lectures in foreign universities across 61 countries including in South America, North America, Asia, Europe and Africa.He Edited several books on Higher Education, ELT and Artificial intelligence. He has done several projects in international and National level.

Index

Symbols

21st-Century Skills 177

A

Academic Performance 14, 21, 47, 57, 85, 87, 92, 94, 97, 102, 105, 109, 113, 114, 118, 122, 123, 143, 170, 176, 177, 188, 216, 244, 262, 267, 280, 281, 284, 297
Adaptive Learning 2, 3, 6, 8, 9, 16, 24, 39, 47, 49, 83, 84, 85, 86, 87, 88, 94, 95, 97, 98, 99, 101, 102, 104, 105, 106, 107, 129, 130, 287
Adaptive Learning Systems 3, 9, 47, 83, 84, 85, 86, 87, 88, 94, 95, 97, 99, 101, 102, 104, 106
AI in Education 11, 14, 24, 26, 30, 31, 32, 35, 63, 69, 70, 71, 75, 76, 105, 126
Analog Resources 209, 210, 211, 213, 215, 216, 217, 218, 219
Artificial Intelligence (AI) 1, 3, 5, 6, 8, 13, 19, 20, 23, 33, 34, 35, 36, 37, 39, 40, 43, 44, 45, 46, 47, 50, 52, 55, 56, 57, 59, 60, 61, 62, 63, 64, 68, 69, 70, 71, 72, 73, 74, 76, 77, 78, 79, 82, 83, 86, 94, 95, 97, 101, 102, 103, 105, 107, 123, 157, 192, 196, 208, 214, 223, 259, 278

C

Climate Emergency 207, 230, 243, 245, 248, 249
Computer Science 1, 2, 3, 5, 7, 8, 9, 11, 12, 25, 39, 40, 41, 42, 43, 44, 45, 46, 47, 49, 50, 56, 57, 151, 226, 262
Conceptual Corpus 63, 68, 69, 70, 71, 72
Critical Thinking 10, 17, 27, 29, 30, 33, 44, 46, 49, 57, 69, 70, 76, 78, 79, 99, 113, 126, 130, 138, 152, 153, 177, 187, 195, 197, 206, 210, 212, 215, 218, 230, 235, 242, 249, 267, 268, 272, 275, 279

D

Data Privacy 1, 13, 17, 25, 30, 32, 33, 41, 46, 48, 57, 79, 93, 98, 102, 157
Descriptive Evaluation 162
Differentiated Instruction 127, 138, 146, 268, 277
Digital Divide 1, 5, 7, 16, 17, 39, 41, 44, 46, 48, 54, 55, 58, 59, 146, 214, 218, 275
Digital Literacy 1, 3, 4, 10, 11, 12, 15, 21, 41, 45, 49, 50, 51, 55, 56, 58, 78, 130, 136, 145, 150, 153, 155, 156, 166, 168, 170, 173, 214, 252, 254, 256, 273, 274, 279, 283, 284
Digital Tools 1, 3, 4, 5, 6, 7, 14, 15, 16, 17, 39, 40, 41, 42, 44, 49, 51, 52, 55, 56, 58, 127, 128, 130, 131, 132, 133, 135, 136, 137, 138, 139, 140, 141, 142, 143, 146, 150, 151, 155, 156, 157, 158, 162, 173, 205, 208, 210, 212, 213, 215, 218, 223
Diverse Learning 32, 155, 207, 213, 252, 253, 254, 257, 259, 260, 264, 266, 268

E

Eco-social Transition 249
Educational Games 216
Educational Technology 11, 24, 34, 35, 36, 39, 50, 52, 59, 63, 66, 74, 80, 85, 105, 106, 124, 125, 144, 145, 146, 161, 162, 220, 226, 261, 263
Educational Transformation 266
E-Portfolio 149, 150, 153, 154, 155, 156, 157, 159, 165, 167, 169, 172, 173

G

Gamification 29, 107, 130, 142, 146, 214, 251, 252, 253, 254, 255, 256, 257, 258, 259, 260, 261, 262, 263, 264, 265, 266, 267, 268, 269, 270, 271, 272, 273, 275, 276, 277, 280, 281, 282, 283, 284, 287, 288, 289, 290,

291, 292, 293, 295, 296, 297
Generation Z 110, 123
Guadalmedina River 229, 230, 231, 232, 233, 235, 236, 237, 240, 245, 247, 248, 249

H

Hidden Curriculum 29
Higher Education 4, 19, 20, 21, 35, 36, 37, 41, 44, 45, 51, 59, 60, 65, 66, 67, 83, 84, 85, 86, 87, 88, 91, 99, 102, 104, 105, 106, 107, 111, 112, 113, 114, 125, 126, 145, 152, 167, 172, 202, 203, 204, 205, 206, 207, 210, 215, 223, 224, 226, 230, 251, 253, 258, 263, 264, 266, 280, 290, 291, 292, 295
Hybrid Learning 107, 208, 209, 210, 211, 212, 213, 215, 216, 217, 219, 225, 226, 273

I

Inclusive Education 155, 210, 211, 215, 254, 262, 264
Interdisciplinary Collaboration 1, 11, 12, 39, 49, 50, 51, 58, 225
Interdisciplinary Teaching 195

K

Knowledge Retention 17, 100, 265

L

Learning Based Project Methodologies 249
Learning Management Systems 3, 4, 13, 43, 83, 87, 129, 157
Learning Outcomes 13, 25, 26, 101, 106, 107, 136, 138, 142, 151, 157, 159, 165, 168, 178, 185, 188, 195, 208, 221, 244, 269, 284, 287, 292, 295, 296, 297

M

Machine Learning 3, 5, 6, 8, 9, 19, 20, 34, 36, 41, 43, 46, 47, 48, 51, 60, 61, 105
Messaging Application 109, 110, 122
Mixed-Methods Research 280

N

New Technologies 4, 155

P

Peer Learning 112, 245
Personalized Learning 1, 2, 11, 16, 19, 26, 30, 47, 51, 104, 130, 167, 213
Professional Development 7, 8, 11, 12, 20, 32, 49, 50, 54, 60, 73, 102, 139, 140, 141, 142, 144, 145, 151, 155, 163, 164, 165, 166, 169, 171, 172, 176, 177, 192, 193, 196, 197, 199, 210, 211, 214, 218, 219, 220, 221, 222, 224, 275, 277
Public Space 229, 230, 233, 236, 237, 238, 240, 241, 249

Q

Qualitative-Descriptive Approach 63, 68
Quantitative Research 133, 135, 175, 178, 179, 180, 182, 201, 202, 203

S

Secondary Education 87, 149, 151, 152, 153, 156, 157, 158, 159, 164, 165, 166, 168, 169, 171, 183, 203
Skill Development 127, 207, 227, 266, 278
Smart Cities 42, 58, 61
Social Network 110
Sociology 11, 23, 25, 49, 57, 251, 252, 254, 258, 259
STEAM Education 203, 205, 206, 208, 209, 210, 211, 212, 213, 215, 217, 218, 219, 220, 221, 223, 224, 225, 227
STEM Education 12, 175, 176, 177, 178, 179, 180, 182, 183, 184, 185, 187, 188, 189, 191, 193, 194, 196, 197, 198, 199, 200, 201, 202, 203, 223, 224, 225, 226, 227
Student Attitudes 25, 28

Student Engagement 5, 12, 21, 48, 61, 83, 84, 95, 102, 127, 130, 137, 142, 147, 185, 192, 200, 202, 206, 208, 211, 216, 217, 222, 243, 265, 266, 269, 277, 280, 281, 284, 285, 287, 288, 291, 296, 297
Student Perceptions 83, 87, 89, 90, 91, 106, 107
Student-Teacher Communication 110, 111, 123
Sustainable Cities 245, 249

T

Teacher Education 124, 144, 145, 202, 205, 206, 209, 210, 211, 217, 221, 227

U

UDL 144, 155, 167, 193, 253, 254, 256, 259, 264
Urban Education 245, 266, 267, 269, 271, 273, 274, 275, 293
Urban Project 229, 243, 249

www.ingramcontent.com/pod-product-compliance
Lightning Source LLC
LaVergne TN
LVHW081533300926
849161LV00006B/1405